THE CHALLENGE OF

Effective Speaking

Fourteenth Edition

Rudolph F. Verderber
University of Cincinnati

Kathleen S. Verderber
Northern Kentucky University

Deanna D. Sellnow
University of Kentucky

WADSWORTH
CENGAGE Learning™

Australia • Brazil • Canada • Mexico • Singapore • Spain • United Kingdom • United States

The Challenge of Effective Speaking, Fourteenth Edition
Rudolph F. Verderber, Kathleen S. Verderber, Deanna D. Sellnow

Publisher: Lyn Uhl

Executive Editor: Monica Eckman

Senior Development Editor: Greer Lleuad

Assistant Editor: Kimberly Gengler

Editorial Assistant: Kimberly Apfelbaum

Associate Technology Project Manager: Jessica Badiner

Marketing Assistant: Mary Anne Payumo

Marketing Manager: Erin Mitchell

Senior Advertising Project Manager: Shemika Britt

Senior Content Project Manager: Lauren Wheelock

Senior Art Director: Maria Epes

Print Buyer: Susan Carroll

Permissions Editor: Roberta Broyer

Production Service: Lachina Publishing Services

Text and Cover Designer: Jerry Wilke

Photo Researcher: Christina Micek

Copy Editor: Lachina Publishing Services

Compositor: Lachina Publishing Services

For more information and technology assistance, contact us at:
Cengage Learning Customer & Sales Support, 1-800-354-9706
For permission to use material from this text or product, submit all requests online at **cengage.com/permissions**
Further permissions questions can be emailed to
permissionrequest@cengage.com

Library of Congress Control Number: 2007931159

ISBN-13: 978-0-495-50217-3
ISBN-10: 0-495-50217-0

ISBN-13: 978-0-495-50348-4
ISBN-10: 0-495-50348-7

Wadsworth
10 Davis Drive
Belmont, CA 94002-3098
USA

Cengage Learning is a leading provider of customized learning solutions with office locations around the globe, including Singapore, the United Kingdom, Australia, Mexico, Brazil, and Japan. Locate your local office at:
international.cengage.com/region

Cengage Learning products are represented in Canada by Nelson Education, Ltd.

For your course and learning solutions, visit **academic.cengage.com**

Purchase any of our products at your local college store or at our preferred online store **www.ichapters.com**

Printed in China
2 3 4 5 6 7 11 10 09 08

Brief Contents

Detailed Contents

Part Two Planning Your Speech

6 Researching Information for Your Speech 90

7 Organizing and Outlining the Speech Body 118

8 Completing the Outline: Creating the Introduction and the Conclusion 140

Part Three   Informative and Persuasive Speaking

Part Four Adapting to Other Occasions
and Formats

Preface

We are delighted to welcome Deanna Sellnow, Ph.D., as our new coauthor for *The Challenge of Effective Speaking*. Professor Sellnow is an accomplished teacher, scholar, and basic course director, as well as a well-respected textbook author. In addition, Dr. Sellnow's voice blends well with ours, as her writing has a delightful conversational quality that keeps the material interesting. We believe our collaboration on this revision has produced a text that you will agree continues to be the best in the market. What makes this collaboration especially noteworthy is the dedication all three of us have to the goal of making *Challenge* a text that is easy to learn from and a joy to teach from.

As with previous editions, we have worked hard to revise the text so that it reflects the speaking challenges today's students will encounter. We began by carefully analyzing feedback received from students and instructors across the country. We also reviewed scholarship and professional publications to see how theories, technology, and practice are evolving, and we updated the text to reflect new trends. In addition, we updated the text's examples and sample speeches so that they reflect current topics of interest, correspond to changes in theory and practice, and incorporate information about the changing technological realities of public discourse. Finally, we have continued to ensure that we are at the forefront of integrating computer-mediated resources into the text so that students are encouraged to be active learners, adept at using the many online resources available to help today's speakers prepare effective speeches.

We are thrilled to have heard both students and instructors confirm that what has become known as the Verderber method for speech preparation really works! This method provides a step-by-step process designed to guide you from topic selection to the rehearsal process to delivery. The six action steps in the book's speech planning process encourage students to complete a sequence of activities designed to help plan an effective speech. From both research and our experience as instructors, we know that speakers who are well prepared feel more confident about speaking, and they usually deliver great speeches. So we advocate that instructors assign the activities as part of the assessment of student speeches, and we encourage students to use the activities even when they are not assigned. Why? Because we know that they work and we want students who are reading our book to be successful. That's why we wrote it!

New to This Edition

Those instructors who have previously used *The Challenge of Effective Speaking* will be pleased with the new material and emphasis in this edition. We made a conscious decision to blend into *Challenge* several of the strengths of *Confident Public Speaking*, Dr. Sellnow's public speaking text. For example, you will notice that in discussions of the speech planning process throughout the book, we have increased the discussion of how a speech can be tailored to a specific audience. Similarly, in this edition, you will notice that we suggest how speakers can adapt their material so that it meets the needs of a diverse audience. For example, we encourage speakers to choose supporting material that addresses multiple learning styles so that audience members who learn in different ways will be able to understand and retain information and arguments. Let's take a look at what's new in this edition.

Speech Snippet boxes throughout the book provide "snippets" of speeches by student speakers working through the myriad issues they must face when preparing a speech. For example, in the Chapter 5 discussions about adapting to an audience, the Speech Snippet boxes highlight how speakers demonstrated personal impact in a speech, addressed timeliness and acknowledged listener attitudes, demonstrated their direct expertise, and established their trustworthiness.

Critical thinking and reflection prompts have been added in the form of What's Ahead questions in the chapter openers and reflection questions in the Spotlight on Speakers boxes. These questions ask students to consider the skills described in the book in context and as they apply to students' own lives.

Chapter 1, "Introduction to Public Speaking," now begins with a brief discussion of general communication contexts that situates public speaking among intrapersonal, interpersonal, group, and mass communication. It introduces students to the concept of the speaking situation, which a speaker should analyze when preparing a speech. Finally, the discussion of speech effectiveness has been strengthened to present five hallmarks of an effective speech.

Chapter 2, "Developing Competence Through the Speech Planning Process," includes a discussion of the role of self-talk in the apprehension process, elaborates on the role of previous experience in creating apprehension, and includes a discussion of cognitive restructuring as a method for overcoming apprehension.

Chapter 3, "Effective Listening," begins by differentiating hearing from listening. New research on listening has been integrated throughout the chapter. The criteria for analyzing a speech critically have been reorganized so that they are grouped as criteria for content, structure, and delivery. The chapter concludes with a comprehensive discussion of how to critique a speech, including how to prepare feedback to the speaker.

Chapter 4, "Identifying an Audience-Centered Speech Goal," has been refocused so that consideration of the audience is central and integrative. A discussion of concept mapping has been added to the section on identifying topics. In the section on audience analysis, we not only discuss how to collect demographic data, but we now include a discussion of how to use demographic data when preparing a speech. Throughout the chapter, more attention is paid to the need to adapt a speech's topic and goal to the audience.

Chapter 5, "Adapting to Audiences," has been reorganized so that the issues a speaker encounters when adapting to an audience are presented in the order in which a speaker is likely to encounter them. In addition, a discussion of learning styles has been added to the section on information comprehension and retention.

Chapter 6, "Researching Information for Your Speech," has been organized so that the sources of information are categorized as personal knowledge, secondary research, or primary research. Discussions of each information source describe any caveats to consider. The chapter presents up-to-date information about conducting research online.

Chapter 7, "Organizing and Outlining the Speech Body," now includes a discussion of the narrative organizational pattern. In addition, we now discuss how to use signposts as well as transitions between main points.

Chapter 8, "Completing the Outline: Creating Introductions and Conclusions," has been revised to emphasize the importance of making the introduction and conclusion audience centered by using listener relevance links in the introduction and a clincher in the conclusion.

Chapter 9, "Constructing and Using Presentational Aids," features a new title that reflects its thorough revision. As we have moved into the media age, audiences have increased their expectations about the quality of audiovisual aids speakers use. In addition to discussing visual aids, the chapter now covers audio and audiovisual aids and provides extensive information on the effective use of computer-mediated presentation aids.

Chapter 10, "Practicing Speech Wording," begins with a discussion of the characteristics of oral style and then describes how to speak accurately, clearly, vividly, and appropriately. In the discussion of vivid language, the coverage of figures of speech has been expanded to include additional types of figures and structures of speech.

Chapter 11, "Practicing Delivery," has been reorganized so that it begins with a discussion of the characteristics of effective delivery before moving on to describe how to use voice and bodily movements to augment a verbal message. The chapter concludes with a discussion of how to adapt to your audience while you are giving the speech.

Chapter 12, "Informative Speaking," includes a brief discussion of the nature of informative speaking and describes the importance of developing material that is suited to different learning styles. The chapter also includes new sample process and expository speeches.

Chapter 13, "Persuasive Speaking: Reasoning with Audiences," begins by using the Elaboration Likelihood Model to explain how audience members process persuasive messages. Discussion of several additional reasoning fallacies has been included, and the refutative pattern has been added to the discussion of organizational patterns for speeches of reason.

Chapter 14, "Persuasive Speaking: Motivating the Audience," now includes guidelines for appealing to emotions and demonstrating credibility. The problem-solution and the problem-cause-solution patterns have been added to the discussion of organizational patterns for speeches to actuate. This chapter also includes a new sample speech to actuate.

Chapter 15, "Ceremonial Speaking: Speeches for Special Occasions," has been reorganized, and the discussion of each speech type simplified.

Chapter 16, "Developing and Delivering Group Presentations," is a new chapter written specifically to help students as they work with others to develop group presentations; it replaces a more generic chapter on problem-solving groups. The chapter describes the responsibilities of group members as they prepare for a group presentation and the problem-solving process groups use to decide on and develop the content of presentations. The formats of symposium, panel discussion, and town hall meeting that groups use to deliver public presentations are explained. In addition, the chapter discusses how to evaluate the contributions of each group member as well as the effectiveness of the presentation itself. The chapter concludes with a group presentation assignment.

Revised Features

◆ **Speech Plan Action Steps** guide students through a step-by-step preparation process that results in significantly better speeches. These Action Step activities are supplemented by in-text and online examples of each activity prepared by other students.

- **Sample student speeches** in Chapters 1, 11, 12, 13, and 14 include adaptation plans, outlines, and transcripts with accompanying analyses. In addition, videos of these and other student speeches are featured in this book's online resources.

- **Spotlight on Speakers** boxes highlight the speaking accomplishments of people from a wide range of backgrounds. These boxes, several of which are new to this edition, complement topics related to concepts discussed in the chapter, helping students to understand and appreciate public speaking outside the classroom.

- **Reflect on Ethics** boxes are short case studies that appear in every chapter. These cases present ethical challenges and require students to think critically, sorting through a variety of ethical dilemmas faced by public speakers. In each case, the dilemma posed focuses on issues raised in the specific chapter.

    In addition, the fourteenth edition includes the following new and updated technological features, all highlighted at the end of each chapter in the *Challenge* Online section:

- The *Challenge of Effective Speaking* **online textbook resources,** which provide students with one-stop access to all the integrated technology resources that accompany the book. These resources include the CengageNOW™ for *Challenge* online study system, chapter-by-chapter resources at the *Challenge* book companion website, the *Challenge* interactive video communication scenarios and speeches, InfoTrac® College Edition, and Speech Builder Express™. All of these resources are referenced in the text and highlighted with an icon. Integrated throughout the chapters—and expanded upon at the ends of chapters in the *Challenge* Online section—these references direct students to numerous online activities while reinforcing and enriching the concepts presented. **Note to faculty:** If you want your students to have access to the online textbook resources, please be sure to order them for your course. The content in these resources can be bundled at no additional charge to your students with every new copy of the text. If you do not order them, your students will not have access to these online resources. *Contact your local Wadsworth sales representative for more details.*

- The **CengageNOW™ for** *Challenge,* available to students when instructors order this online textbook resource packaged with the text. Using chapter-by-chapter diagnostic pretests that identify concepts students don't fully understand, this online system creates a personalized study plan for each chapter. Each plan directs students to specific resources designed to improve their understanding, including pages from the text in e-book format. Chapter posttests give them an opportunity to measure how much they've learned and let them know if they are ready for graded quizzes and exams. In addition, CengageNOW provides students with a multitude of text-specific learning aids, including interactive electronic versions of all the Speech Planning Action Steps. From this resource, students can download speech evaluation checklists as well as complete activities online, e-mail them to their instructors if requested, and compare their responses to activities with models provided by the authors. For instructors, CengageNOW is available on WebCT and Blackboard, allowing them to provide virtual office hours, post syllabi, set up threaded discussions, and track student progress.

- The revised *Challenge* **book companion website,** available to students at no additional charge when instructors order this online textbook resource packaged with the book. The website features study aids such as chapter outlines, flash cards and other resources for mastering glossary terms, and chapter quizzes that help students check their understanding of key concepts.

◆ The *Challenge* **interactive video activities,** available to students at no additional charge when instructors order this online textbook resource packaged with the book. This resource features videos of all the sample student speeches featured in the text, as well as evaluation worksheets and critical thinking questions for each speech.

◆ **Web Resource web links,** available to students at no additional charge when instructors order this online textbook resource packaged with the book. These links have been integrated into the text to expand skills practice and learning online. Highlighted in the text with colored text and icons, they are easily accessed from the *Challenge* online textbook resources. All the web links are monitored to ensure that they remain active.

◆ Many of the Speech Planning Action Steps can be completed with the **Speech Builder Express organization and outlining program,** available to students at no additional charge when instructors order this online textbook resource packaged with the book. This interactive web-based tool coaches students through the speech organization and outlining process. By completing interactive sessions based on the in-text Speech Planning Action Steps, students can prepare and save their outlines—including a plan for visual aids and a works cited section—formatted according to the principles presented in the text. Both text and video models reinforce students' interactive practice.

Supplementary Materials

In addition to the *Challenge* online textbook resources just described, the fourteenth edition can be packaged with a suite of integrated resources for students and instructors.

Student Resources

◆ **eAudio Study Tool for *The Challenge of Effective Speaking.*** This text's eAudio mobile content provides a fun and easy way for students to review chapter content whenever and wherever. For each chapter of the text, students will have access to a five- to seven-minute review consisting of a brief summary of the main points in the text and five to seven review questions. Students can purchase the eAudio for *Challenge* through iChapters (see below) and download files to their computers, iPods, or other MP3 players.

◆ **InfoTrac College Edition.** An easy-to-use online library, available to students for four months at no additional charge when instructors order this online textbook resource packaged with the book. This extensive, easy-to-use database of more than 18 million reliable, full-length articles (not abstracts) from 5,000 top academic journals and popular sources is ideal for helping students master online research and is especially useful when students are preparing speeches.

◆ **Student Workbook** *by Kristen A. G. McIntyre, University of Arkansas at Little Rock, and J J McIntyre, University of Central Arkansas.* The student workbook offers chapter-by-chapter skill-building exercises, vocabulary lists, quizzes, and copies of the speech evaluation checklists featured in the text.

- **iChapters.com.** This online store provides students with exactly what they've been asking for: choice, convenience, and savings. A 2005 research study by the National Association of College Stores indicates that as many as 60 percent of students do not purchase all required course material; however, those who do are more likely to succeed. This research also tells us that students want the ability to purchase "à la carte" course material in the format that suits them best. Accordingly, iChapters.com is the only online store that offers eBooks at up to 50 percent off, eChapters for as low as $1.99 each, and new textbooks at up to 25 percent off, plus up to 25 percent off print and digital supplements that can help improve student performance.

- **The Art and Strategy of Service-Learning Presentations** *by Rick Isaacson and Jeff Saperstein, both of San Francisco State University.* This handbook is an invaluable resource for students in a basic course that integrates or is planning to integrate a service learning component. The handbook provides guidelines for connecting service learning work with classroom concepts as well as advice for working effectively with agencies and organizations. The handbook also provides model forms and reports and a directory of online resources.

- **A Guide to the Basic Course for ESL Students** *by Esther Yook, Mary Washington College.* This guide assists the nonnative speaker. It features FAQs, helpful URLs, and strategies for accent management and overcoming speech apprehension.

Instructor Resources

- **Instructor's Resource Manual with Test Bank** *by Brian L. Heisterkamp, California State University, San Bernardino.* This indispensable manual features changes from the thirteenth edition to the fourteenth edition, sample syllabi, chapter-by-chapter outlines, summaries, vocabulary lists, suggested lecture and discussion topics, classroom exercises, assignments, and a comprehensive test bank with answer key and rejoinders.

- **Instructor's Resource CD-ROM** *by Amber Finn, Texas Christian University.* This CD-ROM contains an electronic version of the Instructor's Resource Manual, ExamView® Computerized Testing, and predesigned Microsoft® PowerPoint® presentations. The PowerPoint presentations contain text and images, and they can be used as is or customized to suit your course needs.

- **Student Speeches for Critique and Analysis.** This multivolume video series offers both imperfect and award-winning sample student speeches. The speeches presented in *Challenge* are available in this series.

- **Election 2004: Speeches from the Campaign.** This CD-ROM allows students to see the power and importance of public speaking and its relevance in our society and includes both full and excerpted speeches from the 2004 U.S. presidential campaign. Students can view speeches from the Democratic and Republican conventions as well as a variety of other speeches delivered throughout the campaign. After students view these speeches, they have the option of evaluating them based on specific speech criteria.

- **JoinIn™ on TurningPoint®.** JoinIn content for Response Systems is tailored to *Challenge,* allowing you to transform your classroom and assess your students' progress with instant in-class quizzes and polls. Turning-

Point software lets you pose book-specific questions and display students' answers seamlessly within the Microsoft PowerPoint slides of your own lecture, in conjunction with the "clicker" hardware of your choice. Enhance how your students interact with you, your lecture, and one another. The JoinIn content for each chapter includes two "conditional branching" scenarios that can be used as in-class group activities.

◆ **Turn-It-In.** This proven online plagiarism-prevention software promotes fairness in the classroom by helping students learn to correctly cite sources and allowing instructors to check for originality before reading and grading papers and speeches. Turn-It-In quickly checks student work against billions of pages of Internet content, millions of published works, and millions of student papers and speeches and within seconds generates a comprehensive originality report.

◆ **TLC Technology Training and Support.** Get trained, get connected, and get the support you need for seamless integration of technology resources into your course with Technology Learning Connected (TLC). This unparalleled technology service and training program provides robust online resources, peer-to-peer instruction, personalized training, and a customizable program you can count on. Visit **academic.cengage.com** to sign up for online seminars, first days of class services, technical support, or personalized, face-to-face training. Our online or on-site trainings are frequently led by one of our Lead Teachers, faculty members who are experts in using Cengage Learning technology and can provide best practices and teaching tips.

◆ **The Teaching Assistant's Guide to the Basic Course** *by Katherine G. Hendrix, University of Memphis.* Based on leading communication teacher training programs, this guide covers general teaching and course management topics as well as specific strategies for communication instruction—for example, providing effective feedback on performance, managing sensitive class discussions, and conducting mock interviews.

Acknowledgments

The book you are holding is the result of a team effort, and we have been privileged to work with the best. First, we want to acknowledge the wonderful students whose speeches appear in this book. We also want to thank our colleagues around the world who have used previous editions of the book and have graciously shared their experiences in teaching from the text with us. We would like to single out the following people who participated in the review process for this edition: Daniel Higgins, Heidelberg College; James Johnson, Canyon College; Frank P. Sesko, Webster University, Crystal Lake; Lori Seward, South Georgia College; Terri K. Sparks, Mesa Community College; Laura Umphrey, Northern Arizona University; Robert W. Wawee, University of Houston, Downtown; and Catherine Wright, George Mason University. As we prepared this revision, we worked with some familiar faces and welcomed several new editorial, marketing, and production team members. We have enjoyed working with our publisher, Lyn Uhl; executive editor, Monica Eckman; assistant editor, Kim Gengler; editorial assistant, Kim Apfelbaum; marketing manager, Erin Mitchell; marketing assistant, Mary Anne Payumo; technology project manager, Jessica Badiner; senior production manager, Michael Burggren; senior content project manager, Lauren Wheelock; photo researcher, Christina Micek; copyeditor, Frank Hubert; and production project manager, Bonnie Briggle. A special thank you to Greer Lleuad, our development editor: She is the consummate professional and always a joy to work with. During this revision, she was not only editor but also wise counsel. As far as we are concerned, she is the best in the business. We also thank Allison Verderber Herriott for helping us create a PowerPoint® presentation to accompany the speech on ethanol in Chapter 12.

Finally, we are indebted to our families, who put up with us when we are writing and not always available to attend to their needs. The Sellnow family supported Deanna as she worked on a crazy, expedited writing schedule while at the same time preparing for a cross-country move. During the writing of this edition, the Verderber family welcomed a new granddaughter, Louisa Christine Herriott. We also celebrated the sixty-fifth wedding anniversary of Kathleen's parents, Louise and John Sheldon, to whom we dedicate this edition.

Introduction to Public Speaking

1

© David Young-Wolff/PhotoEdit

All the great speakers were bad speakers at first.

Ralph Waldo Emerson, "Power,"
***The Conduct of Life* (1860)**

What's Ahead

HERE'S WHAT'S AHEAD IN THIS CHAPTER:

1. At what point(s) should you consider your audience in the speech planning and speech making processes?

2. In what ways might you adapt your speech based on the setting in which you will present your speech?

3. What are some ways in which effective public speaking skills will empower you?

4. What does it mean to be an ethical speaker?

5. Why is it necessary to cite sources orally while presenting your speech?

When Tom Simmons, a candidate for council, was invited to speak at the University Forum, he presented his views on the role of government in education.

As Marquez, Bill, and Glenna drove home from the movie they had seen, Bill said he thought the movie deserved an Academy Award nomination and asked the others if they agreed. Marquez listened carefully and then gave two reasons he thought the movie failed to portray characters realistically.

As Heather and Gavin were eating dinner, Heather tried to explain why she was upset with the attention he was paying to Susan.

At the monthly meeting of the Engineering Department, Nancy Bauer, a purchasing clerk, gave a speech on how to fill out the new online requisition form all engineers would be using when ordering parts for newly designed machines.

Who would you identify in these four situations as giving a speech? You're probably thinking that since Tom and Nancy knew that they were expected to speak to a group, they prepared, so they certainly were giving a speech. True. But isn't it likely that since Heather had been thinking about Gavin's attentiveness to Susan for a while, she had prepared as well? And since Marquez was asked a direct question, didn't he have to come up with an answer that made sense, an answer that he had probably been mulling over as he watched the movie?

The point? This course focuses on developing your public speaking skills, but you will be able to draw on these skills across a variety of settings, including work-related meetings, personal business transactions (such as negotiating to buy a new car), and personal relationships. In short, practicing public speaking skills will help you present your ideas more informatively and more persuasively in any setting.

In this chapter, we begin by situating public speaking within various settings we call communication contexts. Next we describe the communication process that occurs during a speech. Then we consider how building public speaking skills empowers us and challenges us to behave ethically.

Communicating in Context

Public speaking is only one context, or setting, in which we communicate. We also communicate in small groups, in one-to-one relationships, on the telephone, over the Internet, and on radio and television, as well as in newspapers, magazines, and newsletters. Communication research reveals five such contexts: intrapersonal, impersonal, interpersonal, small group, and public.[1] Public speaking occurs in the public communication context. To select the most appropriate strategies for communicating in a public context, it is important to understand public communication as it relates to the other contexts.

Intrapersonal communication is communicating with yourself. Usually this is not done orally but by thinking through choices, strategies, and the possible consequences of taking action. When you sit in class and consider what you'll have for dinner tonight, you are communicating intrapersonally. Much of our intrapersonal communication occurs subconsciously.[2] When you drive into your driveway "without thinking," you're communicating intrapersonally on a subconscious level. When you present a speech, intrapersonal communication might occur when you notice confused looks on your listeners' faces as you explain a complex process and, subsequently, you decide to rephrase your explanation.

Impersonal communication is communication between two people about general information.[3] When you say "hi" to a passing stranger or when you talk about the weather with a grocery store checker, you are communicating impersonally. When you present a speech, impersonal communication might occur when you share introductory remarks about current events or the speaking occasion before you move on to the actual body of your speech. These impersonal comments don't relate directly to the speech but can signal to your audience that they need to get ready to listen.

Interpersonal communication is communication between two people who already have an identifiable relationship with each other.[4] When you stop to chat with a friend between classes about weekend plans, how your family is, or what you did last night, you are engaging in interpersonal communication. You are also communicating interpersonally when you have a heart-to-heart talk with a close friend or family member. Interpersonal communication sometimes occurs in a public speech when a speaker supports a main point by telling a story about his or her experiences.

Small group communication is communication that occurs in a group of about three to ten people.[5] There are many kinds of small groups; examples include a family, a group of friends, a group of classmates working together on a class project, and a management team in the workplace.[6] Some research suggests there are more small groups in the United States than there are people! In the public communication context, small group communication occurs when a group of people is asked to make a public presentation. When you are part of such a group, your own success is directly related to how effectively group members work together to develop ideas and how effectively the group functions in presenting those ideas.

Public communication takes place among audiences of more than about ten people. One form of public communication is mass communication, defined as communication produced and transmitted via media to large audiences. Another form is a **public speech,** or **oration,** defined as a sustained formal presentation made by a speaker to an audience. When you give oral presentations in class, you are essentially giving a public speech. Teachers engage in public speaking when they lecture. So do masters of ceremonies who introduce other speakers or entertainers, actors who accept awards, and corporate managers when they run large meetings. Presiding officers of clubs engage in public speaking when they conduct meetings; so do parents when presenting their ideas about educational issues to school boards or other officials. And the list goes on.

Public speaking is much more prevalent in our day-to-day lives than most of us realize. Improving our ability to speak effectively in public is crucial to achieving important goals for ourselves, our families, and our communities. As you read this book and give speeches in class, you'll learn all the steps you need to take to build and improve your public speaking skills. To get you started, let's take a quick look at what makes up the process of public speaking.

public speech, or oration a sustained formal presentation made by a speaker to an audience

Public Speaking Is an Audience-Centered Process

More than 2,000 years ago, the Greek philosopher Aristotle observed, "The audience is the end and object of the speech." What he meant was that the eloquence of your words is irrelevant if the words are not heard by, are not understood by, or do not affect the people to whom you are speaking. The same is true today. As a speaker, you have a specific goal in mind that you want to achieve when you speak. How effective you are at attaining that goal will depend on whether people in your audience listen to, understand, and perhaps act on what you say.

The public speaking effectiveness process model (Exhibit 1.1) depicts the central role played by your audience during both speech planning and speech making. During the speech planning process, your careful analysis of the audience, the speaking context, and your speech planning skills will guide you as you develop your speech action plan. During the speech making process, you can use the audience feedback you receive to alter your planned speech so that your audience is better able to listen, understand, or be motivated to act. Let's briefly discuss each element of this model: audience, speaking context, speaker, speech planning process, speech making process, and speech effectiveness.

audience the specific group of people to whom the speech is directed

audience analysis a study made to learn about the diverse characteristics of audience members and then, based on these characteristics, to predict how audience members are apt to listen to, understand, and be motivated to act on your speech

Audience

The **audience** is the specific group of people to whom your speech is directed. An effective speech planning process begins with studying your audience. **Audience analysis** is a study made to learn about the diverse characteristics of audience members and then, based on these characteristics, to predict how audience members are apt to listen to, understand, and be motivated to act on your speech. Armed with an understanding of your specific audience, you are in a better position to develop a speech plan whose specific goal, organizational

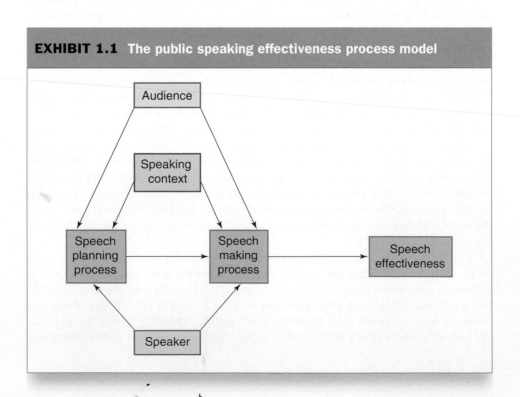

EXHIBIT 1.1 The public speaking effectiveness process model

pattern, and examples, statistics, and other supporting material are suited to your particular audience's needs. For example, if the audience analysis reveals that most audience members are younger than 25, a speaker who has decided to speak on the internment of Japanese Americans during World War II may need to provide more detailed background information than would be needed for an audience whose members were adults during World War II.

During the speech making process, your audience members give you **audience feedback**—nonverbal and occasionally verbal cues that indicate audience members' reactions to what the speaker is saying. If you pay attention to these cues, you can deviate from your speech plan to help meet audience needs that the feedback communicates. For example, after quickly defining a key term and giving a short example, Ethan notices a number of audience members looking quizzical. Even though he had not planned to do so, Ethan should use this feedback and redefine the term using simpler words and even give another detailed example. In this way, he alters his speech plan to meet a need he has identified through audience feedback.

Speaking Context

The **speaking context** is comprised of physical, cultural, historical, and psychological factors in the setting in which your speech is presented. The speaking context affects how your audience members perceive the speech.

The **physical setting** includes location, size of room, seating arrangement, distance between audience and speaker, time of day, room temperature, and lighting. These factors work together to create a physical context that can aid or detract from your speech. For example, if an audience of 50 people listens to a speech you present in a dimly lit auditorium with a capacity of 500 people where you are on a raised platform at a distance from the audience and use a microphone, they are likely to perceive you as impersonal and find it difficult to remain attentive to what you are saying. But an audience of 50 that listens to you give that same speech in a well-lit room designed for 60 people, where you stand within five feet of the first row and use only a small lectern to hold a few notes, is likely to perceive you as personable and pay better attention to what you say.

The **cultural setting** is comprised of the values, beliefs, meanings, and social mores of specific groups of people to which your audience members belong that help members of that group form and interpret messages. During the speech preparation process, you will try to understand how your cultural background meshes with that of your audience and adapt the speech message to ensure that it can be accurately interpreted within your audience members' cultural frame. Because early U.S. immigrants came from western European countries, U.S. public speaking practices have been rooted in western European culture. Today, we are a more diverse country with more heterogeneous cultural backgrounds. As a result, you may no longer expect that the members of your audience subscribe to western European imperatives. Understanding not only who is in the audience, but also how their cultural background differs from yours, is important during speech preparation and presentation. For example, in western European culture, feedback to speakers is primarily nonverbal. It would be considered rude for an audience member to speak out during a public address. In African American and other cultural settings, however, it is common for audience members to provide verbal feedback during a speech. Generally, this feedback affirms and encourages the speaker.

The **historical setting** is comprised of events that have occurred prior to the speech that are related to your speech topic, to you as a speaker, to previous speeches given by you with which audience members are familiar, or other

audience feedback nonverbal and verbal cues that indicate audience members' reaction to what the speaker is saying

speaking context the physical, cultural, historical, and psychological factors in the setting in which your speech is presented

physical setting the location, size of room, seating arrangement, distance between audience and speaker, time of day, room temperature, and lighting

cultural setting the values, beliefs, meanings, and social mores of specific groups of people to which your audience members belong

historical setting events that have already occurred that are related to your speech topic, to you as a speaker, to previous speeches given by you with which audience members are familiar, or to other encounters that audience members have had with you

How do the setting and the occasion dictate what a speaker will talk about at a graduation ceremony?

© Bob Daemmrich/PhotoEdit

encounters that audience members have had with you. The historical setting can predispose an audience toward or against your topic or you as a speaker. For example, a speech on police–community cooperation given by the long-established local president of the Fraternal Order of Police is likely to be viewed differently from a similar speech given by a newly elected president.

The **psychological setting** is comprised of the moods, feelings, attitudes, and beliefs of the individual audience members that affect how your speech message is perceived. As you prepare your speech, you need to consider how individual audience members' psychological makeup is likely to affect how they listen to your speech. For example, a professor who has just returned a test on which most students performed poorly may have a rough time engaging their attention in the lecture that follows. Student audience members may feel resentment toward the professor and have trouble listening to what is said.

Speaker

The **speaker** is the source or originator of the speech. As the speaker, what you discuss and the language you use to express those ideas will depend on your own interests, beliefs, background, and public speaking skills. You will choose topics that you care about, know something about, and want to inform or persuade others about. Your experiences will influence the attitudes and beliefs that you express in the speeches you give. For example, after a drunk driver killed her daughter, Candace Lightner began speaking out about the lenient treatment afforded those who drove drunk. Her speeches on this issue led her to become a cofounder of MADD, Mothers Against Drunk Driving. Although your speeches may not lead you to found a social movement, how well you communicate your ideas will depend on your public speaking skills. In this course, you will learn the skills you will need to craft and deliver effective speeches and presentations.

psychological setting the feelings, attitudes, and beliefs of individual audience members that affect how your speech message is perceived

speaker the source or originator of the speech

Speech Planning Process

Whereas most of our day-to-day interactions occur without much forethought on our part, most of the speeches and presentations that we give are based on preparation. The **speech planning process** is the system that you use to prepare a speech. All of us have heard lectures, speeches, and presentations that were disorganized, boring, and difficult to follow. We may have even commented that the speaker needed to do more to prepare. In this course, you will learn a proven six-step process that will enable you to plan effective speeches. The six steps in this process are (1) selecting a specific speech goal that is appropriate for your audience and occasion, (2) developing a strategy for audience adaptation, (3) gathering and evaluating information to use in your speech, (4) organizing and developing information into a well-structured outline, (5) choosing visual and other presentational aids that are appropriate for your audience, and (6) practicing your speech wording and delivery. You will learn more about these six steps in Chapter 2.

speech planning process the system that you use to prepare a speech

Speech Making Process

Once you have carefully prepared your speech, you still have to deliver it to your audience. **Speech making** is this process of actually presenting a speech to the intended audience. Although you may be nervous before an audience, your planning will give you confidence and allow you to focus on helping the audience understand your message rather than focusing your attention on your discomfort. During your presentation, you will be conscious of what you have planned to say, but you will also respond to audience feedback and adjust to how your audience is receiving your speech. When you are well prepared, you will be comfortable deviating from your planned material to expand on definitions, offer additional examples, or vary your pace in response to audience members' needs.

Speech Effectiveness

When you give a speech, your goal is to communicate with your audience members. You will be effective if, when you have finished speaking, the members of your audience have remained attentive, have understood what you have said, remember the main ideas you have spoken about, and are motivated to use what they have learned from you. Thus, **speech effectiveness** is the extent to which audience members listen to, understand, remember, and are motivated to act on what a speaker has said. All effective public speeches have one thing in common: They are audience-centered. More specifically, they are audience-centered in their content, their structure, and their delivery. Later chapters will go into much more detail about these speech qualities, but let's take a quick look at them now.

AN EFFECTIVE SPEECH IS AUDIENCE-CENTERED

Effective public speakers are **audience-centered**. Being audience-centered means considering who your listeners are and how your message can best be tailored to their interests, desires, and needs.[7] When listening to an audience-centered speech, audience members sense that the speaker cares about them enough to offer ideas in ways that make sense, are relevant, reflect careful research, and sound interesting. Essentially, you are audience-centered when you demonstrate honesty and respect for your listeners by selecting an appropriate topic, developing and organizing the content in a way that is easy for your audience to hear, rehearsing your delivery, and presenting the speech so that it meets your audience's needs.

AN EFFECTIVE SPEECH INCLUDES AUDIENCE-APPROPRIATE CONTENT

The content of a speech is the information and ideas you present. It encompasses your purpose for giving the speech, the main ideas you will present, and the evidence you use to develop your main ideas. Evidence clarifies, explains, or supports your main ideas. It includes facts, expert opinions, and elaborations, and it comes from your own experiences as well as from research materials you collect. Effective evidence has sufficient breadth and depth. *Breadth* refers to the amount and types of evidence you use. *Depth* is the level of detail you provide from each piece of evidence. The ideas you choose to present depend on what is appropriate for your audience, and you adapt your content so that it includes listener-relevance links, which are statements of how and why the ideas you offer are of interest to your listeners.

speech making the process of presenting a speech to the intended audience

speech effectiveness the extent to which audience members listen to, understand, remember, and are motivated to act on what a speaker has said

audience-centered considering who your listeners are and how your message can best be tailored to their interests, desires, and needs

SPEECH SNIPPET

Being Audience-Centered

Kris's first speech was a speech of self-introduction. Her audience was her classmates, a diverse group of men and women with a variety of life experiences. In planning what to say, Kris decided to concentrate on how who she is led to her major. In this way, she hoped to help her audience know her by comparing her academic journey to their own.

SPEECH SNIPPET

Content

Kris decided to talk about how growing up in a resort town influenced her plans to study hospitality management; how being an identical twin contributed to her decision to attend this college; and how she hoped to use her major to work in a ski resort where she could help children with disabilities learn to snowboard. She made sure her content was audience-centered by focusing on the importance of pursuing one's dreams when selecting a major and a career goal.

Macrostructure

Kris decided that the most logical way to present her main ideas was chronologically. She would begin by talking about being a twin, then discuss how her upbringing influenced her choice of majors, and she'd conclude with her dream of teaching kids with disabilities to snowboard. She planned to use people's curiosity about twins to pique interest during her introduction, and she planned a conclusion that would challenge her audience to pursue their passions.

macrostructure the overall framework you use to organize your speech content

microstructure the specific language and style choices you use as you frame your ideas and verbalize them to your audience

SPEECH SNIPPET

Microstructure: Rhetorical Devices

Kris wanted to maintain her audience's attention as she began her first main point, so she practiced using the rhetorical device called *hypophora*, when the speaker raises a question to pique the audience's curiosity and then answers it: "Have you ever looked into a mirror, seen your reflection, and then realized that the reflection in the mirror wasn't really you? No? Well, as weird as it may seem to you, I've had this experience many times in my life. You see, I have an identical twin sister."

AN EFFECTIVE SPEECH IS WELL STRUCTURED

The structure of a speech is the framework that organizes the content. A clear structure helps your listeners follow your ideas so they can understand the points you are making.[8] You will develop a clear structure by working on both the macrostructure and the microstructure of your speech.

Macrostructure is the overall framework you use to organize your speech content. It has four elements: the introduction, body, conclusion, and transitions. The introduction is the beginning segment of the speech and should be structured so that you build audience interest in your topic and preview what you are going to say (you tell them what you are going to tell them). The speech body contains the main ideas and supporting material you have decided to present; it is organized into a pattern that makes the ideas easy for the audience to understand and remember (you tell them). The conclusion ends the speech, reminds the audience of your main ideas, and motivates them to remember or act upon what you have said (you tell them what you told them). The macrostructure of your speech also includes transitions, which are the words or phrases you use to move from one idea to the next.

You have studied macrostructure throughout your education as you learned to write. Now, however, you will be learning how to adapt it to oral messages. You'll see that careful attention to macrostructure is more important when you craft a speech than when you write an essay. A reader can easily reread a poorly written essay to try to understand your intent, but an audience does not usually have the opportunity to rehear your speech. So, as you prepare each of your speeches, you will need to develop an organizational framework that enables your audience to quickly understand and easily remember the ideas you present. In Chapters 7 and 8, you will learn how to develop a macrostructure suited to your topic and audience.

Whereas macrostructure is the overall framework you design for your speech, **microstructure** is the specific language and style choices you use as you frame your ideas and verbalize them to your audience. Pay careful attention to microstructure while practicing and delivering your speech so that you can present your ideas with words that are instantly intelligible and guide your audience to thoughts that are consistent with your own. Practicing and using words that are accurate, clear, vivid and appropriate will help you accomplish your speaking goal.

As your practice wording, you can also plan to use microstructural rhetorical devices. These language techniques are designed to create audience attention, hold interest, and aid memory. Again, from your composition classes, you may be familiar with techniques such as alliteration, onomatopoeia, personification, and other rhetorical devices. In Chapter 10, you will learn how to frame your ideas using effective rhetorical devices that make it easy for your audience to understand and remember the ideas in your speech.

AN EFFECTIVE SPEECH IS DELIVERED ENTHUSIASTICALLY

Delivery is how you use your voice and body to present your message. The manner in which a speech is delivered can dramatically affect the audience's ability to listen to, understand, remember, and act on the ideas presented. Speakers whose voice and body actions have a conversational quality encourage audience members to listen. When speakers use appropriate volume, rate, pronunciation, and enunciation, they make their message easier for the audience to understand. When speakers are expressive and enthusiastic, listeners are more likely to remember and act on what has been said. In fact, listeners often are more persuaded by the manner in which a speech is delivered than by the words used.[9]

Speaking conversationally means sounding as though you are having a spontaneous conversation with your audience rather than simply reading to them or performing in front of them. **Speaking expressively** means using various vocal techniques so you sound a bit more dramatic than you would in casual conversation. Some common vocal techniques used in speeches include speaking more quickly or loudly to underscore your attitudes or emotional convictions, stressing key words or phrases, and pausing strategically to call attention to important ideas.

As you may already know, nonverbal communication is just as important as verbal communication in conveying messages. Effective speakers know this and use their eyes, face, stance, and hands to help them deliver a speech. For example, they make eye contact with audience members rather than focusing solely on their notes, and they use appropriate facial expressions to reflect their conviction about their topic. They stand with poise and confidence, they avoid fidgeting, and they use gestures to reinforce important points.

For an example of a speech of self-introduction, read Kris's outline for her entire speech at the end of this chapter. There you'll see the culmination of her efforts to make her speech audience-centered and well structured.

SPOTLIGHT ON SPEAKERS

Frederick Douglass *This Fourth of July Is Yours, Not Mine*

Portrait of Frederick Douglass (1817–95) (oil on canvas) Frederick Douglass National Historic Site, Washington, USA, American School, The Bridgeman Art Library

The U.S. Constitution makes it clear that we are to be a nation of free people. Yet throughout much of the nineteenth century, Frederick Douglass felt anything but free. Born into slavery and separated from his parents at birth, Douglass managed to escape and then devoted his life to addressing the moral, legal, and ethical issues of this wicked social system. Douglass saw in speech making a way to empower himself and his people who were still enslaved. Much sought after as a lecturer, Douglass was invited to give a speech in 1852 in Rochester, New York, at a Fourth of July celebration where the audience was primarily white.

In his speech "What to the Slave Is the Fourth of July?" Douglass gives a powerful oration on the meaninglessness of this day. In this short excerpt, notice how Douglass uses the irony of this situation to his advantage:

Your high independence only reveals the immeasurable distance between us. The blessings in which you, this day, rejoice, are not enjoyed in common. The rich inheritance of justice, liberty, prosperity and independence, bequeathed by your fathers, is shared by you, not by me. The sunlight that brought light and healing to you, has brought stripes and death to me. This Fourth [of] July is yours, not mine. You may rejoice, I must mourn.

Through this moral appeal, Douglass shares his personal testimony and alludes to his vision for change. Like Douglass, you too can be *empowered* by the speaking process. Frederick Douglass's vision and his single voice earned him the respect and honor of many, including an appointment as adviser to President Lincoln. But more important, his strong words helped bring about change—an amendment—to a constitution that claimed liberty for all.

To Think About

✦ What social issue today is particularly important to you and why?

✦ What type of speech might you prepare about this issue?

✦ How would doing so serve to empower you?

Public Speaking Skills Empower

You may be taking this course because it is required, but we believe this may be the single most important course you take during your college career. Why? Because developing public speaking skills empowers you in four ways.

First, developing public speaking skills empowers you to communicate complex ideas and information in a way that all members of the audience can understand. Many of us have had the experience of understanding something but being unable to explain it clearly to others. Most of us have had an unfortunate experience with a teacher who "talked over our heads." The teacher understood the material but was unable to express it clearly to us. When we can express our ideas clearly, we are more likely to share them. When others understand our ideas, they learn from us.

Second, developing public speaking skills empowers you to influence the attitudes and behavior of other people. We seem to be trying constantly to influence others. Have you ever tried to get a classmate to lend you her notes? Or tried to get an airline to change a reservation without charging a fee? Have you tried to get your boss to give you an extra shift at work? Or tried to get a professor to change a grade you received? When we thoughtfully articulate the reasons for our positions and requests, others are more likely to comply with our wishes. Public speaking skills equip us to fashion arguments that others may find compelling.

Third, mastering public speaking skills empowers you to achieve your career goals. Studies show that for almost any job, one of the most highly sought-after skills in new hires is oral communication skills.[10] So, whether you aspire to a career in business, industry, government, education, or almost any other field you can name, communication skills are a likely prerequisite to your success. Moreover, most jobs require people to present oral reports and proposals and to train coworkers. Although you might be hired on the basis of your technical competence, your ability to earn promotions will depend on your ability to communicate what you know to others, including your boss, your clients, and your colleagues.

Fourth, public speaking skills empower you to participate in our democratic processes. Free speech is a hallmark of our democracy. The strategies and policies our government adopts are a direct result of the debate that occurs across the nation and in our executive, legislative, and judicial branches of government. When you are equipped with sound public speaking skills, you will have the confidence to speak out in town hall meetings and other settings and voice your ideas on important public issues.

Public Speaking Challenges Us to Behave Ethically

Today, as in times past, we expect a speaker to behave ethically. **Ethics** are a set of moral principles that a society, group, or individual holds that differentiate right from wrong and good behavior from bad behavior. (To read a thorough discussion about ethics and what they involve, go to your CengageNOW for *Challenge* to access **Web Resource 1.1: The Basics of Ethics**. To learn how to get started with your CengageNOW and other online textbook resources, see the inside front and back covers of this book.) Regardless of whether the setting for your speeches is a classroom, a boardroom, the campaign trail, or the floor of a legislative body, you have ethical responsibilities to your listeners.

Speakers are ethical when they conform to standards of moral behavior that are expected in public speaking situations. What standards are we expected to conform to? Five generally agreed upon standards are honesty (not to lie, cheat, or steal), integrity (holding sound moral principles), fairness (behaving justly), respect (showing consideration), and responsibility (being accountable). If you look at these closely, you'll see that these terms are quite general and abstract. But there are two specific behaviors that are fundamental to ethical speaking:

1. Ethical speakers tell the truth. Telling the truth is showing honesty in behavior. An audience expects that what you tell them will be true—not made

ethics a set of moral principles that a society, group, or individual holds that differentiate right from wrong and good behavior from bad behavior

up, not your personal belief presented as fact, and not an exaggeration. If, during or after your speech, members of your audience doubt the accuracy of something you have said, they are likely to reject all of your ideas. To make sure that what you say is truthful, you will want to research your topic carefully and present both sides of controversial issues accurately.

2. Ethical speakers fully credit sources for their ideas. Fully **crediting ideas**—giving the sources of the information you use—is ethical. Presenting others' ideas as your own or refraining from identifying questionable sources is unethical. For instance, saying "The overwhelming majority of people have a pessimistic view of ethics and morality in this country" is less ethical than saying "According to a Gallup poll cited in a June 28, 2003, *Christian Century* article, 'Seventy-seven percent of Americans rated current ethics and morality as fair or poor.'"[11]

crediting ideas giving the sources of information you use

In many cases, failing to cite sources is **plagiarism**—stealing and passing off the ideas, words, or created works of another as one's own without crediting the source. Unfortunately, plagiarism is all too common. According to a 2002–2003 survey of 3,500 graduate students at U.S. and Canadian universities, "23 percent to 25 percent of students acknowledged one or more instances of 'cutting and pasting' from Internet sources and/or published documents."[12] Moreover, 38 percent of undergrads admit to committing such online plagiarism in the past year (2003).[13] In the classroom setting, plagiarism can lead to failing an assignment or the course or to suspension from school. In public speaking settings, it can undermine speaker credibility, result in lawsuits, and ruin promising careers.

plagiarism the unethical act of representing another person's work as your own

How can you recognize and avoid plagiarism? Caroline McCullen cites three common methods of plagiarism:[14]

1. If you change a few words at the beginning, in the middle, or at the end of the material, but copy much of the rest, you are plagiarizing.

2. If you paraphrase the unique ideas of another person and do not credit that person, you are plagiarizing.

3. If you purchase, borrow, or use a speech prepared by another and present it as original, you are plagiarizing.

Crediting sources is also important because where ideas originate is often as important as the ideas themselves. For example, the faith that an audience may place in a statistic on global warming will depend on the source. If the statistic comes from an article by a renowned scientist in a respected peer-reviewed journal, it is likely to have more credibility than if it comes from the personal web page of someone with unknown credentials. Ethical speakers are careful to acknowledge the sources of controversial ideas, especially when the information is damaging to an individual or institution.

Throughout this text, we will continue to discuss ethical standards for public speaking. Likewise, we will consider more specific ethical issues as we discuss topic selection, audience analysis, selection and use of supporting information, construction and use of visual aids, speech language, delivery, reasoning, use of emotional appeals, establishing credibility, and refutation.

Most of the ethical principles we will present are drawn from what is commonly accepted to be ethical behavior in the United States. But we will note where standards differ across cultures and how these differences lead to alter-

© Christopher Morris/Black Star/PictureQuest

Ethical speakers embody the behaviors they advocate for others. President Jimmy Carter and his wife, Rosalynn, have long advocated for Habitat for Humanity, an organization they both volunteer for.

native ethics. Because ethical behavior is central to public speaking, in each chapter you will find a Reflect on Ethics box like the one on this page. These short cases challenge you to think through your ethical responsibilities as a speaker.

To learn more about ethics, check out the website for the Markkula Center for Applied Ethics at Santa Clara University. Go to your CengageNOW for *Challenge* to access **Web Resource 1.2: Ethics Connection**. (To learn how to get started with your CengageNOW and other online textbook resources, see the inside front and back covers of this book.)

REFLECT ON ETHICS

Nalini sighed loudly as the club members of Toastmasters International took their seats. It was her first time meeting with the public speaking group, and she didn't want to be there, but her mom had insisted that she join the club in the hopes that it would help Nalini transfer from her community college to the state university. It wasn't that the idea of public speaking scared Nalini. She had already spent time in front of an audience as the lead singer of the defunct emo band Deathstar. To Nalini's mind, public speaking was just another type of performance, like singing or acting, albeit a stuffy form better suited to middle-aged men and women than people her own age, a sentiment that explained why she wanted to be elsewhere at the moment.

After the club leader called the meeting to order, he asked each of the new members to stand, introduce themselves, and give a brief speech describing their background, aspirations, and reasons for joining the club. "Spare me," Nalini muttered loud enough for those next to her to hear. The club leader then called on a young woman to Nalini's left, who rose and began to speak about her dream of becoming a lawyer and doing public advocacy work for the poor. After the young woman sat down, the club members applauded politely. Nalini whistled and clapped loudly and kept on clapping after the others had stopped.

The club leader, somewhat taken aback, called on Nalini next. She rose from her seat and introduced herself as the secret love child of a former president and a famous actress. Nalini then strung together a series of other fantastic lies about her past and her ambitions. She concluded her speech by saying that she had joined the club in the hopes that she could learn how to hypnotize audiences into obeying her commands. After Nalini sat, a few of the club members applauded quietly, while others cast glances at each other and the club leader.

1. Is mocking behavior in a formal public speaking setting, either by an audience member or a speaker, an ethical matter? Explain your answer.
2. What ethical obligations does an audience member have to a speaker? What about a speaker to his or her audience?

SPEECH ASSIGNMENT

Speech of Self-Introduction

Prepare a two- to three-minute speech of self-introduction. Tell us about the following:

1. Your personal background
2. Something that makes you unique
3. Why you chose your major

As you prepare your speech, use the Speech Evaluation Checklist that follows to check that your speech includes all the elements of an effective speech.

General Criteria

You can use this checklist to critique a speech of self-introduction that you hear in class. (You can also use it to critique your own speech.) As you listen to the speaker, consider what makes a speech effective. Then answer the following questions.

Content

_____ **1.** Were all three main points addressed per the assignment?

_____ **2.** Were two to three pieces of evidence provided for each main point?

_____ **3.** Was one extended piece of evidence provided for each main point?

_____ **4.** Were listener-relevance links provided for each main point?

_____ **5.** Did the speech fall within the time constraints of the assignment?

Structure

1. Did the speech provide all the basic elements of an effective speech: introduction, body, conclusion, and transitions? *(macrostructure)*

2. Did the introduction _____ catch the audience's interest? _____ state the topic of the speech? _____ preview the main points of the speech?

3. Were the main points organized in a way that helped the audience understand and remember the ideas in the speech?

4. Were transitions provided between each main point?

5. Did the conclusion _____ remind the audience of the main points? _____ motivate the audience to remember the main ideas of the speech?

6. Did the speaker use words that were _____ accurate and clear? _____ vivid and emphatic? _____ appropriate and inclusive? *(microstructure)*

7. Did the speaker use rhetorical devices that _____ gained the audience's attention? _____ held the audience's interest? *(microstructure)*

Delivery

1. Did the speaker use the appropriate _____ volume? _____ rate of speaking?

2. Did the speaker use proper _____ pronunciation? _____ enunciation?

3. Was the speaker's voice _____ intelligible? _____ conversational? _____ expressive?

4. Did the speaker look up from his or her notes most of the time and make eye contact with the audience?

5. Did the speaker use appropriate facial expressions and gestures to reinforce important points?

6. Was the speaker poised and confident?

You can use your CengageNOW for *Challenge* to access this checklist, complete it online and compare your feedback to that of the authors, or print a copy to use in class. (To learn how to get started with your CengageNOW and other online textbook resources, see the inside front and back covers of this book.)

Speech of Self-Introduction

Mirror Image

by Kris Treinen[15]

Use your CengageNOW for *Challenge* to watch a video clip of Kris presenting her speech in class. (See the inside back cover of this book for how to access the *Challenge* speech videos through CengageNOW.)

Introduction

I. Have you ever looked into a mirror and seen your reflection, and realized that the reflection in the mirror wasn't really you? I have, many times. *(catch audience's interest)*

II. As you listen to my speech today, I believe you'll begin to understand how important I believe it is to believe in yourself, your family and friends, and most important, your dreams. *(listener-relevance link)*

III. Today, I'd like to introduce myself to you by talking about why my mirror image makes me unique, how where I grew up influenced my choice of majors, and how, ultimately, my major has helped shape my career goal. *(preview of main points)*

Body

I. When I was a child, I had a mirror image that wasn't really me and I still have it today.

    A. My mirror image isn't really an "it" but a "her."

        1. Her name is Karla, and she is my identical "mirror image" twin sister.

        2. Every day I am away from her, I realize how easy it was to take her and my family for granted. *(listener-relevance link)*

    B. My sister and I were born right here at a local hospital in Fargo, North Dakota.

        1. We were born three minutes apart.

        2. I was born first, so I'm the oldest.

    C. We were known as the "good" twin and the "evil" twin.

        1. Here is a story about me as the "good" twin.

        2. Here is a story about her as the "evil" twin.

Transition: Now that you know how having my own mirror image—my twin—makes me unique, let's talk a bit about how where I grew up influenced my choice of a major.

II. I spent most of my life growing up in the lakes area of Brainerd, Minnesota—perhaps you'll want to visit this area after you hear about it today. *(listener-relevance link)*

    A. I grew up in a small town called Nisswa, Minnesota.

        1. I moved to Nisswa when I was three years old.

        2. We lived in a house that was very special to me.

    B. As I grew up in an area known for lots of snow in the winter, I got involved in snowboarding.

        1. I started snowboarding recreationally.

        2. Then I competed as a snowboarder.

        3. Eventually, I taught snowboarding as a part-time job.

Transition: So my upbringing led me to realize I love to snowboard and to teach snowboarding, which is why I chose to come to school here at North Dakota State University (NDSU).

III. I chose to further my education with a major in hospitality management. *(listener-relevance link)*

    A. NDSU has a reputable program.

    B. The winters in the Fargo area allow me to continue to pursue snowboarding.

    C. Ultimately, my degree will help me pursue my goal to work in a ski resort area and help children with disabilities learn to snowboard.

Conclusion

I. Now that you know a little bit about me as a twin and why I chose to major in hospitality management, I hope you'll be inspired to also follow your career dreams. *(reminder of main points)*

II. I hope you now see why I have learned to look beyond the reflection I see in the mirror to understand who I really am on the way to who I will one day become. *(motivation to remember main ideas)*

Summary

Public speaking is important to success in nearly every walk of life. Speeches—oral presentations that are usually given without interruption—occur at formal occasions where an audience has assembled expressly to listen, in less formal employment contexts, and during our informal daily conversations.

Public speaking is an audience-centered process that occurs within a speaking context comprised of physical, cultural, historical, and psychological factors. The speaker uses a six-part speech plan process that includes selecting a goal, developing a strategy for audience adaptation, gathering and evaluating information, organizing the information, choosing visual and other presentational aids, and practicing speech wording and delivery. How effective a speech is depends on how well audience members listen to, understand, remember, and are motivated to act on what the speaker has said. Effective speeches are audience-centered with appropriate content, clear structure, and enthusiastic delivery.

Public speaking skills empower us to communicate ideas and information in a way that all members of the audience can understand. They enable us to influence the attitudes and behaviors of others, to achieve career goals, and to participate in our democratic society.

Public speaking challenges us to behave ethically. Ethics—a set of moral principles that differentiate right from wrong and good behavior from bad behavior—rely on standards of honesty, integrity, fairness, respect, and responsibility. Specifically, ethical speakers fully credit sources for their ideas to avoid plagiarism, as well as to demonstrate honesty and respect for their listeners.

CHALLENGE ONLINE

CENGAGENOW

Now that you've read Chapter 1, use your Cengage-NOW for *The Challenge of Effective Speaking* for quick access to the electronic resources that accompany this text. Your CengageNOW gives you access to the Web Resources activities featured in this chapter, Speech Builder Express, InfoTrac College Edition, and online study aids such as a digital glossary and review quizzes. To learn how to get started with your CengageNOW and other online textbook resources, see the inside front and back covers of this book.

Your *Challenge* CengageNOW is an online study system that helps you identify concepts you don't fully understand, allowing you to put your study time to the best use. Using chapter-by-chapter diagnostic pretests, the system creates a personalized study plan for each chapter. Each plan directs you to specific resources designed to improve your understanding, including pages from the text in e-book format. Chapter posttests give you an opportunity to measure how much you've learned and let you know if you are ready for graded quizzes and exams.

KEY TERMS

Go to your CengageNOW for *Challenge* to access your online glossary for Chapter 1. Print a copy of the glossary for this chapter and test yourself with the electronic flash cards or complete the crossword puzzle to help you master these key terms:

audience (4)
audience analysis (4)
audience-centered (7)
audience feedback (5)
crediting ideas (11)
cultural setting (5)
ethics (10)

historical setting (5)
macrostructure (8)
microstructure (8)
physical setting (5)
plagiarism (11)
psychological setting (6)
public speech, or oration (3)

speaker (6)
speaking context (5)
speaking conversationally (9)
speaking expressively (9)
speech effectiveness (7)
speech making (7)
speech planning process (6)

WEB RESOURCES

Go to your CengageNOW for *Challenge* to access the Web Resources for this chapter.

1.1 The Basics of Ethics (10)
1.2 Ethics Connection (12)

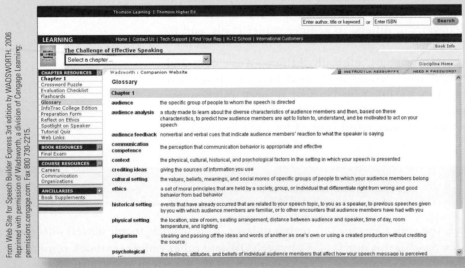

Developing Confidence through the Speech Planning Process

Courage is resistance to fear, mastery of fear, not absence of fear.

Mark Twain, *Pudd'nhead Wilson*

What's Ahead

HERE'S WHAT'S AHEAD IN THIS CHAPTER:

1. What is public speaking apprehension?

2. Why do we experience public speaking apprehension?

3. What can we do to manage public speaking apprehension?

4. In what ways does careful planning help reduce public speaking apprehension?

5. What are the six steps in an effective speech action plan?

Professor Montrose begins class by saying, "Let's look at some of the key points of the chapter that you were assigned to read for today." He then points to Paul and asks, "What were the keys to solving the Kingston problem effectively?" Paul, sputtering and turning red, begins to sweat and stammers, "Well, uh, I guess that, well . . ." Professor Montrose then points to the next student and asks, "Sylvia, what would you say about this?" Sylvia looks at Professor Montrose and answers, "According to the text, there are three steps involved." She goes on to list the steps and then discusses each of the three.

You might think, "Poor, Paul. He just got so nervous when Professor Montrose pointed at him and asked him the question that he couldn't remember a thing." And perhaps he did suffer from severe speech anxiety—or stage fright. But then why was Sylvia able to look Professor Montrose in the eye, tell him there are three steps, and then discuss each? One answer might be, "Well, she doesn't suffer stage fright, so she was able to answer the question." Although that might well be true, there's another answer as well: Paul hadn't prepared well for class, while Sylvia had not only read the text material but had also outlined the key points and reviewed them over a cup of coffee before class.

Recall the title of this chapter: "Developing Confidence through the Speech Planning Process." Although stage fright is normal in public settings, even the most frightened person whose heart is pounding will perform better when he or she is well prepared. In fact, as many as 76 percent of experienced public speakers claim to feel fearful before presenting a speech.[1] For example, did you know that award-winning actor Meryl Streep, singer Barbra Streisand, and evangelist Billy Graham all experience fear of public speaking? In spite of their fear, all are effective public speakers because they employ the strategies for managing nervousness that we will share with you in this chapter.

We begin this chapter by explaining what scholars call "public speaking apprehension" or what you might call "stage fright." Then we discuss how you can manage anxiety successfully and, most important, how careful preparation can help you develop confidence when you speak. At the end of the chapter, we consider the narrative speech, a common first speech assignment in this course.

Understanding Public Speaking Apprehension

People have feared speaking in public since they first began doing it. And those who teach others to speak publicly have been concerned with helping students overcome their fears almost as long. **Public speaking apprehension,** a type of communication anxiety, is the level of fear a person experiences when anticipating or actually speaking to an audience. Almost all of us have some level of public speaking apprehension, but about 15 percent of the U.S. population experiences high levels of apprehension.[2] Yet this apprehension hardly ever stops people from speaking! In our teaching careers, we have only had two students whose stage fright was so severe that they could not complete a speech. One walked to the front of class, looked at the audience, and ran back

public speaking apprehension a type of communication anxiety; the level of fear a person experiences when anticipating or actually speaking to an audience

to his seat. The other paused, turned pale, sat down, and then walked back to her seat. Today, we can benefit from a significant wealth of research studies that have identified methods for helping us overcome our nervousness.

Signs of Public Speaking Apprehension

The signs of pubic speaking apprehension vary from individual to individual, and symptoms range from mild to debilitating. Symptoms may include physical, emotional, and mental reactions. Physically, you may experience stomach upset (or butterflies), flushed skin, sweating, shaking, lightheadedness, rapid or heavy heartbeats, and verbal dysfluencies including stuttering and vocalized pauses ("like," "you know," "ah," "um"). Emotionally, you may feel anxious, worried, or upset. You might also experience specific negative thought patterns. For example, a highly apprehensive person might dwell on thoughts such as "I'm going to make a fool of myself" or "I just know that I'll blow it."

Luckily, the level of public speaking apprehension we experience seems to vary and gradually decreases as we speak. Researchers have identified three phases of reaction that we proceed through: anticipation reaction, confrontation reaction, and adaptation reaction.[3] Exhibit 2.1 depicts this cycle visually.

Anticipation reaction is the level of anxiety you experience prior to giving the speech, including the nervousness you feel while preparing and waiting to speak. Your **confrontation reaction** is the surge in your anxiety level that you feel as you begin your speech. This level begins to fall about a minute or so into your speech and will level off at your prespeaking level about five minutes into your presentation. Your **adaptation reaction** is the gradual decline of your anxiety level that begins about one minute into the presentation and results in your anxiety level's declining to its prespeaking level in about five minutes. Research has found that most of us experience moderate levels of both anticipation and confrontation reactions.[4] So, it's normal to be nervous before you speak.

There are many ways to measure your level of public speaking apprehension. Exhibit 2.2 presents one short survey that is widely used by researchers. You can complete the six questions and score them to gauge your level of apprehension.

anticipation reaction the level of anxiety you experience prior to giving the speech, including the nervousness you feel while preparing and waiting to speak

confrontation reaction the surge in your anxiety level that you feel as you begin your speech

adaptation reaction the gradual decline of your anxiety level that begins about one minute into the presentation and results in your anxiety level's declining to its prespeaking level in about five minutes

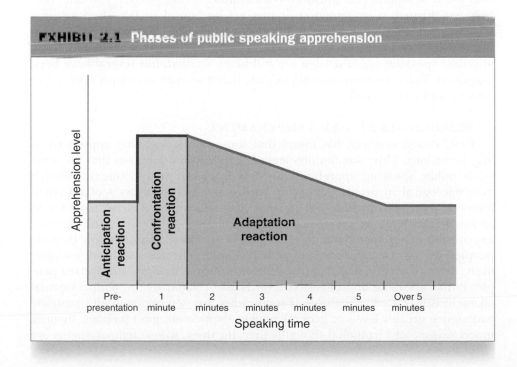

EXHIBIT 2.1 Phases of public speaking apprehension

Causes of Public Speaking Apprehension

self-talk thoughts about success or failure that go through one's mind prior to or during a particular situation

Public speaking apprehension is most commonly caused by negative self-talk.[5] **Self-talk** is defined as the thoughts about success or failure that go through your mind in a particular situation. For example, telling yourself you can't possibly get through a presentation or that you're bound to fail when giving a speech is self-defeating because it increases your anxiety. Where do these negative thoughts come from? The roots of negative self-talk that ultimately result in public speaking apprehension are still being studied, but several have been suggested. These roots include biologically based temperament, previous experiences, and level of skills.

BIOLOGICALLY BASED TEMPERAMENT

First, recent research has found that some public speaking apprehension may be inborn. This "communibiological" explanation proposes that for some of us public speaking apprehension stems from our temperament, which is neurobiological in origin. According to this theory, two aspects of inherited temperament, extroversion–introversion and neuroticism, blend together to create higher levels of public speaking apprehension.[6] People who are more extroverted experience lower levels of public speaking apprehension than do people who are introverted. Extroverted people generally are more sociable, lively, active, assertive, dominant, and adventuresome than are introverted people. Public speaking apprehension level is also related to the temperamental characteristic called *neuroticism*. People who are temperamentally neurotic experience greater levels of general anxiety, depression, guilt feelings, shyness, mood swings, and irrational thoughts than do those whose temperaments are stabler. According to the communibiological theory, public speaking apprehension is likely to be higher for those of us who are both more introverted and more neurotic. Does this mean that if you are temperamentally predisposed toward high public speaking apprehension, you are doomed to be ineffective in your speaking efforts? Of course not, but it does suggest that you will be "working against the grain" and may need special help in learning how to control some of the negative aspects of your temperament.[7]

PREVIOUS EXPERIENCE

Second, our level of apprehension may also result from our experiences with public speaking while growing up. In other words, some of us learned to fear public speaking! Research tells us that most public speaking apprehension stems from such socialization.[8] We are socialized in primarily two ways: through modeling and reinforcement. *Modeling* is learning through watching and then imitating the behaviors and reactions of those you admire or are close to.[9] *Reinforcement* is learning from personal experiences so that past responses to our behavior shapes our present behavior and expectations about how our future behavior will be received.[10]

Consider your past. How did modeling affect your current communication behavior? What was oral communication like in your home when you were a child? What was it like in your community? Did your parents talk freely with each other in your presence? Did family or community members talk with each other a great deal, or were they quiet and reserved? What was it like around the dinner table or at community events? Did any of your family members do much public speaking? What were their experiences? Did they avoid public speaking if they could? If your family tended to be quiet and reserved and avoided speaking in public or showed fear about it, your own preferences and fears may stem from modeling. Modeling an aversion to speaking freely in public influenced noted *Boston Globe* columnist Diana White, who remarked, "In my family, looking for attention was one of the worst sins a child could commit. 'Don't make a spectacle of yourself' was a familiar phrase around our house."[11]

How you have been reinforced by others in your speaking efforts also influences how well you believe you performed in the past and affects how apprehensive you feel about future speaking occasions. We have all had many "public speaking" experiences, from reading aloud during second grade, to giving an oral report in science class, to accepting a sports award at a banquet. If the responses to your speaking in the past were generally positive, you probably learned to feel confident of your ability. If, on the other hand, the responses were negative, you probably learned to feel fearful of public speaking. So, if your second-grade teacher humiliated you when you read aloud, if you flubbed that science report, or if friends laughed at your acceptance speech, you will probably be more apprehensive about speaking in public than if you had been praised for your efforts. However, the public speaking apprehension you feel because of negative past experiences, though uncomfortable, does not have to handicap your future performances. There are strategies you can use as you prepare to speak that will help you reduce your apprehension and be more effective. We will discuss some of these strategies in the next section.

LEVEL OF SKILLS

An important source of public speaking apprehension comes from having underdeveloped speaking skills. This "skill deficit" theory was the earliest explanation for apprehension and continues to receive the attention of researchers. It suggests that most of us become apprehensive because we don't know how to (or choose not to) plan or prepare effectively for a public presentation.

Effective speech planning is an orderly process that is based on a set of skills. If you do not know or apply these skills, you are likely to have higher

© Chuck Savage/Corbis

Although most speakers confess to nervousness at the prospect of giving an important speech, the goal is not to eliminate nervousness but to learn how to manage it effectively.

anticipation reaction levels. On the other hand, as you become skilled at using the six-step speech planning process previewed later in this chapter, your preparation will give you confidence and your anticipation reaction will be lower than if you were ill prepared. The goal of this course is to help you become skilled and, in so doing, help you become a more confident speaker.

Ideal Level of Apprehension

Many of us believe that we would be better off if we could be totally free from nervousness and apprehension. But based on years of study, Professor Gerald Phillips has concluded that nervousness is not necessarily negative. He noted that "learning proceeds best when the organism is in a state of tension."[12] In fact, it helps to be a little nervous to do your best: If you are lackadaisical about giving a speech, you probably will not do a good job.[13]

Because at least some tension is constructive, the goal is not to eliminate nervousness but to learn how to manage it. According to Phillips, studies that followed groups of students taking speaking courses found that nearly all of them still experienced tension, but almost all of them had learned to manage the nervousness. Phillips concludes that "apparently they had learned to manage the tension; they no longer saw it as an impairment, and they went ahead with what they had to do."[14] So let's look at how you can manage apprehension and use it to your advantage.

Overcoming Public Speaking Apprehension

Because our public speaking apprehension has multiple causes, there are both general methods and specific techniques that can help us reduce our anxiety and manage our nervousness.

General Methods

Some methods are targeted at reducing the apprehension that results from our worrisome thoughts and irrational beliefs. Other methods are aimed at reducing the physical symptoms of anxiety that we experience. Still others focus on helping us overcome the skill deficiencies that lead to our anxiety. In this section, we consider five common methods for reducing public speaking apprehension.

1. Communication orientation motivation (COM) techniques are designed to reduce anxiety by helping us adopt a "communication" rather than a "performance" orientation toward our speeches.[15] According to Michael Motley, public speaking anxiety increases when we hold a **performance orientation,** viewing public speaking as a situation that demands special delivery techniques to impress our audience "aesthetically"[16] or viewing audience members as hypercritical judges who will not forgive even our minor mistakes. On the other

communication orientation motivation (COM) techniques designed to reduce anxiety by helping the speaker adopt a "communication" rather than a "performance" orientation toward the speech

performance orientation viewing public speaking as a situation demanding special delivery techniques to impress an audience aesthetically or viewing audience members as hypercritical judges who will not forgive even our minor mistakes

hand, if we approach public speaking from a **communication orientation,** we view our speech as just an opportunity to talk with a number of people about a topic that is important to us and to our audience. When we have a communication orientation, we are focused on getting our message across to people in our audience rather than on how the people in our audience are judging or reacting to us as a speaker.

So, one way for performance-oriented individuals to reduce public speaking apprehension is to gain a basic understanding of public speaking apprehension, understand how their performance orientation adds to their apprehension, and consciously adopt a communication orientation. When we recognize that public speaking is very much like casual conversations, in which we focus on our message and the people who are listening, and when we recognize that our audience is concerned with understanding the content of the speech, not with judging us, we have adopted a communication rather than performance orientation, and our public speaking apprehension will be reduced.

2. Visualization is a method that reduces apprehension by helping us develop a mental picture of ourselves giving a masterful speech. Like COM techniques, visualization helps us overcome the mental and emotional causes of apprehension. Joe Ayres and Theodore S. Hopf, two scholars who have conducted extensive research on visualization, have found that if people can visualize themselves going through an entire speech preparation and speech making process, they will have a much better chance of succeeding when they are speaking.[17]

Visualization has been used extensively with athletes to improve sports performances. In a study of players trying to improve their foul-shooting percentages, players were divided into three groups. One group never practiced, another group practiced making foul shots, and a third group "practiced" by visualizing themselves making foul shots. As we would expect, those who physically practiced improved far more than those who didn't practice at all. What seems amazing is that those who simply *visualized* practicing improved almost as much as those who actually practiced.[18] Imagine what happens when you visualize and practice as well!

By visualizing the process of speech making, not only do people seem to lower their general apprehension, but they also report fewer negative thoughts when they actually speak.[19] So, you will want to use visualization activities as part of your speech preparation. To complete a visualization activity that will help you prepare your speeches, use your CengageNOW for *Challenge* to access **Web Resource 2.1: Visualizing Your Success**. This audio activity will guide you through a visualization in which you will imagine that you successfully accomplish the complete speech preparation and presentation process. (To learn how to get started with your CengageNOW and other online textbook resources, see the inside front and back covers of this book.)

3. Systematic desensitization is a method that reduces apprehension by gradually having people visualize increasingly more frightening events. Individuals first learn procedures for relaxation and then learn to apply these to each of the anxiety-producing events that they visualize. Thus, they learn to remain relaxed when they encounter these anxiety-producing situations in real life.[20] This method is used to help people overcome the physical symptoms of public speaking apprehension. Research tells us that more than 80 percent of those who try this method reduce their level of anxiety.[21] Since "relaxing" is easier said than done, these programs focus on teaching you deep muscle relaxation procedures. The process involves consciously tensing and then relaxing muscle groups to learn to recognize the difference between the two states. Then, while in a relaxed state, you imagine yourself in successively more stressful speech planning and speech making situations—for example, researching a speech

communication orientation viewing a speech as just an opportunity to talk with a number of people about a topic that is important to the speaker and to the audience

visualization a method that reduces apprehension by helping speakers develop a mental picture of themselves giving a masterful speech

systematic desensitization a method that reduces apprehension by gradually having people visualize increasingly more frightening events

topic in the library, practicing the speech out loud in front of a roommate, and delivering the final speech to your audience. Lastly, you engage in progressively more stressful public speaking situations while maintaining the learned state of calmness. The ultimate goal of systematic desensitization is to transfer the calm feelings we attain while visualizing to the actual speaking event. Calmness on command—and it works.

cognitive restructuring a process designed to help you systematically rebuild your thoughts about public speaking

4. **Cognitive restructuring** is a process designed to help you systematically rebuild your thoughts about public speaking. The goal is to replace anxiety-arousing negative self-talk with anxiety-reducing positive self-talk. The process consists of four steps.

✦ To change your negative thoughts, you must first identify them. Write down all the fears that come to mind when you know you must give a speech.

✦ Second, consider whether or not these fears are rational. Most fears about public speaking are, in fact, irrational because public speaking is not life threatening.

✦ Third, develop positive coping statements to replace each negative self-talk statement. There is no list of coping statements that will work for everyone; only you can determine what your negative self-talk statements are, why each is irrational, and what positive coping statement you can use to replace it. Psychologist Richard Heimberg of the State University of New York at Albany asks his clients to consider just how many listeners in an audience of 100 would even notice or care if the clients did what they're afraid of doing when giving a speech. Ultimately, he concludes with the question, "Can you cope with the one or two people who [notice or criticize or] get upset?"[22]

✦ The final step is to incorporate your positive coping statements into your life so that they're second nature. You can do this by writing your statements down and reading them aloud to yourself each day, as well as before you give a speech. The more you repeat your coping statements to yourself, silently and aloud, the more natural they will become and the more unnatural your negative thoughts will seem.

EXHIBIT 2.3 Negative self-talk versus positive coping statements

Beth decided to try cognitive restructuring to reduce her anxiety about giving speeches in front of her classmates. Here is how she worked through the process:

Negative self-talk
1. I'm afraid I'll stumble over my words and look foolish.
2. I'm afraid everyone will be able to tell that I'm nervous.
3. I'm afraid my voice will crack.
4. I'm afraid I'll sound boring.

Positive coping statements
1. Even if I stumble, I will have succeeded as long as I get my message across.
2. They probably won't be able to tell I'm nervous, but as long as I focus on getting my message across, that's what matters.
3. Even if my voice cracks, as long as I keep going and focus on getting my message across, I'll succeed at what matters most.
4. I won't sound bored if I focus on how important this message is to me and to my audience. I don't have to do somersaults to keep their attention because my topic is relevant to them.

For an activity that will help you develop positive coping statements to replace negative self-talk, use your CengageNOW to access **Web Resource 2.2: Restructure Your Expectations**. (To learn how to get started with your Cengage-NOW and other online textbook resources, see the inside front and back covers of this book.)

5. Public speaking skills training is the systematic teaching of the skills associated with the processes involved in preparing and delivering an effective public speech with the intention of reducing public speaking apprehension. Skills training is based on the assumption that some of our anxiety about speaking in public is due to our realization that we do not know how to be successful, that we lack the knowledge and behaviors to be effective. Therefore, if we learn the processes and behaviors associated with effective speech making, then we will be less anxious.[23] Public speaking skills include those associated with the processes of goal analysis, audience and situation analysis, organization, delivery, and self-evaluation.[24]

All five of these methods for reducing public speaking apprehension have successfully helped people reduce their anxiety. Researchers are just beginning to conduct studies to identify which techniques are most appropriate for a particular person. A study conducted by Karen Kangas Dwyer suggests that the most effective program for combating apprehension is one that uses a variety of techniques but individualizes them so that the techniques are used in a sequence that corresponds to the order in which the individual experiences apprehension.[25] So, for example, if your immediate reaction when facing a speaking situation is to think worrisome thoughts ("I don't know what I'm supposed to do," "I'm going to make a fool of myself"), which then lead you to feel nervous, you would be best served by first undergoing skills training or COM techniques. Another person who immediately feels the physical sensations of apprehension (such as nausea and rapid heartbeat) would benefit from first learning systematic desensitization techniques before working with visualization or receiving skills training. So, to reduce your public speaking apprehension, you may need to use all five techniques in a sequence that matches the order in which you experience apprehension.

If you think you'll experience public speaking apprehension in this course, which of these techniques do you think might help you? Have you already tried some of them in other situations? If they helped, do you think you could apply them to reduce your anxiety about giving a speech?

Specific Techniques

Along with the five general methods just discussed as ways of systematically overcoming public speaking apprehension, public speaking instructors generally recommend several specific techniques to novice speakers.

1. Allow sufficient time to prepare. During the first few days of class, you will receive a course syllabus, a plan for what will occur in class each day. Your instructor will let you know both how many and what kinds of speeches you will be giving this term. Armed with this information, you can develop a schedule based on preparing each speech over one or two weeks. If you have a topic at

public speaking skills training systematic teaching of the skills associated with the processes involved in preparing and delivering an effective public speech with the intention of improving speaking competence as a means of reducing public speaking apprehension

© Jeff Greenberg/PhotoEdit

If people can visualize themselves going through an entire process, they will have a much better chance of succeeding when they are in the situation.

least a week or ten days prior to your assigned presentation, you should be able to allow enough time to prepare for your speech.

2. Practice your speech aloud. When you practice your speech aloud, you get comfortable hearing yourself talk about your topic. You identify sections of the speech where your ideas may not flow and where you need to do additional preparation. By the third or fourth time you have practiced aloud, you will notice your delivery becoming easier, and you will gain confidence in your ability to present your ideas to others.

Many successful speakers not only practice aloud alone but also practice in front of trusted friends who serve as a "practice" audience and give the speaker feedback. On the night before your speech, review your speech plan immediately before you go to sleep. That way, as you sleep, your mind will continue to prepare.[26]

3. Choose an appropriate time to speak. In some classes, the date on which you speak will be assigned, but the order of speakers for the day is voluntary. Some students become more nervous when they sit and listen to others, so they are better off speaking early in the class period. Other students find that listening to their peers calms them, so they are better off speaking later in the class period. If given a chance, choose to speak at the time that is optimal for you.

4. Use positive self-talk. Immediately prior to getting up to speak, coach yourself with a short "pregame pep talk." Remind yourself about the importance of what you have to say. Remember all the hard work you have done to be prepared and recall how good you are when you are at your best. Remind yourself that nervousness is normal and useful. Tell yourself that you are confident and ready.

5. Face the audience. Face the audience with confidence. When it is time, walk purposefully to the front. Take a second or two to look at the audience. Take a deep breath as you smile and begin your well-rehearsed introduction.

6. Focus on your message. Although you may feel nervous, your audience is unlikely to "see" it. Continue to focus on sharing your ideas with the audience rather than focusing on your nerves.

Gaining Confidence through Effective Speech Planning

Whether you are a marketing account manager presenting an advertising campaign idea to your corporate clients, a coach trying to motivate your team in its game with your arch rival, or a student giving a speech in class, you will have more confidence in your likelihood of success when you have developed an effective **speech plan**—a strategy for achieving your goal.

speech plan a strategy for achieving your goal

An effective speech plan is the result of a six-step process:

1. Selecting a specific speaking goal that is appropriate for the audience and occasion
2. Understanding your audience and adapting to it
3. Gathering and evaluating information to use in the speech
4. Organizing and developing ideas into a well-structured speech outline
5. Choosing visual and other presentational aids that are appropriate for the audience
6. Practicing the speech wording and delivery

In Part Two of this book, you will learn the skills associated with each of these steps. As you practice the skills, you will gain confidence in your ability to present your ideas effectively. Let's briefly preview what you will learn in each step.

Step 1: Select a Speech Goal That Is Appropriate for the Audience and Occasion

Your **speech goal** (or speech purpose) is a statement of what you want your audience to know, believe, or do. To arrive at such a goal, you begin by selecting a topic. Regardless of whether you are a renowned speaker or are preparing your very first speech, the advice is the same: Choose a topic that you know something about and that interests you or is important to you. Although there could be times in your life when you must speak on a topic that is unfamiliar to you, in this class *and* in the great majority of real-life speaking experiences, you will be speaking on topics that meet these tests.

Because your speech will be given to a particular audience, before you get very far you need to think about your specific audience: Who are they? What do they need to know about your topic? What do they already know? To answer these questions, you need to make a preliminary audience analysis based on their gender, culture, average age, education level, occupation, income level, and group affiliation. As you study these factors, you can assess the kinds of material the audience is likely to know and the information they are likely to respond to.

Likewise, you need to consider the speaking context: What is the size of the audience? When will the speech be given? Where will the speech be given? What is the time limit for the speech? What is the specific assignment? Since you will be speaking in the same classroom all term, you can determine any peculiarities of the room that you need to take into consideration.

Once you have a topic and have analyzed the audience and setting, you can phrase your speech goal. Every speech has a general and a specific goal. For most of your in-class speeches, your general goal is likely to be assigned. You will probably be giving either an informative speech, in which you want your audience to understand information, or a persuasive speech, in which you want your audience to believe something or act in a particular way. But in a setting outside of class, your general goal is based on what is appropriate for your particular audience on the particular occasion.

Your specific speech goal articulates exactly what you want your audience to understand, believe, or do. For instance, for an informative speech, Glen, a member of the basketball team, might phrase his goal, "I want my audience to understand how to shoot a jump shot." Ling, an art history major, might phrase her goal, "I want the audience to have an appreciation of Ming porcelain."

speech goal a statement of what you want your listeners to know, believe, or do

Step 2: Understand Your Audience and Adapt to It

Once you have a clear speech goal, you begin the task of understanding your specific audience and how to adapt your speech to it. **Audience adaptation** is the process of tailoring your speech's information to the needs, interests, and expectations of your listeners. As you prepare for a speech, you will consider your specific audience's needs and seek to meet these needs continually as you develop your ideas.

For any speech, it is important to consider the audience's initial level of interest in your goal, their ability to understand the content of the speech, and their attitude toward you and your topic.

audience adaptation the process of tailoring your speech's information to the needs, interests, and expectations of your listeners

Suppose you were giving a speech on rationing during World War II. Your adaptation challenges would differ between the audience pictured here and an audience composed of young college students.

© Bill Aron/PhotoEdit

If you believe your audience has very little interest in your speech topic, you will need to adapt to them so that they understand why the topic is important. For instance, if Ling is talking with an audience that she believes has very little interest in understanding Ming porcelain, she may pique their interest by recounting how someone took an old vase to the *Antiques Road Show* TV program and discovered that it was from the Ming period and worth $40,000!

Not only will you need to adapt your speech by piquing audience interest, but if you believe that your audience doesn't know much about your topic, you will want to provide the basic information they need to understand your speech. For instance, if Ling is speaking to an audience that is unfamiliar with porcelain, she may need to explain briefly how porcelain is made and how it differs from other pottery before they will be able to understand how to identify Ming era vases.

Finally, you will need to adapt to your audience's initial attitudes toward your topic. If Kelly has chosen to speak on repealing the death penalty, she will need to understand where her audience stands on this topic before she begins. If the majority of her audience is pro–death penalty, then as she prepares, she will adapt by selecting arguments and evidence that can be accepted by the audience.

Step 3: Gather and Evaluate Information to Use in the Speech

For most of your speeches, you will need additional information from research sources. You will also want to use some humorous, exciting, or interesting experiences and stories to illustrate your points. When you select a topic, although you already know something about it, you will usually need more information that you can get from printed or interview sources. Regardless of the sources of your information, you will need to evaluate the information you gather and select the items you deem valid and truthful. The more you know about your topic, the easier it is to evaluate the information you uncover in your research. For instance, Nora, who is a member of the local volunteer Life Squad, will be able to give a better speech on CPR than a person with no practical experience who has learned about CPR from reading and interviewing others. Why? Because in the course of her volunteer work, Nora has actually used this skill and has real experiences to draw from. Likewise, as a student of art history, Ling is able to explain the characteristics of Ming porcelain because she has studied it in her History of Chinese Art class.

For your major class assignments, you may draw on material from your own knowledge and experiences, observations, interviews, surveys, and research.

Step 4: Organize and Develop Ideas into a Well-Structured Speech Outline

You begin the process of organizing your speech by identifying the three or four major ideas you want your audience to remember. If the audience understands and remembers these main points, you will have achieved your speech goal. These main points are written in full sentences. Once you have identified these key ideas, you will combine them with your speech goal into a succinct thesis statement that describes specifically what you want your audience to understand when you have finished speaking. This process provides the initial framework, or macrostructure, of your speech.

Main points must be carefully worded, and then they must be arranged in an organizational pattern that helps the audience understand and remember them. Two of the most basic organizational patterns are chronological and topical order. In later chapters, we'll consider several types of organization that you may want to use in your informative and persuasive speeches. Chronological means following an order that moves from first to last. So, Nora, who is planning to speak on how to perform CPR on a child, will organize her speech following the steps (what is done first, second, and third) involved in administrating CPR. In some circumstances, you may find that your speech is best presented topically. Topical means following an order of headings. For instance, Ling, who decides to inform her audience about the three characteristics that distinguish Ming vases from others, might choose to talk about the characteristics in ascending order with the most important characteristic last.

Having identified, phrased, and ordered the main points, you are now ready to outline the body of the speech. Although it is tempting to work out a speech as it comes to mind, speeches are not essays, and you will be more effective if you prepare a thorough outline.

After you have outlined the body of the speech, which includes noting elaborations, you can outline your introduction and conclusion. Your introduction should both get attention and lead into the body of the speech. Because there are never any guarantees that your audience is ready to pay full attention to the speech, an effective introduction draws the audience into what you are saying.

In your conclusion, you will want to remind the audience of your main points and speech goal. You should do this in a creative way that helps the audience remember.

When you think you are finished, review the outline to make sure that the parts are relevant to your goal. A written outline allows you to test the logic and clarity of your proposed organization. In Chapters 7 and 8, you will learn how to develop a complete outline comprised of the introduction, the main points, major subpoints of the body and key support, section transitions, and the conclusion, plus a list of sources. The length of your outline will depend on the length of your speech. In a speech of three to five minutes, the outline may contain up to 50 percent or more of the words in the speech; for a five- to eight-minute speech, up to 33 to 50 percent. And in speeches given in public later in life (often thirty to forty-five minutes), the speech outline may contain as few as 20 percent of the words.

Although an expert who has spoken frequently on a topic may be able to speak effectively from a mental outline or a few notes, most of us benefit from the discipline of organizing and developing a complete speech outline.

Step 5: Choose Visual and Other Presentational Aids That Are Appropriate for the Audience

"One picture is worth a thousand words" is an old saying with a lot of wisdom. So, even for a very short speech, you may decide to create a visual or other aid that will help clarify, emphasize, or dramatize what you say. Because audiences understand and retain information better when they have received that information through more than one sense, objects, models, charts, pictorial representations, projections, and computer graphics maximize the effect of high-quality information.

As you get ready to practice your speech, make sure you consider when to use visual aids, how long to use them, and how to show visual aids so that everyone can see them. Likewise, a very brief excerpt from a song, film, or television program can sometimes capture your intent more succinctly than words alone.

Step 6: Practice the Wording and Delivery of the Speech

In your practice sessions, you need to choose the wording of main points and supporting materials carefully. If you have not practiced various ways of phrasing your key ideas, you run the risk of missing a major opportunity for communicating your ideas effectively. In practice sessions, work on clarity, vividness, emphasis, and appropriate language. Recall that these wording choices make up the microstructure of your speech.

Although a speech is comprised of words, how effective you will be is also largely a matter of how well you use your voice and gestures in delivering your speech. You will want to present the speech enthusiastically, with vocal variety and emphasis, using good eye contact (look at members of the audience while you are speaking).

Very few people can present speeches effectively without considerable practice. The goal of practice is to give you confidence that you can talk comfortably with your audience and accomplish your speech goal within the time limit. Don't try to memorize the speech. Trying to memorize your speech is likely to add to your stage fright because you may also fear forgetting what you planned to say. Instead, deliver your speech extemporaneously—that is, practiced until the ideas of the speech are firmly in mind, but varying the wording from practice to practice and in the actual delivery. Engaging in effective practice sessions enables you to become comfortable with your main points, the supporting material you use to explain them, and the transitioning from one point to another. We will consider detailed information about methods of practice in Chapter 11.

Exhibit 2.4 summarizes the six action steps of an effective speech plan in outline form. These steps will be explained in Part Two of this book. As you read, you will see specific speech preparation activities that are related to each action step. By completing all of these activities, you will gain confidence in your ability to be effective when you give your speech.

1 | Goals

I. Determine an audience-centered speech goal

2 | Audience

II. Develop a strategy for audience adaptation

3 | Research

III. Gather Information

4 | Organization

IV. Organize and develop your material

5 | Visual Aids

V. Create visual and other presentational aids

6 | Delivery

VI. Practice speech wording and delivery

I. Identify a specific speech goal that is audience-centered and appropriate for the occasion. (Chapter 4)
   A. Select a topic from a subject area you know something about and that is important to you.
   B. Analyze your audience to assess their familiarity with and interest in your topic.
   C. Consider how your speech setting affects what is appropriate for you to talk about.
   D. Choose a topic that you know about and are interested in.
   E. Develop a speech goal statement tailored to your audience and the occasion.

II. Understand your audience and recognize opportunities for audience adaptation. (Chapter 5)
   A. Understand audience diversity.
   B. Understand audience interests so that material relates to them.
   C. Adjust content so it is appropriate for your audience's current understanding of this topic.
   D. Understand your audience's attitude toward your topic.
   E. Determine how you will establish your credibility with your audience.

III. Gather and evaluate information you can use to reach your speech goal. (Chapter 6)
   A. Survey manual and electronic sources of information and evaluate the quality of the information found.
   B. Observe and interview sources of information.
   C. Record on research cards information that is relevant to your specific speech goal.

IV. Organize and develop ideas into a well-structured speech outline. (Chapters 7 and 8)
   A. Write a thesis statement that identifies the specifics of your speech goal.
   B. Outline main points as complete sentences that are clear, parallel, and meaningful.
   C. Choose an organizational pattern that orders the main points in a way that aids audience understanding.
   D. Create section transitions to help the audience follow your organization.
   E. Create an introduction that gets attention, establishes listener relevance, states your thesis, establishes your credibility, and creates goodwill
   F. Create a conclusion that both summarizes the material and leaves your audience with a vivid impression.
   G. Review and complete the speech outline.

V. Choose presentational aids that are appropriate for the audience.
   A. Consider drawings, maps, charts, and graphs.
   B. Make sure your printed elements are large enough to be seen—use upper- and lowercase letters.
   C. Plan when to use presentational aids and how to show them so that everyone can see them. (Chapter 9)

VI. Practice the speech wording and delivery.
   A. Practice until the wording is accurate, clear, vivid, and appropriate. (Chapter 10)
   B. Practice until the delivery is animated and conversational. (Chapter 11)
   C. Continue practicing until you can deliver it extemporaneously within the time limit. (Chapter 11)

Cicero *Do As the Romans*

© Mary Evans Picture Library/Alamy

As you study the speech planning process, you should be aware that these canons (or rules) date back to ancient Rome. Like many philosophers of his time, the great statesman, politician, and orator Marcus Tullius Cicero (106 B.C.– 43 B.C.) had much to say about effective public speaking and issues of speech invention, arrangement, language, and delivery. Included in his recommendations were the following:

On invention/research: "Before beginning, prepare carefully."

On invention/speech goals: "The aim of Forensic Oratory is to teach, to delight, to move."

On invention/goodwill: "We were born to unite with our fellow men, and to join in community with the human race."

On language: "We should be as careful of our words as of our actions, and as far from speaking ill as from doing ill."

On arrangement/time: "When you wish to instruct, be brief. . . . Every word that is unnecessary only pours over the side of a brimming mind."

On faulty reasoning and evidence: "It is the act of a bad man to deceive by falsehood."

On poor speaker credibility: "Praise coming from so degraded a source, was degrading to me, its recipient."

On delivery: "They are eloquent who can speak of low things acutely, and of great things with dignity, and of moderate things with temper."

On delivery: "Great is our admiration of the orator who speaks with fluency and discretion."

On delivery: "A good orator is pointed and impassioned."

On confidence: "Confidence is that feeling by which the mind embarks in great and honorable courses with a sure hope and trust in itself."

To Think About

✦ Compare Cicero's quotes to the guidelines you're using for your speeches. Do you challenge yourself to be "classically" effective, as he suggests?

✦ Based on Cicero's quotes, what are one or two things you can do to improve your speeches?

Preparing a Narrative/Personal Experience Speech

narrative/personal experience speech a presentation in which you recount an experience you have had and the significance you attach to that experience

The **narrative/personal experience speech** is a presentation in which you recount an experience you have had and the significance you attach to that experience. This speech is an excellent opportunity for you to try out the basic speech preparation action steps we have just introduced. Let's look at how Eric Wais applied these steps to prepare his speech "The Funeral."

The first step is to develop a speech goal that meets audience needs. For his personal experience speech assignment, Eric considered several experiences that he thought the class would enjoy hearing about. For his topic, he finally chose the story of Dan's funeral.

Although funerals are not something that most people think of as enjoyable, Eric thought that his class would relate to his experience, which dramatized what can happen when someone gives a eulogy about a person he didn't really know.

He knew that the speech would be for an audience of about fifteen class-mates who were all traditional-age college students, that the assignment was a narrative/personal experience speech, and that the time limit was two to three minutes.

His general goal was to dramatize. Specifically, Eric wanted the audience to appreciate what can happen when the speaker knows less about the subject than do members of the audience.

His strategy for audience adaptation included using personal pronouns and other means of creating common ground by telling his personal experience.

He also tried to be as specific as possible in relating the details so that the audience would have a clear and vivid mental picture of the events.

Because it was a personal experience narrative, Eric didn't need additional research; he only needed to reconstruct the details of the funeral experience.

Eric organized and developed his story in a way that dramatized his goal. He began his speech with a description of his friend, then recounted the funeral experience, and concluded by reinforcing the point of his story.

When you use narratives/personal experiences as a speech or in a speech, remember the following elements:

✦ A narrative usually has a point to it, a climax to which the details build up. Think carefully about the point of your story and make sure it is appropriate.

✦ A narrative is developed with supporting details that give background to and embellish the story so that the point has maximum effect. Try to select and develop details that heighten the impact.

✦ Narrative drama can be increased by using dialogue. Dialogue gives an audience the experience of "being there" and increases their interest and involvement.

✦ A narrative is often emotional. Most narratives dramatize because they recount emotional incidents. They may be funny, tragic, or frightening, but effectively told personal experiences establish an emotional bond between speaker and audience.

Although Eric used no visual aids, some narratives can be enhanced with pictures of the event described, and of course, effective narratives use language and nonverbals to paint vivid pictures of what happened. Eric used clear and vivid language to tell his story. He also practiced his speech several times until he was comfortable with his ability to tell the story. You can use your Cengage-NOW for *Challenge* to see a video of Eric giving his speech in class, as well as read a transcript of his speech and see the outline he created for it. As you watch the speech, notice how his delivery enhances or detracts from the speech he planned. Use the evaluation checklist provided with the video to identify some of the strengths of Eric's speech. Then compare your answers to those of the authors. (To learn how to get started with your CengageNOW and other online textbook resources, see the inside front and back covers of this book.)

REFLECT ON ETHICS

Paul is scheduled to give his first speech in which he is supposed to talk about a personal experience. Paul realizes that his nervousness is being heightened by the personal nature of the topic—he thinks his experiences are really ordinary and that he'll bore the class. He remembers one of his high school buddies, James. Now *James* had interesting personal experiences, and he had a million awesome stories. So Paul thinks, hey, I'll just pretend that the "dead rat incident" happened to me—no one in my speech class knows it didn't. So, Paul develops his speech around this experience James had. It's a great story, he delivers it well, and he receives an excellent response from his professor and class.

Is it ethical for Paul to relate James's experience as his? Explain.

Summary

This chapter discusses public speaking apprehension, how careful preparation can help you develop confidence when you speak in public, and how to prepare a narrative/personal experience speech.

Public speaking apprehension is the level of fear a person experiences when speaking. Signs of public speaking apprehension include physical, emotional, and cognitive reactions that vary from person to person. The level of apprehension varies over the course of speaking. The root of apprehension, negative self-talk, has three causes: biologically-based temperament, previous experience, and level of skill.

Several methods are available for overcoming public speaking apprehension. General methods include communication orientation motivation (COM) techniques, visualization, systematic desensitization, cognitive restructuring, and public speaking skills training. Specific techniques include allowing sufficient time to prepare, practicing the speech aloud, choosing an appropriate time to speak, using positive self-talk, facing the audience with confidence, and focusing on sharing your ideas.

Gaining confidence through effective speech planning reduces public speaking apprehension and increases speaking effectiveness. An effective speech plan is the product of six action steps. People are most likely to gain confidence in speaking by following this six-step process. The first step is to select a speech goal that is appropriate for the audience and occasion. The second step is to understand your audience and adapt material to it. The third step is to gather and evaluate information to use in the speech. The fourth step is to organize and develop ideas into a well-structured speech outline. The fifth step is to choose visual and other presentational aids that are appropriate for the audience. And the sixth step is to practice the speech until delivery is accurate, clear, vivid, appropriate, conversational, and animated.

A good opening assignment is a narrative/personal experience speech in which you recount an experience you have had and the significance you attach to it. A narrative is a speech that has a point to it, a climax to which the details build up. It is developed with supporting details that give background to and embellish the story so that the point has maximum effect. A narrative often includes dialogue and is often humorous.

CHALLENGE ONLINE

Now that you've read Chapter 2, use your Cengage-NOW for *The Challenge of Effective Speaking* for quick access to the electronic resources that accompany this text. Your CengageNOW gives you access to the video, transcript, and outline of Eric's speech discussed on pages 33–34, an evaluation checklist and analysis questions to help you identify the strengths of his speech, the Web Resources activities featured in this chapter, Speech Builder Express, InfoTrac College Edition, and online study aids such as a digital glossary and review quizzes. To learn how to get started with your CengageNOW and other online textbook resources, see the inside front and back covers of this book.

Your *Challenge* CengageNOW is an online study system that helps you identify concepts you don't fully understand, allowing you to put your study time to the best use. Using chapter-by-chapter diag-nostic pretests, the system creates a personalized study plan for each chapter. Each plan directs you to specific resources designed to improve your understanding, including pages from the text in e-book format. Chapter posttests give you an opportunity to measure how much you've learned and let you know if you are ready for graded quizzes and exams.

KEY TERMS

Go to your CengageNOW for *Challenge* to access your online glossary for Chapter 2. Print a copy of the glossary for this chapter and test yourself with the electronic flash cards or complete the crossword puzzle to help you master these key terms:

adaptation reaction (19)
anticipation reaction (19)
audience adaptation (27)
cognitive restructuring (24)
communication orientation (23)
communication orientation motivation (COM) (22)

confrontation reaction (19)
narrative/personal experience speech (32)
performance orientation (22)
public speaking apprehension (18)
public speaking skills training (25)

self-talk (20)
speech goal (27)
speech plan (26)
systematic desensitization (23)
visualization (23)

WEB RESOURCES

Go to your CengageNOW for *Challenge* to access the Web Resources for this chapter.

2.1 Visualizing Your Success (23)
2.2 Restructure Your Expectations (25)

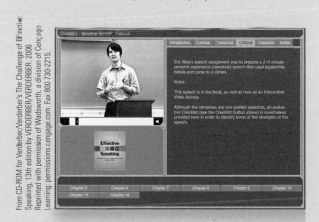

3

Listening Effectively

© Colin Anderson/Brand X Pictures/Alamy Images

What's Ahead

HERE'S WHAT'S AHEAD IN THIS CHAPTER:

1. Why is it important to study listening in a public speaking course?

2. What is the difference between listening and hearing?

3. What are some strategies you can employ to improve your listening skills?

4. What are some strategies you can employ to improve your constructive critiquing skills?

When Professor Norton finished her point on means of evaluating social legislation, she said, "Let me remind you that the primary criterion is the value to the general public at large, not the profit people can make from exploiting legislation."

As Ben, Shawna, and Tim were walking from the class, Ben said, "I was glad to hear that Professor Norton recognized the importance of making profit from social legislation."

"That wasn't her point," said Shawna. "She said that the emphasis is on the value to the general public."

"I'm sure she emphasized profitability," responded Ben. "Tim, what do you think she said?"

"Man, I don't even know what you're talking about. I was thinking about my math test this afternoon."

Does this conversation sound familiar? Have you had times when you'd swear that you heard right when you didn't? If your answer is "Not me," then we congratulate you, for this example illustrates three of the most common listening problems: missing what was said, hearing it but misunderstanding, and not remembering what was said.

In the last chapter, we previewed the speech planning process that you will learn to use to prepare speeches. You learned that for communication to be effective, a speaker must present the message clearly and compellingly. Equally important, however, is that you as a *listener* understand and accurately remember what the speaker said.

Obviously, before you can listen, you must first hear what is said. Although listening depends on hearing, the two are not the same. **Hearing** is simply the biological process that occurs when the brain detects sound waves. Sometimes people do not hear well. There are several common reasons for this: First, when a person is deaf or hard of hearing, his or her brain does not receive sound waves very well or at all. Second, messages transmitted at a low volume are difficult to hear. Third, when other stimuli compete for the brain's attention—such as a passing fire engine, someone talking on a cell phone, or another external "noise"—it gets in the way of a person hearing a message.

hearing the biological process that occurs when the brain detects sound waves

In contrast to hearing, listening occurs after the brain has detected the sound waves and is sorting out what those waves mean. According to the International Listening Association, "**Listening** is the process of receiving, attending to, constructing meaning from, and responding to spoken or nonverbal messages."[1] Listening is important because, of our time spent communicating, 50 percent or more is spent listening.[2] Although all of us have spent a great deal of time learning to read and write, fewer than 2 percent of us have had any formal listening training.[3] In fact, even when they try to listen carefully, most people remember only about 50 percent of what they hear shortly after hearing it and only about 25 percent two days later.[4] Yet effective listening is a key to success in most occupations. One survey of top-level North American executives revealed that 80 percent believe listening is one of the most important skills needed in the corporate environment.[5] It simply makes sense to improve listening skills.

listening the process of receiving, attending to, constructing meaning from, and responding to spoken or nonverbal messages

How effective are your listening skills? To find out, complete an inventory of your listening skills. Use your CengageNOW for *Challenge* to access **Web Resource 3.1: Listening Inventory**. The information you glean from this inventory can help you pinpoint the specific skills you need to improve.

In this class, in addition to learning about how to prepare and deliver effective speeches, you will also become more effective at listening to the speeches of others. During this term, you will give perhaps five or six speeches, but you will probably hear more than sixty. As you listen to these speeches, you can practice the skills of effective listening.

In this chapter, we describe how you can (1) improve your attention when listening to speeches, (2) improve your understanding and memory of the information you have heard, (3) critically analyze what has been said, and (4) assess the effectiveness of a speech. Finally, we will explain how, by giving effective post-speech feedback, you can fulfill your responsibilities to your classmates.

Attending to the Speech

attending paying attention to what the speaker is saying regardless of extraneous interferences

Attending is paying attention to what the speaker is saying regardless of extraneous interferences. Poor listeners have difficulty exercising control over what they attend to, often letting their mind drift to thoughts totally unrelated to the speech. One reason for this stems from the fact that people typically speak at a rate of about 120 to 150 words per minute, but our brains can process between 400 and 800 words per minute.[6] This means we usually assume we know what a speaker is going to say before he or she finishes saying it. That gives our minds time to wander from the message. Remember Tim's response to the question of which interpretation was more on target: "Man, I don't even know what you're talking about. I was thinking about my math test this afternoon."

Not only does the gap between speaking rate and processing create opportunities for inattention, but research suggests that the average attention span for adults today is twenty minutes or less.[7] Consider your own experiences listening to speeches, such as your professors' class lectures. Toward the end of class, do you find yourself more prone to daydreaming? Do you want to find out how long your attention span is? If so, use your CengageNOW for *Challenge* to access **Web Resource 3.2: Attention Span Self-Test**.

Four techniques can help you maintain your attention when you are listening to speeches (or other lengthy presentations).

1. Get physically and mentally ready to listen. Suppose that a few minutes after class begins your professor says, "In the next two minutes, I'm going to cover some material that is especially important—in fact, I can guarantee that it will be on the test." What can you do to increase your attention? Well, physically, you can alter your posture and sit upright in your chair, lean slightly forward, and stop any random physical movement. You can also look directly at the professor because by making eye contact you increase the amount of information you get.[8] You can also react mentally by focusing all of your attention on what the professor is saying and blocking out the miscellaneous thoughts that constantly pass through your mind.

2. Suspend judgment while you hear the speaker out. Far too often, we let a person's mannerisms and words "turn us off." If you find yourself upset by a speaker's ideas on gay marriage, abortion, or any controversial topic, instead of tuning out or getting ready to argue, work that much harder to listen objectively so that you can understand the speaker's position before you respond. Likewise, even when a speaker uses language that is offensive to you, you need to persevere and not be distracted. If we are not careful, we may become annoyed when a speaker mutters, stammers, or talks in a monotone. We need to focus instead on what is being said and overlook the speaker's dysfluency.

3. Adjust to the listening goals of the situation. When you are listening to an after-dinner speaker for pleasure, you can afford to listen without much intensity. Unfortunately, many people approach all speech situations as if they were listening to pass the time of day. But in public forums, in business settings, and in class, your goal is to understand and retain information or to listen critically to be able to evaluate what speakers say and how they say it. In the remainder of this chapter, we consider guidelines for adjusting your listening to meet the demands of these goals.

4. Identify the benefits of attending to the speaker's words. At times, we do this almost automatically, especially when your professor says something like, "Pay attention to this explanation—I'll tell you right now, it will be the basis for one of the major test questions." But even if such a statement is not made, you can provide your own motivation. As you listen, ask yourself why and how you might use the specific information in the near future. For instance, you may be able to use the information in a discussion with your friends, to help you solve work-related problems, or to improve personally. Identifying benefits can motivate you to apply each of the three previous behaviors even more regularly.

Understanding and Remembering Speech Information

The second aspect of listening to speeches is to understand and remember what the speaker is saying. **Understanding** is the ability to assign accurate meaning to what was said. **Remembering** is being able to retain and recall information that you have heard. Both understanding and remembering are facilitated by the use of active listening behaviors. **Active listening** includes identifying the organization of ideas, asking questions, silently paraphrasing, attending to nonverbal cues, and taking notes. To help you both understand better and retain more, let's consider these five active listening behaviors.

1. Determine the speaker's organization. Determining the organization helps you establish a framework for understanding and remembering the information.[9] In any extended message, an effective speaker has an overall organizational pattern for the information being presented. This organization includes a goal, the main points that develop the goal, and details that are presented to develop the main points. Effective listeners mentally (or physically) outline the organization so that when the speech is over they can cite the goal, the main points, and some of the key details.

For instance, during a PTA meeting, Gloria Minton, a teacher, gives a short presentation on the problem of bullying. Her goal is to explain what can be done in school to deter this behavior. In her speech, she presents two main ideas: what teachers can do and what students who are harassed can do. She gives examples, statistics, and specific recommendations to develop each of the points she has made. When she is finished, audience members who have listened carefully are able to remember her goal and state steps that teachers and harassed students can take even though they may not remember the specific examples and statistics that she used to develop each point.

Although effective speakers organize their speeches so that it is easy to identify their goal, key points, and details, not all speakers are well organized. As a result, we as listeners have to pay close attention to grasp the main ideas. As you listen to a speech, ask yourself, "What does the speaker want me to know or

understanding the ability to assign accurate meaning to what was said

remembering being able to retain and recall information that you have heard

active listening identifying the organization of ideas, asking questions, silently paraphrasing, attending to nonverbal cues, and taking notes

do?" (goal); then ask, "What are each of the main points?"; and finally, ask, "What details explain or support each of the main points?"

In classroom lectures, feel free to ask the professor to supply any information you believe has not been presented clearly. (With student speeches or major speeches you hear in other settings, you are unlikely to be able to ask such questions.)

2. Ask yourself questions. As we have seen, asking yourself questions helps you identify key aspects of the speech. But asking yourself questions can also help you determine whether enough information was presented. For instance, if a speaker says, "Swimming is an activity that provides exercise for almost every muscle," active listeners might inwardly question "how?" and then pay attention to the supporting material offered or request it if the speaker does not supply it.

3. Silently paraphrase key information. Silent paraphrases help listeners understand material. A **paraphrase** is a statement in your own words of the meaning you have assigned to a message. It is not simply repeating what has been said. After you have listened to a message, you should be able to summarize your understanding. So, after the speaker explains the criteria for judging diamonds, you might say to yourself, "In other words, it's a trade-off—the bigger the diamond, the poorer the quality." If you cannot paraphrase a message, either the message was not clearly explained or you were not listening carefully enough.

paraphrase a statement in your own words of the meaning you have assigned to a message

Note taking is an important method for improving your memory of what you have heard in a speech.

4. Attend to nonverbal cues. You can interpret messages more accurately by observing the nonverbal behaviors accompanying the words. So, regardless of the topic, you should pay attention to the speaker's tone of voice, facial expression, and gestures. For instance, the director of parking might tell a freshman that he stands a good chance of getting a parking sticker for the garage, but the sound of the person's voice may suggest that the chances are not really that good.

5. Take good notes. Note taking is a powerful method for improving your memory of what you have heard in a speech. Not only does note taking provide a written record that you can go back to, but also by taking notes, you take a more active role in the listening process.[10] In short, whenever you are listening to a speech, take notes.

What constitutes good notes varies by situation. For a short speech, good notes may consist of a statement of the goal, a brief list of main points, and a few of the most significant details. For a lengthy and rather detailed presentation (such as a class lecture), good notes will not only record the goal and the main points but will also include subpoints of main points and more detailed statements of supporting material. Outlining is a useful note-taking strategy because it creates the structure of the information you have received and want to retain. Outlining helps you distinguish among main points, subpoints, and supporting material.

Ideally, the notes you produce will be similar to the outline notes the speaker used. Review the basics of effective listening and note taking by using your CengageNOW for *Challenge* to access **Web Resource 3.3: Effective Listening and Note Taking**.

CENGAGENOW™

Critically Analyzing a Speech

As we have seen, to get the most out of a speech, we must not only pay attention to what is said but must also do what we can to understand and remember it. But good listening doesn't stop here. The third step in effective listening is **critical analysis** of a speech—the process of evaluating what you have heard to determine its completeness, usefulness, and trustworthiness. Critical analysis is especially important when the speaker expects you to believe, support, or act on what was said. If you don't critically analyze what you hear, you risk going along with ideas that violate your values. When you analyze any speech you hear, consider the following:

critical analysis the process of evaluating what you have heard to determine a speech's completeness, usefulness, and trustworthiness

1. **Speaker credibility**

   How did the speaker gain expertise on this subject? Does the speaker appear to be knowledgeable?

   What did the speaker do or say that made you believe what was said? Why should you trust this speaker?

2. **Quality of content**

   Did the speaker convey enough high-quality information to ensure understanding?

   Did the speaker present enough examples and other supporting details and explanations to enable you to apply the information?

   Did the speaker present facts to support the ideas or just give opinions?

   Did the speaker identify the sources of the ideas, facts, and other material that were presented?

   Were the sources relevant? recent? varied? distributed throughout the speech?

   Did the speaker present both sides of controversial issues?

   Was enough information or evidence presented to support controversial ideas?

3. **Quality of structure**

   Did you understand the point of the speech? What were the main ideas?

   Were the speaker's ideas well ordered?

REFLECT ON ETHICS

As they were returning from a rally at the University Field House in which they heard candidates for the two congressional districts that surrounded the university, Nikita asked Lance what he thought of the speech given by Steve Chabot, the Republican candidate for office in the first district.

"Chabot? He's just like any Republican; he's going to make sure that big business is all right."

"I didn't hear him talking about big business. I thought he was talking about the importance of limiting the amount of federal government intrusion in state matters."

"Sure, that's what he said, but we know what he really meant."

"I asked you what you thought of the speech. What ideas did he present that turned you off?"

"Listen, you don't really have to listen to any Republican speaking. Everyone knows that Republicans are for big business and only Democrats are going to watch out for people like us."

1. Is Lance's failure to listen critically an ethical issue? If so, why?

2. If Lance really had been listening critically, what should he be discussing with Nikita?

EXHIBIT 3.1 Effective and ineffective listening behaviors

	Effective listening behavior	Ineffective listening behavior
Attending to the speech	Physically and mentally focusing on what is being said, even when information doesn't seem relevant	Seeming to listen, but looking out the window and letting your mind wander
	Adjusting listening behavior to the specific requirements of the situation	Listening the same way regardless of type of material
Understanding/remembering speech information	Determining organization by identifying goals, main points, and supporting information	Listening to individual bits of information without regard for structure
	Asking yourself questions to help you identify key aspects of the speech	Seldom or never reconsidering what was said
	Silently paraphrasing to solidify understanding	Seldom or never paraphrasing
	Seeking out subtle meanings based on nonverbal cues	Ignoring nonverbal cues
	Taking good notes	Relying on memory alone
Critically analyzing speeches	Assessing speaker credibility, quality of content, quality of structure, and quality of delivery	Relying on gut reactions to the speech

Did they follow logically from one another?

Were important ideas missing that should be considered?

Did the speaker use clear, vivid, and compelling language and phrasing so that you understood each point?

Did the speaker's conclusion seem to follow logically from the main ideas?

4. **Quality of delivery**

Did the speaker sound sincere, informed, and trustworthy?

Did the speaker use appropriate facial expressions and gestures?

Did the speaker seem to convey a confident attitude?

By critically analyzing the speaker's credibility, as well as the quality of the content, structure, and delivery, effective listeners thoughtfully consider if they understand, believe, support, or want to act on what they have learned in the speech.

Exhibit 3.1 summarizes effective and ineffective listening behaviors related to attending to what is said, understanding and remembering information, and critically analyzing the speech.

Evaluating Speech Effectiveness: The Constructive Critique

In most communication situations outside the classroom, it is sufficient to attend to, understand, and retain information in a speech so that you can consider it critically for yourself. But at times, you may be asked to provide a formal assessment, or critique, of a speech or a presentation for a classmate, a colleague, or an employee. Usually, this type of assessment requires you to analyze and evaluate a speech's effectiveness according to how well the speaker meets specific key criteria. A **constructive critique** is an analysis of a speech or a presentation that evaluates how well a speaker meets a specific speaking goal while following the norms for good speaking and that recommends how the presentation could be improved. Essentially, a critique allows you to provide a speaker with meaningful postspeech feedback.

constructive critique an analysis of a speech or presentation that evaluates how well a speaker meets a specific speaking goal while following the norms for good speaking and that recommends how the presentation could be improved

Guidelines for Constructive Critiques

Constructive critiques follow four guidelines. First, effective critiques communicate specific observations. Comments like "great job" or "slow down" are too vague to truly help a speaker improve. Instead, describe specific things the speaker did to make you conclude that the speech was great. For example, did she use transitions in a way that helped you follow her train of thought? Or point out specific places where you would have liked the speaker to present the material at a slower pace.

Second, effective critiques begin with observations about what a speaker did well before turning to observations about what the speaker could do better. Begin with positive observations so that you reinforce what the speaker did well. When we are reinforced for what we have done, we are more likely to continue doing it. By the same token, there is room for improvement in any speech. Since the goal of a critique is to help the speaker improve, describe the specific problems you observe in the speech and then offer suggestions for overcoming them.

Third, effective critiques follow observation statements with explanations about how and why the observed behavior affected the speech. For example, if you suggest that the speaker slow down while previewing the speech's main points, your statement will be more helpful if you also explain that the speaker's rate did not allow the audience time to remember the points.

Finally, effective critiques are phrased so that it's clear they reflect your personal perceptions, not "truth." You can ensure this by using "I" rather than "you" language. For example, instead of using "you" language to say, "You need to slow down," use "I" language. For example, "During the preview of main points, I had trouble listening because they were presented faster than I could understand and remember them."

Content of Constructive Critiques

A constructive critique offers observations about a speech's content, structure, and delivery. Comments on content focus on the speaker's analysis of the topic and supporting material. For example, you might comment on how effectively the speaker used reasoning, or comment on the breadth and depth of the information used to develop each main idea. You might observe how relevant, recent, or credible the speaker's evidence seemed to be. Exhibit 3.2 illustrates ineffective and effective constructive critique comments regarding content.

EXHIBIT 3.2   Ineffective and effective comments about content

Ineffective	Effective
◆ Interesting stories.	◆ I liked the story about your trip to the carnival. The many details you provided made it sound really fun!
◆ Too short.	◆ I would have liked to hear another example for each main point. This would have helped me better understand why the carnival was so significant to you.

EXHIBIT 3.3 Ineffective and effective comments about structure

Ineffective	Effective
◆ Nice transitions.	◆ Your transitions reminded me of the main point.
	◆ You finished and introduced the upcoming main point. I found it easy to follow your ideas as a result.
◆ Boring introduction.	◆ I would have tuned in to the speech more quickly if you had begun with a great story about the carnival to capture my attention before stating your thesis.

Comments on structure focus on macrostructure or microstructure, including how the speaker organized and expressed his or her ideas (content). You might consider the clarity of the speaker's goal, transitions, summary, or ordering of main ideas. You might also talk about the speaker's language and style choices. Exhibit 3.3 offers some examples of ineffective and effective constructive critique comments regarding structure.

Comments on delivery focus on the speaker's use of his or her voice and body. In commenting on voice, you might consider how intelligible, conversational, and emotionally expressive the speaker was. Regarding use of body, focus on poise, gestures, facial expression, and eye contact. Consider if the speaker's mannerisms distracted you from the speech's message or enhanced it. Comment on the specific behaviors that contributed to your opinion of the speaker's use of body. Exhibit 3.4 provides a couple of examples of ineffective and effective constructive critique comments regarding delivery.

Certainly, you can help other speakers improve by offering effective constructive critiques. You can also help yourself by completing a self-critique after each speech you give, using the same approach you use to critique others. Begin by noting one or two specific things you did well in terms of content, structure, and delivery. Then consider one thing you'll focus on improving for your next speech. This self-critique approach is actually a form of cognitive restructuring that can help reduce your anxiety because it forces you to temper negative self-talk with positive criticism immediately after your speech. Exhibit 3.5 presents the general criteria for giving a constructive critique. You can use these criteria as a starting point for giving feedback to a speaker or critiquing your own speech.

As we will see later in this text, for each speech you give this term (and for the different kinds of speeches you will hear in real-life situations), there are additional aspects of content, delivery, and structure you will want to consider in your constructive critique. We will provide additional criteria in speech specific checklists you can use to evaluate each type of speech you study in this

EXHIBIT 3.4 Ineffective and effective comments about delivery

Ineffective	Effective
◆ Great gestures!	◆ I really liked how you gestured while you stated your transitions. It made it even clearer to me that we were moving to the next main point.
◆ Slow down.	◆ I didn't hear the preview of the main points. For me, it would be helpful to slow down during that opening sentence so I could process the main points. That way, I would have followed along better throughout the speech.

EXHIBIT 3.5   General criteria for a constructive critique

1. **Content of the speech**
   Does the speaker establish common ground and adapt the content to the audience's interests, knowledge, and attitudes?
   Does the speaker seem to have expertise in the subject areas?
   Does the speaker have high-quality sources for the information given in the speech?
   Does the speaker reveal the sources of the information?
   Are the sources relevant? recent? varied? distributed throughout the speech?
   Does the information presented explain or support each of the main points?
   Are visual and other presentational aids appropriate and well used?
   Is each main point supported with breadth? depth? listener relevance?

2. **Structure of the speech**
   Does the introduction of the speech get attention, build, and lead into the topic?
   Has the speaker stated a clear goal for the speech?
   Are the main points of the speech clearly stated, parallel, and meaningful?
   Do transitions lead smoothly from one point to another?
   Does the information presented explain or support each of the main points?
   Does the speaker use language that is accurate, clear, vivid, and appropriate?
   Does the speaker use a compelling style?
   Does the conclusion summarize the main points and end the speech on a high note?

3. **Delivery of the speech**
   Does the speaker sound intelligible? conversational? enthusiastic?
   Does the speaker show sufficient vocal expressiveness? Is the presentation spontaneous? conversational?
   Is the presentation fluent?
   Does the speaker look at the audience?
   Does the speaker use appropriate facial expression?
   Were the pronunciation and articulation acceptable?
   Does the speaker have good posture?
   Does the speaker have sufficient poise?

text. These customized critique sheets will include the primary criteria (specific skills) your instructor is expecting speakers to demonstrate in the particular speech as well as general criteria in Exhibit 3.5, skills that speakers will attempt to meet in all speeches.

SPEECH EVALUATION CHECKLIST

General Criteria Checklist for Providing Constructive Critique

_____ 1. Did you offer specific comments about your observations? (Consider what, where, and how.)

_____ 2. Did you begin with observations about what the speaker did well, reinforcing positive behavior?

_____ 3. Did you offer specific suggestions for what the speaker could do to improve? (Consider what, where, and how.)

_____ 4. Did you provide an explanation for each comment you made?

_____ 5. Did you focus on the *speech*, using "I" language to phrase each statement as a personal perception?

_____ 6. Did you avoid focusing on the *speaker personally* and avoid using "you" language, which can sound like a personal attack?

Preparing a Constructive Critique

Use your CengageNOW for *Challenge* to access and watch Tiffany's speech, "Meat Free and Me." Prepare a constructive critique of this speech, using the general criteria offered in this chapter. Be sure to offer specific comments about positive aspects of the speech, provide specific suggestions for improvement, explain your observations, and use nonthreatening "I" language.

Summary

Listening is the process of receiving, attending to, constructing meaning from, and responding to spoken or nonverbal messages. Effective listening in public speaking settings is an active process that requires the skills of attending, understanding and remembering, analyzing critically, and evaluating speech effectiveness.

The process of attending to a message is sharpened by getting ready to listen, hearing the speaker out regardless of your thoughts or feelings, adjusting attention to the listening goals of different situations, and identifying benefits of attending to the speaker.

Understanding and remembering are enhanced by determining the speaker's organization, asking rhetorical questions, silently paraphrasing, paying attention to nonverbal cues, and taking good notes.

Critical analysis is the process of determining how truthful, useful, and trustworthy you judge a speaker and the speaker's information to be. Critical analysis requires assessing the speaker's credibility, as well as judging the quality of the content, structure, and delivery of the speech.

In public speaking classes, effective listeners provide feedback by critiquing the speeches of others. Because overall speaking effectiveness is complex, effective critics base their evaluation on how well the speaker meets the specific criteria related to the type of speech that has been given. Constructive critiques cite specific strengths of speeches, suggest ways in which speakers can improve, provide clear explanations of observations, and use nonthreatening "I" language.

CHALLENGE ONLINE

Now that you've read Chapter 3, use your Cengage-NOW for *The Challenge of Effective Speaking* for quick access to the electronic resources that accompany this text. Your CengageNOW gives you access to the video, transcript, and outline of Tiffany's speech discussed in the speech assignment above, an evaluation checklist and analysis questions to help you prepare a critique of her speech, the Web Resources activities featured in this chapter, Speech Builder Express, InfoTrac College Edition, and online study aids such as a digital glossary and review quizzes.

Your *Challenge* CengageNOW is an online study system that helps you identify concepts you don't fully understand, allowing you to put your study time to the best use. Using chapter-by-chapter diagnostic pretests, the system creates a personalized study plan for each chapter. Each plan directs you to specific resources designed to improve your understanding, including pages from the text in e-book format. Chapter posttests give you an opportunity to measure how much you've learned and let you know if you are ready for graded quizzes and exams.

KEY TERMS

Go to your CengageNOW for *Challenge* to access your online glossary for Chapter 3. Print a copy of the glossary for this chapter and test yourself with the electronic flash cards or complete the cross-word puzzle to help you master these key terms:

active listening (39)　　**constructive critique** (43)　　**paraphrase** (40)
attending (38)　　**hearing** (37)　　**remembering** (39)
critical analysis (41)　　**listening** (37)　　**understanding** (39)

WEB RESOURCES

Go to your CengageNOW for *Challenge* to access the Web Resources for this chapter.

3.1 Listening Inventory (38)　　3.3 Effective Listening and Note Taking (40)
3.2 Attention Span Self-Test (38)

From Web Site or Verderber/Verderber's The Challenge of Effective Speaking, 13th edition by VERDERBER/VERDERBER. 2006 Reprinted with permission of Wadsworth, a division of Cengage Learning: permissions.cengage.com. Fax 800 730-2215.

Identifying an Audience-Centered Speech Goal

The secret of success is constancy to purpose.

Benjamin Disraeli, speech (June 24, 1870)

© James Marshall/Corbis

What's Ahead

HERE'S WHAT'S AHEAD IN THIS CHAPTER:

1. What strategies can you use to brainstorm for speech topics?

2. What should you consider about your audience when determining your speech goal?

3. How can you find out about your audience before giving your speech?

4. In what ways might the location and occasion for your speech influence your speech goal?

5. How should you phrase your specific speech goal?

Donna Montez is a marine biologist. She knows that her audience wants to hear her talk about marine biology, but she doesn't know what aspect of the topic she should focus on.

Romeo Brown has been invited to speak to a student assembly at the inner-city middle school he attended. He has a lot he could say to these students who are so much like him, but he really wants them to understand what they need to do now to have a shot at going to college.

Dan Wong is taking a public speaking class. His first speech is scheduled for two weeks from tomorrow. As of today, he doesn't have the foggiest idea what he is going to talk about.

1 | Goals   ACTION STEP 1

Identifying an audience-centered speech goal

A. Brainstorming and concept mapping for topics
B. Analyzing your audience
C. Analyzing your setting
D. Choosing a topic
E. Articulating your goal by tailoring it to your audience and the occasion

In real-life settings, people are invited to speak because they have expertise on a particular subject or have some relationship to the audience. Nevertheless, choosing exactly what to speak about is usually left in the hands of the speaker. So, although Donna and Romeo may have an inkling about what the audience expects, they, like Dan, will need to take the first action step, which is to determine a specific speech goal that is adapted to the audience and setting.

You must determine your specific speech goal in light of your **speaking situation,** the circumstances under which you deliver your speech. As Exhibit 4.1 illustrates, these circumstances include the speaker (you), the audience (in this course, your classmates), and the occasion (purpose of the speech). Because the audience is a crucial component of the speaking situation, your specific speech goal must be based on **audience analysis,** the study of the intended audience for your speech, and **audience adaptation,** the process of tailoring your speech's information to the needs, interests, and expectations of your listeners. Of course, effective speakers continually adjust their analysis of their audience and adapt their speech accordingly throughout the speech planning and speech making process, but these steps begin at the point of determining your specific speech goal.

In this chapter, we explain each of the five substeps that help speakers determine a specific speech goal that is adapted to the audience and speaking situation. These five substeps are identifying possible topics, analyzing your audience, understanding the speech setting, choosing a topic, and finally, developing a specific speech goal. Although we discuss each task separately, in practice they overlap and can be completed in a different order.

speaking situation the circumstances under which you deliver your speech

audience analysis the study of the intended audience for your speech

audience adaptation the process of tailoring your speech's information to the needs, interests, and expectations of your listeners

Identifying Topics

What do you know a lot about? What has interested you enough so that you have gained some expertise? Our speech topics should come from subject areas in which we already have some knowledge and interest. What is the difference between a subject and a topic? A **subject** is a broad area of expertise, such as movies, cognitive psychology, computer technology, or the Middle East. A **topic** is a narrow, specific aspect of a subject. So, if your broad area of expertise is movies, you might feel qualified to speak on a variety of topics such as how the Academy Awards nomination process works, the relationships between movie producers, directors, and distributors, or how technology is changing movie production.

subject a broad area of expertise, such as movies, cognitive psychology, computer technology, or the Middle East

topic some specific aspect of a subject

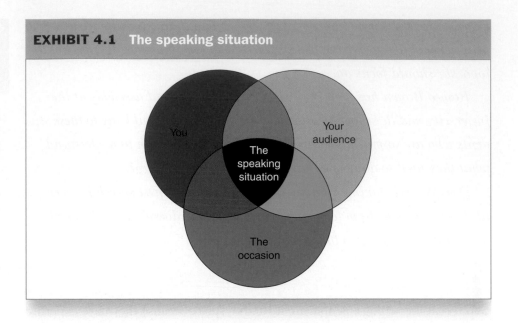

EXHIBIT 4.1   The speaking situation

You

Your audience

The speaking situation

The occasion

In this section, you will learn how to identify subject areas in which you have interest and knowledge and then, from those subject areas, to identify and select potential specific topics that you can use for the speeches you will be assigned to present in class.

Listing Subjects

You can identify potential subjects for your speeches simply by listing those areas that (1) are important to you and (2) you know something about. These areas will probably include such things as your probable vocations or areas of formal study (major, prospective profession, or current job), your hobbies or leisure activities, and special interests (social, economic, educational, or political concerns). So, if sales and marketing are your actual or prospective vocations, skateboarding and snowboarding are your favorite activities, and problems of illiteracy, substance abuse, and immigration are your special concerns, then these are subject areas from which you can identify topics for your speeches.

At this point, it is tempting to think, "Why not just talk on a subject I know an audience wants to hear about?" But in reality, all subject areas can interest an audience when speakers use their expertise or insight to enlighten the audience on a particular subject. If you speak on a topic that really interests you, you will find it easier to prepare for and be enthusiastic about speaking.

Exhibit 4.2 contains subjects that Holly, a beginning speech student, listed as she began thinking about subjects for upcoming class speeches. She chose to

EXHIBIT 4.2   Holly's subject lists

Major or vocational interest	Hobby or activity	Issue or concern
teaching	tennis	literacy
early childhood education	day care	affordable child care
curriculum development	reading	abstinence education
coaching	soccer	obesity
motherhood	photography	cancer research funding

Angela Perez Baraquio *Beauty and the Speech*

When Angela Perez Baraquio was asked why she thought the judges selected her to be Miss America, her response was, "I think they looked for someone who was . . . confident, genuine, and sincere." Baraquio, awarded the pageant title in 2001, is convinced she won the crown because she spoke with conviction about her topic, character education for children. "I had work experience, not just book knowledge. I have personal connections with my platform," she explains.*

Baraquio's comments echo what research on speech apprehension supports: Speaking on a topic that you know something about helps reduce stage fright. As she continues to make appearances speaking about character education, the platform on which she won her title, Baraquio is able to call upon her experience as a teacher to address any type of audience, from schoolchildren to professional educators.

*"Just Ask Angela," *Houston Advertiser*, November 19, 2000.

It goes without saying that we feel more confident when we look good, but this doesn't mean that only beauty queens can be effective speakers. As Baraquio explains, "the emphasis is not on being the prettiest, but to be well-rounded and articulate. You have to have self-expression. You show that you're comfortable in your skin."

It's hard to argue with this Miss America. Selecting a speech topic you know and care about will go a long way toward earning your audience's respect—if not a crown!

To Think About

✦ Identify one or two issues you feel strongly about, and explain why you feel as you do about them. (You can visit the following website to see and search some common social issues: http://lii.org/search/file/society.)

✦ If you were to make a speech about one of these topics, what would you want your listeners to understand about it?

✦ How does the thought of giving a speech about something you feel strongly about influence your desire to be articulate and expressive?

---

organize her subjects by using three broad headings: (1) major or vocational interests, (2) hobbies or activities, and (3) issues or concerns.

Brainstorming for Topic Ideas

Recall that a topic is a specific aspect of a subject, so from one subject you can list numerous topics by **brainstorming**—an uncritical, nonevaluative process of generating associated ideas. When you brainstorm, you list as many ideas as you can without evaluating them. Brainstorming allows you to take advantage of the basic commonsense principle that just as it is easier to select a correct answer to a multiple-choice question than to think of the answer to the same question without the choices, so too it is easier to select a topic from a list than to come up with a topic out of the blue.

Holly decided she wanted to give a speech on the subject of tennis. By brainstorming, she was able to come up with a list of possible topics that included types of serves, net play, types of courts, player rating systems, and equipment improvements. For practice brainstorming, use your CengageNOW for *Challenge* to access **Web Resource 4.1: Brainstorming**.

brainstorming an uncritical, nonevaluative process of generating associated ideas

Concept Mapping for Topic Ideas

A second tool you can use to identify specific topics from a general subject area is concept mapping. **Concept mapping** is a visual means of exploring connections between a subject and related ideas.[1] To generate connections, you might ask yourself questions about your subject, focusing on who, what, where, when, and how. Keisha used concept mapping to help her identify topics related to

concept mapping a visual means of exploring connections between a subject and related ideas

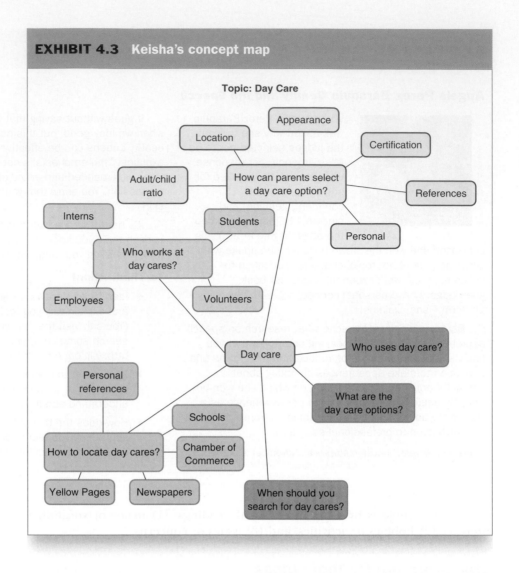

EXHIBIT 4.3 Keisha's concept map

Topic: Day Care

- Location
- Appearance
- Certification
- Adult/child ratio
- How can parents select a day care option?
- References
- Personal
- Interns
- Students
- Who works at day cares?
- Employees
- Volunteers
- Personal references
- Day care
- Who uses day care?
- What are the day care options?
- Schools
- How to locate day cares?
- Chamber of Commerce
- Yellow Pages
- Newspapers
- When should you search for day cares?

her job at a day-care center. In Exhibit 4.3, you can see an example of what Keisha's concept map looked like. If you want to practice concept mapping, go to your CengageNOW for *Challenge* to access **Web Resource 4.2: Create Your Own Concept Map**.

Speech Planning Action Step 1, Activity 1A: Using Brainstorming and Concept Mapping to Identify Speech Topics, on page 53, is designed to help you develop a list of topic ideas you can use for your speeches in this course. To see a sample of what one student who completed this exercise came up with, see the Student Response to Activity 1A on page 54.

Analyzing the Audience

Because speeches are presented to a particular audience, before you can finally decide on your topic, you need to understand who will be in your prospective audience. Recall that audience analysis is the study of the intended audience for your speech. During your audience analysis, you will want to develop a demographic profile of your audience that includes age, gender, socioeconomic background, race, ethnicity, religion, geographic uniqueness, and language. You will also want to understand audience members' knowledge of and attitudes toward your topic. This information will help you choose from your

SPEECH PLANNING   ACTION STEP 1

ACTIVITY 1A Using Brainstorming and Concept Mapping to Identify Speech Topics

The goal of this activity is to help you identify prospective topics for speeches.

1. Develop a subject list.
   a. Divide a sheet of paper into three columns. Label column 1 "major or vocational interest," label column 2 "hobby or activity," and label column 3 "concern or issue."
   b. Working on one column at a time, identify subjects of interest to you. Try to identify at least three subjects in each column.
   c. Place a check mark next to the one subject in each list that you would most enjoy speaking about.
   d. Keep the lists for future use in choosing a topic for an assigned speech.
2. For each subject you have checked, brainstorm a list of topics that relate to that subject.
3. Then, for each subject you have checked, develop a concept map to identify smaller topic areas and related ideas that might be developed into future speeches.

You can go online to print a worksheet that will help you complete this activity. Use your CengageNOW for *Challenge* to access Action Step Activity 1A.

topic lists one that is appropriate for most audience members. You will use your audience analysis to tailor your speech to meet the needs, interests, and expectations of your listeners. To read an interesting article on the importance of careful audience analysis, use your CengageNOW for *Challenge* to access **Web Resource 4.3: Defining Your Audience.**

Types of Audience Data Needed

The first step in analyzing the audience is to gather audience demographic data and subject-specific information to determine in what ways audience members are similar to and different from you and from each other.

DEMOGRAPHIC INFORMATION

Helpful demographic information about your audience includes each member's age, education, gender, income, occupation, race, ethnicity, religion, geographic uniqueness, and language. It is also important to know about your audience members' level of knowledge and attitude toward your subject. You will use the demographic information you collect for several purposes.

First, demographic information helps you choose a specific topic and the main ideas you will present. The information you collect about your audience enables you to make educated inferences about what they know about your subject area and what their attitudes are toward it. These inferences can then help you narrow your focus and choose an appropriate specific topic. For example, imagine that you want to talk about some aspect of the Internet, which is a very broad subject. Your audience analysis reveals that your audience is comprised of college students, most of whom are under twenty-one years old, so you decide to talk about the dangers of blogging. You choose this topic based on the reasonable assumption that traditional-age college students are web savvy and understand what blogging is.

ACTIVITY 1A   Using Brainstorming and Concept Mapping to Identify Speech Topics

Brainstorming list

Major or vocational interest	Hobby or activity	Concern or issue
accounting	traveling	global warming ✓
financial planning ✓	gardening	school violence
stock trading	golfing ✓	college tuition
retail management	singing	illegal downloading
banking	NASCAR	censorship

Concept map

Second, demographic information can help you discover the ways in which your audience members are similar to and different from one another and from you. This information will help you tailor your speech to your audience. In planning your speech, it is just as important to recognize and adapt to differences as it is to acknowledge similarities. For example, while the majority of your classroom audience may be composed of traditional-age college students, you may have several audience members who are "nontraditional" students and somewhat older. If you begin your speech on the dangers of blogging with the assumption that everyone in the audience is familiar with blogging and base all your examples on today's youth culture, you may marginalize audience members who grew up in an earlier era; they may not understand your cultural references or be familiar with the practice of blogging. **Marginalizing** is the practice of ignoring the values, needs, and interests of certain audience members, leaving them feeling excluded from the speaking situation.

marginalizing ignoring the values, needs, and interests of certain audience members, leaving them feeling excluded from the speaking situation

Third, understanding who is in your audience will help you develop appropriate **listener relevance links,** statements of how and why the ideas you offer are of interest to your listeners. For example, during your speech on the dangers of blogging, you might provide this listener relevance link, which would be appropriate for audience members who have blogged as well as for those who haven't: "If you have blogged, you may not be aware of the long-term potential dangers in this practice. And if you have not yet blogged, you probably know and care about someone who has. So what I am about to say might prevent you or someone you care about from making a costly mistake."

Analyzing your audience and using demographic information to adapt your speech to your audience are invaluable tools in the speech making process. But be aware of one of the dangers of using demographic information: stereotyping.[2] **Stereotyping** is assuming all members of a group behave or believe alike simply because they belong to the group. General demographic information like age and education can help you make reasonable assumptions about your audience. But to minimize the chance of incorrectly stereotyping your audience, be sure to recognize and acknowledge the demographic diversity your audience analysis reveals. **Demographic diversity** is the range of demographic characteristics represented in an audience. Collecting audience data that are directly related to your subject can also help you minimize stereotyping. For example, if you're not sure your audience understands what blogging is, your audience analysis can include a question that asks them what they know about this topic.

Exhibit 4.4 presents a list of questions to answer when acquiring demographic information about an audience.

listener relevance links statements of how and why the ideas you offer are of interest to your listeners

stereotyping assuming all members of a group behave or believe alike simply because they belong to the group

demographic diversity the range of demographic characteristics represented in an audience

---

EXHIBIT 4.4   Demographic audience analysis questions

Age. What is the age range of your audience, and what is the average age?

Education. What percentage of your audience has a high school, college, or postgraduate education?

Sex. What percentage of your audience is male? female?

Socioeconomic background. What percentage of your audience comes from high-, middle-, or low-income families?

Occupation. Is a majority of your audience from a single occupational group or industry, or do audience members come from diverse occupational groups?

Race. Are most members of your audience of the same race, or is there a mixture of races?

Ethnicity. What ethnic groups are in the audience? Are most audience members from the same cultural background?

Religion. What religious traditions are followed by audience members?

Geographic uniqueness. Are audience members from the same state, city, or neighborhood?

Language. What languages do a significant number of members of the audience speak as a first language? What language (if any) is common to all audience members?

Knowledge of subject. What can I expect the audience already knows about my subject? How varied is the knowledge level of audience members?

Attitude toward subject. What can I expect my audience's feelings to be about my subject?

SUBJECT-RELATED AUDIENCE DATA

Not only will you want to understand the demographic makeup of your audience, but you will also want to learn about the average knowledge level your audience members have on your subject, their interest in the subject, their attitudes toward the subject, and their perceptions of your credibility. Knowing this information will help you reach your goals of (1) forming reasonable generalizations about your audience and (2) adapting your speech to embrace subject-related diversity. Let's take a closer look at each of these pieces of information.

1. **Audience knowledge.** What can you expect your average audience member to already know about your subject? What topics are likely to provide new information for most of them? It is important that you choose a topic geared to the background knowledge you can expect audience members to have. When you choose a topic that most audience members already know about, you will bore them if you are not really creative. On the other hand, if you choose a topic for which your audience has insufficient background, you will have to provide it or risk confusing them. For instance, if your subject is music, you can expect that an audience of traditional-age college students will know the general history of rock-'n'-roll, including the major performers. So the topic "A Brief History of Rock-'n'-Roll" is unlikely to offer them much new information. However, a speech on the contributions of girl bands to the development of rock-'n'-roll would draw on the audience's background knowledge but offer new information to most audience members.

2. **Audience interest.** How attracted are audience members likely to be to your subject? For instance, suppose you would like to speak on the subject of cancer drugs. If your audience is made up of health-care professionals, you can assume that because of their vocations they will be curious about the subject. But if your audience is this beginning public speaking class, then unless they have had a personal experience with cancer, they may not naturally relate to your subject. So you can either choose another topic or make an extra effort to determine why cancer drugs are important to your audience and articulate this relevance in your speech.

3. **Audience attitude toward the subject.** How does your audience feel about your subject? This is especially important when you want to influence their beliefs or move the audience members to action. You can determine your audience's attitudes toward your subject directly by surveying them, which we will discuss in the next section. If you cannot survey the audience directly, you might try to see if published opinion polls related to your subject are available. Then you can estimate your audience members' attitudes by studying these opinion polls and extrapolating their results to your audience. To access links to one of the world's most respected polling organizations, use your CengageNOW for *Challenge* to access **Web Resource 4.4: Public Opinion Polls**. Finally, in some cases, you will be forced to estimate the audience's attitudes from the speaking occasion and the demographic information you have acquired. Once you understand your audience's attitude toward your subject, you can choose a topic that will allow you to influence rather than alienate the audience. For example, a speech calling for strict gun control is likely to be perceived differently by classmates who grew up in an urban environment where gang violence is a problem than by those who grew up in a suburb where gun crimes are relatively rare or in a rural area where many people are hunters.

4. **Audience attitude toward you as a speaker.** Will your audience recognize you as a subject matter expert? Will they know that beforehand, or will you have to establish your credibility as you speak? **Credibility** is based on the perception

credibility the perception that you are knowledgeable, trustworthy, and personable

that you are knowledgeable (have the necessary understanding that allows you to explain the topic well), trustworthy (are honest, dependable, and ethical), and personable (show enthusiasm, warmth, friendliness, and concern for audience members). You will want to choose a topic that allows the audience to perceive you as credible and to believe that you know what you are talking about.

Methods for Gathering Audience Data

1. You can collect data through surveys. Although it is not always possible, the most direct way to collect audience data is to survey the audience. A **survey** is a questionnaire designed to gather information directly from people. Some surveys are done as interviews; others are written forms that are completed by the participants. The four kinds of items or questions most likely to be used in a survey are called two-sided, multiple-response, scaled, and open-ended.

- **Two-sided items** force the respondent to choose between two answers, such as yes/no, for/against, or pro/con. Suppose you wanted to understand your audience members' attitudes on the subject of TV. You might phrase several questions with two-sided answers, such as:

    Do you believe prime-time TV shows contain too much violence?

    _____ Yes _____ No

    Do you watch any of the *Law and Order* TV shows?

    _____ Yes _____ No

    Two-sided items are easy to use in an interview, and the answers are easy to sort during analysis.

- **Multiple-response items** give the respondent several alternative answers from which to choose. These items are especially useful for gathering demographic data. For example:

    Which best describes your religious tradition?

_____ Protestant	_____ Evangelical	_____ Catholic
_____ Jewish	_____ Buddhist	_____ Muslim
_____ Atheist	_____ Other	

    Multiple-response items can also be used to assess the extent of knowledge that audience members have about a topic. For example, a speaker might assess audience members' knowledge about diamonds with the following question:

    Please indicate what you know about diamonds by placing an X next to each topic you already know about.

    _____ How to value a diamond

    _____ How diamonds are made

    _____ How to tell the difference between a diamond and a fake

    _____ Blood diamonds

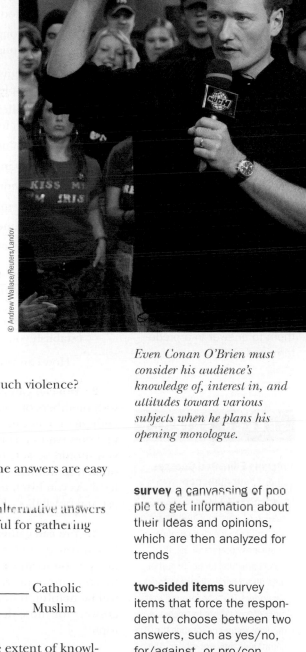

Even Conan O'Brien must consider his audience's knowledge of, interest in, and attitudes toward various subjects when he plans his opening monologue.

survey a canvassing of people to get information about their ideas and opinions, which are then analyzed for trends

two-sided items survey items that force the respondent to choose between two answers, such as yes/no, for/against, or pro/con

multiple-response items survey items that give the respondent several alternative answers from which to choose

scaled items survey items that measure the direction and/or intensity of an audience member's feeling or attitude toward something

- **Scaled items** measure the direction or intensity of an audience member's feeling or attitude toward something. For example:

  Indicate the extent to which you agree or disagree with the following statement:

  There is too much violence on prime-time TV.

  _____ Strongly agree   _____ Agree   _____ Neutral   _____ Disagree
  _____ Strongly disagree

  Scaled items can also be used to assess audience interest in a subject. For example:

  Please indicate, by checking the appropriate response, how interested you are in learning about each of the following.

  How to value diamonds:

  ____ Very interested   ____ Somewhat interested   ____ Uninterested

  How diamonds are cut:

  ____ Very interested   ____ Somewhat interested   ____ Uninterested

  Blood diamonds:

  ____ Very interested   ____ Somewhat interested   ____ Uninterested

open-ended items survey items that encourage respondents to elaborate on their opinions without forcing them to answer in a predetermined way

- **Open-ended items** encourage respondents to elaborate on their opinions without forcing them to answer in a predetermined way. These items yield rich information, but the wide variety of responses make them difficult to analyze. For example, to determine what you would need to do to establish your credibility on the subject of TV violence you might ask:

  How can you tell if someone is an expert on TV violence?

2. You can gather data through informal observation. If you are familiar with members of your audience (as you are with members of your classroom audience), you can get much of the important data about them through informal observation. For instance, after being in class for even a couple of sessions, you should be able to estimate the approximate age or age range and the ratio of men to women. Because you are all in college, you know the educational level. As you listen to your classmates talk, you will learn more about their interest in, knowledge of, and attitudes about many issues.

3. You can gather data by questioning the person who invited you to speak. When you are invited to speak to a group you are unfamiliar with, ask your contact person to answer the demographic questions in Exhibit 4.5. Even when the person cannot provide answers to all of the questions, the information you get will be helpful. If necessary, probe your contact person to at least estimate answers for those demographics that are likely to be most important for your topic.

4. You can make educated guesses about audience demographics and attitudes. If you can't get information in any other way, you will have to make educated guesses based on such indirect information as the general makeup of the people who live in a specific community and belong to a group like this or the kinds of people who are likely to attend the event or occasion. Suppose, for example, that you are asked by a nonprofit group you support to give a speech on volunteer opportunities with this charity to a meeting of high school guidance counselors who oversee community service projects for students. You can infer a number of things about audience members. First, all will be college-educated high school counselors from your city. They will all speak English. There are likely to be more women than men, and their ethnic backgrounds can be assumed to

---

SPEECH SNIPPET

Making Educated Guesses about Your Audience

Karlie was asked to give a speech on universal health care to a local service club comprised of business professionals. It wasn't practical for her to gather data about her audience before her speech, but she inferred that most of them probably received medical insurance through the companies they worked for. She made her topic relevant to them by talking about the advantages and disadvantages of universal health care relative to private insurance options. In that way, she was able to acknowledge the value of private insurance for those who have it and then move on to compare the two options for society overall.

EXHIBIT 4.5 **Audience analysis summary form**

My subject is _____

Data were collected:

_____ by survey

_____ by direct observation

_____ by questioning the person who invited me

_____ by educated guessing

Demographic Data

1. The average audience member's education level is _____ high school _____ college _____ postgraduate.

2. The ages range from _____ to _____. The average age is about _____.

3. The audience is approximately _____ percent male and _____ percent female.

4. My estimate of the average income level of the audience is _____ upper _____ middle _____ lower.

5. Most audience members are of _____ the same occupation/major (which is _____) _____ different occupations/majors.

6. Most audience members are of _____ the same race (which is _____) _____ a mixture of races.

7. Most audience members are of _____ the same religion (which is _____) _____ a mixture of religions.

8. Most audience members are of _____ the same nationality (which is _____) _____ a mixture of nationalities.

9. Most audience members are from _____ the same state _____ the same city _____ the same neighborhood _____ different areas.

10. Most audience members _____ speak English as their first language _____ English as a second language (ESL).

Subject-Specific Data

1. The average audience member's knowledge of the subject is likely to be _____ extensive _____ moderate _____ limited because _____
_____.

2. The average audience member's interest in this subject is likely to be _____ high _____ moderate _____ low because _____
_____.

3. The average audience member's attitude toward my subject is likely to be _____ positive _____ neutral _____ negative because _____
_____.

4. My initial credibility with the audience is likely to be _____ high _____ medium _____ low because _____
_____.

Conclusion

Based on these data _____
_____,

which relate to my speech topic in the following ways: _____
_____,

I will tailor my speech in the following ways: _____
_____

be similar to that of your community. They will be interested in your topic, but their knowledge of the specific opportunities at your agency will vary.

Whether you survey your audience, rely on informal observation, question the person who invited you to speak, or make educated guesses about audience demographics and subject-related information, you will want to record the information in a form that is convenient to use. Exhibit 4.5 presents an audience analysis summary form you can use to summarize your findings.

Now that you understand audience analysis, you can complete Speech Planning Action Step 1, Activity 1B: Analyzing Your Audience. To see an example of what a completed survey might look like, see the Student Response to Activity 1B.

SPEECH PLANNING	**ACTION STEP 1**
1 | Goals	

ACTIVITY 1B Analyzing Your Audience

1. Decide on a method for gathering audience data.
2. Collect the data.
3. Copy or duplicate the Audience Analysis Summary Form (Exhibit 4.5).
4. Use the information you have collected to complete the form.
5. Write two short paragraphs to describe your initial impression of audience demographics, knowledge, and attitudes toward your subject.
6. Save the completed form. You will refer to this audience analysis information to address listener relevance throughout the speech planning process.

You can download an online copy of this form. Use your CengageNOW for *Challenge* to access the chapter resources for Chapter 4; then click Audience Analysis Summary Form.

STUDENT RESPONSE	**ACTION STEP 1**

ACTIVITY 1B Analyzing Your Audience

Audience Analysis Summary Form
Demographic Data
1. The average audience member's education level is _____ high school _X_ college _____ postgraduate.
2. The ages range from _19_ to _24_. The average age is about _20_.
3. The audience is approximately _65_ percent male and _35_ percent female.
4. My estimate of the average income level of the audience is _____ upper _X_ middle _____ lower.
5. Most audience members are of _X_ the same occupation/major (which is **communication students**) _____ different occupations/majors.
6. Most audience members are of _X_ the same race (which is **white**) _____ a mixture of races.
7. Most audience members are of _X_ the same religion (which is **Judeo-Christian tradition**) _____ a mixture of religions.
8. Most audience members are of _X_ the same nationality (which is **American**) _____ a mixture of nationalities.

(continued)

9. Most audience members are from _____ the same state _____ the same city _____ the same neighborhood __X__ different areas.
10. Most audience members speak __X__ English as their first language _____ English as a second language (ESL).

Summary description of key audience characteristics: *From these data, I conclude that most audience members are similar to each other and to me. We are all students at U.C. Most of us are around twenty years old, which suggests that we have a common generational view. Since U.C. is a commuter school, most of us are probably middle to lower socioeconomic class. There are more men than women in the class, and we are mostly white middle-class Americans. Although we have some religious diversity, most of us come from Judeo-Christian religious traditions.*

Subject-Specific Data

1. The average audience member's knowledge of the subject is likely to be _____ extensive _____ moderate __X__ limited because *my audience members are mostly communication students, not geology or mineralogy students* .
2. The average audience member's interest in this subject is likely to be _____ high __X__ moderate _____ low because *without encouragement, they have no need to know about this subject. Mineralogy is hardly a trendy subject* .
3. The average audience member's attitude toward my subject is likely to be _____ positive __X__ neutral _____ negative because *the audience doesn't really have any information about the topic* .
4. My initial credibility with the audience is likely to be _____ high _____ medium __X__ low because *this is our first speech and they don't know I am a geology major whose family owns a jewelry store* .

Summary: *Most audience members don't know a lot about diamonds and have only a moderate interest in the subject, although it is not a controversial subject. So I will need to make sure to address listener relevance and include listener relevance links throughout the speech to maintain my audience's interest during the entire speech.*

Analyzing the Setting

The location and occasion make up the speech **setting.** The answers to several questions about the setting should guide your topic selection and other parts of your speech planning.

setting the location and occasion for a speech

   1. **What are the special expectations for the speech?** Every speaking occasion is surrounded by expectations. At an Episcopalian Sunday service, for example, the congregation expects the minister's sermon to have a religious theme. At a national sales meeting, the field representatives expect to hear about new products. For your classroom speeches, a major expectation is that your speech will meet the assignment requirements. Whether the speech assignment is defined by purpose (to inform or to persuade), by type (expository or demonstration), or by subject (book analysis or current event), your topic should reflect the nature of that assignment.

   2. **What is the appropriate length for the speech?** The time limits for classroom speeches are usually quite short, so you will want to choose a topic that is narrow enough to be accomplished in the time allotted. "Two Major Causes of Environmental Degradation" can be presented in five minutes, but "A History of Human Impact on the Environment" cannot. Problems with time limits are not peculiar to classroom speeches. Any speech setting includes actual or implied time limits. For example, the expected length for the sermon in a Protestant Sunday service may be twenty to thirty minutes; the expected length for a homily in a Roman Catholic Mass may be only ten minutes. It is important to understand and adhere to audience expectations regarding time limits—this

demonstrates respect for your listeners. For example, consider when you attended a concert or other public event that required an expensive ticket. If the main event was too short, it probably failed to meet your expectations about how much entertainment you should get for your money, and you probably felt cheated. Or consider when a teacher kept you in class longer than the allotted time. You were likely frustrated because it seemed the instructor failed to respect your other classes, your job, or the other commitments you juggled along with that particular course.

3. How large will the audience be? If you will be speaking to a small audience (fewer than fifty people), you will be physically close enough to them to talk in a normal voice and to move about. In contrast, if you will be speaking to a large audience, you will probably need a microphone, and you'll be less likely to be able to move about.

4. Where will the speech be given? Because classrooms vary in size, lighting, seating arrangements, and the like, consider the factors that may affect your presentation. In a long, narrow room, you may need to speak louder than usual to reach the back row. In a dark room, make sure the lights are on and that the blinds or shades are open to bring in as much light as possible.

Venues outside school settings offer even greater variations in conditions. Ask for specific information about seating capacity, shape, number of rows, nature of lighting, existence of a speaking stage or platform, distance between speaker and first row, and so on before you speak. If possible, visit the place and see it for yourself.

5. When will the speech be given? A speech given early in the morning requires a different approach from one given right after lunch or in the evening. If a speech is scheduled after a meal, for instance, the audience may be lethargic, mellow, or even on the verge of sleep. As a result, it helps to insert more "attention getters" (examples, illustrations, and stories) to counter potential lapses of attention.

6. Where in the program does the speech occur? If you are the only speaker or the featured speaker, you have an obvious advantage: You are the focal point of audience attention. In the classroom, however, and at some rallies, hearings, and other events, there are many speeches, and your place on the schedule may affect how you are received. For example, if you go first, you may need to "warm up" the listeners and be prepared to meet the distraction of a few audience members' strolling in late. If you speak last, you must counter the tendency of the audience to be weary from listening to several speeches.

The setting of your speech should guide the topic you select.

7. What equipment is necessary to give the speech? For some speeches, you may need a microphone, a chalkboard, an overhead or slide projector and screen, or a hookup for your laptop computer. In most instances, speakers have some kind of speaking stand, but it is wise not to count on it. If the person who has invited you to speak has any control over the setting, be sure to explain what you need, but always have alternative plans in case what you have asked for is unavailable. It is frustrating to plan a computer PowerPoint presentation, for example, and then discover that there's no place to plug in the computer!

Complete Speech Planning Action Step 1, Activity 1C: Analyzing the Setting. Analyze the setting so that you understand your setting and take it into consideration as you choose your topic and develop your speech. To see how one student completed this activity, see the Student Response to Activity 1C.

SPEECH PLANNING   **ACTION STEP 1**

ACTIVITY 1C Analyzing the Setting

The goal of this activity is to help you understand your speech setting. Fill in answers to the following questions:

1. What are the special expectations for the speech? _____
2. What is the appropriate length for the speech? _____
3. How large will the audience be? _____
4. Where will the speech be given? _____
5. When will the speech be given? _____
6. Where in the program does the speech occur? _____
7. What equipment is necessary to give the speech? _____

Write a short paragraph mentioning which aspects of the setting are most important for you to consider in speech preparation and why.

You can complete this activity online, print it, and if requested, e-mail it to your instructor. Use your CengageNOW for *Challenge* to access Action Step Activity 1C.

STUDENT RESPONSE   **ACTION STEP 1**

ACTIVITY 1C Analyzing the Setting

1. What are the special expectations for the speech? __*informative or persuasive*__
2. What is the appropriate length for the speech? __*4–6 minutes*__
3. How large will the audience be? __*13–15 people*__
4. Where will the speech be given? __*614 Dyer Hall*__
5. When will the speech be given? __*9:30 a.m., Tuesday*__
6. Where in the program does the speech occur? __*I will try to go first.*__
7. What equipment is necessary to give the speech? __*Overhead and chalkboard*__

Time is certainly important: Four to six minutes is not very long. I plan to time my speech when I practice to make sure I stay within the expected time limits. Also, I want to make sure that I am one of the first speakers.

Selecting a Topic

Armed with your topic lists and the information you have collected on your audience and setting, you are ready to select a topic that will be appropriate to the audience and the setting.

As you review your list of topics, compare each to your audience profile. Are there some topics that are too simple for this audience's knowledge base? too difficult? Are some topics likely to be more interesting to the audience? How do the audience's age, ethnicity, and other demographic features mesh with each topic? By asking these and similar questions, you will be able to identify topics that are appropriate for the audience. Then consider the setting. Are some topics too broad for the time allotted? Are there topics that won't meet the special expectations? Answers to these and other questions will help you identify the topics that are appropriate to your setting. Speech Planning Action Step 1, Activity 1D: Selecting a Topic will aid you in selecting your topic. To see how one student responded to this activity, see the Student Response to Activity 1D.

| **SPEECH PLANNING** | **ACTION STEP 1** |

1 | Goals

ACTIVITY 1D Selecting a Topic

Use your responses to Action Step Activities 1A, 1B, and 1C to complete this activity.
1. Write each of the topics that you checked in Activity 1A on the lines below:

_____   _____   _____

_____   _____   _____

_____   _____   _____

2. Using the information you compiled in Activity 1B, the audience analysis, compare each topic to your audience profile. Eliminate topics that seem less appropriate. Write each of the topics that remain on the lines below:

_____   _____   _____

_____   _____   _____

3. Using the information you compiled in Activity 1C, your analysis of the setting for this speech, compare each of the remaining topics to your setting profile. Eliminate topics that seem less appropriate. Write each of the topics that remain on the lines below:

_____   _____   _____

4. Each of the remaining topics is appropriate to your audience and setting; you can be confident that you can develop an appropriate speech from any of these. So, from the topics that remain, select the one that you are most excited about sharing with others. My topic will be _____

You can go online to complete this activity and print out a worksheet that will help you select your topic. Use your CengageNOW for *Challenge* to access Action Step Activity 1D.

ACTIVITY 1D Selecting a Topic

1. Write each of the topics that you checked in Activity 1A on the lines below:

volcanoes	*history of lacrosse*	*habitat destruction*
diamond tests	*lacrosse skills*	*oil wells*
hydrology	*lacrosse strategy*	*littering*

2. Using the information you compiled in Activity 1B, the audience analysis, compare each topic to your audience profile. Eliminate topics that seem less appropriate. Write each of the topics that remain on the lines below:

volcanoes	*lacrosse skills*	*habitat destruction*
diamond tests	*lacrosse strategy*	

3. Using the information you compiled in Activity 1C, your analysis of the setting for this speech, compare each of the remaining topics to your setting profile. Eliminate topics that seem less appropriate. Write each of the topics that remain on the lines below:

diamond tests	*lacrosse skills*	*habitat destruction*

4. Each of the remaining topics is appropriate to your audience and setting; you can be confident that you can develop an appropriate speech from any of these. So, from the topics that remain, select the one that you are most excited about sharing with others. My topic will be *diamond tests* .

Writing a Speech Goal

Once you have chosen your topic, you are ready to identify and write the general speech goal you hope to achieve in the speech and then the specific goal that is tailored to the audience and the setting.

Understanding General and Specific Speech Goals

The **general goal** is the overall intent of the speech. Most speeches intend to entertain, to inform, or to persuade, even though each type of speech may include elements of other types. Consider the following examples: Conan O'Brien's opening monologue is intended to entertain, even though it may include material that is seen as persuasive. Likewise, John Kerry's political campaign speeches were intended to persuade, even though they also may have been very informative.

The general goal is usually dictated by the setting, particularly the occasion. (In this course, your instructor is likely to specify it.) Most speeches given by adults as part of their job or community activities have the general goal of informing or persuading. But occasionally, such as when giving a toast at a wedding, the purpose is to entertain.

Whereas the general goal is often determined by the setting in which a speech is given, the **specific goal,** or specific purpose of a speech, is a single statement that identifies the exact response the speaker wants from the audience. For a speech on the topic "Evaluating Diamonds," one might state the specific goal as, "I would like the audience to understand the four major criteria used for evaluating a diamond." For a speech on "Supporting the United

general goal the overall intent of the speech

specific goal a single statement that identifies the exact response the speaker wants from the audience

Way," a specific goal might be stated as, "I would like the audience to donate money to the United Way."

In the first example, the goal is informative: The speaker wants the audience to understand the criteria. In the second example, the goal is persuasive: The speaker wants to convince the audience to donate money.

Phrasing a Specific Speech Goal

The setting (or in the case of this class, the assignment) usually dictates the nature of your general speech goal. A specific speech goal, however, must be carefully crafted because it lays the foundation for organizing the speech.

The following guidelines can help you craft a well-worded specific goal.

In deciding on a general speech goal, you will have to balance your desires against the needs of your audience and the setting.

1. Write a draft of your general speech goal using a complete sentence that specifies the type of response you want from the audience. Julia, who has been concerned with and is knowledgeable about the subject of illiteracy, drafts the following statement of her general speech goal.

I want my audience to understand the effects of illiteracy.

Julia's draft is a complete sentence, and it specifies the response she wants from the audience: *to understand* the effects of illiteracy. Her phrasing tells us that she is planning to give an informative speech.

© Royalty-free/Corbis

2. Revise the statement (and the infinitive phrase) until it indicates the specific audience reaction desired. If your objective is to explain (to inform), the infinitive that expresses your desired audience reaction could be "to understand," "to recognize," "to distinguish," or "to identify." If you see the goal of your speech as changing a belief or calling the audience to action, then your general goal is persuasive and can be reflected by the use of such infinitives as "to believe," "to accept," "to change," or "to do." If Julia wanted to persuade her audience, her specific goal might be worded:

I want my audience to believe that illiteracy is a major problem.

3. Make sure that the goal statement contains only one idea. Suppose Julia had first written

I would like the audience to understand the nature of illiteracy and its effects on the individual and society.

This statement is not a good specific goal because it includes two distinct ideas: understanding the nature of illiteracy and understanding the specific effects that may follow from being illiterate. Either one is a worthy goal—but not both in one speech. Julia needs to choose one of these ideas. If your goal statement includes the word *and*, you have more than one idea.

4. Revise your statement until it describes the precise focus of your speech (the infinitive phrase articulates the

complete response you want from your audience). Julia's draft "I want my audience to understand the effects of illiteracy" is a good start, but the infinitive phrase "to understand the effects of illiteracy" is vague. Exactly what about illiteracy is it that Julia wants her audience to understand? Here is where you need to consider your audience analysis and adapt your specific goal in ways that address listener relevance. What is it about illiteracy your particular audience should know and why?

At this point, Julia may need to begin doing some research to focus her ideas and refine her goal statement. Since Julia knows her classmates all have the goal of becoming gainfully employed after graduating, and because she knows how illiteracy places people in the workplace at a disadvantage, she might rephrase her specific goal to read

> I want the audience to understand three ways illiteracy hinders a person's effectiveness in the workplace.

This statement meets the criteria for a good specific goal statement because it indicates the specific desired audience reaction and it contains only one explicit idea that is the focus of the speech.

A good specific goal statement is important because it will guide your research as you prepare the speech. Once you have completed your research, you will expand your specific goal statement into a thesis statement, which will be the foundation on which you will organize the speech.

Exhibit 4.6 gives several additional examples of general and specific informative and persuasive goals.

By completing Speech Planning Action Step 1, Activity 1E: Writing a Specific Goal on page 68, you will develop a well-written specific goal statement for your speech. To see how one student responded to this activity, see the Student Response to Activity 1E.

EXHIBIT 4.6 General and specific speech goals

Informative Goals

General goal: To inform the audience about techniques of handwriting analysis.

Specific goal: I want the audience to understand the differences between two major techniques graphologists use to analyze handwriting.

General goal: To inform the audience about forms of mystery stories.

Specific goal: I want the audience to be able to identify the three basic forms of mystery stories.

Persuasive Goals

General goal: To persuade the audience that drug testing by businesses should be prohibited.

Specific goal: I want the audience to believe that required random drug testing of employees by businesses should be prohibited.

General goal: To persuade the audience to donate to a food bank.

Specific goal: I want to persuade the audience to make a donation of $5 or more to Second Harvest.

ACTIVITY 1E Writing a Specific Goal

Type of speech: _____

1. Write a draft of your general speech goal using a complete sentence that specifies the type of response you want from the audience.
2. Revise the infinitive to make it reflect the specific audience response you desire.
3. Check the number of ideas expressed in the statement. If the statement contains more than one idea, select one and rewrite the statement.
4. Improve the statement so that it describes the precise focus of your speech as it relates to your intended audience.

Write the final draft of the specific goal:

_____

_____

_____

You can complete this activity online with Speech Builder Express, a speech outlining and development tool that will help you complete the action steps in this book to develop your speech. See the inside back cover of this book for instructions on how to access Speech Builder Express.

STUDENT RESPONSE

ACTION STEP 1

ACTIVITY 1E Writing a Specific Goal

Type of speech: _informative_

1. Write a draft of your general speech goal using a complete sentence that specifies the type of response you want from the audience.

   I want the audience to have an understanding of the skills necessary to play lacrosse.

2. Revise the infinitive to make it reflect the specific audience response you desire.

   I want the audience to recognize the skills necessary to play lacrosse.

3. Check the number of ideas expressed in the statement. If the statement contains more than one idea, select one and rewrite the statement.

   I want my audience to recognize the basic skills necessary to play lacrosse.

4. Improve the statement so that it describes the precise focus of your speech as it relates to your intended audience.

   I want my audience to recognize the three basic skills needed to begin playing lacrosse.

Write the final draft of the specific goal:

   I want my audience to recognize the three basic skills necessary to play the game of lacrosse.

Although Glen and Adam were taking the same speech course, they were in sections that had different instructors. One evening when Adam was talking with Glen about his trouble finding a topic, Glen mentioned that he was planning to speak about home pages. Because the number of different speech goals for this topic seemed unlimited, he didn't see any harm in showing Adam his bibliography, so he brought it up on his computer screen.

As Adam was looking at it, Glen went down the hall to get a book he had lent to a friend earlier that morning. While Glen was away, Adam thought he'd take a look at what else Glen had in the file. He was soon excited to see that Glen had a complete outline on the goal "I want the class to understand the steps in designing a home page." Figuring he could save himself some time, Adam printed the outline; he justified his action on the basis that it represented a good start that would give him ideas. As time ran short, Adam decided to just use Glen's outline for his own speech.

Later in the week, Glen's instructor happened to be talking to Adam's instructor about speeches she had heard that week. When she mentioned that Glen had given a really interesting speech on home pages, Adam's teacher said, "That's interesting. I heard a good one just this morning. Now what did you say the goal of the speech you heard was?" When the goals turned out to be the same, Glen's instructor went back to her office to get the outline that she would be returning the next day. As the two instructors went over the outlines, they saw that the two speeches were exactly the same. The next day, they left messages for both Adam and Glen to meet with them and the department head that day.

1. What is the ethical issue at stake?
2. Was there anything about Glen's behavior that was unethical? anything about Adam's?
3. What should be the penalty, if any, for Glen? for Adam?

Summary

The first step of effective speech preparation is to identify a topic. You begin by selecting a subject that is important to you and that you know something about, such as a job, a hobby, or a contemporary issue that concerns you. To arrive at a specific topic, brainstorm a list of related words under each subject heading. When you have brainstormed at least fifteen topics under each heading, you can check two or three specific topics under each heading that are most meaningful to you. You might also use concept mapping to brainstorm a variety of topics related to your subject.

The second step is to analyze the audience to decide how to shape and direct your speech. Audience analysis is the study of the intended audience for your speech. Gather specific data about your audience to develop a demographic profile that includes age, education, gender, background, occupation, race, ethnicity, religion, geographic uniqueness, language, knowledge of subject, and attitude toward subject. To ensure that you don't unintentionally marginalize or stereotype your listeners based on demographic characteristics, you may want to validate your predictions by surveying your classroom audience using two-sided, multiple-response, scaled, or open-ended questions. You may also gather data through informal observation, by questioning the person who invited you to speak, and by making educated guesses about audience demographics and attitudes.

The third step is to analyze the setting of the speech, which will affect your overall speech plan, by asking such questions as: What are the special expectations for the speech? What is the appropriate length for the speech? How large will the audience be? Where will the speech be given? When will the speech be given? Where in the program does the speech occur? What equipment is necessary to give the speech?

The fourth step is to select a topic that is appropriate for your audience members and the setting.

The final step is to write your speech goal. The general goal of a speech (the overarching purpose) is to entertain, to inform, or to persuade. The specific goal is a single statement that identifies the exact response the speaker wants from the audience. Writing a specific speech goal involves the following four-step procedure: (1) Write a first draft of your speech goal using a complete sentence that specifies the type of response you want from your audience. (2) Revise the statement (and the infinitive phrase) until it indicates the specific audience reaction desired. (3) Make sure that the goal statement contains only one idea. (4) Revise your statement until it describes the precise focus of your speech as it relates to the knowledge, interests, and values of your listeners.

CHALLENGE ONLINE

Now that you've read Chapter 4, use your CengageNOW for *The Challenge of Effective Speaking* for quick access to the electronic resources that accompany this text. Your CengageNOW gives you access to the Web Resources activities featured in this chapter, Speech Builder Express, InfoTrac College Edition, and online study aids such as a digital glossary and review quizzes.

Your *Challenge* CengageNOW is an online study system that helps you identify concepts you don't fully understand, allowing you to put your study time to the best use. Using chapter-by-chapter diagnostic pretests, the system creates a personalized study plan for each chapter. Each plan directs you to specific resources designed to improve your understanding, including pages from the text in e-book format. Chapter posttests give you an opportunity to measure how much you've learned and let you know if you are ready for graded quizzes and exams.

KEY TERMS

Go to your CengageNOW for *Challenge* to access your online glossary for Chapter 4. Print a copy of the glossary for this chapter and test yourself with the electronic flash cards or complete the crossword puzzle to help you master these key terms:

audience adaptation (49)
audience analysis (49)
brainstorming (51)
concept mapping (51)
credibility (57)
demographic diversity (55)
general goal (65)

listener relevance links (55)
marginalizing (54)
multiple-response items (57)
open-ended items (58)
scaled items (58)
setting (61)
speaking situation (49)

specific goal (65)
stereotyping (55)
subject (49)
survey (57)
topic (49)
two-sided items (57)

WEB RESOURCES

Go to your CengageNOW for *Challenge* to access the Web Resources for this chapter.

4.1 Brainstorming (51)
4.2 Create Your Own Concept Map (52)
4.3 Defining Your Audience (53)
4.4 Public Opinion Polls (56)

SPEECH PLANNING ACTION STEPS

Access the Action Step activities for this chapter online at your CengageNOW for *Challenge*. Select the chapter resources for Chapter 4; then click on the activity number you want. You may print your completed activities, and you should save your work so you can use it as needed in later Action Step activities.

1A Using Brainstorming and Concept Maps to Identify Speech Topics (53)

1B Analyzing Your Audience (60)
1C Analyzing the Setting (63)

1D Selecting a Topic (64)
1E Writing a Specific Goal (68)

From Web Site for Verderber/Verderber's The Challenge of Effective Speaking 13th edition by VERDERBER/VERDERBER. 2006 Reprinted with permission of Wadsworth, a division of Cengage Learning: permissions.cengage.com. Fax 800 730-2215.

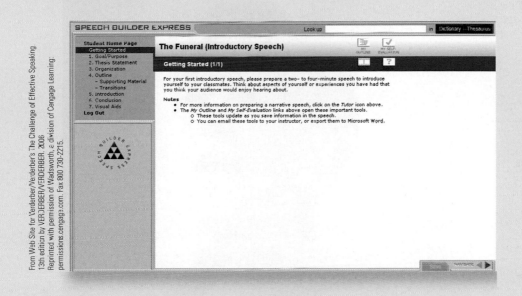

Adapting to Audiences

You persuade a man only inso-far as you can talk his language by speech, gesture, tonality, order, image, attitude, idea, identifying your ways with his.

Kenneth Burke, *A Rhetoric of Motives* (1950)

© Justin Sullivan/Getty Images

What's Ahead

HERE'S WHAT'S AHEAD IN THIS CHAPTER:

1. Why is it important in your speech to articulate its relevance to your audience?

2. What should you do if your audience does not share your attitude about the topic of your speech?

3. What can you do to help your audience see you as trustworthy and knowledgeable about your topic?

4. Why is it important to address diverse learning styles in your speech?

5. What can you do to overcome language and cultural differences between you and your audience?

Nathan had asked his friend George to listen to one of his speech rehearsals. As he finished the final sentence of the speech, "So, watching violence on TV does affect children in at least two ways—it not only desensitizes them to real violence, but it also influences them to behave more aggressively." He asked George, "So, what do you think?"

"You're giving the speech to your classmates, right?"

"Yeah."

"And they're mostly mass media majors?"

"Uh-huh."

"Well, it was a good speech, but I didn't hear anything that showed that you had media majors in mind."

Nathan may have chosen his topic with his audience in mind, but as he prepared, he forgot that an effective speech is one in which what is said is geared to the specific audience. In the previous chapter, we saw how audience and setting considerations help you to choose a speech topic. In this chapter, we describe how you can use audience analysis to tailor what you say in the speech to the audience who will listen to it. The second Speech Planning Action Step is to identify audience adaptation strategies.

Audience adaptation is the process of tailoring your speech's information to the needs, interests, and expectations of your listeners. Your concerns about adapting to your audience will inform your research efforts, your choice of main points to cover in the speech, the supporting material that you will use to develop those points, and even the jokes you might want to tell. So recognizing audience adaptation needs during Action Step 2 lays the foundation for the work that follows. In the rest of this chapter, we describe the issues of adaptation, including demonstrating the relevance of your topic, acknowledging initial audience disposition toward your topic, establishing common ground, gaining credibility, ensuring information comprehension and retention, and dealing with cultural and language differences. Your consideration of these issues will enable you to formulate a specific blueprint that you will use as you plan your speech.

Relevance

The first issue you face is demonstrating **relevance**—adapting the information in a speech so that audience members view it as important to them. Listeners pay attention to and are interested in ideas that have a personal impact ("What does this have to do with me?") and are bored when they don't see how what is being said relates to them. You help an audience see how your topic is relevant to them when you demonstrate the timeliness, proximity, and personal impact that the ideas in your speech have for your audience.

Demonstrate Timeliness

Information has **timeliness** when it is useful now or in the near future. You can increase the relevance of the information you present by showing how it is

audience adaptation the process of tailoring your speech's information to the needs, interests, and expectations of your listeners

ACTION STEP 2

1 | Goals

Recognizing opportunities for audience adaptation

relevance adapting the information in a speech so that audience members view it as important to them

timeliness showing how information is useful now or in the near future

David Young Wolff/PhotoEdit

Reactions such as applause, laughter, head nodding, and smiles are all signs that your audience is relating well to what you are saying.

timely for a particular audience. For example, in a speech about the hazards of talking on cell phones while driving, J. J. quickly established the topic's relevance to the audience with this introduction:

> Most of us in this room, as many as 90 percent of us in fact, are a danger to society. Why? Because we talk or text message on our cell phones while driving. Although driving while phoning (DWP) seems harmless, a study conducted in January 2007 by the Nationwide Mutual Insurance Company reports that DWP is the most common cause of accidents today. Another study published in 2005 by the Insurance Institute for Highway safety reveals that motorists who use cell phones are four times as likely to get into crashes serious enough to injure themselves or others. So this issue is far from harmless and is certainly one each of us should take seriously.

To see an excellent example of how timeliness can impact a message—President Ronald Reagan's 1986 speech on the *Challenger* space shuttle disaster—use your CengageNOW for *Challenge* to access **Web Resource 5.1: Demonstrating Timeliness**.

Demonstrate Proximity

proximity the relevance of information to personal life space

Listeners are more likely to be interested in information that has **proximity** to them—that is, it is relevant to their personal life space. Psychologically, we are more interested in information that affects our "territory" than to information that is remote from us. So we are likely to be more attentive to information when it is related to our family, neighborhood, city, state, or country. The more "distant" the information, the less it interests us.

As you prepare to speak, consider how to make your information more proximal for your audience. You have probably heard speakers say, "Let me bring this close to home for you . . ." and then make their point by using a local example. As you research your speech, you will want to look for statistics and examples that are proximal for your audience. For example, if you give a speech on the problem of homelessness in our country, you can address proximity by talking about the statistics of homelessness in your community and sharing a story or two from someone you interviewed at a local shelter.

Demonstrate Personal Impact

When you present information on a topic that can have a serious physical, economic, or psychological impact on audience members, they will be interested in what you have to say. For example, notice how your classmates' attention picks up when your instructor states that what is said next "will definitely be on the test." Your instructor understands that this "economic impact" (not paying attention can "cost") is enough to refocus most students' attention on what is said.

As you research and prepare your speech, you will want to find and incorporate ideas that create personal impact for your audience. In a speech on toxic waste, you might show a serious physical impact by providing statistics on the effects of toxic waste on the health of people in your state. You may be able to demonstrate serious economic impact by citing the cost to the taxpayers of a recent toxic waste cleanup in your city. Or you might be able to illustrate a serious psychological impact by finding and recounting the stresses faced by one family (that is demographically similar to your audience) with a long-term toxic waste problem in their neighborhood.

Initial Audience Disposition

Initial audience disposition is the knowledge of and opinions about your topic that your listeners have before they hear you speak. Adapting to the initial audience disposition means creating a speech that takes into account how much audience members already know about your topic and what their attitudes are toward it. As part of your audience analysis, you identified the initial attitude you expected most of your audience members to have toward your topic. During your speech preparation, you will choose specific supporting material with these initial attitudes in mind so that your speech provides your audience with new information.

Adapting to listeners' attitudes is obviously important for persuasive speeches, but it is also important for informative speeches. For example, a speech on refinishing wood furniture is meant to be informative. However, you may face an audience whose initial attitude is that refinishing furniture is difficult, uninteresting, or complicated. On the other hand, you may face an audience of young homeowners who are addicted to HGTV and who are really looking forward to your talk. Although the refinishing process you describe in both situations would be the same, your approach to explaining the steps would need to take the audience's initial disposition into account. If you know your audience thinks refinishing furniture is complicated and boring, you will need to adjust what you say so that you pique their interest and convince them that the process is really simpler than they initially thought. And if you know you have an audience of new homeowners and have found out through a simple show of hands that most of them enjoy watching HGTV, you can play upon their interest as you speak—by making reference to some of the most popular shows on HGTV. In Chapter 13, Persuasive Speaking: Reasoning with Your Audience, we will examine strategies for dealing with listeners' attitudes in depth.

Common Ground

Each person in the audience is unique, with different knowledge, attitudes, philosophies, experiences, and ways of perceiving the world. Your listeners may or may not know others in the audience. So it is easy for them to assume that

SPEECH SNIPPET

Demonstrating Personal Impact

In her speech about her reasons for being a vegetarian, Tiffany demonstrated personal impact by citing U.S. health statistics related to consuming too much fat and not enough fruits and vegetables, such as obesity, heart disease, and high cholesterol.

initial audience disposition the knowledge of and opinions about your topic that your listeners have before they hear you speak

SPEECH SNIPPET

Addressing Timeliness and Acknowledging Listener Attitudes

In her introductory remarks, Tiffany addressed timeliness and acknowledged listener attitudes in her speech "Meat Free and Me": "With Thanksgiving just around the corner, many of you are probably anticipating a feast complete with a flavorful, juicy turkey as the main course. I am too, but many of you would find my menu bizarre—I'm planning to feast on rice pilaf with grilled vegetables and garlic-roasted tofu." In this way, Tiffany establishes timeliness by relating her topic to the traditional holiday dinner and acknowledges that her audience will find her menu odd. This sets the stage for her discussion of meat-free dining.

they have nothing in common with you or with other audience members. Yet when you speak, you will be giving one message to that diverse group. **Common ground** is the background, knowledge, attitudes, experiences, and philosophies that audience members and the speaker share. Effective speakers use audience analysis to identify areas of similarity and then apply the adaptation techniques of using personal pronouns, asking rhetorical questions, and drawing on common experiences to create common ground.

Use Personal Pronouns

The simplest way of establishing common ground is to use **personal pronouns**—"we," "us," and "our"—to directly link the speaker to members of the audience. For example, in a speech to an audience whose members are known to be sympathetic to legislation limiting violence in children's programming on TV, notice the effect of using a personal pronoun:

> I know that most people worry about the effects that violence on TV is having on young children.

> I know that most of us worry about the effects that violence on TV is having on young children.

By using "us" instead of "people," the speaker includes the audience members and thus gives them a stake in listening to what follows.

Ask Rhetorical Questions

A second way of developing common ground is to pose **rhetorical questions**—questions phrased to stimulate a mental response rather than an actual spoken response on the part of the audience. Rhetorical questions create common ground by alluding to information that is shared by audience members and the speaker. They are often used in the introduction to a speech but can also be effective as transitions and in other parts of the speech. For instance, notice how this transition, phrased as a rhetorical question, creates common ground:

> When you have watched a particularly violent TV program, have you ever asked yourself, "Did they really need to be this graphic to make the point?"

Rhetorical questions are meant to have only one answer that highlights similarities between the speaker and audience members and leads them to be more interested in the content that follows. So, as the speaker, you should choose rhetorical questions that are in line with the information you have gleaned from the audience analysis. You don't want audience members to answer silently in a way opposite to what you intend. When this happens, instead of listening to your speech, audience members may begin silently debating what you say.

Draw from Common Experiences

A third way of developing common ground is selecting and presenting personal experiences, examples, and illustrations that embody what you and the audience have in common. For instance, in a speech about the effects of television violence, you might allude to a common viewing experience:

> Remember how sometimes at a key moment when you're watching a really frightening scene in a movie you may quickly shut your eyes? I remember doing that over and over again. I vividly remember slamming my eyes shut during the snake scenes in *Raiders of the Lost Ark*.

In this example, the audience members recall their own personal moment of fear and then relate it to the snake scene experience of the speaker.

To create material that draws on common experiences, you must study the audience analysis to understand how you and audience members are similar in the exposure you have had to the topic or in other areas that you can then compare to your topic. For example, suppose you are going to give a narrative/personal experience speech on skydiving. If most of your audience members have never jumped out of a plane, it would be difficult for them to imagine the sensation unless you can create a common-ground experience. So you might try relating the immediate sensation of leaving the plane to a more common experience:

> The first thing you feel when you finally jump is that stomach-in-the-mouth sensation that is similar to something we've all experienced when we have lurched because we've missed a step going down a staircase or when we have momentarily gone airborne in a car from approaching the crest of a hill too fast.

Speaker Credibility

Credibility is the confidence that an audience places in the truthfulness of what a speaker says. There are several theories as to how speakers develop credibility. You can read a summary of these theories by using your CengageNOW for *Challenge* to access **Web Resource 5.2: Holistic Theory of Speaker Credibility**.

Some famous people are widely known as experts in a particular area and have proven to be trustworthy and likable. When these people give a speech, they don't have to adapt their remarks to establish their credibility. For example, in May 2007 Ben Bernanke, chairman of the Federal Reserve Board of the United States, spoke before the Montana Economic Development Summit on the subject of the future of small business in the global economy—no one listening would have questioned his credibility.

However, most of us, even though we may be given a formal introduction that attempts to acquaint the audience with our credentials and character prior to our speech, still need to adapt our remarks to build audience confidence in the truthfulness of what we are saying. Three adaptation techniques can affect how credible we are perceived to be: demonstrating knowledge and expertise, establishing trustworthiness, and displaying personableness.

Demonstrate Knowledge and Expertise

When listeners perceive you to be a knowledgeable expert, they will perceive you as credible. Their assessment of your **knowledge and expertise** depends on how well you convince them that you are qualified to speak on this topic. You can demonstrate your knowledge and expertise through direct and indirect means.

You establish your expertise directly when you disclose your experiences with your topic, including formal education, special study, demonstrated skill, and your "track record." For example, in a speech on driving while phoning, J. J. explained:

> I became interested in the issue of driving while phoning (DWP) after being involved personally in an accident caused by a driver who was talking on the phone. Since then, I've done a great deal of research on the subject and am involved in a grass-roots organization devoted to passing legislation to ban driving while phoning in our state.

Of course, to make claims like this, you must have had experiences that give you "standing" to speak on your topic. This is why it was critical for you to choose a topic you knew something about. When you can demonstrate your personal involvement with your topic, your audience begins to trust that you

credibility the perception that you are knowledgeable, trustworthy, and personable

knowledge and expertise how well you convince your audience that you are qualified to speak on the topic

Tiffany demonstrated direct expertise with her topic when she declared, "About five years ago, I made a decision to stop eating meat, which has changed my life in several ways. Living a vegetarian lifestyle is an important aspect of who I am today."

trustworthiness the extent to which the audience can believe that what you say is accurate, true, and in their best interests

Establishing Trustworthiness

Tiffany established trustworthiness in her speech by framing it as an explanation about why she chose to live a vegetarian lifestyle rather than trying to convince her listeners to make that same choice: "In the next few minutes, we'll talk about how I made this choice to live meat-free, some of the family issues I've dealt with as a result of this choice, and some of the specific ways this choice continues to affect my life today."

personableness the extent to which you project an agreeable or pleasing personality

understand the material you are presenting. Needless to say, you will be perceived as more credible if you demonstrate to the audience that you have real experience with your topic.

Audience members will also assess your expertise through indirect means, such as how well prepared you seem and how much you demonstrate firsthand involvement by using personal examples and illustrations. Audiences have an almost instinctive sense of when a speaker is "winging it," and most audiences distrust a speaker who does not appear to have command of the material. Speakers, who are overly dependent on their notes or who hem and haw fumbling to find ways to express their ideas, undermine the confidence of the audience. On the other hand, when your ideas are easy to follow and clearly expressed, audience members perceive you to be more credible.

Similarly, when the audience hears a speech in which the ideas are developed through specific statistics, high-quality examples, illustrations, and the personal experiences of the speaker, they are likely to view the speaker as credible. Recall how impressed you are with instructors who always seem to have two or three perfect examples and illustrations and who are able to recall statistics without looking at their notes. Compare this to your experiences with instructors who seem tied to the textbook and don't appear to know much about the subject beyond their prepared lecture. In which instance do you perceive the instructor to be more knowledgeable?

Establish Trustworthiness

A second way to enhance your credibility as a speaker is to directly establish your **trustworthiness**—the extent to which the audience can believe that what you say is accurate, true, and in their best interests. The more your audience sees you as trustworthy, the more credible you will be. People assess others' trustworthiness by judging their character and their motives. So you can establish yourself as trustworthy by following ethical standards and by honestly explaining what is motivating you to speak.

As you plan your speech, you need to consider how to demonstrate your character—that you are honest, industrious, dependable, and a morally strong person. For example, when you credit the source of your information as you speak, you confirm that the information is true—that you are not making it up—and you signal your honesty by not taking credit for someone else's ideas. Similarly, if you present the arguments evenly on both sides of an issue, instead of just the side you favor, audience members will see you as fair-minded.

How trustworthy you appear to be will also depend on how the audience views your motives. If people believe that what you are saying is self-serving rather than in their interests, they will be suspicious and view you as less trustworthy. Early in your speech, then, it is important to show how audience members will benefit from what you are saying. For example, in his speech on toxic waste, Brandon might describe how one community's ignorance of toxic waste disposal dangers allowed a toxic waste dump to be located in their community and the serious health issues that subsequently arose. He can then share his motive by saying something like this: "My hope is that this speech will give you the information you need to thoughtfully participate in decisions like these that may face your community."

Display Personableness

We have more confidence in people that we like. **Personableness** is the extent to which you project an agreeable or pleasing personality. The more your listeners like you, the more inclined they are to believe what you tell them. We quickly decide how much we like a new person based on our first impression of

The audience's perception of your trustworthiness results from their assessment of your character and your apparent motives for speaking.

© Ken James/Corbis

him or her. Although first impressions can be inaccurate, we still use them. And first impressions are based on what we infer about people from what we see, such as how they dress, how physically attractive we find them, how well they speak, whether they smile and appear friendly, and how they carry themselves.

Politicians running for office provide excellent (and at times humorous) examples of adapting to be liked. When a candidate takes off his jacket and tie, rolls up his sleeves, and dons a baseball cap emblazoned with "AFL-CIO" before speaking to a rally of union workers to solicit their votes, he is trying to be "like them" to be liked. As a speaker trying to build credibility with an audience, you should look for ways to adapt your personal style to one that will help the audience like you and perceive you as credible.

Besides dressing appropriately for the audience and occasion, you can increase the chances that the audience will like you by smiling at individual audience members before beginning your remarks and by looking at individuals as you speak, acknowledging them with a quick nod. You can also demonstrate personableness by using appropriate humor. We'll talk more about appropriate and inappropriate humor in Chapter 10, Practicing Speech Wording.

Information Comprehension and Retention

Although audience analysis helps you select a topic that is appropriate for your audience's current knowledge level, you will still need to adapt the information you present so that audience members can easily follow what you are saying and remember it when you are through. Six techniques that can aid you are appealing to diverse learning styles, orienting or refamiliarizing the audience with basic information, defining key terms, creating vivid examples to illustrate new concepts, personalizing information, and comparing unfamiliar ideas with those the audience recognizes.

Appeal to Diverse Learning Styles

A **learning style** is a person's preferred way of receiving information. As you might expect, people differ in how they learn, so as a speaker, try to present your ideas in ways that hold the interest of different types of learners. Models for understanding learning styles have been developed by a number of scholars across many disciplines.[1] One prominent model, called Kolb's cycle of learning,

learning style a person's preferred way of receiving information is based on the fact that people differ in how much they prefer to learn by watching versus doing and by feeling versus thinking.[2]

Some people prefer to learn by "watching" and easily understand and remember things they see and hear. People who prefer to learn by watching relate to well-designed visual aids and vivid examples that they can picture. Others prefer to learn by "doing." For these people, hands-on activities aid their comprehension and memory. People who prefer to learn by doing relate well when speakers provide real-life applications and clearly state how the speech topic is relevant to their personal or professional lives.

Some people find it difficult to understand and remember factual material and learn better if their feelings are engaged. These people learn well from stories and other supporting material that appeals to their emotions or senses. Other people learn well by absorbing and considering factual material. People who prefer to learn by thinking connect well when your ideas are supported with detailed definitions, explanations, facts, and statistics.

Exhibit 5.1 depicts how the watching-doing and feeling-thinking dimensions of the cycle of learning theory result in four types of learners. Although each of us has a favored learning style, research has revealed that all people learn most effectively when ideas are presented in diverse ways that "round" the entire cycle of learning.[3] So as you consider what information you will provide, adapt to diverse learning styles by presenting new information in ways that appeal to both those who prefer to learn by watching and feeling and those who prefer to learn by doing and thinking.

For example, suppose you are trying to make the point that for the large numbers of Americans who are functionally illiterate, understanding simple directions can be a problem. Here's an illustration that develops this idea:

> For instance, a person who is functionally illiterate might not be able to read or understand a label that says, "Take three times a day after eating."

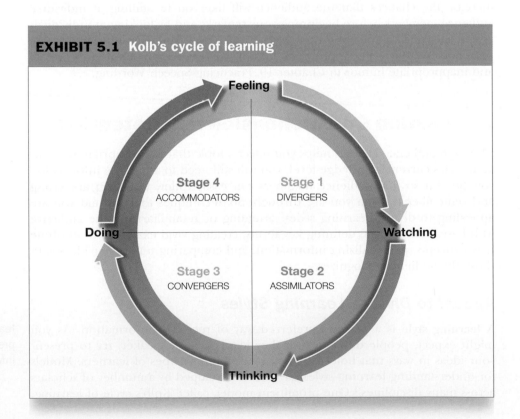

EXHIBIT 5.1   Kolb's cycle of learning

Feeling

Doing

Watching

Thinking

Stage 4
ACCOMMODATORS

Stage 1
DIVERGERS

Stage 3
CONVERGERS

Stage 2
ASSIMILATORS

Now look at how much richer this illustration becomes when we enhance the statement by using supportive material that rounds the cycle of learning:

> A significant number of Americans are functionally illiterate. That is, about 35 million people, 20 percent of the adult population, have serious difficulties with common reading tasks. *(thinking)* That means that one of every five people you see today may struggle with basic reading tasks. *(watching)* They cannot read well enough to understand how to bake a frozen pizza, how to assemble their children's bicycle from the printed instructions, or which bus to catch from the signs at the stop. *(feeling)* Many functionally illiterate people don't read well enough to follow the directions on this bottle [show an enlarged image of the label on a medicine bottle that reads, "Take three times a day after eating"]. *(doing)* So the directions on a prescription bottle like this [show visual aid of enlarged prescription bottle with directions written in garbled nonsense words] are basically meaningless.

You will find it easier to adapt to different learning styles if when you research your topic, you search for material that can appeal to watching and doing, feeling and thinking. And then, when you choose specific material to support your ideas, work consciously to include various types of evidence designed to appeal to the different learning preferences.

Orient Listeners

When listeners become confused or forget basic information, they lose interest in what is being said. Therefore, you will want to quickly review the basic ideas that are critical to understanding the speech. For example, if your speech concerns U.S. military involvement in Iraq, you can be reasonably sure that everyone in your audience is aware that the United States and Great Britain were participants in the coalition, but many may not remember the other countries that participated. So, before launching into the roles of various countries, remind your listeners by listing the nations that have provided troops and where they were stationed.

There may be some audience members who do not need the reminder, so to avoid offending them by appearing to talk down to them and to save face for those who need the reminder, you should acknowledge that they probably already remember the information. Phrases such as "As you will remember," "As we all probably learned in high school," and "As we have come to find out" are ways of prefacing reviews so that they are not offensive.

To see an excellent example of orienting listeners—former President Bill Clinton's speech outlining the reasons for NATO involvement in Kosovo—use your CengageNOW for *Challenge* to access **Web Resource 5.3: Orienting Listeners**.

CENGAGENOW™

Define Key Terms

Words have many meanings, so you should ensure audience members' comprehension of ideas by defining key terms that may be unfamiliar to them or are critical for understanding your speech. This becomes especially important when you are using familiar words whose commonly accepted meanings have been altered. For instance, in a speech on the four major problems faced by functionally illiterate people in the workplace, it will be important for your audience to understand what you mean by "functionally illiterate." So, early in the speech, you can offer your definition: "By 'functionally illiterate,' I mean people who have trouble accomplishing simple reading and writing tasks."

Illustrate New Concepts with Vivid Examples

Vivid examples help audience members understand and remember abstract, complex, and novel material. One vivid example can help us understand a complicated concept. So, as you prepare your speech, you will want to adapt by finding or creating real or hypothetical examples and illustrations to help your audience understand new information you present. For example, in the previous definition of functionally illiterate, the description "people who have trouble accomplishing simple reading and writing tasks" can be made more vivid by adding the following example: "For instance, a functionally illiterate person could not read and understand the directions on a prescription label that states, 'Take three times a day with a glass of water. Do not take on an empty stomach.'"

Personalize Information

personalize to present information in a frame of reference that is familiar to the audience

We **personalize** information by presenting it in a frame of reference that is familiar to the audience. Devon, a student at the University of California, is to give a speech on how the Japanese economy affects U.S. markets at the student chapter of the American Marketing Association. He wants to help his audience understand geographic data about Japan. He could just quote the following statistics from the 2004 *World Almanac*.[4]

> Japan is small and densely populated. The nation's 128 million people live in a land area of 146,000 square miles, giving them a population density of 877 persons per square mile.

Although this would provide the necessary information, it is not adapted to an audience comprised of college students in California, a large state in the United States. Devon can easily adapt the information to the audience by personalizing it for this student audience.

> Japan is a small, densely populated nation. Its population of 128 million is nearly half that of the *United States*. Yet the Japanese are crowded into a land area of only 146,000 square miles—roughly the same size as *California*. Just think of the implications of having half the population of the *United States* living *here in California*, where 30 million people—about one-fifth of that total—now live. In fact, Japan packs 877

Sometimes we can personalize information with a presentational aid like this one that compares the size of a dinosaur egg, which is unfamiliar to most audience members, with the commonly seen chicken egg.

persons into every square mile of land, whereas in the *United States* we average about 74 persons per square mile. Overall, then, Japan is about 12 times as crowded as the *United States.*

This revision adapts the information by personalizing it for this audience. Even though most Americans do not have the total land area of the United States on the tip of their tongue, they do know that the United States covers a great deal of territory. Likewise, a California audience would have a sense of the size of their home state compared to the rest of the nation. Personalized information is easier for audience members to understand and remember, so as you research and prepare your speech, you will want to look for ways to personalize the information. For Devon to personalize his information, he had to research the statistics on the United States and California. If Devon were speaking to an audience from another part of the country, he could adapt to them by substituting information from that state.

Compare Unknown Ideas with Familiar Ones

When you understand who is in your audience, you can help them with new ideas by making comparisons to things with which they are familiar. So, as you prepare your speech, you will want to identify places where you can use adaptive comparisons. For example, if I want an audience of Generation Xers to feel the excitement that was generated when telegrams were first introduced, I might compare it to the change that was experienced when e-mail became widely available. In the speech on functional illiteracy, if you want the audience of literates to sense what functionally illiterate people experience, you might compare it to the experience of surviving in a country where one is not fluent in the language:

> Many of us have taken a foreign language in school. So we figure we can visit a place where that language is spoken and "get along," right? But when we get to the country, we are often appalled to discover that even the road signs are written in this "foreign" language! And we can't quite make the signs out, at least not at sixty kilometers an hour! I was in France last summer, equipped with my three years of high school French, and I saw a sign that indicated that the train station I was looking for

REFLECT ON ETHICS

"Kendra, I heard you telling Jim about the speech you're giving tomorrow. You think it's a winner, huh?"

"Absolutely, Omar. Professor Bardston's going to give me an A for sure."

"You sound pretty confident."

"I am *so* confident. See, Professor Bardston's been talking about how important audience adaptation is. These last two weeks that's all we've heard—adaptation, adaptation."

"What does she mean?"

"Talking about something in a way that really relates to people personally."

"Okay. So how are you going to do that?"

"Well, I'm giving this speech on abortion, and Bardston let it slip that she's pro-life. So I'm going to give

this informative speech on the Right to Life movement. But I'm going to discuss the major beliefs of the movement in a way that'll get her to think I'm a supporter. I'm going to mention aspects of the movement that I know she'll like."

"But I've heard you talk about how you're pro-choice."

"I am—all the way. But by keeping the information positive, I'll make her think I'm a supporter. It isn't as if I'm going to be telling any lies or anything."

1. In a speech, is it ethical to adapt in a way that resonates with your audience but isn't in keeping with what you really believe?

2. Could Kendra have achieved her goal by using different methods? If so, how?

was "à droit"—"to the right," or is it "to the left"? I knew it was one or the other. Unfortunately, I couldn't remember and took a shot that it was to the left. Bad move. By the time I figured it out, I was ten miles in the wrong direction and ended up missing my train. At that moment, I could imagine how tough life must be for functionally illiterate people. So many "little details" of life require the ability to comprehend written messages.

Language and Cultural Differences

Western Europeans' speaking traditions inform the approach to public speaking we discuss in this book. However, public speaking is a social and cultural act, so as you would expect, public speaking practices and their perceived effectiveness vary. As they prepare and present speeches, speakers from various cultures and subcultures draw on the traditions of their speech communities, and speakers who address audiences comprised of people from ethnic and language groups different from their own face two additional challenges of adaptation: being understood when speaking in a second language and having limited common experiences on which to establish common ground.

Overcome Linguistic Problems

When the first language spoken by the audience is different from that of the speaker, audience members may not be able to understand what the speaker is saying because of mispronunciations, accents, vocabulary mistakes, and idiomatic speech meaning. Fear of making these mistakes can make second-language speakers self-conscious. But most audience members are more tolerant of mistakes made by second-language speakers than they are of those made by native speakers. Likewise, most audience members will work hard to understand a second-language speaker.

Nevertheless, second-language speakers have an additional responsibility to make their speech as understandable as possible. You can help your audience by speaking slowly and articulating as clearly as you can. By slowing your speaking rate, you give yourself additional time to pronounce what seem like awkward sounds and choose words whose meanings you know. This will also give your audience members additional time to "adjust their ear" so they can more easily process what you are saying. You can use visual aids to reinforce key terms and concepts as you move through your speech. Doing so assures listeners that they've heard you correctly, even with your accent. But be careful not to include too much information on your visual aids. Your visual aids should never replace your speech, but they can help ensure that key terms are understood equally by all.

One of the best ways for second-language speakers to improve giving a speech is to practice the speech in front of friends and associates who are native speakers. These "trial audience members" should be instructed to take note of words and phrases that are mispronounced or misused. They can work with you to correct your pronunciation or help you choose alternative words that better express your ideas. They can also review your visual aids to make sure they are appropriate. Keep in mind that the more practice you get speaking a language other than your native language, the more comfortable you will become with it and with your ability to relate to audience members.

Choose Culturally Sensitive Material

Although overcoming linguistic problems can seem daunting, those whose cultural background is significantly different from that of their audience members

When you are speaking to audiences who are vastly different from you, you must learn as much as you can about their culture so you can adapt your material to them.

also face the challenge of having few common experiences from which to draw. Much of our success in adapting to the audience hinges on establishing common ground and drawing on common experiences. But when we are speaking to audiences who are vastly different from us, we must learn as much as we can about the culture of our audience so that we can develop the material in a way that is meaningful to them. This may mean conducting additional library research to find statistics and examples that will be meaningful to the audience. Or it may require us to elaborate on ideas that would be self explanatory in our own culture. For example, suppose that Maria, a Mexican American exchange student, is giving a narrative/personal experience speech for her speech class at Yeshiva University in Israel on the *quiencianera* party she had when she turned fifteen. Because students in Israel don't have any experience with the Mexican coming-of-age tradition of *quiencianera* parties, they would have trouble understanding the significance of this event unless Maria was able to use her knowledge of the bar mitzvah and bat mitzvah coming-of-age ritual celebrations in Jewish culture and relate it to those.

Forming a Specific Plan of Audience Adaptation

You now understand the challenges that speakers face in developing and maintaining audience interest and understanding, and you have read about the adaptation techniques that can overcome these challenges. You have also completed your audience analysis. So you are ready to think about the adaptation challenges you will face in your speech as well as how you might adapt to them. At this point in your preparation process, identifying the challenges you face with your audience and planning how you might meet them will provide a guide to direct your research efforts and aid you as you develop the speech. Your adaptation plan should answer the following questions:

   1. How relevant will the audience find this material? How can I demonstrate that the material is timely, proximate, and has personal impact for audience members?

2. What is my audience's initial disposition toward my speech topic likely to be? What can I do to create or enhance audience interest in my topic or sympathy for my argument?

3. What common ground do audience members share with each other and with me? How and where can I use personal pronouns, rhetorical questions, and common experiences to enhance the perception of common ground?

4. What can I do to enhance my credibility? How did I develop my expertise on this topic, and how can I share that with the audience? How can I demonstrate my trustworthiness as I speak? What will I do to help the audience find me personable so they will like me?

5. How can I make it easier for audience members to comprehend and remember the information I will share? What types of material can I find and use to appeal to different types of learning styles? Given my topic and audience, what ideas will the audience need to be oriented to? What key terms will I need to define? What new concepts might be developed through vivid examples? What new ideas might I want to compare to ones the audience is already familiar with? How can I personalize the information I present?

6. What language or cultural differences do audience members have with each other and with me? If I will be speaking in a second language, how do I plan to increase the likelihood that the audience will understand me? What cultural differences do I need to be sensitive to, and what culturally appropriate material might I search for and use?

SPEECH PLANNING | ACTION STEP 2

2 | Audience

ACTIVITY 2 Recognizing Opportunities for Audience Adaptation

To identify opportunities for audience adaptation and lay a groundwork for applying information from the next several chapters, state your potential topic and then answer the following questions.

Potential topic: _____

1. How relevant will the audience find this material? How can I demonstrate that the material is timely, proximate, and has personal impact on the members of this audience?
2. What is my audience's initial disposition toward my speech topic likely to be?
3. What common ground do audience members share with each other and with me?
4. What can I do to enhance my credibility?
5. How can I make it easier for audience members to comprehend and remember the information I will share?
6. What language or cultural differences do audience members have with each other and with me?

You can complete this activity online, view another student sample of this activity, and if requested, e-mail your completed activity to your instructor. Use your Cengage-NOW for *Challenge* to access Action Step Activity 2.

To see how one student responded to this activity, see the Student Response to Activity 2.

ACTIVITY 2 Recognizing Opportunities for Audience Adaptation

Potential topic: _The criteria for evaluating diamonds_

1. How relevant will the audience find this material?

Initially, they are not likely to see it as relevant.

How can I demonstrate that the material is timely, proximate, and has personal impact on the members of this audience?

Because they are in their early twenties, I can make the information timely and give it personal impact by putting it in the context of buying an engagement ring. I can make it proximate by using examples of people in this area who have been ripped off because they didn't know what to look for.

2. What is my audience's initial disposition toward my speech topic likely to be?

Most audience members will be only mildly interested in and not well informed about this topic when I begin, but by tying the information to buying an engagement ring, I hope to pique their interest.

3. What common ground do audience members share with each other and with me?

Because most audience members are my age and are from the same national culture, we share areas of common ground that I can draw on. First, a diamond engagement ring is part of our shared culture. We are all about the same age, so we are looking for life mates and may be in the market for a diamond soon. So using personal pronouns and rhetorical questions to create common ground will be pretty easy. We are different in that I have a very strong interest in gemstones, and I will have to work hard not to become too technical and to assume that audience members are more knowledgeable than they are.

4. What can I do to enhance my credibility?

As I am introducing my speech, I need to work in my credentials. I need to tell the audience that I became interested in diamonds when I got to tour a diamond mine in South Africa while we were visiting family. I also need to share that I work for a jeweler and that I am majoring in geology. I can demonstrate trustworthiness by making sure that I tell the audience where the standards for evaluating diamonds came from. Although I have several friends who will be in the audience, most of the audience does not know me, so I will try to be personable by getting to the presentation early to meet and talk with audience members as they arrive.

5. How can I make it easier for audience members to comprehend and remember the information I will share?

I will orient the audience by reminding them of the different diamond shapes. I figure most people know these but may have forgotten some of them. I will need to define terms such as cut, clarity, occlusion, and carat. I think that I will need to create vivid examples and personalize some of the more technical information I present. I will know better how to do this once I have decided on all of the main ideas I will present.

6. What language or cultural differences do audience members have with each other and with me?

I will not be speaking in a second language, but I will need to be careful not to use too many technical terms that as a geology major I am comfortable with but would be "jargon" to my audience. Although most audience members are U.S.

nationals, there are three foreign students in class whose cultural engagement practices may not include giving a diamond ring. To adapt to them without singling them out, I may say something like, "As we all know, in the United States, it is tradition that when we become engaged the woman receives a diamond ring from the man."

Summary

Audience adaptation is the process of customizing your speech material to your specific audience.

One part of audience adaptation is to help the audience see the relevance of your material by demonstrating timeliness (showing how the information is useful now or in the near future), demonstrating proximity (showing relevance to personal life span), and demonstrating personal impact on audience members.

The second part of the adaptation process is to acknowledge the audiences initial disposition by framing the speech in a way that takes into account how much audience members know about your topic and what their attitudes are about it.

The third part is to develop common ground by using personal pronouns, asking rhetorical questions, and drawing from common experiences.

The fourth part is to build speaker credibility by demonstrating knowledge and expertise, establishing trustworthiness, and displaying personableness.

The fifth part is to increase audience comprehension of information by creating material that appeals to diverse learning styles, orienting listeners, defining key terms, creating vivid examples to illustrate new concepts, presenting information in a frame of reference that is familiar to the audience, personalizing information, and comparing unknown ideas with familiar ones.

The sixth part is to take into account language and cultural differences by overcoming linguistic problems and choosing culturally sensitive material.

As you consider each part of audience adaptation, you can write down the specific actions you will take. This list becomes a written strategy that you can consult as you move forward in the speech planning process. Effective speakers are able to use adaptation techniques to develop unique speeches sharing a common speech goal but tailored to the specific needs of different audiences.

CHALLENGE ONLINE

Now that you've read Chapter 5, use your CengageNOW for *The Challenge of Effective Speaking* for quick access to the electronic resources that accompany this text. Your CengageNOW gives you access to the Web Resources and Speech Planning activities featured in this chapter, Speech Builder Express, InfoTrac College Edition, and online study aids such as a digital glossary and review quizzes.

Your *Challenge* CengageNOW is an online study system that helps you identify concepts you don't fully understand, allowing you to put your study time to the best use. Using chapter-by-chapter diagnostic pretests, the system creates a personalized study plan for each chapter. Each plan directs you to specific resources designed to improve your understanding, including pages from the text in e-book format. Chapter posttests give you an opportunity to measure how much you've learned and let you know if you are ready for graded quizzes and exams.

KEY TERMS

Go to your CengageNOW for *Challenge* to access your online glossary for Chapter 5. Print a copy of the glossary for this chapter and test yourself with the electronic flash cards or complete the crossword puzzle to help you master these key terms:

audience adaptation (73)
common ground (76)
credibility (77)
initial audience disposition (75)
knowledge and expertise (77)

learning styles (79)
personableness (78)
personal pronouns (76)
personalize (82)
proximity (74)

relevance (73)
rhetorical questions (76)
timeliness (73)
trustworthiness (78)

WEB RESOURCE

Go to your CengageNOW for *Challenge* to access the Web Resources for this chapter.

5.1 Demonstrating Timeliness (74)

5.2 Holistic Theory of Speaker Credibility (77)

5.3 Orienting Listeners (81)

SPEECH PLANNING ACTION STEP

Access the Action Step activities for this chapter online at your CengageNOW for *Challenge*. Select the chapter resources for Chapter 5; then click the activity number you want. You may print your completed activities, and you should save your work so you can use it as needed in later Action Step activities.

2 Recognizing Opportunities for
  Audience Adaptation (87)

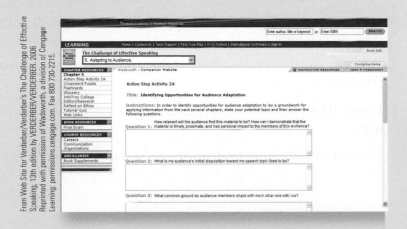

Researching Information for Your Speech

An empty bag cannot stand upright.

Benjamin Franklin, *Poor Richard's Almanac* (1740)

© Ilja C. Hendel/Visum/The Image Works

What's Ahead

HERE'S WHAT'S AHEAD IN THIS CHAPTER:

1. Where could you look for information related to your speech goal?

2. How can you go about conducting an interview with an expert on your speech topic?

3. How can you determine whether the source of your information is reliable?

4. How will you record relevant information as you research your speech topic?

5. How do you cite sources in a speech, and why is doing so important?

Jeremy was concerned. He was scheduled to give his first speech in a week, but he hadn't begun to find information. When he was in high school, he had written a term paper on media violence, and he was really taken with the subject. Just a couple of months ago, he had read a recent article in a magazine at the doctor's office, but he couldn't remember the issue of the magazine the article was in. He hadn't kept a copy of his term paper, but he was still really interested in the subject. But he wasn't sure exactly what to do to find the information he would need for a speech.

3 | Research   ACTION STEP 3

Gather Information
A. Locating and evaluating information sources
B. Preparing research cards
C. Citing sources

Jeremy's experience is not unlike that of many of us. We have strong opinions that we've formed over time as we have read and interacted with others, but we don't have the sources that support our knowledge or viewpoints at our fingertips. So, when we decide to present these ideas in a public forum, we need to do some research.

You are likely to be assigned three or more major speeches during this term, and you are likely to find yourself in need of information to prepare those speeches. In this chapter, we explain the many ways you can use to locate information sources, identify and select relevant information, and prepare to cite key sources in your speech.

Locate and Evaluate Information Sources

How can you quickly find the best information related to your specific speech goal? It depends. Speakers usually start by assessing their own knowledge, experience, and personal observations. Then they move to **secondary research,** which is the process of locating information about your topic that has been discovered by other people. This research includes doing electronic searches for relevant books, articles, general references, and websites. If the information you find from secondary sources is insufficient, you may turn to conducting **primary research,** or conducting your own study to acquire the information you need.

secondary research the process of locating information that has been discovered by other people

primary research the process of conducting your own study to acquire the information you need

Personal Knowledge, Experience, and Observation

If you have chosen to speak on a topic you know something about, you are likely to have material that you can use as examples and personal experiences in your speech. For instance, musicians have special knowledge about music and instruments, entrepreneurs about starting up their own businesses, and marine biologists about marine reserves. So Erin, a skilled rock climber, can draw on material from her own knowledge and experience for her speech on "Rappelling Down a Mountain."

For many topics, the knowledge you've gained from experience can be supplemented with careful observation. If, for instance, you are planning to talk about how a small claims court works or how churches help the homeless find shelter and job training, you can learn more by attending small claims sessions or visiting a church's outreach center. By focusing on specific behaviors and taking notes on your observations, you will have a record of specifics that you can use in your speech.

Careful observation is an often overlooked research strategy. In addition to facts, observation can provide the kinds of specific details that make your topic come alive for an audience.

© Nano Calvo/V&W/The Image Works

credentials your experiences or education that qualifies you to speak with authority on a specific subject

Sharing your personal knowledge, experience, and observations can also bolster your credibility if you share your **credentials**—your experiences or education that qualifies you to speak with authority on a specific subject. For Erin, establishing her credentials means briefly mentioning her training and expertise as a rock climber before she launches into her observations about unqualified climbers.

Secondary Research

The process of locating information about your topic that has been discovered by other people is called secondary research. Libraries house various sources of secondary research, and many of these sources are available on electronic databases. Keep in mind that electronic library systems and procedures change frequently to incorporate advances in technology. When you visit a library for the first time, you can avoid losing time and frustrating yourself by asking a librarian for help or taking advantage of a short seminar on research offered at the library. Librarians are free resources, experts who can demystify thorny research problems as well as direct you to short courses or workshops designed to make your research endeavors productive and efficient. When at the library, most speakers find information in books, articles, and other specialized sources.

BOOKS

If your topic has been around for more than six months, there are likely to be books written about it. Although books are excellent sources of in-depth material about a topic, most of the information in a book is likely to be at least two years old when it is published. So books are not a good resource if your topic is very recent or if you're looking for the latest information on a topic. Most libraries have their book holdings listed in an online catalog by title, author, and subject. Although you may occasionally know the title or author of a book you want, more often you will be looking for books using a subject label, such as "violence in the mass media."

In addition to searching by author, title, and subject, most online catalogs now allow you to search by entering "keywords." Even with this user-friendly system, you may find it useful to brainstorm for keywords to search. For instance, Jeremy wanted to find information on the subject "violence in the mass media." With a few minutes of brainstorming, he came up with several keyword designations that brought a variety of "hits"—that is, books available. Notice the different number of hits he found using different keywords:

media violence	95
violence in mass media	57
violence television	88

Under "violence in mass media," one book listed was *The 11 Myths of Media Violence.* Exhibit 6.1 shows the information about the book that was in the database. Not all of the information will be useful to you. But you certainly will want to note the book's *location* (many libraries have multiple branch locations and not all books are available at all locations), *call number* (the book's physical "address" in the library), and *status* (whether it is immediately available for use or on loan to someone else, archived, or otherwise unavailable).

Another bit of useful information, found under "Note," is whether the book includes bibliographical references and an index. In addition to the information it contains, a book on your topic often leads you to additional sources. For instance, Exhibit 6.1 shows that the *11 Myths* book has twenty pages of bibliographical references, so Jeremy might find several excellent additional sources just from this book's bibliography.

In addition to searching the online database for books, you can use the call number for one book to physically locate other books on the same subject. For example, having found the *11 Myths* book through an electronic search, when Jeremy goes to the library to retrieve it, he will find that other books on that topic have very similar call numbers (in this case, P96 V5 P678 2003) and are shelved together. He can then quickly thumb through them to check their usefulness.

ARTICLES

Articles are published in **periodicals**—magazines and journals that appear at fixed periods. The information in periodical articles is often more current than that published in books because many periodicals are published weekly,

periodicals magazines and journals that appear at fixed periods

EXHIBIT 6.1 Library card (online catalog)

Author:	Potter, W. James	
Title:	The 11 myths of media violence	
Pub Info:	Thousand Oaks, CA: Sage Publications, c2003	
Location	**Call No.**	**Status**
Langsam stacks	P96 V5 P678 2003	Available
Description:	xviii, 259p.; 24 cm	
Note:	Includes bibliographical references (pp. 229–249) and index	
Subject:	Violence in mass media	
OCLC#:	51095835	
ISBN:	0761927344 (hard)	
LCCN:	2002008802	

biweekly, or monthly. So a periodical article is likely to be a better source if a topic is one that's "in the news." However, articles do not provide as much in-depth information and may not provide basic information, assuming that the reader is already somewhat familiar with the topic. Articles are likely to be the best source of information for highly specialized topics where there may not be sufficient information for books.

Most libraries subscribe to electronic databases that index periodical articles. Check with your librarian to learn what electronic indexes your college or university subscribes to. Four frequently available databases that index many popular magazines, such as *Time* and *Newsweek*, as well as some of the popular academic journals, such as *Communication Quarterly* and *Journal of Psychology*, are:

- **InfoTrac College Edition** is the electronic index that you can access from the Internet this semester through the electronic resources that accompany this textbook. InfoTrac College Edition indexes about 18 million articles in popular magazines and academic journals. See the inside cover of this book for how to access and use InfoTrac College Edition.

- **InfoTrac University Library** is an expanded version of InfoTrac College Edition. Available online through most college and university libraries, it provides access to several hundred additional popular magazines and academic journals.

- **Periodical Abstract,** another electronic database available online in most college and university libraries, provides access to articles in more than 1,000 popular magazines and academic journals.

- **EBSCO**, also available online at many college and university libraries, is another database that provides access to many popular magazines and academic journals.

Access to these online catalogs is likely to vary from place to place, so it is wise to check with a librarian to see which of these and other catalogs are part of your university library.

When using most online indexes, you begin by entering the subject heading that you are researching. The search of an index's database will result in a list of articles related to your subject. From these, you can then choose to read or print the individual articles or use the list of citations to locate hard copies of the original articles in your library's periodical section.

For instance, Rhonda has identified prescription drug abuse as a topic on her brainstorming list. Rhonda's tentative speech goal is, "I want my audience to understand the dangers of prescription drug abuse." Working from her computer at home, Rhonda opens EBSCO on her university library home page and types in "prescription drug abuse." She finds 108 references, including the following:

Prescription drug abuse rises globally. Kuehn, Bridget M. *Journal of the American Medical Association.* 2007, v.297 i.12, p. 1306.

The doctor is not a criminal. Jacob Sullum. *National Review,* May 23, 2005, v.57 i.9, pp. 27–30.

Controlled prescription drug abuse at epidemic level. *Journal of Pain and Palliative Care Pharmacotherapy,* 2006, v.20 i.2, pp. 61–64.

Rhonda finds that the complete text of each of these articles can be printed on her own printer. At the University of Cincinnati college library, Rhonda could open the extended InfoTrac University Library index or Periodical Abstracts and find article lists that include some of these same articles as well as others.

At times, a search may identify articles that cannot be downloaded to your own printer. You will need to go to your library's journal and magazine index to see whether the library has hard copies of the journal articles you want. Then you can manually access those journals.

NEWSPAPERS

Newspaper articles are excellent sources of facts about and interpretations of both contemporary and historical issues. Keep in mind, however, that authors of newspaper articles are typically journalists who draw on interviews or the work of others and are probably not experts themselves. Also keep in mind that at times journalists will insert their own opinions in an article or present only one side of a controversial issue. So, although information from newspapers can be useful in your speech, it is best not to rely exclusively on them for your information.

In the past, it was sometimes difficult to access past issues of newspapers. But today, most newspapers are available online, which makes them much more accessible to anyone anywhere. Most major newspapers are also now specifically indexed. The *New York Times*, the *Wall Street Journal*, and *USA Today*, for example, each index their back issues and content. Three electronic newspaper indexes that are most useful if they are available to you are (1) the *National Newspaper Index*, which indexes five major newspapers: the *New York Times*, *Wall Street Journal*, *Christian Science Monitor*, *Washington Post*, and *Los Angeles Times*; (2) *Newsbank*, which provides not only the indexes but also the text of articles from more than 450 U.S. and Canadian newspapers; and (3) InfoTrac College Edition's *National Newspaper Index*.

ENCYCLOPEDIAS

An encyclopedia can be a good starting point for your research. Encyclopedias give an excellent overview of many subjects and can acquaint you with the basic terminology and ideas associated with a topic. But because encyclopedias are designed to provide only overviews of a topic, you certainly should never limit your research to encyclopedias. General encyclopedias contain short articles about a wide variety of subjects. In addition, there are many specialized encyclopedias to choose from in areas such as art, history, religion, philosophy, and science. For instance, a college library is likely to have the *African American Encyclopedia*, *Latino Encyclopedia*, *Asian American Encyclopedia*, *Encyclopaedia Britannica*, *Encyclopedia Americana*, *World Book Encyclopedia*, *Encyclopedia of Computer Science*, *Encyclopedia of Women*, *Encyclopedia of Women in American Politics*, and many more.

Many libraries have encyclopedias available online, and some encyclopedias can be accessed from the Internet. However, not all online encyclopedias are the best sources of accurate information. Traditional encyclopedias use a careful process to select the authors of each entry—these authors are respected experts. But Wikipedia, an online encyclopedia that has become very popular, does not review its authors or its entries as carefully. As a result, there is often no way to confirm the credibility of the people posting information in Wikipedia entries. So, although Wikipedia may be an easy starting point for your research, especially for topics from popular culture, check what you learn from this source against other more reliable sources of information. For a list of encyclopedias that are available on the web, use your CengageNOW for *Challenge* to access **Web Resource 6.1: Online Encyclopedias**.

STATISTICAL SOURCES

Statistical sources present numerical information on a wide variety of subjects. When you need facts about demography, continents, heads of state, weather, or similar subjects, access one of the many single-volume sources that report such data. Two of the most popular sources in this category are *The Statistical Abstract of the United States* (available online), which provides numerical

CENGAGENOW™

information on various aspects of American life, and *The World Almanac and Book of Facts.* You will find almanacs and other statistical resources at your library in the reference section. For links to web-based statistical sources, use your CengageNOW for *Challenge* to access **Web Resource 6.2: Online Statistics**. And to read an interesting essay on the improper uses of statistics, access **Web Resource 6.3: Bad Uses of Statistics and Polling**.

BIOGRAPHICAL REFERENCES

When you need accounts of a person's life, from thumbnail sketches to reasonably complete essays, you can turn to one of the many available biographical references. Although you can access some biographical information online, you will find information of more depth and breadth by reading full-length biographies and by consulting biographical references such as *Who's Who in America* and *International Who's Who.* Your library is also likely to carry *Contemporary Black Biography, Dictionary of Hispanic Biography, Native American Women, Who's Who of American Women, Who's Who Among Asian Americans,* and many more. For links to web-based collections of biographical references, use your CengageNOW for *Challenge* to access **Web Resource 6.4: Online Biographical References**.

BOOKS OF QUOTATIONS

A good quotation can be especially provocative as well as informative, and there are times you want to use a quotation from a respected person. *Bartlett's Familiar Quotations* is a popular source of quotes from historical as well as contemporary figures. But many other collections of quotations are also available. Some you may find at your library include *The International Thesaurus of Quotations; Harper Book of American Quotations; My Soul Looks Back, 'Less I Forget: A Collection of Quotations by People of Color; The New Quotable Woman;* and *The Oxford Dictionary of Quotations.* For links to web-based collections of quotations, use your CengageNOW for *Challenge* to access **Web Resource 6.5: Online Quotations**.

U.S. GOVERNMENT PUBLICATIONS

primary source a document that details a firsthand account

Some government publications are especially useful for locating **primary sources,** or documents that detail firsthand accounts. The *Federal Register* publishes daily regulations and legal notices issued by the U.S. executive branch and all federal agencies. It is divided into sections, such as rules and regulations and Sunshine Act meetings. Of special interest are announcements of hearings and investigations, committee meetings, and agency decisions and rulings. The *Monthly Catalog of United States Government Publications* covers publications of all branches of the federal government. It has semiannual and annual cumulative indexes by title, author/agency, and subject. For links to several frequently used U.S. federal government documents, use your Cengage-NOW for *Challenge* to access **Web Resource 6.6: Online Government Publications**. Online documents for other countries and for states and cities can be found by using a search engine.

INTERNET RESOURCES

Internet an international electronic collection of thousands of smaller networks

In addition to printed resources (most of which you can access online), you may find resources for your speech that are only available on the **Internet,** an international electronic collection of thousands of smaller networks. The World Wide Web (WWW) is one network that houses information on a broad range of topics. You can access the Internet through your college or university library, campus computer labs, or your own personal computer. Public libraries also usually provide Internet access. On the Internet, you can access electronic databases, bulletin boards, and scholarly and professional electronic discussion groups, as well as websites and web pages authored by individuals and groups.

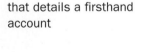

To find information on your topic, you will use a search engine, a program that locates information housed on the web. Google, InfoSeek, Excite, HotBot, Yahoo!, and AltaVista are some of the more popular search engines. You use search engines by typing in keywords for your topic. If you want to be more effective, find out which computer symbols help limit and focus your search. For example, if Jeremy uses AltaVista and puts quotation marks around the words "media violence," he will only get hits in which these two words appear together. If he does not use quotation marks, he will get hits in which either word appears, which will produce lots of "hits" that aren't relevant to his speech.

Just as there are different types of print resources, so too there are several types of electronic resources. A **newsgroup,** or **bulletin board,** is "an electronic gathering place for people with similar interests."[1] To communicate in a newsgroup, a user posts a message (called an article) about some topic that is appropriate for the site. Other users read these articles and, when so disposed, respond. The result is a kind of ongoing discussion in which users (ten, fifty, or maybe even hundreds) may participate. Today, many college classes require students to share their ideas and opinions about course-related topics in class-specific newsgroups. Bulletin boards and newsgroups maintained by scholarly organizations can be a source of new information that has yet to be published in other sources.

Hosted websites, personal web pages, and blogs can also be good sources of information for speeches. Most commercial and nonprofit organizations host websites that provide information on the organization and on issues of interest to the organization and its members. For example, the Sierra Club website at http://sierraclub.org/ provides updates on a variety of environmental issues. Hosted websites can be comprised of numerous web pages and may also provide links to other related sites. When considering information on a hosted website, be sure to take into account the viewpoint or bias of the host. For example, if you were preparing a speech on global warming, what bias might be expected on the Sierra Club website versus a website maintained by the World Coal Institute? Personal web pages and blogs are created and maintained by individuals who can post any information they choose. On the personal sites or blogs of some noted scholars, you can find links to their professional papers. On other personal sites and blogs, you can find posts that support causes or points of view advocated by the site creator. As with hosted websites, consider the credentials and bias of the site or of the creator of the blog.

For more information on evaluating websites as sources of information, use your CengageNOW for *Challenge* to access **Web Resource 6.7: Evaluating Internet Sources.**

Primary Research

When there is little secondary research available on your topic or on a main idea you want to develop in your speech, consider conducting your own study. But keep in mind that primary research is much more labor intensive and time consuming than secondary research—and, in the professional world, much more costly. If after making an exhaustive search of secondary sources you cannot locate the information you need, try getting it through a survey or an interview, by examining artifacts or original documents, or by experimenting.

SURVEYS

A **survey** is a canvassing of people to get information about their ideas and opinions, which are then analyzed for trends. Surveys are especially effective for discovering the attitudes, values, and beliefs generally held by a group of people. Surveys may be conducted in person, over the phone or Internet, or in writing. At times, you will be able to find secondary sources of surveys that have been conducted by other people or organizations and that provide information

newsgroup (bulletin board) an electronic gathering place for people with similar interests

survey a canvassing of people to get information about their ideas and opinions, which are then analyzed for trends

secondary source a document written about a topic, citing both primary sources and other secondary sources

interviewing the skillful asking and answering of questions

---

relevant to your topic. A **secondary source** is a document written about a topic, citing both primary sources and other secondary sources. At other times, you may want to conduct your own survey. If you decide to conduct your own survey, use your CengageNOW for *Challenge* to access **Web Resource 6.8: Conducting Surveys**, which will provide you with important tips for collecting good information.

INTERVIEWS

Like media reporters, you may get some of your best information for your speech from **interviewing**—the skillful asking and answering of questions. How relevant interviewing is to getting information for your speech will of course depend on your topic. To be effective, you'll want to select the best person to interview and have a list of good questions to ask.

1. Selecting the best person. Somewhere on campus or in the larger community are people who have expertise in the topic area of your speech and who can provide you with information. Usually a few telephone calls will lead you to the person who would be best to talk with about your topic. For instance, for a speech on "The Effects of Media Violence on Viewers," Jeremy could interview a professor of mass communication or sociology who studies violence in the media. When you have decided whom you should interview, make an appointment; you cannot walk into an office and expect the prospective interviewee to drop everything just to talk to you. Be forthright in your reasons for scheduling the interview. Whether your interview is for a class speech or for a different audience, say so.

If you are trying to get an interview with someone on campus, you might proceed as follows:

Hello, my name is _____. I am taking a college course in fundamentals of speech, and I'm preparing a speech on the effects of mass media violence on viewers. I understand that you are an expert on this subject. If possible, I'd like to make an appointment to talk with you. Would you be available to talk with me for fifteen or twenty minutes during the next few days?

At the end of the conversation, thank the person, repeat the date and time of the interview, and confirm the office location. If you make the appointment more than a few days ahead, it is usually wise to call the day before the interview to confirm the appointment.

In general, you should not waste your expert's time by asking questions whose answers can be easily obtained through print or electronic sources. Try to formulate a list that stays on the subject so that you can get the information you need without taking up too much time.

How many questions you plan to ask depends on how much time you have for the interview. Keep in mind that you never know how a person will respond. Some people are so talkative and informative that in response to your first question they answer every question you were planning to ask in great detail; other people will answer each question with just a few words.

Early in the interview, plan to ask some questions that can be answered easily and that will show your respect for the person you are interviewing. In an interview with a professor, you might start with background questions such as, "How did you get interested in doing research on the effects of media violence?" The goal is to get the interviewee to feel at ease and talk freely.

The body of the interview includes the major questions you have prepared. You may not ask all the questions you planned to, but you don't want to end the interview until you have the important information you intended to get. The questions are designed to get the information necessary to achieve your goal.

Before interviewing the expert, make sure that you have done other research on the topic. Interviewees are more likely to talk with you if you appear informed; moreover, familiarity with what has been written on the subject will enable you to ask better questions.

2. Writing good questions. The heart of an effective interviewing plan is a list of good questions. They are likely to be a mix of open and closed questions, both primary and follow-up, phrased to be neutral rather than leading.

Primary questions are those main-point questions that the interviewer plans ahead of time. **Follow-up questions** are designed to pursue the answers given to primary questions. Although some follow-ups are planned ahead by anticipating possible answers, more often than not they are composed as the interview goes along. Some ("And then?" "Is there more?") encourage further comments; others ("What does 'frequently' mean?" "What were you thinking at the time?") probe; still others ("How did it feel to win the prize?" "Were you worried when you didn't find her?") plumb the feelings of the interviewee. All are designed to motivate a person to enlarge on an answer.

Open questions are broad-based questions that ask the interviewee to provide perspective, ideas, information, or opinions as the question is answered ("What kinds of people are likely to be most affected by television violence?" "What are some kinds of behaviors that viewers exhibit as a result of viewing violence?" "What would you recommend be done about violence on TV?" "What research studies would you recommend?"). Open questions enable the interviewer to find out about the person's perspectives, values, and goals, but they do take time to answer.[2]

Closed questions are narrowly focused and require only very brief answers. Some require a simple yes or no ("Are young children affected by TV violence more than older children?"); others need only a short response ("What behavior seems to be most affected by television violence?"). By asking closed questions, interviewers can control the interview and obtain large amounts of information in a short time. On the other hand, the closed question seldom enables the interviewer to know why a person gave a certain response, nor is the closed question likely to yield much voluntary information.[3]

For the most part, questions should be phrased neutrally. **Neutral questions** are phrased in ways that do not direct a person's answers—for example, "Do you believe television violence has a major effect on children's behavior?" By contrast, **leading questions** are phrased in a way that suggests the interviewer has a preferred answer—for example, "Television violence has a major effect on children's behavior, doesn't it?"

Exhibit 6.2 lists some of the questions you might ask to get information on the effects of television violence on viewers.

primary questions questions the interviewer plans ahead of time

follow-up questions questions designed to pursue the answers given to primary questions

open questions broad-based questions that ask the interviewee to provide perspective, ideas, information, or opinions

closed questions narrow-focus questions that require only very brief answers

neutral questions questions phrased in ways that do not direct a person's answers

leading questions questions phrased in a way that suggests the interviewer has a preferred answer

---

EXHIBIT 6.2 Sample interview questions

Background Information
How did you get interested in doing research on the effects of media violence?

Findings
Does your research show negative effects of television violence on viewers?
Are heavy viewers more likely to show negative effects than light viewers?
Have you found evidence that shows major effects on aggressiveness? desensitization?
Have you found evidence that shows effects on civility? How is violence on TV changing?
How are these changes likely to impact heavy viewers?

Action
Are effects great enough to warrant limiting viewing of violent programming for children?
Do you have any recommendations that you would offer the viewing public?

3. **Conducting the interview.** The following guidelines provide a framework for ensuring an effective interview.

◆ **Arrive five to ten minutes early and dress professionally.** Doing so demonstrates respect for the person taking the time to talk with you.

◆ **Introduce yourself and repeat the purpose of the interview.** This quick reminder is a polite way to immediately focus the conversation.

◆ **Be courteous during the interview.** Start by thanking the person for taking the time to talk with you. Throughout the interview, respect what the person says regardless of what you may think of the answers.

◆ **Listen carefully.** In addition to listening to what is said, also pay attention to how it is said. A person's tone of voice, facial expression, and gestures often communicate as much or more than what the person says. If you don't understand, take time to ask questions. If you're not sure you understand, tell the person what you think he or she meant, such as, "If I understand you correctly, you're saying that older and younger children react differently to television violence."

◆ **Keep the interview moving.** Although some people will get so involved that they will not be concerned with the amount of time spent, most people will have other important business to attend to.

◆ **Make sure that your nonverbal reactions—facial expressions and gestures—are in keeping with the tone you want to communicate.** Maintain good eye contact with the person. Nod to show understanding. And smile occasionally to maintain the friendliness of the interview.

◆ **End on time.** If you suggested the amount of time intended for the interview, respect the interviewee by finishing within the allotted time.

◆ **Confirm your interviewee's credentials.** Revealing the credentials of the expert you interview in your speech is just as important as revealing your own credentials when offering personal experience. Before you leave the interview, be sure to confirm your interviewee's professional title, the company or organization he or she works with, and the spelling of his or her name (in case you want to include it on a visual aid). You'll need these details when explaining why you chose to interview this person.

◆ **Thank the interviewee for his or her time.** Acknowledge that your interviewee took time out of a busy schedule to speak with you.

4. **Processing the interview.** Because your interview notes were probably taken in an outline or shorthand form and may be difficult to translate later, sit down with your notes as soon as possible after the interview and make individual research cards of the information you want to use in the speech. (Research cards will be discussed in detail later in this chapter.) If at any point you are not sure whether you have accurately transcribed what the person said, take a minute to telephone or e-mail the person to double-check. You do not want to risk your credibility by misquoting an expert.

EXAMINING ARTIFACTS OR ORIGINAL DOCUMENTS

Sometimes the information you need may not have been published. Rather, it may exist in an original unpublished source, such as an ancient manuscript, a diary, personal correspondence, or company files. Or you may need to view an object to get the information you need, such as a geographic feature, a building, a monument, or an artifact in a museum.

EXPERIMENTING

You can design a study to test a hypothesis you have. Then you can report the results of your experiment in your speech. Keep in mind that experiment-

Interviews are a good source of personal narratives that can be used to support key ideas.

© Jeff Greenberg/Alamy

ing takes time, and you must understand the principles of the scientific process of experimentation to be able to trust your results.

Skimming to Determine Source Value

Because you are likely to uncover far more information than you can use, you will want to skim sources to determine whether or not to read them in full. **Skimming** is a method of rapidly going through a work to determine what is covered and how.

skimming a method of rapidly going through a work to determine what is covered and how

If you are evaluating an article, spend a minute or two finding out whether it really presents information on the exact area of the topic you are exploring and whether it contains any documented statistics, examples, or quotable opinions. (We will examine the kind of information to look for in the next section.) If you are evaluating a book, read the table of contents carefully, look at the index, and skim pertinent chapters, asking the same questions as you would for a magazine article. Skimming helps you decide which sources should be read in full, which should be read in part, and which should be abandoned. Minutes spent in such evaluation will save hours of reading.

If you are using an electronic periodical index, you may be able to access short abstracts for each article identified by your search. Reading these abstracts can help you decide which sources you want to read in their entirety. Once you have the sources in hand, however, you still need to follow a skimming procedure.

Criteria for Judging Sources

When you rely on printed sources for the information in your speech, you can have some confidence that the information you are using is reliable if it has been published by a reputable publishing house and chosen by professional librarians to be part of the collection. You should be more cautious in using information that you find on the Internet because it contains information from a wide variety of sources and no one oversees the accuracy of the information or honesty of the people who produce it.

For instance, as the authors of *Researching Online* note, "While the universality of the Internet can be good in that it allows previously marginalized voices to be heard, it also adds a new layer of difficulty for researchers."[4] What does this mean? Editors of academic articles and books "have always made it a relative certainty that any source in a college library meets a basic standard of reliability and relevance." They go on to say, "Since the Internet lacks those gatekeepers, you're just as likely to encounter uninformed drivel there as you are to find a unique resource that's unavailable in any other form."[5]

With this warning in mind, it's important for you to critically evaluate the information and authorship of the material you find. In evaluating any source, you will want to use four criteria that have been suggested by a variety of research librarians: authority, relevance, objectivity, and currency.

AUTHORITY

The first test of a resource is the expertise of its author or the reputation of the publishing or sponsoring organization. For example, Dan's adviser is an authority because she is an expert in bioluminescence research. Books and articles published by reputable companies are also credible, but books, articles, and pamphlets published privately might not be credible unless you can verify the credentials of their authors. Websites that don't acknowledge the source of the information presented should be viewed skeptically. On the Internet, the first filter of quality is the type of URL. Those ending in ".gov" (governmental), ".edu" (educational), and ".org" are noncommercial sites with institutional publishers. The URL ".com" indicates that the sponsor is a for-profit organization. The second test of information is the qualifications of the source or the author. When an author is listed, you can check the author's credentials through biographical references or by seeing if the author has a home page listing professional qualifications. Use the electronic periodical indexes to see whether the author has other related articles that show expertise, or check the Library of Congress to see whether the author has published books in the field.[6]

At some sites, you will find information that is anonymous or credited to someone whose background is not clear. In these cases, your ability to trust the information depends on evaluating the qualifications of the sponsoring organization. If you do not know whether you can trust the source, do not use the information.

RELEVANCE

A second test of the information is how relevant it is to your speech topic. During your research, you will likely come across a great deal of interesting information. Whether that information is appropriate for your speech is another matter. Relevant information is directly related to your topic and supports your main points, making your speech easier to follow and understand. Irrelevant information will only confuse listeners, leading them to believe you're addressing points other than those you previewed in your introduction. So you should avoid using irrelevant information, no matter how interesting it is.

OBJECTIVITY

A third test of the information is how impartially it is presented. All authors have a viewpoint, but you will want to be wary of information that is overly slanted. Web documents that have been created under the sponsorship of some business, government, or public interest groups should be carefully scrutinized for obvious biases or good "public relations" fronts. For example, commercial websites often include corporate histories and biographical essays on founders that present the company and founders in a favorable light. So you will need other sources to give you a more accurate picture of both the company's and founders' strengths and weaknesses. Similarly, as mentioned earlier, although the Sierra Club is a well-respected environmental organization, the articles on its website are unlikely to present a balanced discussion of the pros and cons of controversial environmental issues.

To evaluate the potential biases in articles and books, read the Preface, or identify the thesis statement. These often reveal the authors' point of view.

When evaluating a website with which you are unfamiliar, look for the purpose of the website. Most home pages contain a purpose or mission statement that can help you understand why the site was created. Armed with this information, you are in a better position to recognize the biases that the information may contain. Remember, at some level, all web pages can be seen as "infomercials," so always be concerned with who created this information and why.[7]

CURRENCY

Finally, newer information is generally more accurate than older. So, when evaluating your sources, be sure to consult the latest information you can find. One of the reasons for using web-based sources is that they can provide more up-to-date information than printed sources.[8] But just because a source is found online does not mean that the information is timely. To determine how up to date the information is, you will need to find out when the information was placed on the web and how often it is revised. Many authors post this information at the end of the page. If there are no dates indicated and no indications for checking the accuracy, the information should not be used.

Even some recent publications use old information. With statistics, especially, you want to know not only when the statistics were published but also when the data were collected. If, for instance, you are talking about the number of women in Congress, you don't want to be using data that are more than two years old. Because congressional elections occur every two years, even data from a recent publication could be wrong.

Web Resource 6.9: Analyzing Information Sources provides information on additional criteria you can use to evaluate your sources. Use your Cengage-NOW to access this resource.

| SPEECH PLANNING | ACTION STEP 3 |

3 | Research

ACTIVITY 3A Locating and Evaluating Information Sources

The goal of this activity is to help you compile a list of potential sources for your speech.

1. Identify gaps in your current knowledge that you would like to fill.
2. Identify a person, an event, or a process that you could observe to broaden your personal knowledge base.
3. Brainstorm a list of keywords that are related to your speech goal.
4. Working with paper or electronic versions of your library's card catalog, periodical indexes (including InfoTrac College Edition), and general references discussed in this chapter, find and list specific resources that appear to provide information for your speech.
5. Using a search engine, identify Internet-sponsored and personal websites that may be sources of information for your speech.
6. Identify a person you could interview for additional information for this speech.
7. Skim the resources you have identified to decide which are likely to be most useful.
8. Evaluate each resource to determine how much faith you can place in the information.

You can complete this activity online, print it, and if requested, e-mail it to your instructor. Use your CengageNOW for *Challenge* to access Action Step Activity 3A.

ACTIVITY 3A Locating and Evaluating Information Sources

Speech goal: *I would like the audience to understand how bioluminescence works.*

1. Identify gaps in your current knowledge that you would like to fill.

   Since I'm a biogenetics engineering major and have done an eight-week internship in the field, I am familiar with the kinds of works I'll need to fill any gaps in knowledge.

2. Identify a person, an event, or a process that you could observe to broaden your personal knowledge base.

   An event I could observe is my adviser explaining to her freshman class how bioluminescence works.

3. Brainstorm a list of keywords that are related to your speech goal.

   bioluminescence, chemistry, physiology, kinetics, luminous fish

4. Working with paper or electronic versions of your library's card catalog, periodical indexes (including InfoTrac College Edition), and general references discussed in this chapter, find and list specific resources that appear to provide information for your speech.

   Journal of Fish Biology, Science, Marine Biology, Biochemistry, Journal of Bioluminescence and Chemiluminescence

5. Using a search engine, identify Internet-sponsored and personal websites that may be sources of information for your speech.

   lifesci.ucsb.edu/, explorations.ucsd.edu/biolum/, www.interscience.wiley.com/jpages/0884-3996/

6. Identify a person you could interview for additional information for this speech.

   I could interview my adviser, Dr. Susan Stromme.

7. Skim the resources you have identified to decide which are likely to be most useful.

8. Evaluate each resource to determine how much faith you can place in the information.

Identify and Select Relevant Information

The information you find in your sources that you will want to use in your speech may include factual statements, expert opinions, and elaborations.

Factual Statements

factual statements information that can be verified

Factual statements are those that can be verified. "A recent study confirmed that preschoolers watch an average of 28 hours of television a week," "The Gateway Solo laptop comes with a CD-ROM drive," and "Johannes Gutenberg invented printing from movable type in the 1400s" are all statements of fact that can be verified. One way to verify whether the information is factual is to check it against material from another source on the same subject. Never use any information that is not carefully documented unless you have corroborating sources.

STATISTICS

Statistics are numerical facts. Statistical statements, such as, "Only five of every ten local citizens voted in the last election" or "The cost of living rose 0.6 percent in January 2003," enable you to pack a great deal of information into a small package. Statistics can provide impressive support for a point, but when they are poorly used in the speech, they may be boring and, in some instances, downright deceiving. Here are some guidelines for using statistics effectively.

statistics numerical facts

1. Use only statistics whose reliability you can verify. Taking statistics from only the most reliable sources and double-checking any startling statistics with another source will guard against the use of faulty statistics.

2. Use only recent statistics so that your audience will not be misled. For example, if you find the statistic that only nine of one hundred members of the Senate, or 9 percent, are women (true in 1999), you would be misleading your audience if you used that statistic in a speech. If you want to make a point about the number of women in the Senate, find the most recent statistics. Check for both the year and the range of years to which the statistics apply.

3. Use statistics comparatively. By themselves, statistics are hard to interpret. When we present comparative statistics, they are easier to understand.

In a speech on chemical waste, Donald Baeder points out that chemicals are measured in parts per billion or even parts per trillion. Notice how he goes on to use comparisons to put the meaning of the statistics in perspective:

> One part per billion is the equivalent of one drop—one drop!—of vermouth in two 36,000 gallon tanks of gin and that would be a very dry martini even by San Francisco standards! One part per trillion is the equivalent of one drop in two thousand tank cars.[9]

4. Limit how many statistics you offer. Although statistics may be an excellent way to present a great deal of material quickly, be careful not to overuse them. A few pertinent numbers are far more effective than a battery of statistics. When you believe you must use many statistics, try preparing a visual aid, perhaps a chart, to help your audience visualize them.

5. Remember that statistics are biased. Mark Twain once said there are three kinds of lies: "lies, damned lies, and statistics."[10] Not all statistics are lies, of course, but consider the source of statistics you'd like to use, what that source

Use statistics from only the most reliable sources, and double-check any startling statistics with another source.

may have been trying to prove with these data, and how that situation might have influenced the way the data were collected and interpreted. For example, in his speech about media violence, Jeremy might think twice about the accuracy of statistics reported by a Hollywood production company claiming that there are 20 percent fewer violent scenes on television today than there were forty years ago. No statistic can represent the truth perfectly, so evaluate them thoughtfully before using them.[11]

EXAMPLES

examples specific instances that illustrate or explain a general factual statement

Examples are specific instances that illustrate or explain a general factual statement. One or two short examples such as the following are often enough to help make a generalization meaningful.

> One way a company increases its power is to acquire another company. In December 2006, AT&T bought Bell South Corporation, creating a premier global communication company.

> Professional billiard players practice many long hours every day. Jennifer Lee practices as many as ten hours a day when she is not in a tournament.

Examples are useful because they provide concrete details that make a general statement more meaningful to the audience.

Although most of the examples you find will be real, you may find hypothetical examples you can use. **Hypothetical examples** are specific instances based on reflections about future events. They develop the idea "What if . . . ?" In the following excerpt, John A. Ahladas presents some hypothetical examples of what it will be like in the year 2039 if global warming continues.

hypothetical examples specific instances based on reflections about future events

> In New York, workers are building levees to hold back the rising tidal waters of the Hudson River, now lined with palm trees. In Louisiana, 100,000 acres of wetland are steadily being claimed by the sea. In Kansas, farmers learn to live with drought as a way of life and struggle to eke out an existence in the increasingly dry and dusty heartland. . . . And reports arrive from Siberia of bumper crops of corn and wheat from a longer and warmer growing season.[12]

Because hypothetical examples are not themselves factual, you must be very careful to check that the facts on which they are based are accurate.

Three principles should guide your use of examples. First, the examples should be clear and specific enough to create a picture the audience can understand. Consider the following generalization and supporting example.

> **Generalization:** Electronics is one of the few areas in which products are significantly cheaper today than they were in the 1980s.

> **Supporting example:** In the mid-1980s, Motorola sold cell phones for $5,000 each; now a person can buy a Motorola cell phone for under $90.

With this single example, the listener has a vivid picture of the tremendous difference in about a twenty-year period.

Second, the examples you use should be representative. If cell phones were the *only* electronics product whose prices had dropped so much over that same period, this vivid example would be misleading and unethical. Any misuse of data is unethical, especially if the user knows better.

Third, use at least one example to support every generalization.

DEFINITIONS

definition a statement that clarifies the meaning of a word or phrase

A **definition** is a statement that clarifies the meaning of a word or phrase. Definitions are often used in speeches to clarify a topic or some aspect of it. Definitions serve to clarify in three ways.

First, definitions clarify the meaning of terminology that is specialized, technical, or otherwise likely to be unfamiliar to your audience. For example, when Dan talked about bioluminescence, he clarified the meaning of the word *bioluminescence* with the following definition: "According to *Encyclopaedia Britannica Online*, bioluminescence is the emission of visible light by living organisms like fireflies." Although dictionaries and encyclopedias contain definitions, your speech topic might be such that you have to find definitions through prominent researchers or professional practitioners. For example, in a speech about eating disorders, you might go to the website of the American Dietetic Association for your definition of the term *eating disorders*.

Second, definitions clarify words and terms that have more than one meaning and might be misconstrued. For example, since *child abuse* is a term that encompasses a broad range of behaviors, you might choose to define it in a way that acknowledges which behaviors you intend to focus on in your speech.

Third, particularly with controversial subjects, definitions clarify your stance on a subject in an effort to draw listeners to interpret it as you do. For example, in a speech about domestic violence against women, former U.S. Secretary of Health and Human Services Donna Shalala defined such violence as "terrorism in the home."[13]

Expert Opinions

Expert opinions are interpretations and judgments made by authorities in a particular subject area. "Watching twenty-eight hours of television a week is far too much for young children," "Having a DVD port on your computer is a necessity," and "The invention of printing from movable type was for all intents

expert opinions interpretations and judgments made by authorities in a particular subject area

---

SPOTLIGHT ON SPEAKERS

Marian Wright Edelman *We Can Do Better*

Evan Agostini/Getty Images

We've lost nearly 90,000 children to guns since 1979. . . . It's safer to be an on-duty police officer or law enforcement officer than a child under ten in America. We can do better.

The idea of "doing better" is what motivates Marian Wright Edelman to speak. "Doing better" pushed young Edelman to defy barriers in the segregated south of the 1940s, and this personal triumph resonates when she speaks. After graduating from Spelman College, Edelman earned a law degree from Yale University and became the first African American woman admitted to the Mississippi Bar. "Doing better" inspired her to work with Martin Luther King Jr. and in 1974 to found the Children's Defense Fund, the most successful advocacy and research organization for child heath care, education, and welfare. "Doing better" is a plea she continues to make when she speaks before parents, corporations, politicians, and presidents. Hers is a relentless voice that effectively uses relevant information born of careful research and vast personal experience to speak to diverse audiences about reality.

She is especially effective at using elaborations to dramatize her points:

This country has had enormous scientific and technological progress. We've sent a man to the moon, we've sent space ships to Mars, we've created a tiny microchip that, you know, has raised billions and trillions of dollars, we have broken the genetic code. Don't tell me we can't figure out and make the commitment to teach every child to read by the third grade, and we just need to make that happen.

Although she has received numerous awards and attained global prominence for her work, Edelman continues to raise her voice to speak, not for her own glory, but on behalf of impoverished children and families.

Quotes: Marian Wright Edelman speaking at the Town Hall Los Angeles luncheon (October 2002).

To Think About

♦ What specific technique(s) did Edelman use to elaborate on her point that we must make a commitment to teach every child to read by the third grade?

♦ To what extent do you believe the United States is committed to Edelman's goal today? Explain.

and purposes the start of mass communication" are all opinions based on the factual statements cited previously. Whether they are expert opinions or not depends on who made the statements.

How do you tell if a source is an expert? First, the expert must be a master of the specific subject. Second, experts have engaged in long-term study of their subject. Third, an expert is recognized by other people in his or her field as being a knowledgeable and trustworthy authority. For instance, a history professor may be an expert in ancient Greek city-states but know little about Aztec civilization.

When you use expert opinions in your speech, you should always cite the credentials of the expert. You should also identify comments from the expert as opinions. For instance, an informative speaker might say, "Temperatures throughout the 1990s were much higher than average. Paul Jorgenson, a space biologist, believes that these higher than average temperatures represent the first stages of the greenhouse effect, but the significance of these temperatures is still being debated."

Although opinions should not take the place of facts, expert opinions can help interpret and give weight to facts that you present.

Elaborations

Factual information and expert opinions can be elaborated on through anecdotes and narratives, comparisons and contrasts, or quotable explanations and opinions.

ANECDOTES AND NARRATIVES

anecdotes brief, often amusing stories

narratives accounts, personal experiences, tales, or lengthier stories

Anecdotes are brief, often amusing stories; **narratives** are accounts, personal experiences, tales, or lengthier stories. Because holding audience interest is important in a speech and because audience attention is likely to be captured by a story, anecdotes and narratives are worth looking for, creating, and using. In a five-minute speech, you have little time to tell a detailed story, so one or two anecdotes or a very short narrative would be preferable.

The key to using stories is to make sure that the point of the story directly states or reinforces the point you are making in your speech. In the following speech excerpt, John Howard makes a point about failure to follow guidelines.

The knight was returning to the castle after a long, hard day. His face was bruised and badly swollen. His armor was dented. The plume on his helmet was broken, and his steed was limping. He was a sad sight.

The lord of the castle ran out and asked, "What hath befallen you, Sir Timothy?"

"Oh, Sire," he said, "I have been laboring all day in your service, bloodying and pillaging your enemies to the West."

"You've been doing what?" gasped the astonished nobleman. "I haven't any enemies to the West!"

"Oh!" said Timothy. "Well, I think you do now."

There is a moral to this little story. Enthusiasm is not enough. You need to have a sense of direction.[14]

Good stories and narratives may be humorous, sentimental, suspenseful, or dramatic.

COMPARISONS AND CONTRASTS

comparison illuminating a point by showing similarities

One of the best ways to give meaning to new ideas is through comparison and contrast. **Comparisons** illuminate a point by showing similarities. Although you can easily create comparisons using information you have found, you should still keep your eyes open for creative comparisons developed by the authors of the books and articles you have found.

Comparisons may be literal or figurative. Literal comparisons show similarities of real things:

> The walk from the lighthouse back up the hill to the parking lot is equal to walking up the stairs of a thirty-story building.

Figurative comparisons express one thing in terms normally denoting another:

> I always envisioned myself as a four-door sedan. I didn't know she was looking for a sports car!

Comparisons make ideas both clearer and more vivid. Notice how Steven Joel Trachtenberg, in a speech to the Newington High School Scholars' Breakfast, uses a figurative comparison to demonstrate the importance of a willingness to take risks even in the face of danger. Although the speech was given years ago, the point is timeless:

> The eagle flying high always risks being shot at by some hare-brained human with a rifle. But eagles and young eagles like you still prefer the view from that risky height to what is available flying with the turkeys far, far below.[15]

Whereas comparisons suggest similarities, **contrasts** highlight differences. Notice how the following humorous contrast dramatizes the difference between "participation" and "commitment."

> If this morning you had bacon and eggs for breakfast, I think it illustrates the difference. The eggs represented "participation" on the part of the chicken. The bacon represented "total commitment" on the part of the pig![16]

QUOTATIONS

When you find an explanation, an opinion, or a brief anecdote that seems to be exactly what you are looking for, you may quote it directly in your speech. Because audiences want to listen to your ideas and arguments, they do not want to hear a string of long quotations. Nevertheless, a well-selected quotation may be perfect in one or two key places.

Quotations can both explain and vivify. Look for quotations that make a point in a particularly clear or vivid way. For example, in his speech "Enduring Values for a Secular Age," Hans Becherer, executive officer at Deere & Company, used this Henry Ford quote to show the importance of enthusiasm to progress:

> Enthusiasm is at the heart of all progress. With it, there is accomplishment. Without it, there are only alibis.[17]

Frequently, historical or literary quotations can reinforce a point vividly. Cynthia Opheim, chair of the Department of Political Science at Southwest Texas State University, in her speech "Making Democracy Work," used this quote from Mark Twain on the frustration of witnessing legislative decision making:

> There are two things you should never watch being made: sausage and legislation.[18]

Quotations may come from a book of quotations, from an article, or from an interview that you have conducted as part of the speech research process. Regardless of the source, however, when you use a direct quotation, you need to verbally acknowledge the person it came from. Using any quotation or close paraphrase without crediting its source is **plagiarism,** the unethical act of representing another person's work as your own.

SPEECH SNIPPET

Using Narratives to Elaborate

Holly used this narrative to elaborate on her point about the benefits of day care: "I will never forget having lunch my first day on the job at the day-care center. . . . I watched in awe as three-year-old children poured their own milk and passed the pitcher along to the next child at the table and, likewise, dished up their own macaroni and cheese, green beans, and so on. The children visited cordially with me as we ate. When everyone was finished eating, each child at the table helped to clear the dishes away. To my amazement, those three-year-olds were behaving in a more civil manner than my roommates do! I cannot help but wonder whether my friends and I could have benefited from learning the social skills these children had mastered as a result of their experiences at a day-care center."

contrast Illuminating a point by highlighting differences

plagiarism the unethical act of representing another person's work as your own

"Dan, I was wondering whether you'd listen to the speech I'm giving in class tomorrow. It will only take about five minutes."

"Sure."

Tom and Dan found an empty classroom and Tom went through his speech. "What did you think?"

"Sounded pretty good to me. I could follow the speech—I knew what you wanted to do. But I was wondering about that section where you had the statistics. You didn't give any source."

"Well, the fact is I can't remember the source."

"You remember the statistics that specifically, but you don't remember the source?"

"Well, I don't remember the statistics all that well, but I think I've got them about right."

"Well, you can check them, can't you?"

"Check them? Where? That would take me hours. And after all, I told you I think I have them about right."

"But Tom, the accuracy of the statistics seem pretty important to what you said."

"Listen, trust me on this—no one is going to say anything about it. You've already said that my goal was clear, my main points were clear, and I sounded as if I know what I'm talking about. I really think that's all Goodwin is interested in."

"Well, whatever you say, Tom. I just thought I'd ask."

"No problem. Thanks for listening. I thought I had it in pretty good shape, but I wanted someone to hear my last practice."

"Well, good luck!"

1. What do you think of Tom's assessment of his use of statistics that "no one is going to say anything about it"?
2. Does Tom have any further ethical obligation? If so, what is it?
3. How and why do you think you might use statistics in a speech for your speech class?

Drawing Information from Multiple Cultural Perspectives

A person's cultural background often influences how facts are perceived and what opinions are held. Therefore, it is important to draw your information from culturally diverse perspectives by seeking sources that have differing cultural orientations and by interviewing experts with diverse cultural backgrounds. For example, when Carrie was preparing for her speech on proficiency testing in grade schools, she purposefully searched for articles written by noted Hispanic, Asian, and African American, as well as European American, authors. In addition, she interviewed two local school superintendents—one from an urban district and one from a suburban district. Because she consciously worked to develop diverse sources of information, Carrie had greater confidence that her speech would more accurately reflect all sides of the debate on proficiency testing.

Record Information

As you find the facts, opinions, and elaborations that you want to use in your speech, you need to record the information accurately and keep a careful account of your sources so that they can be cited appropriately during your speech as you give it.

Preparing Research Cards

How should you keep track of the information you plan to use? Although it may seem easier to record all material from one source on a single sheet of paper (or to photocopy source material), sorting and arranging material is much easier when each item is recorded separately. So it is wise to record information on index cards that allow you to easily find, arrange, and rearrange each item of information as you prepare your speech.

In the research card method, each factual statement, expert opinion, or elaboration, along with the bibliographical information on its source, is recorded on a four-by-six-inch or larger index card containing three types of information. First, each card should have a heading or keywords that identify the subcategory to which the information belongs. Second, the specific fact, opinion, or elaboration statement should be recorded on the card. Any part of the information item that is quoted directly from the source should be enclosed in quotation marks. Third, the bibliographical publication data related to the source should be recorded.

The bibliographical information you will record depends on whether the source is a book, a periodical, a newspaper, an interview, or a website. For a book, include the names of authors, the title of the book, the place of publication and the publisher, the date of publication, and the page or pages from which the information is taken. For a periodical or newspaper, include the name of the author (if given), the title of the article, the name of the publication, the date, and the page number from which the information is taken. For online sources, include the URL for the website, the credentials of the site host, the heading under which you found the information, and the date that you accessed the site. Be sure to record enough source information so that you can relocate the material if you need to and cite the source appropriately during your speech. Exhibit 6.3 shows a sample research card.

As your stack of research cards grows, you can sort the material and place each item under the heading to which it is related. For instance, for a speech on bioluminescence, you might have a stack of research cards related to the biological process of bioluminescence, species that are bioluminescent, and causes of bioluminescence. The card in Exhibit 6.3 would be indexed under the heading "species that are bioluminescent."

The number of sources you will need depends in part on the type of speech you are giving and your own expertise. For a narrative/personal experience speech, you obviously will be the main, if not the only, source. For informative reports and persuasive speeches, however, speakers ordinarily draw from multiple sources. For a five-minute speech on Ebola in which you plan to talk about causes, symptoms, and treatment, you might have two or more research cards under each heading. Moreover, the research cards should come from at least three different sources. Avoid using only one source for your information because this often leads to plagiarism; furthermore, basing your speech on one or two sources suggests that you have not done sufficient research. Selecting and using information from several sources allow you to develop an original approach to your topic, ensure a broader research base, and make it more likely that you will have uncovered various opinions related to your topic.

EXHIBIT 6.3 A sample research card

Topic: Bioluminescence

Heading: Uses

Fireflies blink to communicate, and each fly has a distinctive blink. Males and females also blink during mating season.

Kathryn Lund Johnson. "Things that go 'blink' in the night." *American Gardener,* Jul./Aug. 2006, v. 85 i.4, pp. 46–47.

ACTIVITY 3B Preparing Research Cards

The goal of this activity is to review the source material that you identified in Action Step Activity 3A and to record on research cards specific items of information that you might wish to use in your speech.

1. Carefully read all print and electronic sources (including website material) that you have identified and evaluated as appropriate sources for your speech. Review your notes and tapes from all interviews and observations.

2. As you read an item (fact, opinion, example, illustration, statistic, anecdote, narrative, comparison–contrast, quotation, definition, or description) that you think might be useful in your speech, record the item on a research card or on the appropriate electronic research card form available at the *Challenge of Effective Speaking* website. (If you are using an article that appeared in a periodical source that you read online, use the periodical research card form.)

You can complete this activity online and, if requested, e-mail it to your instructor. You can also use online forms to prepare your own research cards and print them for use in preparing your speech. Use your CengageNOW for *Challenge* to access Action Step Activity 3B.

ACTIVITY 3B Preparing Research Cards

Speech goal: *I would like the audience to agree that domestic violence is a problem, realize some of its underlying causes, and be convinced of strategies to reduce domestic violence in the United States today.*

Card 1
Topic: *The problem*
Heading: *Scope*

3 million women per year are physically abused by their husbands or boyfriends. And about 31 percent of American women report being sexually or physically abused by a male partner during her lifetime. (In other words, of the twenty women in my speech class, about six will be assaulted by a male partner during her lifetime!)

Family Violence Prevention Fund Website (2007). "Domestic violence is a serious, widespread social problem in America: The facts." http://www.endabuse.org/ resources/facts. Accessed April 17, 2007.

Card 2
Topic: *The problem*
Heading: *Severity*

Domestic violence is the number-one reason for emergency room visits by women.

Gordon, J. S. (1998). Helping survivors of domestic violence: The effects of medical, mental health, and community services. *New York: Garland Publishing.*

Card 3
Topic: *Causes*
Heading: *Power and control*

Men often resort to violence to gain power over women when they feel threatened and subordinate and want to maintain a sense of control.

Johnson, Michael P., and Ferraro, Kathleen J. (2000). "Research on domestic violence in the 1990s: Making distinctions." Journal of Marriage and Family, 62(4), pp. 948–963.

Card 4
Topic: *Causes*
Heading: *Power and control*

Most abused women would leave if human capital such as housing and employment were more readily available to them.

Christy-McMullin, K., and Shobe, M. A. (2007). "The role of economic resources and human capital with woman abuse." Journal of Policy Practice, 6(1), pp. 3–26.

Citing Sources In the Speech

In your speeches, as in any communication in which you use ideas that are not your own, you need to acknowledge the sources of your ideas and statements. Specifically mentioning your sources not only helps the audience evaluate the content but also adds to your credibility. In addition, citing sources will give concrete evidence of the depth of your research. Failure to cite sources, especially when you are presenting information that is meant to substantiate a controversial point, is unethical. Furthermore, failure to cite sources orally during your speech constitutes plagiarism. Just as you would provide footnotes in a written document, you must provide oral footnotes during your speech. **Oral footnotes** are references to an original source, made at the point in the speech where information from that source is presented. The key to preparing oral footnotes is to include enough information for listeners to access the sources themselves and to offer enough credentials to enhance the credibility of the information you are citing. Exhibit 6.4 gives several examples of appropriate speech source citations.

oral footnote reference to an original source, made at the point in the speech where information from that source is presented

EXHIBIT 6.4 Appropriate speech source citations

Books
Cite the title of the book and the name of its author. You may cite the book's publication date or the author's credentials if doing so boosts credibility.

> "Thomas Friedman, noted international editor for the *New York Times*, stated in his book *The World Is Flat* . . ."

> "But to get a complete picture we have to look at the statistics. According to the 2007 *Statistical Abstract*, the level of production for the European Economic Community rose from . . ."

(continued)

EXHIBIT 6.4 **Appropriate speech source citations** (*continued*)

Journal or magazine articles

Cite the name and date of the publication in which you found the article. You may cite the article's author and title if doing so adds credibility.

> "According to an article about the Federal Reserve in last week's *Newsweek* magazine . . ."

> "In the latest Gallup poll cited in the February 10 issue of *Newsweek* . . ."

> "Timothy Plax, professor of communication at California State University, Long Beach, wrote in an article published in April 2006 in *Communication Education* that . . ."

Newspapers

Cite the name of the newspaper and date of the article. You may cite the article's author and his or her credentials if it adds credibility.

> "According to a May 2007 article in the *Wall Street Journal* . . ."

Interviews

Cite the name and credentials of the person interviewed and the date the interview took place. If you cite the interview more than once, you need only cite the interviewee's name in subsequent oral footnotes.

> "In an interview with *New Republic* magazine in December 2006, Governor Arnold Schwarzenegger stated . . ."

> "In my telephone interview on September 29 with Dr. Susan Nissen, physician for physical medicine in Kansas City, Kansas, I learned that . . ."

Internet sources

Cite the website's author, his or her credentials, and the date of the site's most recent revision. If there is no author, cite the credentials of the website's sponsoring organization. Do not cite the URL as part of your oral footnote.

> "According to a January 2007 posting on the official website of the American Dietetic Association . . ."

Television programs

Cite the name of the program and the date of the original broadcast. You may also cite the name of the reporter for news programs if it boosts credibility.

> "According to a May 1995 CNN special broadcast called 'Cry Hatred . . .'"

Public speeches

Cite the name and credentials of the speaker, as well as the occasion and date of the speech.

> "In a speech on business ethics delivered to the Public Relations Society of America last November, Preston Townly, CEO of the Conference Board, said . . ."

ACTIVITY 3C **Citing Sources**

On the back of each research card, write a short phrase that you can use in your speech as an oral footnote for the material on this card.

STUDENT RESPONSE   ACTION STEP 3

ACTIVITY 3C **Citing Sources**

According to J. S. Gordon in his book, Helping Survivors of Domestic Violence: The Effects of Medial, Mental Health, and Community Services, *domestic violence is the number-one reason for emergency room visits by women.*

Summary

Effective speaking requires high-quality information. You need to know where to look for information, what kind of information to look for, how to record it, and how to cite sources in your speeches.

To find material, begin by exploring your personal knowledge, experience, and observations. Then work outward by looking for primary or secondary sources through library and electronic sources, interviewing, and surveying. Look for material in books, articles in periodicals, newspapers, encyclopedias, statistical sources, biographical references, U.S. government publications, and the Internet. You may also need to conduct primary research if secondary sources are insufficient. You may conduct surveys, interview people who are knowledgeable on your subject, examine original sources and artifacts, or conduct experiments. By skimming written material, you can quickly evaluate sources to determine whether or not to read them in full. Four criteria for judging sources are authority, relevance, objectivity, and currency.

Two major types of material for speeches are factual statements and expert opinions. Factual statements are presented in the form of examples, statistics, and definitions. Expert opinions are interpretations of facts and judgments made by qualified authorities. Depending on your topic and speech goal, you may use facts and opinions and elaborate them with examples, anecdotes, narratives, comparisons, contrasts, and quotations.

A good method for recording material that you may want to use in your speech is to record each bit of data along with necessary bibliographical documentation on a separate research card. As your stack of information grows, sort the material under common headings. During the speech, cite the sources for the information on your research cards in the form of oral footnotes.

Now that you've read Chapter 6, use your Cengage-NOW for *The Challenge of Effective Speaking* for quick access to the electronic resources that accompany this text. Your CengageNOW gives you access to the Web Resources and Speech Planning activities featured in this chapter, Speech Builder Express, Info-Trac College Edition, and online study aids such as a digital glossary and review quizzes.

Your *Challenge* CengageNOW is an online study system that helps you identify concepts you don't fully understand, allowing you to put your study time to the best use. Using chapter-by-chapter diagnostic pretests, the system creates a personalized study plan for each chapter. Each plan directs you to specific resources designed to improve your understanding, including pages from the text in e-book format. Chapter posttests give you an opportunity to measure how much you've learned and let you know if you are ready for graded quizzes and exams.

KEY TERMS

Go to your CengageNOW for *Challenge* to access your online glossary for Chapter 6. Print a copy of the glossary for this chapter and test yourself with the electronic flash cards or complete the crossword puzzle to help you master these key terms:

anecdotes (108)
closed questions (99)
comparison (108)
contrast (109)
credentials (92)
definition (106)
examples (106)
expert opinions (107)
factual statements (104)
follow-up questions (99)

hypothetical examples (106)
Internet (96)
interviewing (98)
leading questions (99)
narratives (108)
neutral questions (99)
newsgroup (bulletin board) (97)
open questions (99)
oral footnote (113)
periodicals (93)

plagiarism (109)
primary questions (99)
primary research (91)
primary source (96)
secondary research (91)
secondary source (98)
skimming (101)
statistics (105)
survey (97)

WEB RESOURCES

Go to your CengageNOW for *Challenge* to access the Web Resources for this chapter.

6.1 Online Encyclopedias (95)
6.2 Online Statistics (96)
6.3 Bad Uses of Statistics and Polling (96)
6.4 Online Biographical References (96)

6.5 Online Quotations (96)
6.6 Online Government Publications (96)
6.7 Evaluating Internet Sources (97)

6.8 Conducting Surveys (98)
6.9 Analyzing Information Sources (103)

Access the Action Step activities for this chapter online at your CengageNOW for *Challenge.* Select the chapter resources for Chapter 6, then click the activity number you want. You may print your com- pleted activities, and you should save your work so you can use it as needed in later Action Step activities.

3A Locating and Evaluating Information Sources (103)

3B Preparing Research Cards (112)

3C Citing Sources (115)

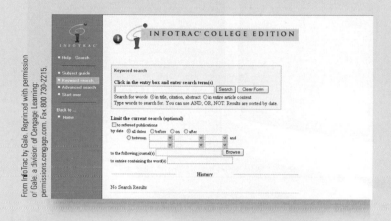

From InfoTrac by Gale. Reprinted with permission of Gale, a division of Cengage Learning; permissions.cengage.com. Fax 800 730-2215.

Organizing and Outlining the Speech Body

Every discourse like a living creature, should be put together that it has its own body and lacks neither head nor feet, middle nor extremities, all composed in such a way that suit both each other and the whole.

Plato, *Phaedrus*

What's Ahead

HERE'S WHAT'S AHEAD IN THIS CHAPTER:

1. Why is it important to limit the number of main points to no more than five?

2. Why should you construct a clear thesis statement?

3. How might you arrange your points in your speech?

4. What are some types of supporting material you can use to elaborate your main points?

5. Why are section transitions important?

"Troy, Mareka gave an awesome speech about recycling paper. I didn't realize the efforts that other universities are making to help the environment, and I haven't heard so many powerful stories in a long time."

"Yeah, Brett, I agree, the stories were interesting. But, you know, I had a hard time following the talk. I couldn't really get ahold of what the main ideas were. Did you?"

"Well, she was talking about recycling and stuff, . . . but now that you mention it, I'm not sure what she really wanted us to think or do about it. I mean, it was really interesting, but kind of confusing too."

Organizing information
A. Identifying main points
B. Writing a thesis statement
C. Developing the main points of your speech
D. Outlining the speech body

Troy and Brett's experience is not that unusual; even well-known speakers can give speeches that aren't as tightly organized as they could or should be. Yet if your speeches are well organized, you are more likely to achieve your speech goal. In the next two chapters, we explain the fourth speech plan action step: Organize your ideas and develop supporting material that achieves your goal and is appropriate for your audience. This chapter describes how to (1) identify main points that are implied in the specific goal statement and write them into a thesis statement for the speech; (2) organize the body of your speech by carefully wording and ordering your main points, and develop each main point with supporting material that is appropriate to the audience; and (3) create transitional statements that move the speech from one main point to the next. In the next chapter, we explain how to create introductions and conclusions that pique audience interest and aid audience understanding. Also in that chapter, you will learn how working with a complete speech outline enables you to test the structure and development of your ideas before you worry about the specific wording or begin practicing the speech aloud.

Construct a Thesis Statement

Once you have analyzed your audience, identified your general goal, created a specific goal, and assembled a body of information on your topic, you are ready to identify the main ideas you wish to present in your speech and to craft them into a well-phrased thesis statement.

Identify Main Points

The **main points** of a speech are complete-sentence statements of the two to five central ideas that will be used in the thesis statement. The number of main points in a well-organized speech is limited to help audience members keep track of the ideas and to allow each idea to be developed with appropriate supporting material. The difference between a five-minute speech and a twenty-five-minute speech with the same speech goal will be the extent to which each main point is developed.

In some cases, identifying the main points is easy. For Speech Planning Action Step 1, Activity 1E, in Chapter 4, Erin *might* have written, "I want the audience to understand the steps in spiking a volleyball." Because she is an

main points complete-sentence statements of the two to five central ideas that will be used in the thesis statement

excellent volleyball player, however, she doesn't need to do much research to identify the steps in this skill, so she is able to write a clear thesis statement: "I want my audience to understand the three major steps in spiking a volleyball—having a proper approach, a powerful swing, and an effective follow-through."

But instead of being in Erin's position, let's say that you are in Emming's. Even though you may have written a goal statement for Activity 1E that is on the right track, you may not be able to turn it into a clearly stated thesis statement at this time. For instance, Emming may have written the specific goal statement "I want the audience to understand the criteria for choosing a credit card." He may even have decided that, because he would probably have time to discuss only a few of these criteria, he would write the specific goal statement "I want the audience to understand three criteria for choosing a credit card." But at this stage, he is not yet ready to write a meaningful thesis statement.

If you find yourself in Emming's shoes, you will need to do some further work. How can you proceed? First, begin by listing the ideas you have found that relate to your specific goal. Like Emming, you may be able to list as many as nine or more. Second, eliminate ideas that your audience analysis suggests this audience already understands. Third, check to see if some of the ideas can be grouped together under a broader concept. Fourth, eliminate ideas for which you do not have strong support in the sources you consulted. Fifth, eliminate any ideas that might be too complicated for this audience to comprehend in the time you have to explain them. Finally, from the ideas that remain, choose two to five that are the most important for your audience to understand if you are to accomplish your specific speech goal.

Let's look at how Emming used these steps to identify the main points for his speech on criteria for choosing a credit card. To begin, Emming had a few ideas about what might be the main points for the speech, but it wasn't until he completed most of his research, sorted through what he had collected, and thought about it that he was able to choose his main points. First, he listed ideas (in this case, nine) that were discussed in the information about choosing a credit card that he had discovered when doing his research.

> what is a credit card
>
> interest rates
>
> credit rating
>
> convenience
>
> discounts
>
> annual fee
>
> rebates
>
> institutional reputation
>
> frequent flyer points

Second, Emming eliminated the idea "what is a credit card" because he knew that his audience already understood this. This left him with eight—still far too many for his first speech. Third, Emming noticed that several of the ideas seemed to be related. Discounts, rebates, and frequent flyer points are all types of incentives that card companies offer to entice people to choose their card. So Emming grouped these three ideas together under the single heading "incentives." Fourth, Emming noticed that several of the sources had provided considerable information on interest rates, credit ratings, discounts, annual fees, rebates, and frequent flyer points but had provided very little information on convenience or institutional reputation, so he crossed these ideas out.

Finally, Emming considered each of the remaining ideas in light of the five-minute time requirement he faced. He decided to cross out "credit rating" because, although it influences the types of cards and interest rates for which a person might qualify, Emming believed that he could not adequately explain this idea in the short time available. Explaining to this audience how a credit rating was determined might take longer than five minutes by itself and wasn't really as basic as some of the other ideas he had listed. When he was finished with his analysis and synthesis, his list looked like this:

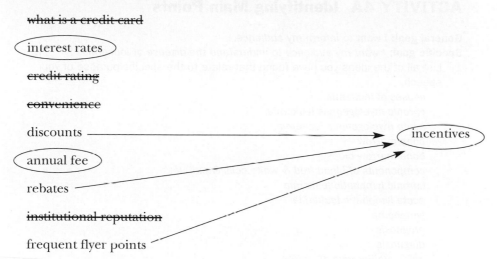

what is a credit card

~~interest rates~~

credit rating

convenience

discounts ⟶ incentives

annual fee

rebates

institutional reputation

frequent flyer points

This process left Emming with three broad-based points that he could develop in his speech: interest rates, annual fee, and incentives.

So, if you find that you want to talk about a topic that includes numerous forms, types, or categories, follow Emming's steps to reduce the number of your main points to two to five. To identify the main points of your speeches, you will want to complete Speech Planning Action Step 4, Activity A: Identifying Main Points. Another example of identifying main points is presented in the Student Response to Speech Planning Action Step 4, Activity A.

SPEECH PLANNING   ACTION STEP 4

4 | Organization

ACTIVITY 4A Identifying Main Points

1. List all of the ideas you have found that relate to the specific purpose of your speech.
2. If you have trouble limiting the number, do the following:
   a. Draw a line through each of the ideas that you believe the audience already understands, that you have no information to support, or that just seems too complicated.
   b. Combine ideas that can be grouped together under a single heading.
3. From those ideas that remain, choose the two to five you will use as main points in your speech.

You can complete this activity online with Speech Builder Express and, if requested, e-mail your completed activity to your instructor. Use your CengageNOW for *Challenge* to access Action Step Activity 4A.

CENGAGENOW™

ACTIVITY 4A Identifying Main Points

General goal: *I want to inform my audience.*
Specific goal: *I want my audience to understand the disease of leukemia.*

1. List all of the ideas you have found that relate to the specific purpose of your speech.

    causes of leukemia
    chronic myelogenous leukemia
    acute myelogenous leukemia
    bone marrow
    bone marrow biopsy
    components of blood (red & white cells & platelets)
    chronic lymphatic leukemia
    acute lymphatic leukemia
    lymphoma
    prognosis
    diagnosis
    myeloproliferative disorders
    types of blood tests

2. If you have trouble limiting the number, do the following:
    a. Draw a line through each of the ideas that you believe the audience already understands, that you have no information to support, or that just seems too complicated.
    b. Combine ideas that can be grouped together under a single heading.

3. From those ideas that remain, choose the two to five you will use as main points in your speech.

    causes of leukemia
    chronic myelogenous leukemia
    acute myelogenous leukemia
    bone marrow
    bone marrow biopsy
    components of blood (red & white cells & platelets) → *types of leukemia*
    chronic lymphatic leukemia
    acute lymphatic leukemia
    lymphoma
    prognosis
    diagnosis → *diagnosis*
    myeloproliferative disorders
    types of blood tests

Main points:
1. There are four types of leukemia.
2. The prognosis depends on the type of leukemia.
3. Leukemia is diagnosed by using blood and bone marrow tests.

thesis statement a one- or two-sentence summary of the speech that incorporates the general and specific goals and previews the main points

Write the Thesis Statement

A **thesis statement** is a one- or two-sentence summary of your speech that incorporates your general and specific goals and previews the main points of the speech. Not only will you write this sentence on your speech outline, but

The general goal, specific goal, and main points of the speech are introduced with a clearly stated thesis statement.

you will also use this sentence as a basis for the transition from the introduction to the body of your speech (see Emming's complete outline in Chapter 8, pages 159–160). Thus, your thesis statement provides a blueprint from which you will organize the body of your speech.

Now let's consider how you arrive at this thesis statement. First, let's look at a situation like Erin's, in which you have enough knowledge to go directly from a specific speech goal to a thesis statement.

Recall that Erin might have written her speech goal as, "I want the audience to understand the steps in spiking a volleyball." In fact, given her knowledge of volleyball, she was able to write: "I want my audience to understand the three major steps in spiking a volleyball—having a proper approach, a powerful swing, and an effective follow-through." Because she knows what the main points will be, she can write the following thesis statement that she will put on her speech outline: "The three major steps in spiking a volleyball are having a proper approach, a powerful swing, and an effective follow-through."

To reach the same level of preparedness as Erin, Emming went through the complete process of determining the ideas for his speech to arrive at his three choices: interest rates, annual fee, and incentives. Based on his specific goal and the main points he had identified, Emming was able to write the following thesis statement: "Three criteria you should use to find the most suitable credit card are level of real interest rate, annual fee, and advertised incentives."

Exhibit 7.1 provides other examples of specific speech goals and thesis statements.

For guidance on writing analytical, expository, and persuasive thesis statements, use your CengageNOW for *Challenge* to access **Web Resource 7.1: Writing Different Types of Thesis Statements**.

Speech Planning Action Step 4, Activity 4B: Writing a Thesis Statement, directs you in writing a thesis statement for your speech. To see an example of a student's response to this activity, see the Student Response to Activity 4B.

SPEECH SNIPPET

Preparing a Thesis Statement

Darla wanted her listeners to understand three different methods for disciplining children, so she phrased her thesis statement in this way: "Today, we'll discuss three unique methods you can use to discipline children. These methods are based on the perspectives of B. F. Skinner, Sigmund Freud, and Benjamin Spock."

EXHIBIT 7.1 Sample speech goals and thesis statements

General goal: I want to inform my audience.
Specific goal: I want my audience to understand how to improve their grades in college.
Thesis statement: Three proven techniques for improving test scores in college are to attend classes regularly, develop a positive attitude, and study efficiently.
General goal: I want to inform my audience.
Specific goal: I want the audience to understand the major characteristics of impressionistic painting.
Thesis statement: Impressionistic painting is characterized by unique subject matter, use of color, and technique.
General goal: I want to persuade my audience.
Specific goal: I want my audience to believe that parents should limit the time their children spend viewing television.
Thesis statement: Parents should limit the time their children spend viewing television because heavy television viewing desensitizes children to violence and increases violent tendencies in children.
General goal: I want to persuade my audience.
Specific goal: I want my audience to believe that they should learn to speak Spanish.
Thesis statement: You should learn to speak Spanish because it will benefit you personally, economically, and practically.

SPEECH PLANNING　　　　　　　　　ACTION STEP 4

4 | Organization

ACTIVITY 4B Writing a Thesis Statement

The goal of this activity is to use your general and specific goals and the main points you have identified to develop a well-worded thesis statement for your speech.
1. Write the specific goal you developed in Activity 4A.
2. List the main points you identified in Activity 4A.
3. Now write one or two complete sentences that combine your specific goal with your main point ideas.

You can complete this activity online with Speech Builder Express, view a student sample of this activity, and if requested, e-mail your completed activity to your instructor. Use you CengageNOW for *Challenge* to access Action Step Activity 4B.

CENGAGENOW™

STUDENT RESPONSE　　　　　　　　ACTION STEP 4

ACTIVITY 4B Writing a Thesis Statement

1. Write the general and specific goals you developed in Activity 4A.
   General goal: *I want to inform my audience.*
   Specific goal: *I want my audience to be able to find the credit card that is most suitable for them.*

Outline the Body of the Speech

An outline of the body of a speech will include three levels of information: (1) main points (I, II, III); (2) a maximum of two sets of subpoints and sub-subpoints (A, B, C; 1, 2, 3) for some or all of your main points; and (3) the elaboration material you choose to develop your main points and subpoints (a, b, c). Why are there two levels of subpoints? In speeches of more than a few minutes, the first level of subpoints (A, B, C) will often require additional explanation, indicated by sub-subpoints (1, 2, 3), before elaboration can begin. Relevant elaborations (a, b, c) will then be noted in appropriate places. Exhibit 7.2 shows the general form of how the speech outline system looks.

If you have developed expertise on your topic and done a lot of research, you will have to choose what subpoints and supporting information to present because the same two to five main points can be developed into a speech that will last for three to five minutes, five to seven minutes, eight to ten minutes, or even become a fifty-minute major presentation! The length of your speech is determined not by the number of main points but by how thoroughly you develop each of them. As you will see, a complex main point may have two, three, or even more subpoints. Each subpoint will be developed through one or more sub-subpoints. And subpoints and/or sub-subpoints may be elaborated with definitions, examples, statistics, personal experiences, stories, quotations, and other items. It's often the number and length of elaborations that determine the length of the speech. In a five-minute speech, you may be limited to only three elaborations of developmental information of fifteen seconds each. But an hour speech may allow six to ten or more elaborations of developmental information of up to several minutes for each.

Now let's look at an example of how three or four levels of points may be shown on your outline. Notice that all main points, subpoints, and sub-subpoints are written in complete sentences.

    I. One criterion for finding a suitable credit card is to examine the level of real interest rate.

        A. Interest rates are the percentages that a company charges you to carry a balance on your card past the due date.

            1. The average credit card charges 16 percent interest.

            2. The interest rate can change for a number of reasons.

What if you believe that the audience needs additional information to understand what this means? During the speech, you may decide to provide an example, present statistics, offer a quotation, tell a story, or provide some other elaboration. But none of these needs to be spelled out in any detail on the outline. The kinds of elaboration you use, length of statements, and the like will be determined during practice sessions. We'll discuss consideration of various points of elaboration further in this section and return to the issue in Chapter 11, Practicing Delivery.

EXHIBIT 7.2 General form for a speech outline

EXHIBIT 7.2 General form for a speech outline

I. Main point one
  A. Subpoint A for main point one
    1. Sub-subpoint one for subpoint A of main point one
    2. Sub-subpoint two for subpoint A of main point one
  B. Subpoint B of main point one
    1. Sub-subpoint one for subpoint B of main point one
    2. Sub-subpoint two for subpoint B of main point one

II. Main point two
  A. Subpoint one for main point two
    1. Sub-subpoint one for subpoint one of main point two
    2. Sub-subpoint two for subpoint one of main point two
  B. Subpoint two of main point two
    1. Sub-subpoint one for subpoint two of main point two
    2. Sub-subpoint two for subpoint two of main point two
    3. Sub-subpoint three for subpoint two of main point two
  C. Subpoint three of main point two
    1. Sub-subpoint one for subpoint three of main point two
    2. Sub-subpoint two for subpoint three of main point two
    3. Sub-subpoint three for subpoint three of main point two

III. Main point three
  A. Subpoint one of main point three
    1. Sub-subpoint one for subpoint one of main point three
    2. Sub-subpoint two for subpoint one of main point three
  B. Subpoint two of main point three
    . . . etc.

Outline Main Points

Once you have a thesis statement, you can begin outlining the main points that will make up the body of your speech. The main points in your outline are complete-sentence representations of the main ideas that you have identified and specified in your thesis statement. It is important to write main points, subpoints, and sub-subpoints as complete sentences because only sentences can fully express the relationship among the main points and between each main point and the specific goal of the speech. Once you have worded each main point, you will choose an organizing pattern.

WORDING MAIN POINTS

Recall that Emming determined that interest rates, annual fee, and advertised inducements are the three major criteria for finding a suitable credit card and that his thesis statement was: "Three criteria that you can use to find a suitable credit card are level of real interest rate, annual fee, and advertised incentives." Suppose he wrote his first draft of main points as follows:

  I. Level of real interest rate

  II. Annual fee

  III. Incentives

From this wording, Emming would have some ideas of the main points he was going to talk about, but he wouldn't have specified clearly how each main point was related to his goal. To make the relationships clear, Emming needs to create complete sentences for each. So Emming might write a first draft of the main points of his speech like this:

I. Examining the level of real interest rate is one criterion that you can use to find a credit card that is suitable for where you are in life.

II. Another criterion that you can use to make sure that you find a credit card that is suitable for where you are in life is to examine the annual fee.

III. Finding a credit card can also depend on weighing the advertised incentives, which is the third criterion that you will want to use to be sure that it is suitable for where you are in life.

Study these statements. Do they seem a bit vague? Notice that we have emphasized that this is a first draft. Sometimes, the first draft of a main point is well expressed and doesn't need additional work. More often, however, we find that our first attempt doesn't quite capture what we want to say. So we need to rework our points to make them clearer. Let's consider Emming's draft statements more carefully. Emming has made a pretty good start. His three main points are complete sentences. Now let's see how Emming might use two test questions to assure himself that he has achieved the best wording for his points.

1. Is the relationship of each main point statement to the goal statement clearly specified? Emming's first main point statement doesn't indicate how we should use interest rates when judging credit cards. So he could improve this statement by stating:

A low interest rate is one criterion that you can use to select a credit card that is suitable for where you are in life.

Similarly, he can improve the second main point statement by stating:

Another criterion that you can use to make sure that you find a credit card that is suitable for where you are in life is to look for a card with no annual fee or a very low one.

The third point might be redrafted to state.

Finding a credit card can also depend on weighing the value of the advertised incentives against the increased annual cost or interest rate, which is the third criterion that you will want to use to be sure that it is suitable for where you are in life.

2. Are the main points parallel in structure? Main points are **parallel** to each other when their wording follows the same structural pattern, often using the same introductory words. Parallel structure helps the audience recognize main points by recalling a pattern in the wording.

Emming notices that each of his main points is worded differently. So he needs to make them parallel:

I. The first criterion for choosing a credit card is to select a card with a low level of real interest rate.

II. A second criterion for choosing a credit card is to select a card with no or a low annual fee.

III. A third criterion for choosing a credit card is to weigh the value of the advertised incentives against the increased annual cost or interest rate.

Parallelism can be achieved in many ways. Emming used numbering: "first . . . second . . . third." Another way is to start each sentence with an active verb.

parallel when wording of points follows the same structural pattern, often using the same introductory words

Wording Main Points

Darla worded her main points on the methods of disciplining children in this way:

I. First, the Skinner disciplinary method is based on behavioral modification.

II. Second, the Freud disciplinary method is rooted in the concepts of the id, the ego, and the superego.

III. Third, the Spock disciplinary method is based on cognitive reasoning.

Suppose Kenneth wants his audience to understand the steps involved in antiquing a table. He might write the following first draft of his main points:

I. Clean the table thoroughly.

II. The base coat can be painted over the old surface.

III. A stiff brush, sponge, or piece of textured material can be used to apply the antique finish.

IV. Then you will want to apply two coats of shellac to harden the finish.

After further consideration, Kenneth might revise his main points to make them parallel in structure by using active verbs (italicized):

I. *Clean* the table thoroughly.

II. *Paint* the base coat over the old surface.

III. *Apply* the antique finish with a stiff brush.

IV. *Harden* the surface with two coats of shellac.

Notice how the similarity of structure clarifies and strengthens the message. The audience can immediately identify the key steps in the process.

Well-written main points help you clarify what you will need to present to develop each point.

SELECTING AN ORGANIZATIONAL PATTERN FOR MAIN POINTS

A speech can be organized in many different ways. Your objective is to find or create the structure that will help the audience make the most sense of the material. Although speeches may follow many types of organization, beginning speakers should learn four fundamental patterns: time order, narrative order, topic order, and logical reasons order.

time order organizing the main points of the speech in a chronological sequence or by steps in a process

1. Time order. Time order, sometimes called *sequential order* or *chronological order,* is a frequently used pattern in informative speeches. When you use time order, you organize your main points in a chronological sequence or by steps in a process. Thus, time order is appropriate when you are explaining how to do something, how to make something, how something works, or how something happened. Kenneth's speech on the *steps* in antiquing a table (clean, paint, apply, harden) is an example of time order. As the following example illustrates, the order of main points is as important for audiences to remember as the ideas themselves.

General goal: I want to inform my audience.

Specific goal: I want the audience to understand the four steps involved in developing a personal network.

Thesis statement: The four steps involved in developing a personal network are to analyze your current networking potential, to position yourself in places for opportunity, to advertise yourself, and to follow up on contacts.

I. First, analyze your current networking potential.

II. Second, position yourself in places for opportunity.

III. Third, advertise yourself.

IV. Fourth, follow up on contacts.

Although the use of "first," "second," and so on, is not required when using time order, their inclusion provides markers that help audience members understand that the *sequence* is important.

narrative order organizing the main points as a story or series of stories

2. Narrative order. A second pattern for arranging your main points is narrative order. **Narrative order** conveys your ideas through a story or series of stories. This pattern is similar to time order because the main points are pre-

Time order is appropriate when you are showing others how to do or make something or how something works.

sented in chronological order, but with narrative order, the entire speech consists of one or more stories that include characters, settings, and plots. Narrative order is particularly effective when you tell stories that are emotionally compelling. The goal of using this pattern is for listeners to accept your conclusion by showing them the validity of what you are saying through description rather than simply telling them. Lonna shared her story about having AIDS to help listeners understand the impact of the disease on one's life.

General goal: I want to inform my audience.

Specific goal: I want my audience to understand how AIDS affects the lives of its victims and their loved ones.

Thesis statement: Today, I want to share the story of my life before contracting AIDS, my life today with AIDS, and my future plans knowing that I have AIDS.

   I. My life before I contracted AIDS was pretty typical for a middle-class white girl.

  II. My life today is anything but typical as I balance my schoolwork and social life with weekly visits to the doctor and daily physical and drug therapy.

 III. My future life plans have changed dramatically because I have AIDS.

Here's how Lonna could also use a narrative pattern that shares several stories:

General goal: I want to inform my audience.

Specific goal: I want my audience to understand how AIDS affects the lives of its victims and their loved ones.

Thesis statement: Today, I want to help you realize the impact AIDS has on its victims and their loved ones by sharing the stories of Robert, Emma, and me.

   I. Robert's story is about a twenty-seven-year-old store manager with AIDS.

  II. Emma's story is about a three-year-old toddler with AIDS.

 III. My story is about a twenty-year-old college student with AIDS.

3. Topic order. A third often used organization for informative speeches is topic order. **Topic order** organizes the main points of the speech by categories or divisions of a subject. This is a common way of ordering main points because nearly any subject can be subdivided or categorized in many different ways. The order of the topics may go from general to specific, move from least important to most important, or follow some other logical sequence.

In the example that follows, the topics are presented in the order that the speaker believes is most suitable for the audience and specific speech goal, with the most important point at the end.

General goal: I want to inform my audience.

Specific goal: I want the audience to understand three proven methods for ridding our bodies of harmful toxins.

Thesis statement: Three proven methods for ridding our bodies of harmful toxins are reducing intake of animal foods, hydrating, and eating natural whole foods.

   I. One proven method for ridding our bodies of harmful toxins is reducing our intake of animal products.

   II. A second proven method for ridding our bodies of harmful toxins is keeping well hydrated.

   III. A third proven method for ridding our bodies of harmful toxins is eating more natural whole foods.

Whereas time order suggests a sequence that must be followed, topic order suggests that, of any possible ideas or methods, two to five are particularly important, valuable, or necessary. Emming's speech on the three criteria that will enable audience members to find the credit card that is most suitable is another example of a speech using topic order.

4. Logical reasons order. Logical reasons order organizes the main points of a persuasive speech by the reasons that support the specific speech goal. It emphasizes why the audience should believe something or behave in a particular way. Logical reasons order is most appropriate for a persuasive speech.

General goal: I want to persuade my audience.

Specific goal: I want the audience to donate money to the United Way.

Thesis statement: Donating to the United Way is appropriate because your one donation covers many charities, you can stipulate which specific charities you wish to support, and a high percentage of your donation goes to charities.

   I. When you donate to the United Way, your one donation covers many charities.

   II. When you donate to the United Way, you can stipulate which charities you wish to support.

   III. When you donate to the United Way, you know that a high percentage of your donation will go directly to the charities you've selected.

As we mentioned earlier, these four organizational patterns are the most common. As you develop your public speaking skills, you may find that you will need to revise one of these patterns or create a totally different one to meet the needs of your particular subject matter or audience. In Chapter 13, Persuasive Speaking: Reasoning with Your Audience, we describe four organizational patterns that are commonly used in persuasive speeches, including the logical reasons pattern.

In summary, then, to organize the body of your speech, (1) turn your speech goal into a thesis statement that combines the general goal and specific goal with a preview of the main points; (2) state the main points in complete sentences that are clear, parallel, meaningful, and limited to a maximum of five in number; and (3) organize the main points in the pattern best suited to your material and the needs of your specific audience.

At this point, you have the structure for your complete outline: a general and specific speech goal, a thesis statement, and an outline of the main points of the speech.

Figure 7.1 shows what Emming's outline would look like at this stage of preparation. Notice that his general and specific speech goals are written at the top of the page. His thesis statement comes right after the goals because later it will become part of his introduction.

Use Speech Planning Action Step 4, Activity 4C: Developing the Main Points of Your Speech, to develop well-written main points for your speech. The Student Response to Activity 4C gives an example of this activity completed by a student in this course.

| SPEECH PLANNING | ACTION STEP 4 |

ACTIVITY 4C Developing the Main Points of Your Speech

The goal of this activity is to help you phrase and order your main points.
1. Write your thesis statement.
2. Underline the two to five main points identified in your thesis statement.
3. For each underlined item, write one sentence that summarizes what you want your audience to know about that idea.
4. Review the main points as a group.
   a. Is the relationship of each main point statement to the goal statement clearly specified? If not, revise.
   b. Are the main points parallel in structure? If not, consider why and revise.
5. Choose an organizational pattern for your main points.
6. Identify the pattern you have used.

You can complete this activity online with Speech Builder Express, view a student sample of this activity, and if requested, e-mail your completed activity to your instructor. Use your CengageNOW for *Challenge* to access Activity 4C.

CENGAGENOW™

| STUDENT RESPONSE | ACTION STEP 4 |

ACTIVITY 4C Developing the Main Points of Your Speech

1. Write your thesis statement.
   The three tests that you can use to determine whether a diamond is real are the acid test, the streak test, and the hardness test.

(continued)

2. Underline the two to five main points identified in your thesis statement.
3. For each underlined item, write one sentence that summarizes what you want your audience to know about that idea.
   I. *One way to identify a diamond is by using the acid test.*
   II. *You can also identify a diamond by using the streak test.*
   III. *You can also identify a diamond by using the hardness test.*
4. Review the main points as a group.
   a. Is the relationship of each main point statement to the goal statement clearly specified? If not, revise.

   No. Purpose of test is to identify whether the diamond is real by using a test. The following revision puts emphasis in the right place.

   Revision:
   I. *One way to identify whether a diamond is real is by using the acid test.*
   II. *You can also identify whether a diamond is real by using the streak test.*
   III. *You can also identify whether a diamond is real by using the hardness test.*

   b. Are the main points parallel in structure? If not, consider why and revise.

   Revision:
   I. *One way to determine whether a diamond is real is to use the acid test.*
   II. *A second way to determine whether a diamond is real is to use the streak test.*
   III. *A third way to determine whether a diamond is real is to use the hardness test.*
5. Choose an organizational pattern for your main points.
   I. *One way to determine whether a diamond is real is to use the acid test.*
   II. *A second way to determine whether a diamond is real is to use the streak test.*
   III. *A third way to determine whether a diamond is real is to use the hardness test.*
6. Identify the type of pattern you have used.
   Topic

Identify and Outline Subpoints

Just as you must identify the main points of your speech, you must also identify the subpoints. As we said earlier, your outline will include complete-sentence statements of each of your subpoints. A main point may have two, three, or even more subpoints depending on the complexity of the main point.

IDENTIFYING SUBPOINTS

You can identify subpoints by sorting the research cards you prepared earlier into piles that correspond to each of your main points. The goal at this point is to see what information you have that supports each of your main points. For example, at the end of sorting his research cards, Emming might find that he has the following items of information that support the first main point:

Main point: The first criterion for choosing a credit card is to select a card with a low interest rate.

Most credit cards carry an average of 8 percent after a specified 0 percent interest period.

Some cards carry as much as 21 percent after the first year.

Some cards offer a grace period.

Department store rates are often higher than bank rates.

Variable rate means that the rate can change from month to month. Fixed rate means that the rate will stay the same.

Even fixed interest rates on some cards can be raised to as much as 32 percent if you make a late payment.

Many companies offer 0 percent interest for up to twelve months. Many companies offer 0 percent interest for a few months.

Once you have listed the items of information that make the point, look for relationships between and among ideas. As you analyze, you can draw lines connecting items of information that fit together logically, cross out information that seems irrelevant or doesn't really fit, and combine similar ideas using different language. Exhibit 7.3 depicts Emming's analysis of the information listed under his first main point.

In most cases, similar items that you have linked can be grouped under broader headings. For instance, Emming has four statements related to specific percentages and two statements related to types of interest rates. For the four statements related to specific percentages, he might create the following heading:

Interest rates are the percentages that a company charges you to carry a balance on your card past the due date.

Then under that heading, he can list the four statements:

Most credit cards carry an average of 8 percent. Some cards carry as much as 21 percent.

Many companies offer 0 percent interest for up to twelve months. Other companies offer 0 percent interest for a few months.

For the two statements related to types of interest rates, he might create the following heading:

Interest rates can be variable or fixed.

Under that heading, he can list the three statements:

Variable rate means that the rate can change from month to month.

Fixed rate means that the rate will stay the same.

Even fixed rates can be raised to as much as 32 percent if you make a late payment.

EXHIBIT 7.3 Editing material supporting the main point

I. The first criterion for choosing a credit card is to select a card with a low interest rate.

> → Most credit cards carry an average of 8 percent after a specified 0 percent interest period.
>
> → Some cards carry as much as 21 percent after the first year.
>
> ~~Some cards offer a grace period.~~
>
> ~~Department store rates are often higher than bank rates.~~
>
> → Variable rate means that the rate can change from month to month.
>
> → Fixed rate means that the rate will stay the same.
>
> Even a credit card with a fixed interest rate can be raised to as much as 32 percent if you make a late payment.
>
> → Many companies offer 0 percent interest for up to twelve months.
>
> → Many companies offer 0 interest for a few months.

You are also likely to have listed information that you decide not to include in the outline. Emming decided to cut the department store point because his emphasis was not on who was offering the rates but on what percentages were charged. Likewise, he thought that the grace period point wasn't directly related to either of the main subpoints he wanted to emphasize.

Sometimes, you'll find you have stated the same point two different ways:

Many companies offer 0 percent interest for the first year.

Some companies offer 0 percent interest for a few months.

Emming might combine the two to read:

Many companies are now offering 0 percent interest rates for anywhere from a few months to a full year.

OUTLINING SUBPOINTS

Subpoints should also be represented on the outline in full sentences. As with main points, they should be revised until they are clearly stated. The items of information listed for Emming's first main point might be grouped and subordinated as follows:

I. The first criterion for choosing a credit card is to select a card with a low interest rate.

    A. Interest rates are the percentages that a company charges you to carry a balance on your card past the due date.

        1. Most credit cards carry an average of 8 percent.

        2. Some cards carry as much as 21 percent.

        3. Many companies quote very low rates (0 to 3 percent) for specific periods.

    B. Interest rates can be variable or fixed.

        1. A variable rate means that the rate can change from month to month.

        2. A fixed rate means that the rate will stay the same.

        3. Even a card with a fixed interest rate can be raised to as much as 32 percent if you make a late payment.

List Supporting Material

supporting material developmental material that will be used in the speech, including personal experiences, examples, illustrations, anecdotes, statistics, and quotations

A good outline will also include short outline statements of **supporting material**—developmental material that will be used in the speech, including personal experiences, examples, illustrations, anecdotes, statistics, quotations, and other forms of supporting material. You will choose these items to meet the needs of your specific audience.

As we have mentioned, supporting material elaborates the main points and subpoints of the speech. Although it is theoretically possible to deliver a speech by merely presenting the outlined main points and subpoints, these points can ordinarily be stated in only a couple of minutes. Thus, if the time limit for your speech is three to five minutes, which includes an introduction and conclusion, you will still have a minute or so for elaboration. The point is that whether a speech is three to five minutes, five to seven minutes, or ten or more minutes may not affect the statement of your main points and subpoints. Making the speech longer will involve your developing (elaborating) your main points and subpoints with various supporting materials.

How to build developmental materials during practice sessions will be discussed at length in Chapter 11, Practicing Delivery.

Create Section Transitions and Signposts

Once you have outlined your main points, subpoints, and potential supporting material, you will want to consider how you will move smoothly from one main point to another. **Transitions** are words, phrases, or sentences that show the relationship between, or bridge, two ideas. Transitions act like tour guides leading the audience from point to point through the speech. **Section transitions** are complete sentences that show the relationship between, or bridge, major parts of the speech. They typically summarize what has just been said in one main point and preview the next main idea. Essentially, section transitions are the glue that holds the macrostructure of your speech together.

For example, suppose Kenneth has just finished the introduction of his speech on antiquing tables and is now ready to launch into his main points. Before stating his first main point, he might say, "Antiquing a table is a process that has four steps. Now let's consider the first one." When his listeners hear this transition, they are signaled to mentally prepare to listen to and remember the first main point. When he finishes his first main point, he will use another section transition to signal that he is finished speaking about step one and is moving on to discuss step two: "Now that we see what is involved in cleaning the table, we can move on to the second step."

You might be thinking that this sounds repetitive or patronizing, but section transitions are important for two reasons. First, they help the audience follow the organization of ideas in the speech. If every member of the audience were able to pay complete attention to every word, then perhaps section transitions would not be needed. But as people's attention rises and falls during a speech, they often find themselves wondering where they are. Section transitions give us a mental jolt and say "Pay attention."

Second, section transitions are important in helping us retain information. We may well remember something that was said once in a speech, but our retention is likely to increase markedly if we hear something more than once. Good transitions are important in writing, but they are even more important in speaking. If listeners get lost or think they have missed something, they cannot check back as they can when reading.

In a speech, if we preview main points, then state each main point, and also provide transitions between points, audiences are more likely to follow and

transitions words, phrases, or sentences that show a relationship between, or bridge, two ideas

section transitions complete sentences that show the relationship between, or bridge, major parts of a speech

Section transitions mentally prepare the audience to move to the next main point.

© Michael Newman/PhotoEdit

signposts words or phrases that connect pieces of supporting material to the main point or subpoint they address

remember the organization. To help you remember and use section transitions, write them in complete sentences on your speech outline.

Signposts are words or phrases that connect pieces of supporting material to the main point or subpoint they address. Sometimes, signposts highlight numerical order: "first," "second," "third," or "fourth." Sometimes, they help the audience focus on a key idea: "foremost," "most important," or "above all." They can also be used to signify an explanation: "to illustrate," "for example," "in other words," "essentially," or "to clarify." Signposts can also signal that an important idea, or even the speech itself, is coming to an end: "in short," "finally," "in conclusion," or "to summarize." Just as section transitions serve as the glue that holds your macrostructure together, signposts serve as the glue that holds your subpoints and supporting material together within each main point.

Complete the outline for the body of your speech by completing Speech Planning Action Step 4, Activity 4D: Outlining the Speech Body. The Student Response to Activity 4D shows Emming's response to this activity.

| SPEECH PLANNING | ACTION STEP 4 |

4 | Organization

ACTIVITY 4D Outlining the Speech Body

The goal of this exercise is to help you get started on the outline for the body of your first speech. Using complete sentences, write the following:

1. The specific speech goal you developed in Activity 1E.
2. The thesis statement you developed in Activity 4A.
3. A transition to the first main point.
4. The first main point you developed in Activity 4B.
5. The outline of the subpoints and support for your first main point that you developed in Activity 4C.
6. A transition from your first main point to your second.
7. The other points, subpoints, support, transition statements, and signposts. Use the format for numeration, spacing, and so on shown in the Student Response to Activity 4D. (Note that the labels Introduction, Conclusion, and Sources are included just to help you understand the requirements for your final outline.) For a sample of a completed outline, see pages 159–160 of Chapter 8.

You can complete this activity online with Speech Builder Express and, if requested, e-mail your completed activity to your instructor. Use your CengageNOW for *Challenge* to access Activity 4D.

CENGAGENOW™

| STUDENT RESPONSE | ACTION STEP 4 |

ACTIVITY 4D Outlining the Speech Body

Here is Emming's outline, including his goal, thesis statement, speech body (complete development of one main point and subpoints), and transitions.

General goal: *I want to inform my audience.*

(continued)

Specific speech goal: *I would like the audience to understand the major criteria for finding a suitable credit card.*

Thesis statement: *Three criteria that will enable the audience to find the credit card most suitable for them are level of real interest rate, annual fee, and advertised incentives.*

Introduction

(Transition: Let's consider the first criterion.)

Body

    I. *The first criterion for choosing a credit card is to select a card with a low interest rate.*

        A. *Interest rates are the percentages that a company charges you to carry a balance on your card past the due date.*

[Then under that heading, he can list the relevant subpoints.]

            1. *Most credit cards carry an average of 8 percent.*

            2. *Some cards carry as much as 21 percent.*

            3. *Many companies offer 0 percent interest rates anywhere from a few months to a full year.*

        B. *Interest rates can be variable or fixed.*

            1. *Variable rates mean that the rate can change from month to month.*

            2. *Fixed rates mean that the rate will stay the same.*

            3. *Even credit cards with a fixed rate can raise the interest rate if you make a late payment.*

(Transition: Now that we've considered interest rates, let's look at the next criterion.)

    II. *A second criterion for choosing a credit card is to select a card with no or a low annual fee.*

(Transition: After considering interest rates and annual fee, you can consider the final criterion.)

    III. *A third criterion for choosing a credit card is to weigh the value of the advertised incentives against the increased annual cost or interest rate.*

Conclusion

Sources

REFLECT ON ETHICS

Carson had done a variety of computer searches for his speech on cloning and had come up with more than seven major articles, but time was getting short. He had three tests the week before his assigned speech, and even though he had taken the time to get an excellent list of sources, the speech itself was due the next morning.

As Carson thought about his problem, it occurred to him that the one magazine article he had read really "said it all." In fact, as far as he could see, most of the key ideas he had noticed in scanning the other articles were included in this one source. Suddenly a "plan" for his speech organization hit him. He would use the organization of this article for his speech and adapt the thesis statement from the article as his own. He would list the other articles in his bibliography. Moreover, because the article actually referenced three of the sources his search had uncovered, his bibliography really did reflect what he had found and what was in the speech.

Quickly then, Carson took the three key paragraphs from the article and outlined them for his speech. He used a story related in the article as his introduction and wrote a short summary of the three main points for the conclusion. "Great," he thought, "in just about fifteen minutes, I've got a great speech for tomorrow." He even had time to read through the three paragraphs about four times before he went to bed. He knew he was in great shape for the speech.

1. Was Carson's method of organizing his speech ethical? Why do you reach this conclusion?
2. How should material from a key article be used?

Summary

A speech that is well organized is likely to achieve its goal. Speech organization begins by writing a thesis statement that articulates your goal to inform, persuade, or entertain and is based on the main points suggested in your specific speech goal. The thesis statement identifies the key ideas that you will present in the speech.

The body of the speech includes main points and subpoints that should be written in complete sentences and checked to make sure that they are clear, parallel in structure, meaningful, and limited in number to five or fewer.

The order in which you present your main points depends on the type of speech you are giving and on the specific nature of the material you want to present. Four fundamental organizational patterns are time, narrative, topic, and logical reasons. You will want to choose an organizational pattern that best helps your audience understand and remember your main points.

The next step in organizing your speech is to choose and order material that you will use to explain each main point. To begin this process, create lists of the information you have that relates to each of your main points. Then review each list, grouping similar information under larger headings and identifying the information that is most important for helping the audience understand and remember the main point. These subpoints should be written in complete sentences and entered on your outline below the main point to which they belong. As a speaker, you will also want to consider such elements as definitions, examples, statistics, personal experiences, stories, and quotations that you can use to elaborate your key subpoints.

Section transitions bridge major parts of the speech and occur between the introduction and the body, between main points within the body, and between the body and the conclusion. Section transitions should be planned and placed in the outline as parenthetical statements where they are to occur. Whereas section transitions serve as the glue that holds together the macrostructural elements of your speech, signposts serve as the glue that holds together the subpoints and supporting material within each main point. Together, these types of transitions serve as a road map for listeners to follow as you present your speech.

CHALLENGE ONLINE

Now that you've read Chapter 7, use your CengageNOW for *The Challenge of Effective Speaking* for quick access to the electronic resources that accompany this text. Your CengageNOW gives you access to the Web Resources and Speech Planning activities featured in this chapter, Speech Builder Express, InfoTrac College Edition, and online study aids such as a digital glossary and review quizzes.

Your *Challenge* CengageNOW is an online study system that helps you identify concepts you don't fully understand, allowing you to put your study time to the best use. Using chapter-by-chapter diagnostic pretests, the system creates a personalized study plan for each chapter. Each plan directs you to specific resources designed to improve your understanding, including pages from the text in e-book format. Chapter posttests give you an opportunity to measure how much you've learned and let you know if you are ready for graded quizzes and exams.

KEY TERMS

Go to your CengageNOW for *Challenge* to access your online glossary for Chapter 7. Print a copy of the glossary for this chapter and test yourself with the electronic flash cards or complete the crossword puzzle to help you master these key terms:

logical reasons order (130)	section transitions (135)	time order (128)
main points (119)	signposts (136)	topic order (130)
narrative order (128)	supporting material (134)	transitions (135)
parallel (127)	thesis statement (122)	

WEB RESOURCE

Go to your CengageNOW for *Challenge* to access the Web Resources for this chapter.

7.1 Writing Different Types of Thesis Statements (123)

SPEECH PLANNING ACTION STEPS

Access the Action Step activities for this chapter online at your CengageNOW for *Challenge*. Select the chapter resources for Chapter 7 and then click the activity number you want. You may print your completed activities, and you should save your work so you can use it as needed in later Action Step activities.

4A Identifying Main Points (121)

4B Writing a Thesis Statement (124)

4C Developing the Main Points of Your Speech (131)

4D Outlining the Speech Body (136)

Completing the Outline: Creating the Introduction and the Conclusion

© Phil Boorman/Taxi/Getty Images

What's Ahead

HERE'S WHAT'S AHEAD IN THIS CHAPTER:

1. Why are solid introductions and conclusions so important to effective public speaking?

2. How can you get your audience's attention in your introduction?

3. Why should you summarize your main points again in the conclusion?

4. How might you motivate listeners to remember your speech in your conclusion?

5. How do you determine which sources to include in your bibliography?

Tiffany asked Amanda to listen to her rehearse her speech. As she stood in front of the classroom where she was practicing, she began, "Today I want to tell you about why I became a vegetarian, some family issues that arose as a result of my decision, and some of the ways being a vegetarian affects my life today."

"Whoa, Tiffany," Amanda said. "That's your introduction?"

"Yes," Tiffany replied. "People know what a vegetarian is. Why shouldn't I just get on with the speech?"

4 | Organization   ACTION STEP 4

Organizing information

E. Creating speech introductions
F. Creating speech conclusions
G. Compiling a list of sources
H. Completing the speech outline

Tiffany's question sounds reasonable—most people know what a vegetarian is. But this doesn't mean that everyone in the audience is ready to listen to a speech about being a vegetarian. People might think the topic is boring, irrelevant to them, or for some other reason not worth their time. For most speeches, how well you start the speech may determine whether most members of the audience even listen, and how well you start and finish your speech can play a major role in the speech's overall success.

One reason for this focus on a speech's introduction and conclusion is what psychologists call the **primacy-recency effect:** We are more likely to remember the first and last items conveyed orally in a series than the items in between.[1] This means listeners are more likely to remember the beginning and end of your speech than what you say in the body! So make sure your introduction and conclusion are strong. Another reason stems from the need for listeners to quickly grasp your goal and main points as they listen to your speech. You can give listeners a preview of the macrostructure of your speech by using the introduction to highlight your goal and preview the main points, and you can reinforce them by restating them in the conclusion.

primacy-recency effect the tendency to remember the first and last items conveyed orally in a series than the items in between

In the previous chapter, we described the first few tasks involved in organizing your speech. These resulted in a complete-sentence outline of the body. In this chapter, we describe how you complete your organizational process by creating an introduction that both gets attention and leads into the body of the speech; creating a conclusion that both summarizes the material and leaves the speech on a high note; writing a title; and completing a list of sources used to develop the speech.

Creating the Introduction

Now that the body of the speech has been developed, you can decide how to begin your speech. Because the introduction establishes your relationship with your audience, you will want to develop two or three different introductions and then select the one that seems best for this particular audience. Although your introduction may be very short, it should gain audience attention and motivate them to listen to all that you have to say. An introduction is generally about 10 percent of the length of the entire speech, so for a five-minute speech (approximately 750 words), an introduction of about thirty seconds (approximately sixty to eighty-five words) is appropriate.

Goals of the Introduction

An effective introduction has three primary goals: to get audience attention, establish listener relevance, and identify your thesis statement, or speech goal

Marcia used a combination of rhetorical questions and a startling statement to get her listeners' attention for her speech on eating disorders: "Who are five of the most important women in your life? Your mother? Your sister? Your daughter? Your wife? Your best friend? Now which one of them has an eating disorder? Before you disregard my question, listen to what research tells us. One in every five women in the United States has an eating disorder."

startling statement a sentence or two that grabs your listeners' attention by shocking them in some way

rhetorical question a question that seeks a mental rather than a direct response

direct question a question that demands an overt response from the audience, usually by a show of hands

story an account of something that has happened (actual) or could happen (hypothetical)

and main points. In addition, effective introductions can help you begin to establish speaker credibility and create a bond of goodwill between you and the audience.

GET ATTENTION

An audience's physical presence does not guarantee that people will actually listen to your speech. Your first goal, then, is to create an opening that will win your listeners' attention by arousing their curiosity and motivating them to continue listening. In this chapter, we discuss eight types of devices you can use not only to get attention but also to stimulate audience excitement for finding out what you have to say: startling statements, questions, stories, jokes, personal references, quotations, action, and suspense. You can determine which attention-getting device to use by considering what emotional tone is appropriate for your topic. A humorous attention getter will signal a lighthearted tone; a serious one signals a more thoughtful or somber tone. For instance, a speaker who starts with a funny story will put the audience in a lighthearted mood. If that speaker then says, "Now let's turn to the subject of abortion" (or nuclear war or drug abuse), the audience will be confused by the speaker's initial words, which signaled a far different type of subject.

1. Make a startling statement. A **startling statement** is a sentence or two that grabs your listeners' attention by shocking them in some way. Startling audience members helps them stop what they were doing or thinking and focus on the speaker. Chris used a startling statement to get his listeners' attention for his speech about how automobile emissions contribute to global warming:

> Look around. Each one of you is sitting next to a killer. That's right. You are sitting next to a cold-blooded killer. Before you think about jumping up and running out of this room, let me explain. Everyone who drives an automobile is a killer of the environment. Every time you turn the key to your ignition, you are helping to destroy our precious surroundings.

Once Chris's startling statement grabbed the attention of his listeners, he went on to state his speech goal and preview his main points.

2. Ask a question. Questions are requests for information that encourage your audience to get involved with your topic. Questions can be *rhetorical* or *direct*. A **rhetorical question** seeks a mental rather than a direct response. Notice how a student began his speech on counterfeiting with these three short rhetorical questions:

> What would you do with this $20 bill if I gave it to you? Take your friend to a movie? Treat yourself to a pizza and drinks? Well, if you did either of these things, you could get in big trouble—this bill is counterfeit!

Unlike a rhetorical question, a **direct question** demands an overt response from the audience, usually by a show of hands. For example, here's how Stephanie introduced her speech about seatbelt safety:

> By a show of hands, how many of you drove or rode in an automobile to get here today? Of those of you who did, how many of you actually wore your seatbelt?

Direct questions can be helpful in getting audience attention because they require a physical response. However, getting listeners to actually comply with your request can also pose a challenge.

3. Tell a story. A **story** is an account of something that has happened (actual) or could happen (hypothetical). Most people enjoy a well-told story, so it makes a good attention getter. One drawback of stories is that they are often lengthy and can take more time to tell than is appropriate for the length of your speech. Use a story only if it is short or if you can abbreviate it so that it is just right for your speech length. Matt used a short story to get audience attention for his speech about spanking as a form of discipline:

> One rainy afternoon, four-year-old Billy was playing "pretend" in the living room. He was Captain Jack Sparrow, staving off the bad guys with his amazing sword-fighting skills. Then it happened. Billy knocked his mother's very expensive china bowl off the table. Billy hung his head and began to cry. He knew what was coming, and sure enough it did. The low thud of his mother's hand on his bottom brought a sting to his behind and a small yelp from his mouth. Billy got a spanking.

With this very short story, Matt was able to get his audience's attention and still have time to state his purpose and preview his main points.

4. Tell a joke. A **joke** is an anecdote or a piece of wordplay designed to be funny and make people laugh. A joke can be used to get audience attention when it meets the *three-r test*: It must be realistic, relevant, and repeatable.[2] In other words, it can't be too far-fetched, unrelated to the speech purpose, or potentially offensive to some listeners. For example, one of your authors gave a speech recently about running effective meetings to a group of business professionals. She began with, "As many of you know, I'm a college teacher, so I just couldn't resist giving you a quiz." Audience members looked slightly uncomfortable. She then handed out a twelve-item personal inventory of learning styles to each audience member. As she distributed the inventory, she explained, "The nice thing about *this* quiz, though, is you can't be wrong. You'll all get 100 percent." The audience laughed with relief. Be careful with humorous introductions—and consider how you will handle the situation if nobody laughs.

5. Supply a personal reference. A **personal reference** is a brief story about something that happened to you or a hypothetical situation that listeners can imagine themselves in. In addition to getting attention, a personal reference can be especially effective at engaging listeners as active participants. A personal reference like this one on exercise is suitable for a speech of any length:

> Say, were you panting when you got to the top of those four flights of stairs this morning? I'll bet there were a few of you who vowed you'd never take a class on the top floor of this building again. But did you ever stop to think that maybe the problem isn't that this class is on the top floor? It just might be that you are not getting enough exercise.

For longer speeches, you can build personal references that tie together the speaker, the audience, and the setting. Let's see how Bruce Cole, chairman of the National Endowment for the Humanities, used a personal reference in the opening of his speech at New York University's "Art in an Age of Uncertainty" conference:

> Good morning. It is an honor and pleasure to be here today. It's been said that a picture is worth a thousand words; as an art historian, I ardently believe this is true. And so I freely confess that nothing I say here today is as meaningful, as momentous, or as memorable as the sight of what lies nearby. We are on hallowed ground.
>
> The magnitude of the horrific events of September 11 is still being realized, the aftershocks still felt. But even in an age of uncertainty there are truths to be discovered, lessons to discern, and hope to share.
>
> Today, I'd like to talk to you about the centrality of the humanities to democratic and civic life; the danger of American amnesia; and the possibilities of recovering our memory and protecting the best of our culture.[3]

Notice how smoothly Cole moves from personal reference into his thesis and preview of his main points.

joke an anecdote or a piece of wordplay designed to be funny and make people laugh

personal reference a brief story about something that happened to you or a hypothetical situation that listeners can imagine themselves in

SPEECH SNIPPET

Introducing a Speech with a Personal Reference and a Startling Statement

In her speech about binge eating and obesity, Jamie used this personal reference and startling statement to get her audience's attention: "Imagine a table full of all the food you eat in one week. *[pause]* That's a lot of food, right? Now, imagine eating all that food in one day! Believe it or not, there are people who do this. They consume many thousands of calories more than the suggested intake of 2,000 per day. This is a condition called binge eating, and it's more common than you might think."

6. Recite a quotation. A **quotation** is a comment made by and attributed to someone other than the speaker. A particularly vivid or thought-provoking quotation can make an excellent attention getter as long as it relates to your topic. Although it is common to quote famous people, a good quotation from *any* source can create interest in your topic. For instance, notice how Sally Mason, provost at Purdue University, used a quotation to get the attention of her audience, the Lafayette, Indiana, YWCA:

> There is an ancient saying, "May you live in interesting times." It is actually an ancient curse. It might sound great to live in interesting times. But interesting times are times of change and even turmoil. They are times of struggle. They are exciting. But, at the same time, they are difficult. People of my generation have certainly lived through interesting times and they continue today.[4]

As the introduction progressed, she introduced her topic about the gender gap in technology.

In a speech about the importance of courage and taking risks, Sonja began with Franklin D. Roosevelt's famous quotation, "The only thing we have to fear is fear itself".[5] This short attention getter provided Sonja with plenty of time to state her purpose and preview her main points.

In the following excerpt from his speech to the National Conference on Media Reform, noted journalist Bill Moyers exemplifies the way a clever speaker can use a quotation to introduce the theme of an entire speech:

> Benjamin Franklin once said, "Democracy is two wolves and a lamb voting on what to have for dinner."
>
> "Liberty," he said, "is a well-armed lamb, contesting the vote."
>
> My fellow lambs—it's good to be in Memphis and find you well armed with passion for democracy, readiness for action, and courage for the next round in the fight for a free and independent press in America. I cherish the spirit that fills this hall, and the camaraderie that we share here.
>
> All too often, the greatest obstacle to reform is the reform movement itself. Factions rise, fences are erected, jealousies mount, and the cause all of us believe in is lost in the shattered fragments of what once was a clear and compelling vision.[6]

If you were a journalist in his audience, wouldn't you be intrigued to hear what he had to say?

7. Perform or motivate an action. You can introduce your topic and gain attention through an **action,** an attention-getting act designed to highlight your topic or purpose. You can perform an action yourself, just as Juan did when he split a stack of boards with his hand to get attention for his speech on karate. Or you can ask volunteers from the audience to perform the action. For example, Cindria used three audience members to participate in breaking a piñata to create interest in her speech on the history of the piñata. If you choose to use audience members, consider soliciting participants ahead of time to avoid the possibility of having no volunteers when you ask during your speech. Finally, you can ask your entire audience to perform some action that is related to your speech topic. In her speech about acupressure, Andria asked her audience to perform this action as she modeled it for them:

> Take the thumb and index finger of your right hand and pinch the skin between the thumb and index finger of your left hand. What you've just done is stimulate a pressure point that can relieve headaches.

After piquing their interest with this action, Andria went on to state her purpose and preview her main points. If you'd like to ask your whole audience to perform an action, realistically assess whether what you are asking is something your audience is likely to comply with.

8. Create suspense. When you **create suspense,** you word your attention getter so that what is described generates uncertainty or mystery during the first few sentences and excites the audience. When you get the audience to ask, "What is she leading up to?" you hook them for the entire speech. The suspenseful opening is especially valuable when your audience is not particularly interested in hearing about your topic. Consider this suspenseful statement:

> It costs the United States more than $116 billion per year. It has cost the loss of more jobs than a recession. It accounts for nearly 100,000 deaths a year. I'm not talking about cocaine abuse—the problem is alcoholism. Today I want to show you how we can avoid this inhumane killer by abstaining from it.

Notice that by introducing the problem, alcoholism, at the end of the statement, the speaker encourages the audience to try to anticipate the answer. And since the audience may well be thinking that the problem is narcotics, the revelation that it is alcoholism is likely to be that much more effective.

For more tips about how to use these and other types of attention getters, use your CengageNOW for *Challenge* to access **Web Resource 8.1: Strategies for Introducing Speeches.**

ESTABLISH LISTENER RELEVANCE

Even if you successfully get the attention of your listeners, to *keep* their attention you will need to motivate them to listen to your speech. You can do this by creating a clear **listener relevance link,** a statement of how and why your speech relates to or might affect your audience. Sometimes, your attention-getting statement will serve this function, but if it doesn't, you will need to provide a personal connection between your topic and your audience. Notice how Tiffany improved her introduction when she created a listener relevance link by asking her audience to consider her topic in relation to their own lives:

> Although a diet rich in eggs and meat was once the norm in our country, more and more of us are choosing a vegetarian lifestyle to help lower blood pressure, reduce cholesterol, and even help prevent the onset of some diseases. So as I describe my experience, you may want to consider how *you* could alter your diet.

When creating a listener relevance link, answer these questions: Why should my listeners care about what I'm saying? In what way(s) might they benefit

creating suspense wording an attention getter so that what is described generates initial uncertainty or mystery and excites the audience

listener relevance link a statement of how and why your speech relates to or might affect your listeners

An effective speech introduction will not only get attention and lead into the body of the speech but will also build goodwill and set the tone for the speech. Telling a brief story is a popular and time-honored way to achieve these objectives.

© Bill Aron/PhotoEdit

from hearing about it? How might my speech relate to my listeners' needs or desires for health, wealth, well-being, self-esteem, success, and so forth?

STATE YOUR THESIS

Because audiences want to know what your speech is going to be about, it's important to state your thesis. Recall from Chapter 7 that your thesis statement introduces your audience to your general goal, specific goal, and main points. Thus, for his speech about romantic love, after Miguel gains attention and establishes relevance, he might draw from his thesis statement and say, "In the next five minutes, I'd like to explain to you that romantic love is comprised of three elements: passion, intimacy, and commitment." Stating your main points in the introduction is necessary unless you have some special reason for not revealing the details of the thesis. For instance, after getting the attention of his audience, Miguel might say, "In the next five minutes, I'd like to explain the three aspects of romantic love," a statement that specifies the number of main points but leaves the details for a preview statement that immediately precedes the main points.

Now let's consider two additional goals for your introduction if you have time in your speech.

ESTABLISH YOUR CREDIBILITY

If someone hasn't formally introduced you before you speak, audience members are going to wonder who you are and why they should pay attention to what you say. So, another goal of the introduction is to begin to build your credibility. For instance, if the audience is likely to question Miguel's qualifications for speaking on the topic of romantic love, after his attention-getting statement he might say, "As a child development and family science major, last semester I took an interdisciplinary seminar on romantic love, and now I'm doing an independent research project on commitment in relationships, so I feel comfortable talking with you about this topic." Remember, your goal is to highlight how you are a credible speaker on this topic, not that you are *the* or even *a* final authority on the subject.

CREATE A BOND OF GOODWILL

In your first few words, you influence how an audience will feel about you as a person. If you're enthusiastic, warm, and friendly and give a sense that what you're going to talk about is in the audience's best interest, it will make them feel more comfortable spending time listening to you.

For longer speeches, you may be able to accomplish all five goals in the introduction. But for shorter speeches, such as those you are likely to give in class, focus on the three primary goals: getting attention, establishing relevance, and stating your thesis. You can then try to build your credibility and develop goodwill as the speech moves along.

Selecting and Outlining an Introduction

Because the introduction is critical in establishing your relationship with your audience, it's worth investing the time to compare different openings. Try working on two or three different introductions; then pick the one you believe will work best for your specific audience and speech goal.

For instance, Emming created three introductions for his speech on evaluating credit cards. The first used a series of rhetorical questions to get attention:

Have you seen the number of agencies that have showered the campus with credit card applications? Sounds good, doesn't it? Take just a few minutes to fill out aapplication, and you'll be in control of your economic destiny. But wait a minute. The road down Consumer Credit Lane is not as smooth as the companies would have

Wendy Liebmann *How America Shops*

Wendy Liebmann is president and founder of WSL Strategic Retail, a marketing consulting firm that helps companies attract and retain shoppers. One of the services WSL Strategic Retail offers is inspirational forums in which Liebmann and her partner, Candace Corlett, give speeches "designed to stimulate ideas, drive action and motivate change within companies and among teams."* In a recent speech, Liebmann got the attention of her audience, members of the Non-Prescription Drug Manufacturers Association, with a series of rhetorical questions:

> Have you wondered of late what's going on with consumers? Why are they so full of contradictions when it comes to spending money? Why will they buy a $500 leather jacket at full price but wait for a $50 sweater to go on sale? Will buy a top-of-the-line sports utility vehicle then go to Costco to buy new tires? Will eagerly pay $3.50 for a cup of coffee but think $1.29 is too expensive for a hamburger? Will spend $2.00 for a strawberry-smelling bath soap but wait for a coupon to buy a $0.99 twin pack of toilet soap?

Next, she established listener relevance and set the tone of her speech:

> The economy is booming. Unemployment is at a 25-year low. Real income has increased. Why isn't everyone out spending like they did in the 1980s—shopping everywhere, buying everything? Why are so many companies struggling? What is this paradox? Is there a paradox?

Finally, she articulated her goal and previewed her main points in a two-sentence thesis. Interestingly, she provided additional listener relevance links in her final introductory remarks:

> Well, that's what we are going to talk about today. This apparent consumer paradox: what it is, what it means and how to make sense out of it. Because if we don't understand it and respond to it, there's a very good chance we won't attract the consumers we want, and a very, very good chance we won't build long-term profitable sales, and a very, very, very good chance we won't all be sitting here this time next year.**

Liebmann's 221-word introduction (about two minutes long) is the type of introduction that would work well for a speech that was ten to fifteen minutes long or even longer. Notice that the series of questions in the first paragraph touches on the behavior of many of us and even introduces some light humor. Right away, she is not only getting attention but also gaining goodwill. Moreover, her lighthearted approach sets the tone for her speech. Then notice that her second series of questions really starts to get the audience to think with her. Finally, notice that she concludes her introduction by telling her audience exactly how the body of her speech will address the questions she asks.

*"Inspirational Forums," *WSL Strategic Retail*, May 29, 2007. http://www.wslstrategicretail.com/services/inspirational.html.

**Wendy Liebmann, "How America Shops," *Vital Speeches*, July 15, 1998, 595.

you believe. Today I'm going to share with you the criteria gained from my reading and personal experience that you'll want to consider for selecting a credit card. (eighty-six words)

The second used a direct question followed by a rhetorical question to get attention:

> I'd like to see a show of hands. How many of you have been hounded by credit card vendors outside the Student Union? They make a credit card sound like the answer to all your dreams, don't they? Today I'm going to share with you the three criteria gained from my reading and personal experience that you'll want to consider for selecting a credit card. (sixty-five words)

The third used a famous quotation to get attention:

> P. T. Barnum once said, "There's a sucker born every minute." Although Barnum wasn't talking about signing up for a credit card, he could have been. Banks and credit unions shower us with incentives to get us to sign up, but we'd be wise to look before we leap. Today I'm going to share with you the criteria that you'll want to consider for selecting a credit card so that you won't end up being one of those "suckers." (seventy-nine words)

Each of these introductions is an appropriate length for a short speech. Which one do you prefer?

For her speech about obesity, Jamie created two introductions. The first used a personal reference for an attention getter. Notice, too, how she established listener relevance and credibility by citing the U.S. Department of Health and Human Services statistic before offering her thesis statement:

> Imagine a table full of all the food you eat in one week. That's a lot of food, right? Now, imagine eating all that food in one day! Believe it or not, there are people who do this. This condition, called binge eating, is contributing to a national epidemic: obesity. According to the U.S. Department of Health and Human Services, obesity may soon overtake tobacco as the leading cause of preventable death. In order to reduce obesity, let's examine the scope of the problem and its causes followed by some practical solutions. (ninety-two words)

Her second introduction used a startling statement and rhetorical question to get attention:

> Tom is a 135-pound male who enjoys playing computer games and loves pizza. Sounds like an average person, right? Well, what would you think if I told you that Tom is only six years old? Obesity is a serious problem in our society and warrants our attention. To prove my point, let's examine the scope of the problem and its causes followed by some practical solutions. (sixty-seven words)

Which of Jamie's introductions do you prefer? Why?

Whether or not your speech introduction meets all three of the primary goals directly, it should be long enough to put listeners in a frame of mind that will encourage them to hear you out, without being so long that it leaves too little time to develop the substance of your speech. Of course, the shorter the speech, the shorter the introduction.

The introduction will not make your speech an instant success, but it can get an audience to look at and listen to you and choose to focus on your topic. That is about as much as a speaker can ask of an audience during the first minute or two of a speech.

By completing Speech Planning Action Step 4, Activity 4E, Creating Speech Introductions, you will develop three choices for your speech introduction. The Student Response to Activity 4E provides an example of a student response to this activity.

SPEECH PLANNING ACTION STEP 4

ACTIVITY 4E Creating Speech Introductions

The goal of this activity is to create choices for how you will begin your speech.
1. For the speech body you outlined earlier, write three different introductions—using a startling statement, a question, a story, a personal reference, a joke, a quotation, action, or suspense—that you believe meet the primary goals of effective introductions and would be appropriate for your speech goal and audience.
2. Of the three introductions you drafted, which do you believe is the best? Why?
3. Write that introduction in outline form.

You can complete this activity online with Speech Builder Express, view a student sample of this activity, and if requested, e-mail your completed activity to your instructor. Use your CengageNOW for *Challenge* to access Activity 4E.

ACTIVITY 4E Creating Speech Introductions

1. For the speech body you outlined earlier, write three different introductions—using a startling statement, a question, a story, a personal reference, a joke, a quotation, action, or suspense—that you believe meet the goals of effective introductions and would be appropriate for your speech goal and audience.

    Specific goal: *I would like the audience to understand the three ways to tell if a diamond is real.*

    (1) *As Dr. Verderber mentioned earlier in the course, we are in the age group where buying or receiving diamonds might be on our minds. I would like to tell you how you can know for sure if your diamond is real.*

    (2) *Men, have you ever wondered if you would know if the diamond that the jeweler is trying to sell you is real? Ladies, have you ever wondered how you would be able to tell if your engagement ring is fake? Today, I am going to share some information that can help you answer these questions.*

    (3) *Calcite, quartz, cubic zirconia, diamond. How can you tell these minerals apart? They are all colorless and can sometimes look alike. But, let me tell you three ways that you can tell if you are holding a diamond.*

2. Of the three introductions you drafted, which do you believe is the best? Why?

    I believe the second one is the best because the rhetorical questions are likely to motivate the audience to listen and it leads into the body of the speech.

3. Write that introduction in outline form.

    I. *Men, have you ever wondered if you would know if the diamond that the jeweler is trying to sell you is real?*

    II. *Ladies, have you ever wondered how you would be able to tell if your engagement ring is fake?*

    III. *Today, I am going to tell you three ways to identify a real diamond.*

REFLECT ON ETHICS

While eating lunch together, Marna asked Gloria, "How are you doing in Woodward's speech class?"

"Not bad," Gloria replied. "I'm working on this speech about product development. I think it will be really informative, but I'm having a little trouble with the opening. I just can't seem to get a good idea for getting started."

"Why not start with a story—that always worked for me in class."

"Thanks, Marna, I'll think on it."

The next day, when Marna ran into Gloria again, she asked, "How's that introduction going?"

"Great. I've prepared a great story about Mary Kay—you know, the cosmetics woman? I'm going to tell about how she was terrible in school and no one thought she'd amount to anything. But she loved dabbling with cosmetics so much that she decided to start her own business—and the rest is history."

"That's a great story. I really like that part about being terrible in school. Was she really that bad?"

"I really don't know—the material I read didn't focus on that part of her life. But I thought that angle would get people listening right away. And after all, I did it that way because you suggested starting with a story."

"Yes, but . . ."

"Listen, she did start the business. So what if the story isn't quite right? It makes the point I want to make—if people are creative and have a strong work ethic, they can make it big."

1. What are the ethical issues here?
2. Is anyone really hurt by Gloria's opening the speech with this story?
3. What are the speaker's ethical responsibilities?

Creating the Conclusion

Shakespeare said, "All's well that ends well." A strong conclusion can heighten the impact of a good speech. Even though the conclusion will be a relatively short part of the speech—seldom more than 5 percent (thirty-five to forty-five words for a five-minute speech)—it is important that your conclusion be carefully planned.

The conclusion of a speech has two major goals. The first is to review the key ideas of the speech so that the audience remembers what you have said. The second is to provide a sense of closure that leaves the audience with a vivid impression so they will understand the importance of what you have said or be persuaded by your arguments.

Parts of the Conclusion

Just as with your speech introduction, prepare two or three conclusions and then choose the one you believe will be the most effective for your audience and speaking occasion. Each of your conclusions should include a summary of your speech goal and main points as well as a clincher, a final statement that helps drive your point home.

SUMMARY

Any effective speech conclusion will include a summary of your speech goal and main points. A summary for an informative speech on how to improve your grades might be, "So I hope you now understand *[informative goal]* that three techniques for helping you improve your grades are to attend classes regularly, to develop a positive attitude toward the course, and to study systematically *[main points]*." Likewise, a short summary for a persuasive speech on why you should lift weights might be, "So remember that three major reasons you should consider *[persuasive goal]* lifting weights are to improve your appearance, to improve your health, and to accomplish both with a minimum of effort *[main points]*."

The conclusion offers you one last chance to hit home with your point. Supplementing a summary with a quote or a short anecdote is often a good way of emphasizing what you want the audience to get from the speech.

© Ed Book/Corbis

CLINCHER

Although summaries help you achieve the first goal of an effective conclusion, you'll need to develop additional material designed to achieve the second goal: leaving your audience with a vivid impression. You can achieve this second goal with a **clincher**—a one- or two-sentence statement that provides a sense of closure by driving home the importance of your speech in a memorable way. Very often, effective clinchers also achieve closure by referring back to the introductory comments in some way. Two effective strategies for developing effective clinchers are using vivid imagery and appealing to action.

To develop vivid imagery in your clincher, you can use any of the devices we discussed for getting your audience's attention: startling statement, question, story, personal reference, joke, quotation, action, or suspense. For example, Emming's clincher drove home his point and referred back to his introduction:

> So, if you exercise care in examining interest rates, annual fee, and incentives, you can choose a credit card that's right for you. Then, your credit card truly may be the answer to your dreams.

In Tiffany's speech about being a vegetarian, she referred back to the personal reference she had made in her introduction about a vegetarian Thanksgiving meal:

> So now you know why I made the choice to become a vegetarian and how this choice affects my life today. As a vegetarian, I've discovered a world of food I never knew existed. Believe me, I am salivating just thinking about the meal I have planned for this Thanksgiving: fennel and blood orange salad; followed by baked polenta layered with tomato, fontina, and Gorgonzola cheeses; an acorn squash tart, marinated tofu; and with what else but pumpkin pie for dessert!

Sounds good doesn't it? Clinchers that foster vivid imagery are appropriate for both informative and persuasive speeches because they leave listeners with a vibrant picture imprinted in their minds.

The appeal to action is a common way to end some persuasive speeches. The **appeal to action** describes the behavior you want your listeners to follow after they have heard your arguments. Notice how David M. Walker, comptroller general of the United States, concludes his speech on fiscal responsibility with a strong appeal to action:

> The truth is that all sectors of society have a dog in this fiscal fight and transformation effort. If government stays on its current course, we'll all end up paying a big price, especially our kids and grandkids.
>
> Over its 200-plus years of existence, the United States has faced many great challenges. We've always risen to those challenges, and I'm confident we'll eventually do so this time as well. After all, it's always a mistake to underestimate American resolve when we set our mind to accomplish something.
>
> But we need to act, and act soon. Baby boomers like myself are on course to become the first generation of Americans who leave things in worse shape than when we found them. Fortunately, such a legacy isn't carved in stone. Turning things around won't be easy, and it's not going to happen overnight. But we all need to be part of the solution. By applying our collective energy, expertise, and experience to looming problems; by making some difficult decisions; and by accepting some degree of shared sacrifice, we can ensure a brighter future for this great nation, for our children and grandchildren, and for those who will follow them.[7]

Jamie drove home her point about obesity by referring back to her story about Tom and then offering an appeal to action:

> Without doubt, obesity is a serious problem that must be addressed by examining its causes and then constructing and implementing workable solutions. Together, we can help people like Tom overcome obesity. If we can, we must—before it's too late.

By their nature, appeals are most relevant for persuasive speeches, especially when the goal is to motivate an audience to act.

clincher a one- or two-sentence statement in a conclusion that provides a sense of closure by driving home the importance of your speech in a memorable way

appeal to action a statement in a conclusion that describes the behavior you want your listeners to follow after they have heard your arguments

Solomon D. Trujillo *Once Lost, Honor Cannot Be Replaced*

Solomon D. Trujillo, chief executive officer and a director of Telstra Corporation Limited, a telecommunications company, has been a well-respected business and community leader for almost thirty years. Committed to fostering and participating in good communication, Trujillo was awarded the prestigious Excellence in Communication Leadership Award (EXCEL) in 2000 by the International Association of Business Communicators, the highest honor the IABC awards to nonmembers. In a speech on corporate responsibility in the Hispanic business community, Trujillo ends with a clincher that dramatizes the importance of acting with honor in business and doing the right thing:

> In closing, there's an old tale called "The Four Elements" from the Hispanic Southwest by my friend Rudolfo Anaya that captures my message.

In the beginning, there were four elements on this earth, as well as in man. These basic elements in man and earth were Water, Fire, Wind and Honor. When the work of the creation was completed, the elements decided to separate, with each one seeking its own way. Water spoke first and said: "If you should ever need me, look for me under the earth and in the oceans." Fire then said: "If you should need me, you will find me in steel and in the power of the sun." Wind whispered: "If you should need me, I will be in the heavens among the clouds." Honor, the bond of life, said: "If you lose me, don't look for me again—you will not find me."

So it is for corporate responsibility. Once lost, honor cannot be replaced. It is the right thing to do . . . it is right for business . . . it is inseparable in our interdependent world. Let's act now to bring Hispanic issues to the forefront of America's agenda.*

*S. D. Trujillo. "The Hispanic Destiny: Corporate Responsibility," *Vital Speeches*, April 15, 2002, 406.

Selecting and Outlining a Conclusion

To determine how you will conclude your speech, create two or three conclusions; then choose the one you believe will best reinforce your speech goal with your audience.

For his short speech on evaluating credit cards, Emming created the following three variations of summaries for consideration. Which do you like best?

> Having a credit card gives you power—but only if you make a good choice. If you decide to apply for a credit card, you'll now be able to make an evaluation based upon sound criteria: interest rates, annual fee, and incentives. Then you can ignore the vendors outside the Student Union, knowing you've made the right choice.

> So, if you exercise care in examining interest rates, annual fee, and incentives, you can choose a credit card that's right for you. Then your credit card may truly be the answer to your dreams.

> Now you see the importance of making sure that you have examined interest rates, annual fee, and incentives before you select a credit card. And instead of having nightmares, you'll rest peacefully with the knowledge that the card you selected is the best one for you.

Because this first speech is relatively short, Emming decided to end his speech with just a couple of sentences. For speeches that are no longer than five minutes, a one- to three-sentence conclusion is often appropriate. You're likely to need as much time as possible to do a good job presenting your main points. But as speech assignments get longer, you'll want to consider supplementing the summary to give the conclusion more impact.

By completing Speech Planning Action Step 4, Activity 4F, Creating Speech Conclusions, you will develop choices for your speech conclusion. The Student Response to Activity 4F provides an example of one student's response to this activity.

ACTIVITY 4F Creating Speech Conclusions

The goal of this activity is to help you create choices for how you will conclude your speech.

1. For the speech body you outlined earlier, write three different conclusions that review important points you want the audience to remember and include a clincher that provides closure by leaving the audience with a vivid impression.
2. Which do you believe is the best? Why?
3. Write that conclusion in outline form.

You can complete this activity online with Speech Builder Express, view a student sample of this activity, and if requested, e-mail your completed activity to your instructor. Use your CengageNOW for *Challenge* to access Activity 4F.

CENGAGENOW™

ACTIVITY 4F Creating Speech Conclusions

1. For the speech body you outlined earlier, write three different conclusions that review important points you want the audience to remember and include a clincher that provides closure by leaving the audience with a vivid impression.

   Specific goal: I would like the audience to understand the three ways to tell if a diamond is real.

   (1) *So, the next time you buy or receive a diamond, you will know how to do the acid, streak, and hardness tests to make sure the diamond is real.*

   (2) *Before making your final diamond selection, make sure it can pass the acid test, streak test, and hardness test. Remember, you want to make sure you're buying a diamond—not paste!*

   (3) *You now know how to tell if your diamond is real. So, folks, if you discover that the gem you're considering effervesces in acid, has a streak that is not clear, or can be scratched, you will know that the person who tried to sell it to you is a crook!*

2. Which do you believe is the best? Why?

   The third one because it restates the characteristics and leaves a vivid impression.

3. Write that conclusion in outline form.

   I. *You now know how to tell if your diamond is real.*
   II. *If it effervesces, streaks, or scratches, the seller is a crook.*

Completing the Outline

At this point, you have a draft outline of your speech. To complete the outline, you will want to compile a list of the source material you will be drawing from in the speech, create a title (if required), and review your draft to make sure that the outline conforms to a logical structure.

Listing Sources

Regardless of the type of speech or how long or how short it will be, you'll want to prepare a list of the sources you are going to use in the speech. Although you may be required to prepare this list for the course you are taking, in real settings this list will enable you to direct audience members to the specific source of the information you have used and will allow you to quickly find the information at a later date. The two standard methods of organizing source lists are alphabetically by author's last name or by content category, with items listed alphabetically by author within each category. For speeches with a short list, the first method is efficient. But for long speeches with a lengthy source list, it is helpful to group sources by content categories.

Many formal bibliographical styles can be used in citing sources (for example, MLA, APA, *Chicago*, CBE); the "correct" form differs by professional or academic discipline. Check to see if your instructor has a preference about which style you use in class.

Regardless of the particular style, the specific information you need to record differs depending on whether the source is a book, a periodical, a newspaper, or an Internet source or website. The elements that are essential to all are author, title of article, name of publication, date of publication, and page numbers. Exhibit 8.1 gives examples of Modern Language Association (MLA) and American Psychological Association (APA) citations for the most commonly used types of sources. To view examples of common citations using the *Chicago Manual of Style*, Turabian, and American Medical Association (AMA) styles, use your CengageNOW for *Challenge* to access **Web Resource 8.2: Citation Styles**.

Speech Planning Action Step 4, Activity 4G, Compiling a List of Sources, helps you compile a list of sources used in your speech. The Student Response to Activity 4G provides an example of a student's response to this activity.

○ ○ ○		
△ △ △	**SPEECH PLANNING**	ACTION STEP 4
□ □ □		
4 | Organization		

ACTIVITY 4G Compiling a List of Sources

The goal of this activity is to help you record the list of sources you used in your speech.

1. Review your research cards, separating those whose information you have used in your speech from those whose information you have not used.
2. Note on your research card or your outline where you'll reference the source during your speech.
3. List the sources whose information was used in the speech by copying the bibliographical information recorded on the research card.
4. For short lists, organize your list alphabetically by the last name of the first author. Be sure to follow a form given in the text. If you did not record some of the bibliographical information on your note card, you will need to revisit the library, database, or other source to find it.

You can complete this activity online with Speech Builder Express, view a student sample of this activity, and if requested, e-mail your completed activity to your instructor. Use your CengageNOW for *Challenge* to access Activity 4G.

	MLA style	APA style
Book	Miller, Roberta B. *The Five Paths to Persuasion: The Art of Selling Your Message.* New York: Warner Business Books, 2004.	Miller, R. B. (2004). *The five paths to persuasion: The art of selling your message.* New York: Warner Business Books.
Edited book	Janzen, Rod. "Five Paradigms of Ethnic Relations." *Intercultural Communication.* 10th ed. Eds. Larry Samovar and Richard Porter. Belmont, CA: Wadsworth, 2003. 36–42.	Janzen, R. (2003). Five paradigms of ethnic relations. In L. Samovar & R. Porter, Eds., *Intercultural communication* (10th ed., pp. 36–42). Belmont, CA: Wadsworth.
Academic journal	Barge, J. Kevin. "Reflexivity and Managerial Practice." *Communication Monographs* 71 (Mar. 2004): 70–96.	Barge, J. K. (2004, March). Reflexivity and managerial practice. *Communication Monographs, 71,* 70–96.
Magazine	Krauthammer, Charles. "What Makes the Bush Haters So Mad?" *Time* 22 Sept. 2003: 84.	Krauthammer, C. (2003, September 22). What makes the Bush haters so mad? *Time,* 84.
Newspaper	Cohen, Richard. "Wall Street Scandal: Whatever the Market Will Bear." *The Cincinnati Enquirer* 17 Sept. 2003: C6.	Cohen, R. (2003, September 17). Wall Street scandal: Whatever the market will bear. *The Cincinnati Enquirer,* p. C6.
Electronic article based on print source	Friedman, Thomas L. "Connect the Dots." 25 Sept. 2003. *The New York Times.* 20 Aug. 2004 <http://www.nytimes.com/2003/09/25/opinion/25FRIED.html>.	Friedman, T. L. (2003, September 25). Connect the dots [Electronic version]. *The New York Times.* Retrieved August 20, 2006, from *http://www.nytimes.com/2003/09/25/opinion/25FRIED.html.*
Electronic article from Internet-only publication	Osterweil, Neil, and Michelle Smith. "Does Stress Cause Breast Cancer?" *Web M.D. Health.* 24 Sept. 2003. WebMD Inc. 20 Aug. 2004. <http://my.webmd.com/contents/article/74/89170.htm?z3734_00000_1000_ts_01>.	Osterweil, N., & Smith, M. (2003, September 24). Does stress cause breast cancer? *Web M.D. Health.* Retrieved August 20, 2006, from http://my.webmd.com/contents/article/74/89170.htm?z3734_00000_1000_ts_01.
Electronic article retrieved from database	Grabe, Mark. "Voluntary Use of Online Lecture Notes: Correlates of Note Use and Note Use as an Alternative to Class Attendance." *Computers and Education* 44 (2005): 409–21. ScienceDirect. Purdue U Lib., West Lafayette, IN. 28 May 2006 <http://www.sciencedirect.com/>.	Grabe, M. (2005). Voluntary use of online lecture notes: Correlates of note use and note use as an alternative to class attendance. *Computers and Education 44,* 409–421. Retrieved May 28, 2006, from ScienceDirect.
Movie	*Pirates of the Caribbean: Dead Man's Chest.* Dir. Gore Verbinksi. Perf. Johnny Depp, Orlando Bloom, Keira Knightly. 2006. DVD. The Walt Disney Company, 2007.	Bruckheimer, J. (Producer), & Verbinksi, G. (Director). (2006). *Pirates of the Caribbean: Dead man's chest* [Motion picture]. United States: Walt Disney Pictures.
Television program	"Truth Be Told." *Dexter.* Showtime. 10 Dec. 2006.	Manos, J., Jr. (Executive Producer). (2006, December 10). Truth be told. *Dexter* [Television series]. New York: Showtime Networks Inc.
Music recording	Nirvana. "Smells Like Teen Spirit." *Nevermind.* Geffen, 1991.	Nirvana. (1991). Smells like teen spirit. On *Nevermind* [CD]. Santa Monica, CA: Geffen.
Personal interview	Mueller, Bruno. Diamond cutter at Fegel's Jewelry. Personal Interview. 19 March 2004.	APA style dictates that no personal interview is included in a reference list. Rather, cite this type of source orally in your speech, mentioning the name of the person you interviewed and the date of the interview.

ACTIVITY 4G Compiling a List of Sources

1. Review your research cards, separating those whose information you have used in your speech from those whose information you have not used.
2. Note on your research card or your outline where you'll reference the source during your speech.
3. List the sources whose information was used in the speech by copying the bibliographical information recorded on the research card.
4. For short lists, organize your list alphabetically by the last name of the first author. Be sure to follow a form given in the text. If you did not record some of the bibliographical information on your note card, you will need to revisit the library, database, or other source to find it.

Sources

Dixon, Dougal. The Practical Geologist. New York: Simon & Schuster, 1992.

Farver, John. Professor of Geology. Personal Interview. 23 June 2004.

Klein, Cornelius. Manual of Mineralogy. 2nd ed. New York: John Wiley & Sons, 1993.

Montgomery, Carla W. Fundamentals of Geology. 3rd ed. Dubuque, IA: Wm. C. Brown, 1997.

Writing a Title

In many classroom situations, speeches are not required to have titles. But in most speech situations outside the classroom, it helps to have a title that lets the audience know what to expect. A title is probably necessary when you will be formally introduced, when the speech is publicized, or when the speech will be published. A good title helps to attract an audience and build interest in what you will say. Titles should be brief, descriptive of the content, and if possible, creative. Most speakers don't settle on a title until the rest of the speech preparation is complete.

Three kinds of titles can be created: a simple statement of subject, a question, or a creative title.

1. Simple statement of subject. This straightforward title captures the subject of the speech in a few words.

Courage to Grow

Selling Safety

The Dignity of Work

America's Destiny

2. Question. To spark greater interest, you can create a title by phrasing your speech goal as a question. A prospective listener may then be motivated to attend the speech to find out the answer.

Do We Need a Department of Play?

Are Farmers on the Way Out?

What Is the Impact of Computers on Our Behavior?

Are We Living in a Moral Stone Age?

3. Creative title. A more creative approach is to combine a familiar saying or metaphor with the simple statement of subject.

Teaching Old Dogs New Tricks: The Need for Adult Computer Literacy

Promises to Keep: Broadcasting and the Public Interest

The Tangled Web: How Environmental Climate Has Changed

Freeze or Freedom: On the Limits of Morals and Worth of Politics

The simple statement of subject gives a clear idea of the topic but is not especially eye- or ear-catching. Questions and creative titles capture interest but may not give a clear idea of content. Creative titles often require subtitles.

Reviewing the Outline

Now that you have created all of the parts of the outline, it is time to put them together in complete outline form and edit them to make sure the outline is well organized and well worded. Use this checklist to complete the final review of the outline before you move into adaptation and rehearsal.

1. Have I used a standard set of symbols to indicate structure? Main points are indicated by Roman numerals, major subdivisions by capital letters, minor subheadings by Arabic numerals, and further subdivisions by lowercase letters.

2. Have I written main points and major subdivisions as complete sentences? Complete sentences help you to see (1) whether each main point actually develops your speech goal and (2) whether the wording makes your intended point. Unless the key ideas are written out in full, it will be difficult to follow the next guidelines.

3. Do main points and major subdivisions each contain a single idea? This guideline ensures that the development of each part of the speech will be relevant to the point. Thus, if your outline contains a point like this:

I. The park is beautiful and easy to get to.

Divide the sentence so that the two parts are separate:

I. The park is beautiful.

II. The park is easy to get to.

Sort out distinct ideas so that when you line up supporting material you can have confidence that the audience will see and understand its relationship to the main points.

4. Does each major subdivision relate to or support its major point? This principle, called subordination, ensures that you don't wander off point and confuse your audience. For example:

I. Proper equipment is necessary for successful play.

A. Good gym shoes are needed for maneuverability.

B. Padded gloves help protect your hands.

C. A lively ball provides sufficient bounce.

D. And a good attitude doesn't hurt.

Notice that the main point deals with equipment. A, B, and C (shoes, gloves, and ball) all relate to the main point. But D, attitude, is not equipment and should appear somewhere else, if at all.

5. Are potential subdivision elaborations indicated? Recall that it is the subdivision elaborations that help to build the speech. Because you don't know how long it might take you to discuss these elaborations, it is a good idea to include more than you are likely to use. During rehearsals, you may discuss each a different way.

6. Does the outline include no more than one-third the total number of words anticipated in the speech? An outline is only a skeleton of the speech—not a complete manuscript with letters and numbers attached. The outline should be short enough to allow you to experiment with different methods of development during practice periods and to adapt to audience reaction during the speech itself. An easy way to judge whether your outline is about the right length is to estimate the number of words that you are likely to speak during the actual speech and compare this to the number of words in the outline (counting only the words in the outline minus speech goal, thesis statement, headings, and list of sources). Because approximate figures are all you need, start by assuming an average speaking rate of 160 words per minute. (Last term, the speaking rate for the majority of speakers in my class was 140 to 180 words per minute.) Thus, a three- to five-minute speech would contain roughly 480 to 800 words, and the outline should be 160 to 300 words. An eight- to ten-minute speech, roughly 1,300 to 1,600 words, should have an outline of approximately 430 to 530 words.

Now that we have considered the various parts of an outline, let us put them together for a final look. The outline in Exhibit 8.2 illustrates the principles in practice. The commentary in the margin relates each part of the outline to the guidelines we have discussed.

4 | Organization	**SPEECH PLANNING**	ACTION STEP 4

ACTIVITY 4H Completing the Speech Outline

CENGAGENOW™

Write and review a complete-sentence outline of your speech using material you've developed so far with the Action Steps in Chapters 4 to 8. You can complete this activity online with Speech Builder Express, view a student sample of this activity, and if requested, e-mail your completed activity to your instructor. Use your Cengage-NOW for *Challenge* to access Activity 4H. For this activity, Emming's complete outline (Exhibit 8.2) will serve as the student response.

Summary

The organization process is completed by creating an introduction and a conclusion, listing the sources you used in the speech, writing a title (if required), and reviewing the draft outline. An effective speech introduction gets audience attention, establishes listener relevance, and introduces the thesis; it may also establish credibility and create goodwill.

A well-designed speech conclusion summarizes the speech goal and main points and leaves the audience with a vivid impression. Informative and persuasive speeches may leave an impression with a clincher, a one- or two-sentence statement that provides a sense of closure by driving home the importance of your speech in a memorable way. Two strategies for effective clinchers are using vivid imagery and appealing to action.

A good outline also includes a list of sources compiled from the bibliographical information recorded on research cards. Short lists are alphabetized

EXHIBIT 8.2 Sample complete outline

General goal: I want to inform my audience.

Specific goal: I would like the audience to understand the major criteria for finding a suitable credit card.

Write your general and specific goals at the top of the page. Refer to the goals to test whether everything in the outline is relevant.

Thesis statement: Three criteria that will enable audience members to find the credit card that is most suitable for them are level of real interest rate, annual fee, and advertised incentives.

The thesis statement states the elements that are suggested in the specific goal. In the speech, the thesis serves as a forecast of the main points.

Introduction

I. How many of you have been hounded by credit card vendors outside the Student Union?

II. They make a credit card sound like the answer to all of your dreams, don't they?

III. Today I want to share with you three criteria you need to consider carefully before deciding on a particular credit card: interest rate, annual fee, and advertised incentives.

The heading *Introduction* sets the section apart as a separate unit. The introduction attempts to (1) get attention and (2) lead into the body of the speech as well as establish credibility, set a tone, and gain goodwill.

Body

I. The first criterion for choosing a credit card is to select a card with a low interest rate.

The heading *Body* sets this section apart as a separate unit. In this example, main point I begins a topical pattern of main points. It is stated as a complete sentence.

A. Interest rates are the percentages that a company charges you to carry a balance on your card past the due date.
   1. Most credit cards carry an average of 8 percent.
   2. Some cards carry as much as 32 percent.
   3. Many companies offer 0 percent interest rates for up to twelve months.
   4. Student credit cards typically have higher interest rates.
   5. Some student credit cards carry APRs below 14 percent.

The two main subdivisions designated by A and B indicate the equal weight of these points. The second-level subdivisions—designated by 1, 2, 3, 4, and 5 for major subpoint A, and 1, 2, and 3 for major subpoint B—give the necessary information for understanding the subpoints.

B. Interest rates can be variable or fixed.
   1. Variable rates mean that the rate can change from month to month.
   2. Fixed rates mean that the rate will stay the same.
   3. Even cards with fixed rates can be raised to as much as 32 percent if you make a late payment.

The number of major and second-level subpoints is at the discretion of the speaker. After the first two levels of subordination, words and phrases may be used in place of complete sentences for elaboration.

(*Transition:* Now that we have considered interest rates, let's look at the next criterion.)

This transition reminds listeners of the first main point and forecasts the second.

(*continued*)

EXHIBIT 8.2 Sample complete outline (*continued*)

Main point II, continuing the topical pattern, is a complete sentence that parallels the wording of main point I. Notice that each main point considers only one major idea.

This transition summarizes the first two criteria and forecasts the third.

Main point III, continuing the topical pattern, is a complete sentence paralleling the wording of main points I and II.

Throughout the outline, notice that main points and subpoints are factual statements. The speaker adds examples, experiences, and other developmental material during practice sessions.

The heading *Conclusion* sets this section apart as a separate unit. The content of the conclusion is intended to summarize the main ideas and leave the speech on a high note. The conclusion also provides closure by referring back to the idea mentioned in the introduction, a credit card is the answer to your dreams.

A list of sources should always be a part of the speech outline. The sources should show where the factual material of the speech came from. The list of sources is not a total of all sources available—only those that were used, directly or indirectly. Each of the sources is shown in proper form.

II. A second criterion for choosing a credit card is to select a card with no annual fee.
  A. The annual fee is the cost the company charges you for extending you credit.
  B. The charges vary widely.
    1. Most cards have no annual fee.
    2. Some companies still charge fees.

(*Transition:* After you have considered interest and fees, you can weigh the incentives that the company promises you.)

III. A third criterion for choosing a credit card is to weigh the incentives.
  A. Incentives are extras that you get for using a particular card.

    1. Some companies promise rebates.
    2. Some companies promise frequent flyer miles.
    3. Some companies promise discounts on "a wide variety of items."
    4. Some companies promise "cash back" on your purchases.
  B. Incentives don't outweigh other criteria.

Conclusion
I. So, if you exercise care in examining interest rates, annual fees, and incentives, you can choose the credit card that's right for you.
II. Then your credit card may truly be the answer to your dreams.

Sources
Bankrate Monitor, http://www.Bankrate.com.
Barrett, Lois. "Good Credit 101," *Black Enterprise,* Oct. 2006,

by authors' last names. Longer source lists group sources by content category before alphabetizing by author.

Although most classroom speeches may not require a title, in most speech situations outside the classroom it helps to have an informative and appealing title. Three kinds of titles are the simple statement of subject, the question, and the creative title.

The complete draft outline should be reviewed and revised to make sure that you have used a standard set of symbols, used complete sentences for main points and major subdivisions, limited each point to a single idea, related minor points to major points, and limited the outline length to no more than one-third the number of words of the final speech.

CHALLENGE ONLINE

Now that you've read Chapter 8, use your Cengage-NOW for *The Challenge of Effective Speaking* for quick access to the electronic resources that accompany this text. Your CengageNOW gives you access to the Web Resources and Speech Planning activities featured in this chapter, Speech Builder Express, Info-Trac College Edition, and online study aids such as a digital glossary and review quizzes.

Your *Challenge* CengageNOW is an online study system that helps you identify concepts you don't

fully understand, allowing you to put your study time to the best use. Using chapter-by-chapter diagnostic pretests, the system creates a personalized study plan for each chapter. Each plan directs you to specific resources designed to improve your understanding, including pages from the text in e-book format. Chapter posttests give you an opportunity to measure how much you've learned and let you know if you are ready for graded quizzes and exams.

KEY TERMS

Go to your CengageNOW for *Challenge* to access your online glossary for Chapter 8. Print a copy of the glossary for this chapter and test yourself with

the electronic flash cards or complete the crossword puzzle to help you master these key terms:

action (144)
appeal to action (151)
clincher (151)
creating suspense (145)
direct question (142)

joke (143)
listener relevance link (145)
personal reference (143)
primacy-recency effect (141)
quotation (144)

rhetorical question (142)
startling statement (142)
story (142)

WEB RESOURCES

Go to your CengageNOW for *Challenge* to access the Web Resources for this chapter.

8.1 Strategies for Introducing Speeches (145)

8.2 Citation Styles (154)

Access the Action Step activities for this chapter online at your CengageNOW for *Challenge*. Select the chapter resources for Chapter 8 and then click the activity number you want. You may print your completed activities, and you should save your work so you can use it as needed in later Action Step activities.

4E Creating Speech Introductions (148) **4G Compiling a List of Sources** (154) **4H Completing the Speech Outline** (158)
4F Creating Speech Conclusions (153)

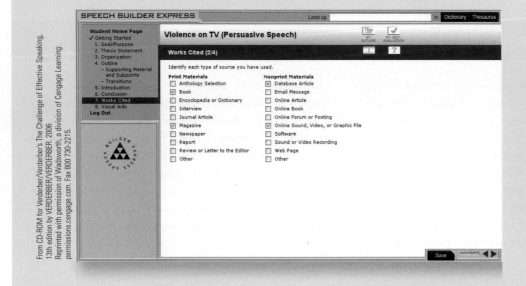

From CD-ROM for Verderber/Verderber's The Challenge of Effective Speaking, 13th edition by VERDERBER/VERDERBER. 2006 Reprinted with permission of Wadsworth, a division of Cengage Learning: permissions.cengage.com. Fax 800 730-2215.

tructing and Using Presentational Aids

A picture is worth a thousand words.

What's Ahead

HERE'S WHAT'S AHEAD IN THIS CHAPTER:

1. Why should you incorporate presentational aids into your speech?

2. What types of presentational aids can you choose from?

3. What are some important considerations to keep in mind when preparing a computerized slide show?

4. Why is it important to limit how much information you include on your presentational aids?

5. What should you consider when you practice presenting with your presentational aids?

"How's it going with the speech, Jeremy?"

"I'm frustrated."

"Why's that?"

"Well, I know we're supposed to think about using visual material with this speech. But I can't think of what I could depict that would be useful."

"What's your topic?"

"Effects of media violence, but I don't see any sense in showing any act of violence."

"Right, but there are lots of other visuals you could show that would be helpful."

"Like what?"

"Well, I'll bet that you're using some statistics about the amount of violence."

"Sure."

"Well, couldn't you show the statistics while you talked about them?"

"But wouldn't showing statistics be just as boring as talking about them?"

Jeremy makes a good point. Just presenting some statistics probably *would* be boring. But the question he really needs to answer is this: How could he use images, audio materials, or audiovisual materials to present those statistics so that the audience would attend to and remember them?

Although there are times when additional materials may not be necessary, we are living in an era when the verbal and visual modes of communicating are merging. Whether it is a TV news program, your professor's lecture, or a sermon you hear at a place of worship, speeches are being fused with media. In business, law, and education, audiences have come to expect computer-enhanced presentations. So you can anticipate facing audiences that expect you to present your ideas in images as well as words.[1] This chapter focuses on identifying, choosing, preparing, and displaying a variety of visual, audio, and audiovisual materials that can accompany your verbal speech and are adapted to your specific audience.

A **presentational aid** is any visual, audio, or audiovisual material used in a speech. The most common form of presentational aid is a **visual aid**—a form of speech development that allows the audience to see as well as hear information. There are several benefits to using presentational aids. First, they enable you to adapt to an audience's level of knowledge by clarifying and dramatizing your verbal message. Second, presentational aids help audiences retain the information they hear. Research has shown that people are likely to remember features of presentational aids even over long periods and that people are likely to learn considerably more when ideas appeal to *both* the eye and the ear.[2] Third, presentational aids enable you to address the diverse learning styles of your audience.[3] Fourth, they can increase the persuasive appeal of your speech. In fact, some research suggests that speakers who use visual aids in their presentations are almost twice as likely to persuade listeners than those who do not.[4] Finally, using presentational aids may help you to feel more com-

presentational aid any visual, audio, or audiovisual material used in a speech

visual aid a form of speech development that allows the audience to see as well as hear information

petent. Speakers report that when they use presentational aids, they tend to be less anxious and have more confidence.[5]

In this chapter, we describe various types of presentational aids, criteria for making choices about which and how many presentational aids to use, ways of designing aids, methods for displaying aids, and guidelines for using them effectively in your speech.

Types of Presentational Aids

Before you can choose what presentational aids you might want to use for a specific speech, you need to recognize the various types of aids that you can choose from. Presentational aids range from those that are simple to use and readily available from some existing source to those that must be custom produced for your specific speech and require practice to use effectively. In this section, we describe types of presentational aids to consider using as you prepare your speech.

Actual Objects

Actual objects are inanimate or animate physical samples of the idea you are communicating. Inanimate objects make good visual aids if they are (1) large enough to be seen by all audience members, (2) small enough to carry to the site of the speech, (3) simple enough to understand visually, and (4) safe. A volleyball or Muslim prayer rug would be appropriate in size for most classroom audiences. A cell phone might be okay if the speech goal is simply to show what a cell phone looks like, but it is probably too small if you want to demonstrate how to use the phone's specialized functions.

Some animate objects also make effective visual aids. For example, on occasion, *you* can be an effective visual aid. For instance, you can use descriptive gestures to show the height of a tennis net; you can use posture and movement to show the motions involved in swinging a golf club; or you can use your attire to illustrate the native dress of a particular country. Sometimes, it can be appropriate to use another person as a visual aid, such as when Jenny used a friend of hers to demonstrate the Heimlich maneuver. Animals can also be effective visual aids. For example, Josh used his AKC Obedience Champion dog to demonstrate the basics of dog training. But keep in mind that animals placed in unfamiliar settings can become difficult to control and can distract from your message.

Models

When an object's size is inappropriate, too complex to understand visually, potentially unsafe, or uncontrollable, a model of the object can be an effective visual aid. A **model** is a three-dimensional scaled-down or scaled-up version of an actual object that may be simplified to aid understanding. In a speech on the physics of bridge construction, a scale model of a suspension bridge would be an effective visual aid. Likewise, in a speech on genetic engineering, a model of the DNA double helix might help the audience understand what happens during microscopic procedures.

Photographs

If an exact reproduction of material is needed, still photographs can be excellent visual aids. In a speech on "smart weapons," before and after photos of target sites would be effective in helping the audience to understand the pinpoint

SPEECH SNIPPET

Avoiding Unsafe Presentational Aids

Lenny wanted to use a twelve-gauge shotgun as a visual aid for his speech on safety practices for hunters. After talking with his instructor, he realized that not only would a shotgun raise safety concerns in class, but it is illegal to bring a gun to campus.

SPEECH SNIPPET

Using an Animal as a Visual Aid

Josey wanted to use her cat as a visual aid for her speech on pet therapy. To avoid having the cat panic and distract her audience from her message, she brought the cat to class in a carrier, sat with him quietly while a few of her classmates gave their speeches so he could get used to the room, and returned him to the carrier after she discussed her first main point.

SPEECH SNIPPET

Using a Photograph as a Visual Aid

In her speech about traditional Muslim dress for women, Marjie projected photographs of Muslim women wearing various types of traditional attire as she explained the cultural significance of the clothing.

actual object an inanimate or animate sample of the idea you are communicating

model a three-dimensional scaled-down or scaled-up version of an actual object

accuracy of these weapons. When choosing photographs, be sure that the image is large enough for the audience to see and that the object of interest in the photo is clearly identified and, ideally, in the foreground. For example, if you are giving a speech about your grandmother and show a photo of her with her college graduating class, you might circle her image so she's easily seen.

Simple Drawings and Diagrams

Simple drawings and diagrams are easy to prepare. If you can use a compass, a straightedge, and a measure, you can draw well enough to prepare a simple diagram. Or with a little practice, you can use a basic computer drawing program to prepare the same drawing. For instance, if you are making the point that water skiers must hold their arms straight, their backs straight, and their knees slightly bent, a stick figure will illustrate the point sufficiently (see Exhibit 9.1). Stick figures may not be as aesthetically pleasing as professional drawings or photographs, but they can still be quite effective. In fact, elaborate, detailed drawings may not be worth the time and effort, and actual photographs may be so detailed that they obscure the point you wish to make. Likewise, a simple **diagram**, a type of drawing that shows how the whole relates to its parts, can be more effective than a photograph because you can choose how much detail to include. Andria's representation of the human body and its pressure points is an example of an effective diagram that clarified her message and helped her meet her speech goal (see Exhibit 9.2).

Maps

Like drawings, maps are relatively easy to prepare. Simple maps allow you to orient audiences to landmarks (mountains, rivers, and lakes), states, cities, land routes, weather systems, and so on. Commercial maps are available, but simple maps can be customized so that audience members are not confused by visual information that is irrelevant to your purpose. Exhibit 9.3 on page 168 shows a map that focuses on weather systems.

Viewing a visual aid, such as a model, can help the audience understand your topic. In this photo, architecture students at the University of Southwestern Louisiana gather around their instructor to view a novel design.

© Philip Gould/Corbis

diagram a type of drawing to show the whole and its parts

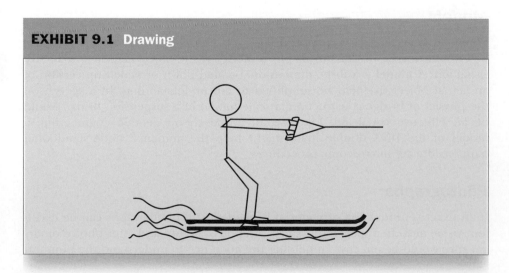

EXHIBIT 9.1 Drawing

Karen planned to give her speech on late-term "partial birth" abortions. As she thought about the content of her speech, she decided to go on the Web to see whether she could come up with any visual ideas. As she searched the links, she found a picture of an aborted fetus. She downloaded it onto her computer and into her PowerPoint file. Later that day, she talked with Paula about how she planned to use the image.

"Wow," Paula replied, "That'll make quite an impression. Go for it."

As Karen rehearsed her speech, she still wondered whether using that particular visual aid was a good idea. But with Paula's apparent encouragement, she went ahead and used it in her speech.

When the audience critiqued Karen's speech in class, one classmate raised the question of the ethics of showing graphic pictures such as aborted fetuses, mutilated bodies, and pornographic images in a speech.

1. Is the use of disquieting graphic images unethical?
2. What ethical arguments support the use of disquieting graphic images?
3. What arguments would hold the use of these images to be unethical?
4. What do you believe is the ethical principle you will follow in making decisions like this?

EXHIBIT 9.2 Diagram

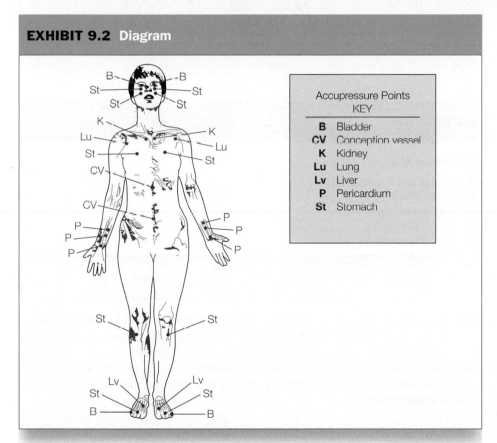

Accupressure Points
KEY

B	Bladder
CV	Conception vessel
K	Kidney
Lu	Lung
Lv	Liver
P	Pericardium
St	Stomach

Charts

A **chart** is a graphic representation that distills a lot of information and presents it to an audience in an easily interpreted visual format. Word charts, flowcharts, and organizational charts are the most common types of charts. A **word chart** is used to preview, review, or highlight important ideas covered in a speech. In a speech on Islam, a speaker might make a word chart that lists the five pillars of Islam, as shown in Exhibit 9.4 on page 168. A **flowchart** uses symbols and

chart a graphic representation that distills a lot of information and presents it to an audience in an easily interpreted visual format

word chart a chart used to preview, review, or highlight important ideas covered in a speech

flowchart a chart that diagrams a sequence of steps through a complicated process

EXHIBIT 9.3 Map

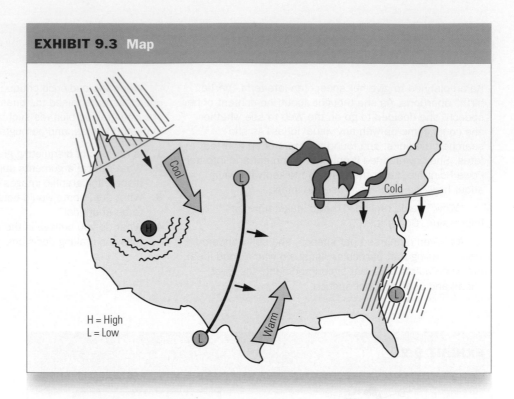

Cool

Cold

H = High
L = Low

Warm

EXHIBIT 9.4 Word chart

Five Pillars of Islam

1. Shahadah: Witness to Faith
2. Salat: Prayer
3. Sawm: Fasting
4. Zakat: Almsgiving
5. Hajj: Pilgrimage

organizational chart a chart that shows the structure of an organization in terms of rank and chain of command

graph a diagram that presents numerical comparisons

bar graph a diagram that uses vertical or horizontal bars to show relationships between two or more variables at the same time or at various times on one or more dimensions

line graph a diagram that indicates changes in one or more variables over time

connecting lines to diagram a sequence of steps through a complicated process. Tim used a flowchart to help listeners move through the sequence of steps to determine whether they might be overweight (see Exhibit 9.5). An **organizational chart** shows the structure of an organization in terms of rank and chain of command. The chart in Exhibit 9.6 on page 170 illustrates the organization of a student union board.

Graphs

A **graph** is a diagram that presents numerical comparisons. Bar graphs, line graphs, and pie graphs are the most common forms of graphs.

A **bar graph** is a diagram that uses vertical or horizontal bars to show relationships between two or more variables at the same time or at various times on one or more dimensions. For instance, Jacqueline used a bar graph to compare the amounts of caffeine found in one serving each of chocolate, coffee, tea, and cola (see Exhibit 9.7 on page 170).

A **line graph** is a diagram that indicates changes in one or more variables over time. In a speech on the population of the United States, for example, the

EXHIBIT 9.5 Flowchart

Assessing Your Weight

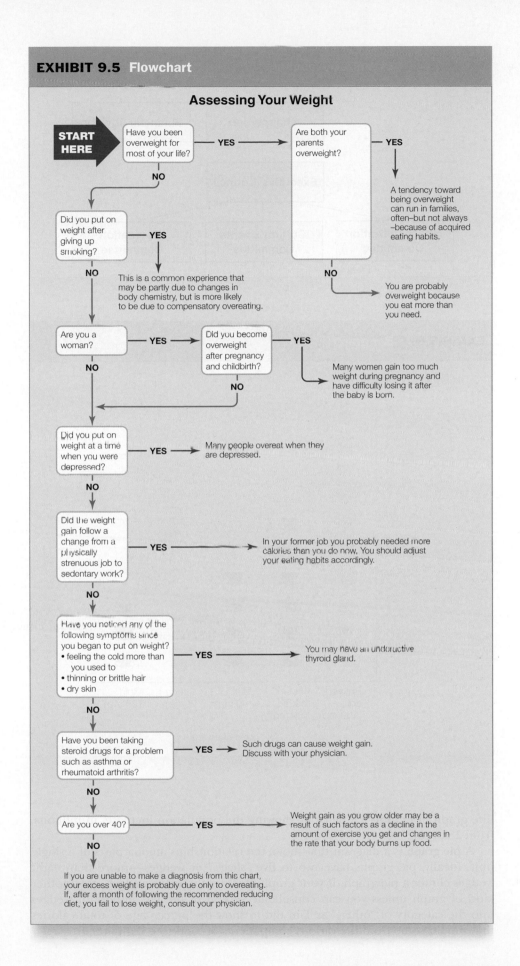

START HERE → Have you been overweight for most of your life? —**YES**→ Are both your parents overweight? —**YES**→

NO↓

A tendency toward being overweight can run in families, often–but not always –because of acquired eating habits.

Did you put on weight after giving up smoking? —**YES**→

This is a common experience that may be partly due to changes in body chemistry, but is more likely to be due to compensatory overeating.

NO (parents) → You are probably overweight because you eat more than you need.

NO↓

Are you a woman? —**YES**→ Did you become overweight after pregnancy and childbirth? —**YES**→

Many women gain too much weight during pregnancy and have difficulty losing it after the baby is born.

NO↓

Did you put on weight at a time when you were depressed? —**YES**→ Many people overeat when they are depressed.

NO↓

Did the weight gain follow a change from a physically strenuous job to sedentary work? —**YES**→ In your former job you probably needed more calories than you do now, You should adjust your eating habits accordingly.

NO↓

Have you noticed any of the following symptoms since you began to put on weight?
• feeling the cold more than you used to
• thinning or brittle hair
• dry skin
—**YES**→ You may have an underactive thyroid gland.

NO↓

Have you been taking steroid drugs for a problem such as asthma or rheumatoid arthritis? —**YES**→ Such drugs can cause weight gain. Discuss with your physician.

NO↓

Are you over 40? —**YES**→ Weight gain as you grow older may be a result of such factors as a decline in the amount of exercise you get and changes in the rate that your body burns up food.

NO↓

If you are unable to make a diagnosis from this chart, your excess weight is probably due only to overeating. If, after a month of following the recommended reducing diet, you fail to lose weight, consult your physician.

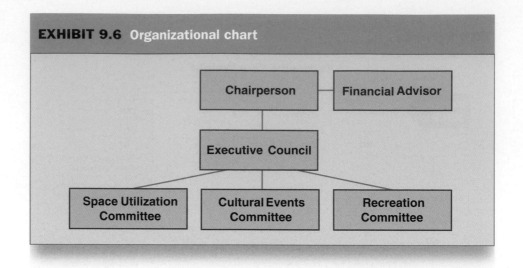

EXHIBIT 9.6 Organizational chart

Chairperson — Financial Advisor

Executive Council

Space Utilization Committee | Cultural Events Committee | Recreation Committee

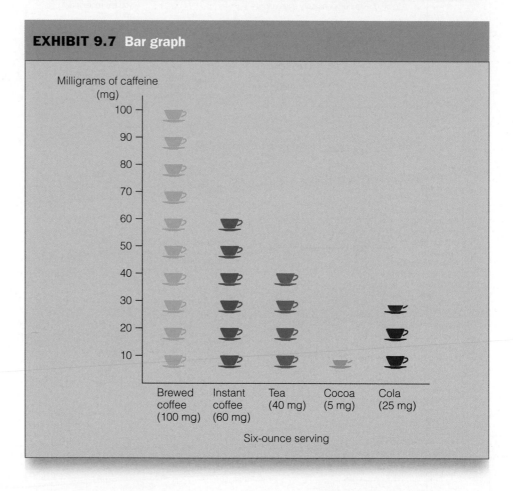

EXHIBIT 9.7 Bar graph

Milligrams of caffeine (mg)

100
90
80
70
60
50
40
30
20
10

Brewed coffee (100 mg) | Instant coffee (60 mg) | Tea (40 mg) | Cocoa (5 mg) | Cola (25 mg)

Six-ounce serving

line graph in Exhibit 9.8 helps by showing the population increase, in millions, from 1810 to 2000.

A **pie graph** is a diagram that shows the relationships among parts of a single unit. Ideally, pie graphs have two to five "slices," or wedges—more than eight wedges clutter a pie graph. If your graph includes too many wedges, use another kind of graph unless you can consolidate several of the less important wedges into the category of "other," as Tim did to show the percentage of total calories that should come from the various components of food (see Exhibit 9.9).

pie graph a diagram that shows the relationships among parts of a single unit

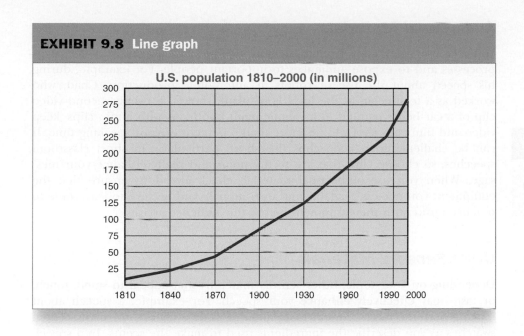

EXHIBIT 9.8 Line graph

U.S. population 1810–2000 (in millions)

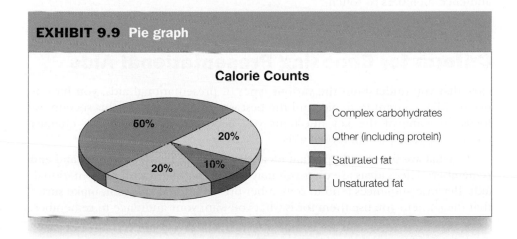

EXHIBIT 9.9 Pie graph

Calorie Counts

- Complex carbohydrates
- Other (including protein)
- Saturated fat
- Unsaturated fat

Audio Materials

Audio materials enhance a verbal message through sound. They are especially useful when it is difficult, if not impossible, to describe a sound in words. For example, in David's speech about the three types of trumpet mutes and how they alter the sounds a trumpet makes, he played his trumpet so listeners could hear what he meant. If you don't want to make your own sounds, you can use audiotaped excerpts from sources such as famous speeches, radio programs, interviews, and recordings of music or environmental sounds, all of which may convey information better than your describing the material or reading it as a quotation. For example, Susan chose to begin her speech on the future of the NASA space program with a recording of Neil Armstrong's first words as he stepped on the surface of the moon: "That's one small step for a man, one giant leap for mankind." Before using audio material, make sure you have enough time to present it (it should make up no more than about 5 percent of your speaking time) and that you have access to a quality sound system.

Audiovisual Materials

You can use short clips from films and videos to demonstrate concepts or processes and to expose audiences to important people. For example, during his speech about the use of robots in automobile production, Chad, who worked as a technician at the local Ford plant, showed a twenty-second video clip of a car being painted in a robotic paint booth. As with audio clips, keep video and film clips short, to no more than 5 percent of your speaking time. It can be challenging to keep clips this short, particularly in short classroom speeches, so choose clips that are to the point and really enhance your message. When you use audiovisual material, check ahead to ensure that the equipment you need is available and operational. And be sure to leave time to practice onsite with the equipment before the audience arrives.

Other Sensory Materials

Depending on your topic, other sensory materials that appeal to smell, touch, or taste may effectively enhance your speech. For example, a speech about making perfume might benefit from allowing your audience to smell scented swatches as you describe the ingredients used to make the scents. In a speech about Braille, Javier handed out copies of his outline written in Braille for audience members to touch.

Criteria for Choosing Presentational Aids

Now that you understand the various types of presentational aids, you have to decide what content to depict and the best way to present it. In this section, we focus on some of the key questions you need to answer to make effective choices for your presentational aids.

1. What are the most important ideas the audience needs to understand and remember? These ideas are ones you may want to highlight with presentational aids. Because audiences tend to remember presentational aids well, make sure that the content you use them for is what you want your audience to remember.

2. Are there ideas that are complex or difficult to explain verbally but easy to understand in visual or audio form? The old saying "One picture is worth a thousand words" is true. For example, demonstrating the correct way to hold a golf club is much easier and clearer than describing the position of each hand and finger.

3. How many presentational aids should I use? Unless you are narrating a slide show in which the total focus of the speech is on visual images, the number of presentational aids you use should be limited so the focus of the audience is on you, the speaker. In addition, you can avoid diluting the impact of your aids by using them only to hold attention, exemplify an idea, or help the audience remember a concept. In a five-minute speech, using just three to five presentational aids is far more effective than using more.

4. Are my presentational aids easy to use and transport? Choose aids that you feel comfortable using and that are easy to transport from home to your speaking site. You want to focus on the content and delivery of your speech, not on how nervous you are using a new technology or transporting a cumbersome or fragile presentational aid.

5. How large is the audience? The kinds of presentational aids that will work for a small group of fifteen or twenty differ from the kinds that will work for an audience of a hundred or more. For an audience of fewer than twenty, as in most of your classroom speeches, you can show relatively small objects and use relatively small models that everyone will be able to see. For larger audiences, you'll want projections that can be seen with ease from 100 or 200 feet away.

6. Is the necessary equipment readily available? At times, you may be speaking in an environment that is not equipped for certain displays. At many colleges and universities, most rooms are equipped with only a chalkboard, an overhead projector, and electrical outlets. Anything else you want to use you will have to bring yourself or schedule through the appropriate school media office. Be prepared! In any situation in which you have scheduled equipment from an outside source, you need to prepare yourself for the possibility that the equipment may not arrive on time or may not work the way you anticipated. Call ahead, get to your speaking location early, practice using your presentational aids with the available equipment, and have an alternative presentational aid to use, just in case.

7. Is there sufficient time to show the aid without having it overtake the speech itself? Remember that presentational aids are meant to supplement and enhance your speech, not replace it. If sharing the aid will take too much time, consider a different sort of aid.

8. Is the time involved in making or getting the presentational aid and equipment cost-effective? Presentational aids are supplements. Their goal is to accent what you are doing verbally. If you believe that a particular aid will help you better achieve your goal, then the time spent is well worth it. You'll notice that most of the presentational aids we've discussed can be obtained or prepared relatively easily. But because some procedures are "so easy," we find ourselves getting lost in making some of them. Presentational aids definitely make a speech more interesting and engaging. However, the best advice we can offer is to "keep it simple."

Designing Effective Presentational Aids

However simple you plan to make your presentational aids, keep in mind that you still have to take the time to design and produce them carefully. You may need to find or create charts, graphs, diagrams, maps, or drawings. You may need to search for and prepare photographs. You may choose to look for audio or video snippets and then need to convert them to a format that you can use at your speech site.

As you approach your design task, you must first determine whether you will design your aids by hand or by using computer presentation software. Depending on the resources available in your classroom, your instructor may stipulate how you are to prepare your presentational aids. Or you may be free to use whatever types of aids you like. In either case, knowing that producing handmade and computer-generated aids require different sets of skills can help you decide which method to use. If you are artistic, can print clearly, and work neatly, then hand-designed aids would be a good choice. If you are comfortable using presentation software, then this method may be more efficient for you. Whatever method you choose, there are several guidelines for producing professional-quality presentational aids.

Designing Effective Presentational Aids by Hand

For most classroom speeches, when you prepare your aids by hand, you will display them on a poster board or a flipchart. Here are some tips to help you make the most of these types of aids.

1. **Limit the reading required of the audience.** The audience should not spend a long time reading your visual aid; you want them listening to you. So limit the total number of lines on an aid to six or fewer, and write points as short phrases rather than complete sentences. The visual aid is meant to reinforce what you say, not repeat what you say. You don't want the audience to spend more than a few seconds "getting" your visual aid.

2. **Customize visuals from other sources so that they're appropriate for your topic and audience.** We often get ideas and information for visual aids from other sources, and the tendency is to simply show the audience all the original material. But if the original source includes information that is irrelevant to your purpose or audience, simplify your visual so that it includes only the information you want to present. For example, as Jia Li prepared a speech on alcohol abuse by young adults, she found a graph titled "Current, Binge, and Heavy Alcohol Use among Persons Aged 12 or Older by Age" in a survey conducted by the U.S. Department of Health and Human Services. The original graph, shown at top in Exhibit 9.10, presents much more information than Jia Li needed. So she simplified the graph, using only the information that pertained to young adults.

3. **Use a photo, a print size, or a type size that can be seen easily by your entire audience.** Create a draft of your aid and then check it for size by moving as far away from it as the farthest person in your audience will be sitting. If you can see the image clearly, read the lettering, and see other details from that distance, your aid is large enough and you can finalize it. If you have trouble seeing the aid, create a larger draft and check it again.

4. **Use a print style that is easy to read.** Avoid printing in highly stylized ways. Although artistic printing may look cool, anything other than simple and basic lettering will be difficult for your audience to read.

5. **Use upper- and lowercase letters.** The combination of upper- and lowercase is easier to read than uppercase only. Some people think that printing in all capital letters creates emphasis. Although that may be true in some instances, ideas printed in all capital letters are more difficult to read—even when the ideas are written in short phrases (see Exhibit 9.11 on page 176).

6. **Make sure information is laid out in a way that is aesthetically pleasing.** Leave sufficient white space around the whole visual so that it's easy to identify each component (white space is the areas of a page without print or pictures), indent subordinate ideas, spell words correctly, and draw and print neatly.

7. **Add pictures or other visual symbols to add interest.** To truly enhance a verbal message, a presentational aid should consist of more than just words.[6] Even on a word chart, visual symbols can increase retention by appealing to diverse learning styles.[7] Most computer graphics packages have a wide variety of clip art that you can import to your document. You can also buy relatively inexpensive software packages that contain thousands of clip art images. A relevant piece of clip art can make the image look both more professional and more dramatic. Be careful, though; clip art can be overdone. Don't let your message be overpowered by unnecessary pictures or animations.

8. **Use color strategically.** Although black and white can work perfectly well for your visual aids, consider using color strategically to emphasize points. Here are some suggestions for incorporating color in your graphics:

- Use color to show similarities and differences between ideas.
- Use bright colors, such as red, to highlight important information.
- Use the same color background for each visual. Or color code backgrounds so that the colors correspond to main points.
- Use black or deep blue for lettering.
- When using yellow or orange for lettering, outline the letters with a darker color so that they can be seen well from a distance.

EXHIBIT 9.10 Complex original graph versus simplified and adapted graph

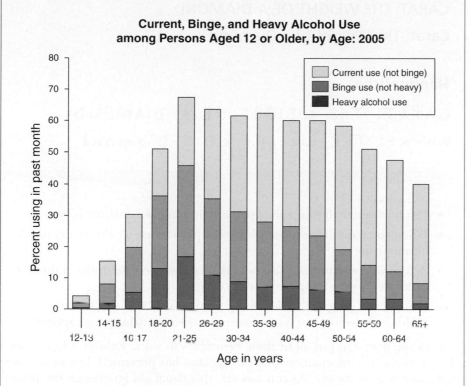

Current, Binge, and Heavy Alcohol Use
among Persons Aged 12 or Older, by Age: 2005

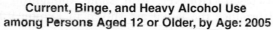

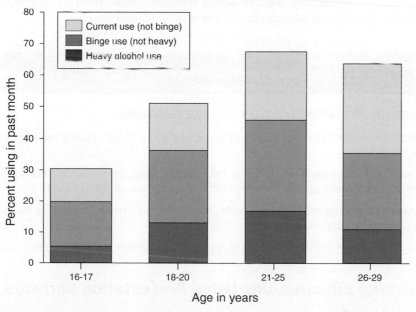

Current, Binge, and Heavy Alcohol Use
among Persons Aged 12 or Older, by Age: 2005

EXHIBIT 9.11 All capitals versus upper- and lowercase letters

Typed

CARAT: THE WEIGHT OF A DIAMOND

Carat: The Weight of a Diamond

Handwritten

CARAT: THE WEIGHT OF A DIAMOND

Carat: The Weight of a Diamond

- ✦ Use no more than four colors per visual; using two or three is best.
- ✦ When you want to use a complex color palette, use a color wheel to select harmonizing colors.
- ✦ Before you prepare your final visual aids, always create drafts of them to make sure you're happy with your color choices.
- ✦ Pretend you are your audience. Sit as far away as they will be sitting, and evaluate the colors you have chosen for their readability and appeal.

Let's see if we can put all of these principles to work. Exhibit 9.12 contains a lot of important information that the speaker has presented, but notice how unpleasant it is to the eye. As you can see, this visual aid ignores all the principles we've discussed. However, with some thoughtful simplification, this speaker could produce the visual aid shown in Exhibit 9.13, which sharpens the focus by emphasizing the key words (reduce, reuse, recycle), highlighting the major details, and adding clip art for a professional touch.

EXHIBIT 9.12 A cluttered and cumbersome visual aid

I WANT YOU TO REMEMBER THE THREE R'S OF RECYCLING

Reduce the amount of waste people produce, like overpacking or using material that won't recycle.

Reuse by relying on cloth towels rather than paper towels, earthenware dishes rather than paper or plastic plates, and glass bottles rather than aluminum cans.

Recycle by collecting recyclable products, sorting them correctly, and getting them to the appropriate recycling agency.

Designing Effective Aids Using Presentation Software

presentation software a computer program that enables you to electronically prepare and store your visual aids using a computer

Presentation software is a computer program that enables you to electronically prepare and store your visual aids using a computer. Microsoft's PowerPoint®, Adobe's Captivate®, and Apple's Keynote 3® are popular commercial presentation software programs. The visuals you create on a computer can become overhead transparencies or handouts, or they can be displayed directly on a screen or TV monitor as a computerized slide show. Aids developed with pre-

EXHIBIT 9.13 A simple but effective visual aid

Remember the Three R's of Recycling

Reduce waste

Reuse
cloth towels
dishes
glass bottles

Recycle
collect
sort
deliver

sentation software give a very polished look to your speech and allow you to develop and deliver the complex multimedia presentations that are expected in many professional settings.

Computerized slide shows have quickly become the presentational aid of choice today. However, too often, these shows do not adhere to the most important function of effective presentational aids, which is to enhance and complement the verbal message. Presentational aids *should not replace a speaker's verbal message,* relegating the speaker to the role of projectionist in the process.[8] On the other hand, well-designed and well-presented computerized slide shows greatly enhance audience interest, understanding, and memory, as well as the audience's perceptions of the speaker's credibility.

When you are unfamiliar with a presentation software package, using it to prepare your presentational aids will be time-consuming. But if you start simply, over time you will become more adept at creating professional-quality visuals. Here are seven tips to help you create interesting and effective computer-generated aids.

1. Plan your aids before you begin using the software. It is easy to get carried away with presentation software and make slide after slide of elaborate visuals with lots of clip art and special effects. This is a waste of valuable time that you can better use practicing your presentation. So, before you sit down at a computer, write or draw a list of the visuals you want to create.

2. Limit the number of visuals you create. Presentation software can lull you into believing that more is better. But if you're not careful, you can create so many visual aids that they become distracting or take the place of your verbal presentation. So a good rule of thumb for a beginning speaker is to limit aids to no more than one aid for every two minutes of speech.

EXHIBIT 9.14 Fonts in eighteen-point regular and boldface

Helvetica	Selecting Typefaces **Selecting Typefaces**
Times	Selecting Typefaces **Selecting Typefaces**
Frutiger	Selecting Typefaces **Selecting Typefaces**
Palatino	Selecting Typefaces **Selecting Typefaces**

3. Use bulleted lists to present additional information that is *not* part of your verbal message. It's a common, but bad, practice to show slide after slide of bulleted text, which amount to nothing more than an outline of the speech.[9] Speakers sometimes use these lists in place of speaking notes and end up simply reading to their audience. A bulleted list can quickly present useful information, but the information in your presentational aids should augment your content, not merely repeat it. For example, in his speech about CEO compensation, George effectively complemented his discussion of runaway compensation packages with a bulleted list of the ten most highly compensated company presidents and their total compensation packages, ordered from the most highly to the least highly paid. He didn't discuss these people in any detail, but the slide helped his audience get a sense of what types of companies reward CEOs too extravagantly.

4. Use a font that is easy to read and pleasing to the eye. Modern software packages come with an extensive variety of fonts (typefaces). Exhibit 9.14 shows a sample of four standard fonts in regular and boldface eighteen-point size. These are the types of fonts you typically see in books and other printed materials; they're simple and easy to read. In general, avoid cursive and overly decorative fonts, which are designed primarily for decorative and illustrative use. Also limit the number of fonts you use per visual aid to only one. Mixing fonts on a single visual tends to obscure key ideas. However, to indicate headings and highlight key ideas, it's okay to use bold and italic fonts in one visual (within moderation).

5. Use fonts of thirty points or more.[10] For audiences of twelve to forty people, the font for the titles of your slides should be at least thirty-six points in size, and the fonts for your text material should be at least thirty points (see Exhibit 9.15). And as with handwritten visuals, use both upper- and lowercase type for easy readability.

6. Consider colors carefully. Strategic use of color on visual aids increases audience retention, but poor color choices can actually reduce readability.[11] Generally, the best color scheme is light text and graphics on a dark back-

EXHIBIT 9.15 Visual aid print sizes

60 Slide titles
48 Heads
30 Text material

ground. Background colors that project well include, blue, green, gray, maroon, and black. Background colors to avoid include purple, yellow, and brown. Text colors should be bright enough to allow for contrast.[12] Finally, avoid using graphics containing red next to green or purple next to blue because audience members who are color-blind will not be able to distinguish them.

7. Keep it simple. Although presentation software programs offer many options for clever clip art and animated graphics, only use those that enhance your message by reinforcing your verbal points. Likewise, avoid using more than one type of slide transition to move from one slide to the next. It can be tempting to play around with combinations of fade-ins, fly-ins, and checker-boards, but using more than one type of transition just distracts and confuses the audience.

Methods for Displaying Presentational Aids

Once you have decided on the specific presentational aids for your speech, you will need to choose the method to display them. Methods for displaying aids vary in the type of preparation they require, the amount of specialized training needed to use them effectively, and the professionalism they convey. Some methods, such as writing on a chalkboard, require little advance preparation. Other methods, such as computerized slide-show presentations, can require extensive preparation. Similarly, it's easy to use an object or a flipchart, but you will need training to properly set up and run computerized slide-show presentations. Finally, the quality of your visual or audio presentation will affect your perceived credibility. A well-run computerized slide show is impressive, but technical difficulties can make you look unprepared. Hand-drawn charts and graphs that are hastily or sloppily developed mark you as an amateur, whereas professional-looking visual aids enhance your credibility. Speakers can choose from the following methods for displaying presentational aids.

Poster Boards

The easiest method for displaying simple drawings, charts, maps, photos, and graphs is by preparing them on or attaching them to stiff cardboard or foam core. Then the visual can be placed on an easel or in a chalk tray when it is referred to during the speech. Because poster boards tend to be fairly small, use them only with smaller audiences.

Whiteboards or Chalkboards

Because a whiteboard or chalkboard is a staple in every college classroom, many novice (and ill-prepared) speakers rely on this method for displaying their visual aids. Unfortunately, a whiteboard or chalkboard is easy to misuse and to overuse. Moreover, they are not suitable for depicting complex material. A whiteboard or chalkboard is appropriate for very short items of information that can be written in a few seconds. Nevertheless, being able to use a whiteboard or chalkboard effectively should be a part of any speaker's repertoire.

Whiteboards or chalkboards should be written on prior to speaking or during a break in speaking. Otherwise, the visual is likely to be either illegible or partly obscured by your body as you write. Or you may end up talking to the board instead of to the audience. Should you need to draw or write on the board while you are talking, you should practice doing it. If you are right-handed, stand to the right of what you are drawing. Try to face at least part of the audience while you work. Although it may seem awkward at first, your effort will allow you to maintain contact with your audience and will allow the audience to see what you are doing while you are doing it.

"Chalk talks" are easiest to prepare, but they are the most likely to result in damage to speaker credibility. It is the rare individual who can develop well-crafted visual aids on a whiteboard or chalkboard. More often, they signal a lack of preparation.

Flipcharts

flipchart a pad of paper mounted on an easel

A **flipchart,** a pad of paper mounted on an easel, can be an effective method for presenting visual aids. Flipcharts (and easels) are available in many sizes. For a presentation to four or five people, a small tabletop version works well; for a larger audience, a larger pad (thirty-by-forty inches) is needed.

Flipcharts are prepared before the speech using colored markers to record the information. At times, a speaker may record some of the information before the speech begins and then add information while speaking.

When preparing flipcharts, leave several pages between each visual on the pad. If you discover a mistake or decide to revise, you can tear out that sheet without disturbing the order of other visuals you may have prepared. After you have the visuals, tear out all but one sheet between each chart. This blank sheet serves as both a transition page and a cover sheet. Because you want your audience to focus on your words and not on visual material that is no longer being discussed, you can flip to the empty page while you are talking about material not covered by charts. Also, the empty page between charts ensures that heavy lines or colors from the next chart will not show through.

For flipcharts to be effective, the information that is handwritten or drawn must be neat and appropriately sized. Flipchart visuals that are not neatly done detract from speaker credibility. Flipcharts can be comfortably used with smaller audiences (fewer than 100 people) but are not appropriate for larger settings. It is especially important when creating flipcharts to make sure that the information is written large enough to be easily seen by all audience members.

Overhead Transparencies

An easy way to display drawings, charts, and graphs is to transfer them to an acetate film and project them onto a screen via an overhead projector. With a master copy of the visual, you can make an overhead transparency using a copy machine, thermograph, or color lift. If the master is a computer document, you can make the transparency with a computer printer. Overheads are easy and inexpensive to make, and the equipment needed to project overheads is easy to operate and likely to be available at most speech sites. Overheads work well in nearly any setting, and unlike other kinds of projections, they don't require dimming the lights in the room. Moreover, overheads can be useful for demonstrating a process because it is possible to write, trace, or draw on the transparency while you are talking. The size at which an overhead is projected can also be adjusted to the size of the room so that all audience members can see the image. It is also a good idea to have transparencies as backups when using computerized slide shows in case the computer system malfunctions.[13]

Handouts

At times, it may be useful for each member of the audience to have a personal copy of the visual aid. In these situations, you can prepare a handout. On the plus side, you can prepare handouts (material printed on sheets of paper) quickly, and all the people in the audience can have their own professional-quality material to refer to and take with them from the speech. On the minus side is the distraction of distributing handouts and the potential for losing audience members' attention when you want them to be looking at you.

Before you decide to use handouts, carefully consider why a handout is superior to other methods. Handouts are effective for information you want listeners to refer to after the speech, such as a set of steps to follow later, useful telephone numbers and addresses, or mathematical formulas. If you do decide on handouts, distribute them at the end of the speech. If you want to refer to information on the handout during the speech, create another visual aid that you can reveal only when discussing it for use during the actual speech. For example, in his speech on obesity, Tim created a handout of his flowchart that shows how to determine if you are overweight. He created the flowchart on a poster board for reference during his speech, saving the handout to distribute to the audience when he'd completed his speech.

Document Cameras

Another simple way to display drawings, charts, photos, and graphs is with a document camera, such as an Elmo®. A document camera allows you to project images without transferring them to an acetate film. Transfer drawings, charts, photos, and graphs from original sources onto sheets of eight-by-eleven-inch paper so you can display them smoothly and professionally.

CD/VCR/DVD Players and LCD Projectors

To show TV, film, and video clips for a classroom speech, a VCR or DVD player and a television monitor should be sufficient. For larger audiences, however, you will need multiple monitors or, ideally, an **LCD multimedia projector.** An LCD projector connects to a VCR player, a DVD player, or a computer and projects images from them onto a large screen, which makes them easy to see, even in a large auditorium. An LCD projector is also ideal for displaying computerized slide shows, such as PowerPoint® presentations.

LCD multimedia projector a projection unit that connects to a VCR player, a DVD player, or a computer and projects images from them onto a screen

Computerized Slide Shows

You can present computerized slide shows using an LCD projector or a large monitor connected to an onsite computer that has presentation software compatible with the software you used to make your aids. Because you can't always anticipate problems with onsite projection equipment, come with backup aids, such as transparencies or handouts. When you present your slide show during your speech, ensure that the audience focuses their attention on you when you're not talking about one of your slides. To redirect their attention from your slide show to you, insert blank screens between your slides or press the B key on your computer to display a blank screen.

ACTIVITY 5A Choosing, Preparing, and Using Presentational Aids

The goal of this activity is to identify information whose visual or audio presentation would increase audience interest, understanding, and retention.

1. Identify the key ideas in your speech for which you believe a visual or audio presentation would increase audience interest, facilitate understanding, or increase retention.
2. For each idea you have identified, list the type of presentational aid you think would be most appropriate to develop and use.
3. For each aid you have identified, decide how you will design it.
4. For each aid you have identified, decide on the method you will use to present it.

You can complete this activity online with Speech Builder Express, download a Presentational Aids Planning Chart to help you organize your aids, and if requested, e-mail your completed activity to your instructor. Use your CengageNOW for *Challenge* to access Activity 5A.

ACTIVITY 5A Choosing, Preparing, and Using Presentational Aids

Speech goal: *I would like my audience to learn to identify common poisonous plants that grow in our area.*

1. Identify the key ideas in your speech for which you believe a visual or audio presentation would increase audience interest, facilitate understanding, or increase retention.
   Leaf shape, size, and color; habitat; signs of contact
2. For each idea you have identified, list the type of presentational aid you think would be most appropriate to develop and use.
   I will use two color photographs of each type of plant. The first will show the entire plant; the second will be a close-up of the leaves. I will also use photos to show the habitat in which each plant is usually found. Finally, I will use photographs to show the reactions that occur as a result of contact with the plants. I will have actual plant samples available for closer inspection after my speech.
3. For each aid you have identified, decide how you will design it.
   I will use my digital camera to take photographs of each plant and the habitats in which I found them. These will be transferred to my computer, and then I will create a computerized slide show using PowerPoint. I will locate images of reactions to each plant online, download them, and add them to the computerized slide show. I will also collect samples of each type of plant and bring them with me to the speech.
4. For each aid you have identified, decide on the method you will use to present it.
   I will bring a CD of the PowerPoint presentation with me and use the computer and LCD projector that is available at the speaking site. I will also have backup overheads of all my photos and slides.

Guidelines for Using Presentational Aids During the Speech

Many speakers think that once they have prepared good presentational aids, they will have no trouble using them in the speech. However, many speeches with good aids have become shambles because the speaker neglected to *practice with them*. You will want to make sure that you practice using presentational aids in your speech rehearsals. During practice sessions, indicate on your notes exactly when you will reveal each aid (and when you will conceal it). Work on statements for introducing the aids, and practice different ways of showing your aids until you are comfortable using them and satisfied that everyone in the audience will be able to see them. Following are several other guidelines for using presentational aids effectively in your speech.

1. Plan carefully when to use presentational aids. As you practice your speech, indicate on your outline when and how you will use each aid. Avoid displaying aids before you begin talking about the specific information to which they relate, as they may distract your audience's attention from important information that precedes the aid. Likewise, if you find that a presentational aid does not contribute directly to the audience's attention to, understanding of, or retention of information on your topic, then reconsider its use.

2. Position presentational aids and audiovisual equipment before beginning your speech. Make sure your aids and equipment are where you want them and that everything is ready and in working order. For example, check to make sure your poster boards or transparencies are in sequence and positioned where all audience members will be able to see them. Test to make sure visual, audio, or audiovisual equipment works and that excerpts are cued correctly. Taking time to position your aids will make you feel more confident and look more professional and at ease.

3. Show or play presentational aids only when talking about them. Because presentational aids will draw audience attention, the basic rule of thumb for using them is this: When the aid is no longer the focus of attention, cover it up, remove it, turn it off, or get rid of it.

4. Talk about the visual aid while showing it. Since you already know what you want your audience to see in a presentational aid, tell your audience what to look for, explain the various parts of the aid, and interpret figures, symbols, and percentages. (For an audio presentational aid, point out what you want your audience to listen for before you play the aid.) When showing a visual aid, such as a transparency projected onto a screen in front of the class, use the following "turn-touch-talk" technique.

+ When you display the visual, walk to the screen—that's where everyone will look anyway. Slightly turn to the visual and touch it—that is, point to it with your arm or a pointer. (Use a pointer carefully.) Then, with your back to the screen and your body still at a slight forty-five-degree angle to the group, talk to your audience about the visual.

+ When you finish making your comments, return to the lectern or your speaking position and turn off the projector or otherwise conceal the visual.

5. Talk to your audience, not to the visual aid. You may need to look at the visual aid occasionally, but it is important to maintain eye contact with your audience as much as possible—in part so that you can gauge how they are reacting to your visual material. When speakers become too engrossed in their visual aids, looking at them instead of the audience, they tend to lose contact with the audience entirely.

Courtesy of InFocus Systems, Inc.

6. Display visual aids so that everyone in the audience can see them. If you hold the visual aid, position it away from your body and point it toward the various parts of the audience. If you place your visual aid on an easel or mount it in some way, stand to one side and point with the arm nearest the visual aid. If it is necessary to roll or fold the visual aid, bring some transparent tape to mount it to the chalkboard or wall so that it does not roll or wrinkle. If the visual aid is projected onto a screen, point with your hand or a pointer to the screen, not to the overhead projector.

7. Avoid passing objects around the audience. People look at, read, handle, and think about whatever they hold in their hands. While they are so occupied, they are not likely to be listening to you. This is why it's best to distribute a handout after your speech, not during it.

To see a video clip of a student speaker presenting visual aids effectively, "Electoral College," use your CengageNOW for *Challenge* to access the chapter resources for Chapter 9.

Summary

Presentational aids allow an audience to see as well as hear information. They are useful when they help audience members understand or remember important information. The most common types of visual aids are objects, models, photographs, simple drawings and diagrams, maps, charts, and graphs. Other types of presentational aids you might use include audio materials, audiovisual materials, and other sensory items. Methods that speakers can use to present presentational aids include computer-mediated presentations, overhead transparencies, flipcharts, poster boards, whiteboards or chalkboards, handouts, and CD, VCR, or DVD players and LCD projectors. Advancements in computer graphics give the speaker a wide range of flexibility in creating professional-quality materials.

Before you start collecting or creating the presentational aids you plan to use, consider a number of questions. What ideas are most important in helping me achieve my speech goal? Are there ideas that are complex or difficult to explain verbally but would be easy for audience members to understand visually? How many presentational aids should I consider? How large is the audience? Is the necessary equipment readily available? Is the time involved in making or getting the visual aid or equipment cost-effective?

Take time to design your visual aids with the following principles in mind: Use a print or font size that can be seen easily by your entire audience. Use a font that is easy to read and pleasing to the eye. Use upper- and lowercase type. Try to limit the lines of type to six or fewer. Include only items of information that you will emphasize in your speech. Make sure information is laid out in a way that is aesthetically pleasing. Add clip art where appropriate. Use color strategically.

When you plan to use presentational aids in a speech, make sure you practice using them as you rehearse your speech. Keep the following suggestions in mind: Carefully plan when you will use each aid during your speech. Position the aids and equipment before beginning your speech. Show presentational aids only when talking about them; when you show a video clip or play an audio clip, talk about it before you play it. Display presentational aids so that everyone in the audience can see them. Talk to your audience, not to your presentational aid. Avoid passing objects around the audience. In short, keep your audience focused on *you* as the speaker as well as your presentational aids.

CHALLENGE ONLINE

Now that you've read Chapter 9, use your Cengage-NOW for *The Challenge of Effective Speaking* for quick access to the electronic resources that accompany this text. Your CengageNOW gives you access to the "Electoral College" video discussed on page 184, the Speech Planning activity featured in this chapter, Speech Builder Express, InfoTrac College Edition, and online study aids such as a digital glossary and review quizzes.

Your *Challenge* CengageNOW is an online study system that helps you identify concepts you don't fully understand, allowing you to put your study time to the best use. Using chapter-by-chapter diagnostic pretests, the system creates a personalized study plan for each chapter. Each plan directs you to specific resources designed to improve your understanding, including pages from the text in e-book format. Chapter posttests give you an opportunity to measure how much you've learned and let you know if you are ready for graded quizzes and exams.

KEY TERMS

Go to your CengageNOW for *Challenge* to access your online glossary for Chapter 9. Print a copy of the glossary for this chapter and test yourself with the electronic flash cards or complete the crossword puzzle to help you master these key terms:

actual object (165)
bar graph (168)
chart (167)
diagram (166)
flipchart (180)
flowchart (167)

graph (168)
LCD multimedia projector (181)
line graph (168)
model (165)
organizational chart (168)

pie graph (170)
presentation software (176)
presentational aid (164)
visual aid (164)
word chart (167)

Access the Action Step activities for this chapter online at your CengageNOW for *Challenge*. Select the chapter resources for Chapter 9, then click the activity number you want. You may print your completed activities, and you should save your work so you can use it as needed in later Action Step activities.

5A Choosing, Preparing, and Using Presentational Aids (183)

From Web Site for Verderber/Verderber's The Challenge of Effective Speaking, 13th edition by VERDERBER/VERDERBER. 2006 Reprinted with permission of Wadsworth, a division of Cengage Learning: permissions.cengage.com. Fax 800 730-2215.

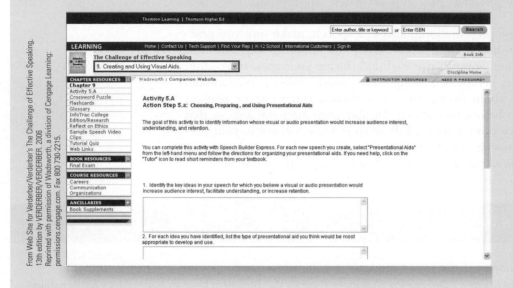

Practicing Speech Wording

© William Thomas Cain/Getty Images

A speech reminds us that words, like children, have the power to make dance the dullest beanbag of a heart.

Peggy Noonan, *What I Saw at the Revolution*, 1990

What's Ahead

HERE'S WHAT'S AHEAD IN THIS CHAPTER:

1. How does oral style differ from written style?

2. What should you consider to make sure your word choices will be interpreted accurately by your audience?

3. What can you do to make sure your message is clear?

4. What are some strategies you can employ to make your ideas vivid for listeners?

5. What can you do when wording your speech to avoid offending some listeners?

Practicing speech wording and delivery

A. Practice until the wording is accurate, clear, vivid, and appropriate

As Rhonda replayed the recording she had made of her first speech practice session, she listened carefully to the section on the effects of Rohypnol. She stopped the tape after she heard herself saying, "Rohypnol leaves many bad effects on people. And a lot of these are really, really terrible. I mean, you can be totally out of it for a long time."

"Yuck," thought Rhonda. "That sounds so vague. I say, 'leaves bad effects,' but I don't specifically state any of the effects. And calling the effects 'really, really terrible' isn't very descriptive. What could I say instead?"

With an outline in hand and your presentational aids prepared, you are ready to practice your speech, switching your focus from the macrostructure (what you plan to say) to the microstructure (how you will say it). Recall that microstructure includes the language you use to convey your message. In the chapter opening, Rhonda is working on developing accurate, clear, vivid, and appropriate wording for her ideas. Once she does this, she will continue to rehearse until she is fluent, enthusiastic, and expressive in her delivery. In this chapter, we explain how you can conduct rehearsal sessions that help you achieve effective wording in your speech.

In a written communication, effective wording evolves through editing and finally appears on the printed page. In a speech, however, effective wording develops through oral practice. The outline of your speech is a skeleton that includes from 35 percent to more than 50 percent of the words that you may use in the speech. During each rehearsal, you fill out the outline to the appropriate speech length. As you continue to rehearse, you will change your wording so that the ideas are presented in language that is clear, accurate, vivid, and appropriate for the audience.

In this chapter, you will learn to use the kind of language that is instantly intelligible to the *ear* so that the audience receives the same meanings as you intend. When a written sentence is unclear, the reader can reread it and puzzle out its meaning, but when a sentence in a speech is unclear, the listener cannot go back, and the meaning may be misunderstood or lost. So, as a speaker, you must focus on how to help the specific audience understand the meaning *as the speech is given.*

Let's begin our discussion by briefly clarifying oral style as it relates to written style. Then we will describe some specific strategies you can use to increase the accuracy, clarity, vividness, and appropriateness of the words you use.

Oral Style

oral style the manner in which one conveys messages through the spoken word

Oral style refers to the manner in which one conveys messages through the spoken word. Oral style differs quite a bit from written style, especially when you're giving a speech. As the speaker, your primary goal is to establish a relationship with your listeners, so your language should reflect a personal tone that encourages listeners to feel you are having a conversation with them. An effective oral style differs from a written style in four important ways.

1. An effective oral style tends toward short sentences and familiar language. Since listeners have only one opportunity to hear your idea, work to make sure the words you use are ones that your particular audience is likely to understand.

2. An effective oral style features plural personal pronouns. Using personal pronouns such as "we," "us," and "our" creates a sense of relationship with the audience, fostering an impression of respect for them as participants in the occasion.

3. A good oral style features descriptive words to sustain listener interest and promote retention. By using colorful adjectives and adverbs, you can draw your listeners into your message and motivate them to stay focused on it.

4. An effective oral style incorporates clear signposts. Because listeners hear a speaker's message only once, signposts such as "first," "second," "third," and "fourth" provide oral markers that enable listeners to follow your train of thought as the speech progresses.

Although it's effective to use a conversational tone during your speech, effective oral style in public speaking differs from the oral style many of us use in casual conversation. For example, in most speech settings, audience members will not interrupt you to ask questions. In addition, you speak longer than would be considered appropriate for a "turn" in a conversation. And because you think about, plan, and practice what you will say and how you will say it, the oral style of a speech is more formal.

Speaking Accurately

Using **accurate language** means using words that convey your meaning precisely. On the surface, speaking accurately seems simple enough. If you select words to represent your meaning, won't audience members interpret your words correctly and understand the meaning you wish to convey? In fact, there are four reasons speaking accurately is not that simple.

accurate language words that convey your meaning precisely

1. Language is symbolic. We use words to represent things, ideas, events, and so forth. Words have no tangible meanings in and of themselves; rather, we attach meaning to them.[1] For example, when you hear the word *dog*, what image forms in your mind? Do you visualize a poodle? A sheepdog? A mutt? There is so much variation in what the word *dog* conjures in our minds because the word *dog* is not the animal. It is a symbol that you use to represent the animal. So if you use the word *dog* in a speech, each member of your audience is likely to picture something different. Since the *word* is not the *thing*, as a speaker you should use accurate words that most closely match the thing or idea you want your audience to see or understand.

2. We are not born knowing a language; we must learn it. Moreover, each generation within a language community learns the language anew. We learn much of our language early in life from our families. We then learn more in school, and we continue to learn more throughout our lives. But we do not all learn to use the same words in the same way.

3. Although every language has a system of syntax and grammar, each utterance of a word is a creative act. When we speak, we use language to create new sentences that represent our own personal meaning. Although on occasion we repeat other people's sentence constructions to represent what we are thinking or feeling, most of our talk is unique.

4. Even though two people may know the same words, they may interpret the meanings of the words differently. Thus, when James tells Chrissie that he liked going to the movies with her the previous night, what Chrissie understands James to mean by "liked" depends on how she interprets the message.

For example, did James mean that he thought the movie was entertaining, or did he mean that he enjoyed spending time with Chrissie?

Using accurate language is crucial to effective speaking because it helps you be **intelligible,** or clearly understood. If listeners don't understand you or what you mean, your attempt to communicate is doomed. To help ensure that the language you use in speeches is accurate, let's take a look at three concepts that affect how words are interpreted: denotation, connotation, and dialect.

intelligible capable of being understood

Denotation

denotation the explicit meaning a language community formally gives a word

The direct, explicit meaning a language community formally gives a word is its **denotation.** A word's denotation is the meaning found in a dictionary. So denotatively, when Melissa said her dog died, she meant that her domesticated canine no longer demonstrates physical life. Keep in mind that in some situations the denotative meaning of a word may not be clear. Why? One reason is that dictionary definitions reflect current and past practices in the language community. In addition, the dictionary uses words to define words. The end result is that words are defined differently in various dictionaries and may include multiple meanings that change over time.

context the position of a word in a sentence and its relationship to other words around it

Moreover, meaning may vary depending on the context in which the word is used. For example, the dictionary definition of *gay* includes both (1) having or showing a merry, lively mood and (2) homosexual. Thus, **context**—the position of a word in a sentence and its relationship to the other words around it—has an important effect on correctly interpreting which denotation of a word is meant. Not only will the other words, the syntax, and the grammar of a verbal message help us to understand the denotative meaning of certain words, but so will the situation in which they are spoken. For example, if you're at the beach and you say you are "surfing," you probably mean you're riding the waves. But if you're sitting at your desk in front of your computer, you probably mean you're searching the Internet for information.

To ensure that listeners assign the denotation you intend, consult a current dictionary to make sure your intended meaning adheres to today's reality and be sure to provide enough context.

Connotation

connotation the feelings or evaluations we associate with a word

The feelings or evaluations we associate with a word, its **connotation,** color the meaning we give it. Thus, our perception of a word's connotation may be even more important than its denotation in how we interpret the meaning of the word. Connotations can be neutral, positive, or negative and can be quite different for different people. For example, describing a woman as a "feminist" can conjure up very different connotations for different people based on previous experiences.

C. K. Ogden and I. A. Richards were among the first scholars to consider the misunderstandings that result from the failure of communicators to realize that their subjective reactions to words will be a product of their life experiences.[2] For instance, when Melissa's dog dies and she tells Trish about it, Trish's understanding of the message depends on the extent to which her feelings about pets and death—her connotations of the words—correspond to the feelings that Melissa has about pets and death. Whereas Melissa, who sees dogs as truly indispensable friends, may be intending to communicate her overwhelming grief, Trish, who has never had a pet and doesn't particularly care for pets in general or dogs in particular, may miss the emotional meaning of Melissa's statement.

Connotations give emotional power to words, so much so that people will even fight and die for them. Consider the connotative meanings people assign to words like *freedom* or *honor* and *right* or *wrong*. For this reason, connotations can be used effectively to increase the emotional appeal of your message. As you practice your wording, be sure to consider how predisposed your audience is likely to be to the words you choose. Use your audience analysis to help you avoid words that arouse unintended connotations, or be sure to explain how you are using a word so that you avoid negative responses to your message.

Dialect

Dialect, a regional variety of a language, can also impact listener understanding of your message. For example, in some places a car's turn signal is called a "blinker," a seesaw is a "teeter-totter," and a soft drink is a "pop" or a "coke." Dialect also affects pronunciation and grammar. For instance, people in some regions pronounce *wash* as "warsh," *hundred* as "hunnert," and *creek* as "crick." And some dialects incorporate what is considered incorrect grammar, such as "he don't," "I says," "this here book," and "beings as he was sick." Speaking in a dialect can interfere with the intelligibility of your message, especially if your audience doesn't share your dialect. To be understood by a greater variety of audiences, practice using **Standard English** in your speeches, the form of English described in the dictionary or an English handbook. It's okay if you still speak with a regional accent, but striving to use Standard English will increase the likelihood that you are understood.

Being aware of and sensitive to denotation, connotation, and dialect are important because regardless of what a speaker says, the only message meaning that counts is the message meaning that is understood by audience members.

Speaking Clearly

Speaking clearly results from reducing your use of ambiguous and confusing language. Compare the clarity of the following two descriptions of the same incident:

> Some nut almost ran into me a while ago.

> Last Saturday afternoon, an older man in a banged-up Honda Civic ran through the red light at Calhoun and Clifton and came within inches of hitting my car while I was waiting to turn left.

Using specific language that is both concrete and precise decreases ambiguity and audience confusion when we speak. Let's look at five strategies for improving clarity: use specific language, choose familiar terms, provide details and examples, limit vocalized pauses, and be sensitive to cultural diversity.

Use Specific Language

Specific language clarifies meaning by narrowing what is understood from a general category to a particular item or group within that category. Often, as we try to express our thoughts, the first words that come to mind are general, abstract, and imprecise. The ambiguity of these words makes the listener choose from many possible images rather than picturing the single, focused image we have in mind. The more listeners are called on to provide their own images, the more likely they are to see meanings different from what we intend.

Specific words are more concrete and precise than are general words. Saying "a banged-up Honda Civic" is more specific than saying "a car." **Concrete words** appeal to the senses. In effect, we can see, hear, smell, taste, or touch what they describe. Thus, we can picture that banged-up Civic. Abstract ideas,

dialect a regional variety of a language

Standard English form of English described in the dictionary or an English handbook

specific language words that clarify meaning by narrowing what is understood from a general category to a particular item or group within that category

concrete words words that appeal to the senses or conjure up a picture

such as justice, equality, or fairness, can be made concrete through examples or metaphors. **Precise words** are words that narrow a larger category. For instance, if in her speech Nevah refers to a "blue-collar worker," you might picture any number of occupations that fall within this broad category. If, instead, she is more precise and says he's a "construction worker," the number of possible images you can picture is reduced. Now you select your image from the subcategory of construction worker, and your meaning is likely to be closer to the one she intended. If she is even more precise, she may say "bulldozer operator." Now you are even clearer on the specific occupation.

In the preceding example, the continuum of specificity goes from blue-collar worker to construction worker to bulldozer operator. Exhibit 10.1 provides another illustration of increasing precision. To see a video clip of a student speaker using specific, concrete, and precise language, use your CengageNOW for *Challenge* to access the chapter resources for Chapter 10. Select the clip called "Shakespeare."

Choosing specific language is easier when you have a large working vocabulary. As a speaker, the larger your vocabulary, the more choices you have from which to select the word you want. As a listener, the larger your vocabulary, the more likely you are to understand the words used by others.

One way to increase your vocabulary is to study one of the many vocabulary-building books on the shelves of almost any bookstore, such as *Word Smart: Building an Educated Vocabulary*.[3] You might also study magazine features such as "Word Power" in the *Reader's Digest*. By completing this monthly quiz and learning the words with which you are not familiar, you could increase your vocabulary by as many as twenty words per month. To take a vocabulary test online, use your CengageNOW for *Challenge* to access **Web Resource 10.1: WordsmartChallenge.**

A second way to increase your vocabulary is to take note of words that you read or that people use in their conversations with you that you don't know and look them up. For instance, suppose you read or hear, "I was inundated with phone calls today!" If you wrote down *inundated* and looked it up in a dictionary later, you would find that it means "overwhelmed" or "flooded." If you then say to yourself, "She was inundated—overwhelmed or flooded—with phone calls today," you are likely to remember that meaning and apply it the next time you hear the word. If you follow this practice, you will soon notice your vocabulary increase.

EXHIBIT 10.1 Levels of precision

Games of skill
Gambling games
Card games
Poker
Seven-card stud

A third way to increase your vocabulary is to use a thesaurus (a book of words and their synonyms) to identify synonyms that are more concrete and precise than the word you may have chosen. But be careful—avoid unfamiliar words that may make you sound intelligent but could reduce your intelligibility. For example, *somnolent* is an interesting word, but most people don't know that it is a synonym for *sleepy*. An easy way to consult a thesaurus is to access Merriam-Webster's online *Collegiate Thesaurus*. For instance, when you type "difficult" into the search box, you'll find such synonyms as "hard," "laborious," "arduous," and "strenuous." Use your CengageNOW for *Challenge* to access **Web Resource 10.2: Merriam-Webster Online.**

Having a larger vocabulary won't help your speaking if you don't have a procedure for accessing it when you speak. So, during practice sessions, you will want to consciously experiment using specific words that precisely reflect your ideas. Suppose you were practicing a speech on registering for classes and said, "Preregistration is awful." If this word isn't quite right, you can quickly brainstorm better words, such as *frustrating, demeaning, cumbersome,* and *annoying.* Then, as you continue to practice, you might say, "Preregistration is a cumbersome process."

Some speakers think that to be effective they must impress their audience with their extensive vocabularies. As a result, instead of looking for specific, concrete, and precise words, they use words that appear pompous, affected, or stilted to the listener. Speaking precisely and specifically does not mean speaking obscurely. The following story illustrates the problem with pretentious words:

> A plumber wrote to a government agency, saying that he found that hydrochloric acid quickly opened drainpipes but that he wasn't sure whether it was a good thing to use. A scientist at the agency replied, "The efficacy of hydrochloric acid is indisputable, but the corrosive residue is incompatible with metallic permanence."
>
> The plumber wrote back thanking him for the assurance that hydrochloric acid was all right. Disturbed by this turn of affairs, the scientist showed the letter to his boss, another scientist, who then wrote to the plumber: "We cannot assume responsibility for the production of toxic and noxious residue with hydrochloric acid and suggest you use an alternative procedure."
>
> The plumber wrote back that he agreed. Hydrochloric acid worked fine. Greatly disturbed by this misunderstanding, the scientists took their problem to the top boss. She wrote to the plumber: "Don't use hydrochloric acid. It eats the hell out of pipes."

To differentiate among individuals in this picture, you would have to be precise, specific, and concrete in your description.

The decision rule is to use a more difficult word *only* when you believe that it is the very best word for a specific context. Let's suppose you wanted to use a more precise or specific word for *building.* Using the guideline of familiarity, you might select *house, apartment, high-rise,* or *skyscraper,* but you would avoid *edifice.* Each of the other choices is more precise or more specific, but *edifice* is neither more precise nor more specific, and in addition to being less well understood, it will be perceived as affected or stilted. Likewise, you would choose *clothing* instead of *apparel, bury* instead of *inter, avoid* instead of *eschew, predict* instead of *presage,* and *beauty* instead of *pulchritude.*

You will know that you have really made strides in improving specificity, precision, and concreteness when you find that you can form clear messages even under the pressure of presenting your speeches.

Calvin and Hobbes © Watterson. Reprinted with permission of Universal Press Syndicate. All rights reserved.

jargon unique technical terminology of a trade or profession that is not generally understood by outsiders

slang informal, nonstandard vocabulary and nonstandard definitions assigned to words by a social group or subculture

Choose Familiar Terms

Using familiar terms is just as important as using specific words. Avoid jargon, slang, abbreviations, and acronyms unless (1) you define them clearly the first time they are used and (2) using them is central to your speech goal.

Jargon is the unique technical terminology of a trade or profession that is not generally understood by outsiders. We might forget that people who are not in our same line of work or who do not have the same hobbies may not understand the jargon that seems such a part of our daily communication. For instance, when Jenny, who is sophisticated in the use of cyberlanguage, starts talking with her computer-illiterate friend Sarah about "social MUDs based on fictional universes," Sarah is likely to be totally lost. If, however, Jenny recognizes Sarah's lack of familiarity with cyberlanguage, she can make her message clear by discussing the concepts in words her friend understands. In short, limit your use of jargon in speeches to general audiences and always define it in simple terms the first time you use it.

Slang refers to informal, nonstandard vocabulary and nonstandard definitions assigned to words by a social group or subculture. For example, today the word *bad*, which has a standard definition denoting something unpleasant or substandard, can mean quite the opposite in some social groups and subcultures.[4] You should generally avoid slang in your public speeches not only because you risk misunderstanding but also because slang doesn't sound professional and it can hurt your credibility. Slang is so pervasive that there are special dictionaries devoted to the specialized vocabulary of different communities. You can even find slang dictionaries online. To access one created by a former student of the University of California, Berkeley, use your Cengage-NOW to access **Web Resource 10.3: Slang Dictionary.**

Overusing and misusing abbreviations and acronyms can also hinder clarity. Even if you think the abbreviation or acronym is a common one, to ensure intelligibility, always define it the first time you use it in the speech. For example, in a speech about NASCAR, refer to it initially by the organization's full name and then provide the acronym: "National Association for Stock Car Auto Racing, or NASCAR." Providing the full and abbreviated forms of the name will ensure clarity for all listeners. If you are assuming right now that everyone knows what NASCAR is, it might benefit you to know one of your authors had to look it up to include it in this book!

Provide Details and Examples

Sometimes, the word we use may not have a concrete or precise synonym. In these situations, clarity can be achieved by adding details or examples. For instance, Linda says, "Rashad is very loyal." The meaning of *loyal* (faithful to an idea, person, company, or other entity) is abstract, so to avoid ambiguity and confusion, Linda might add, "He defended Gerry when Sara was gossiping about her." By following up her use of the abstract concept of loyalty with a concrete example, Linda makes it easier for her listeners to "ground" their idea of this personal quality in a concrete or "real" experience.

Likewise, providing details can clarify our messages. Saying "He lives in a really big house" can be clarified by adding, "He lives in a fourteen-room Tudor mansion on a six-acre estate."

Limit Vocalized Pauses

Vocalized pauses are unnecessary words interjected into sentences to fill moments of silence. Words commonly used for this purpose are "like," "you know," "really," "basically," as well as "um" and "uh." We sometimes refer to vocalized pauses as "verbal garbage" because they do not serve a meaningful purpose and actually distract listeners from the message. Although a few vocalized pauses typically don't hinder clarity, limit their use by practicing your speech without using them.

vocalized pause unnecessary words interjected into sentences to fill moments of silence

Be Sensitive to Cultural Differences

Verbal communication rules and expectations about clarity of language vary from culture to culture. One major theory used to explain similarities and differences in language and behavior is individualism versus collectivism.[5] In general, individualistic cultures emphasize individual goals more than group goals because these cultures value uniqueness. Many individualistic cultures are found in Western Europe and North America. In contrast, collectivistic cultures emphasize group goals more than individual goals because these cultures value harmony and solidarity. Many collectivistic cultures are found in Asia, Africa, and Latin America.[6]

Individualistic cultures tend to use low-context communication, in which information is (1) embedded mainly in the messages transmitted and (2) presented directly. Collectivistic cultures tend to use high-context communication, in which people (1) expect others to know how they're thinking and feeling and (2) present some messages indirectly to avoid embarrassing the other person. Thus, speakers from low-context cultures such as the United States operate on the principle of saying what they mean and getting to the point. They prize clear and direct messages that do not depend on an interpretation of the context to be understood. Their approach may be characterized by such expressions as "Say what you mean" and "Don't beat around the bush."[7] In contrast, speakers from high-context cultures such as China form messages with language that is intentionally ambiguous and indirect; to interpret these messages correctly, listeners need to understand not only the message but the context in which it is uttered.

What does this mean to you as a student of public speaking? When you are a member of a cultural group that operates differently from that of the majority of your audience members, you need to adapt your language so that it is clear and appropriate for your audience. If you are uncertain, then during your rehearsals ask someone from the same cultural group as the majority of your audience to listen to the parts of your speech in which your wording is raising questions and to suggest ways your wording can be adapted to the audience. For speaking to low-context audiences, this may mean using more concrete examples so that your audience members will be more likely to get the same meanings that you intend. For high-context audiences, it may mean stating certain parts of your message indirectly and trusting that the context will enable them to understand your meaning.

To read more about how to adapt to audiences from other cultures, use your CengageNOW for *Challenge* to access **Web Resource 10.4: Speaking to International Audiences.**

Speaking Vividly

vivid language language that is full of life—vigorous, bright, and intense

Because listeners cannot "reread" what you have said, you must speak in ways that help them remember your message. Speaking vividly is one effective way to maintain your audience's interest and help them remember what you say. **Vivid language** is full of life—vigorous, bright, and intense. For example, a mediocre baseball announcer might say, "Jackson made a great catch," but a better commentator's vivid account might be, "Jackson leaped and made a spectacular one-handed catch just as he crashed into the center field wall." The words *leaped, spectacular, one-handed catch,* and *crashed* paint an intense verbal picture of the action. You can make your ideas come to life by using sensory language and by using figures and structures of speech.

Use Sensory Language

sensory language language that appeals to the senses of seeing, hearing, tasting, smelling, and feeling

© Ken Redding/CORBIS

You can help listeners remember by appealing to the senses.

Sensory language is language that appeals to the senses of seeing, hearing, tasting, smelling, and feeling. Vivid sensory language begins with vivid thought. You are much more likely to express yourself vividly if you can physically or psychologically sense the meanings you are trying to convey. If you feel the "bite of the wind" or "the sting of freezing rain," if you hear and smell "the thick, juicy sirloin steaks sizzling on the grill," you will be able to describe these sensations. Does the cake "taste good"? Or do your taste buds "quiver with the sweet double-chocolate icing and velvety feel of the rich, moist cake"?

To develop vivid sensory language, begin by considering how you can re-create what something, someone, or some place *looks like.* Consider, too, how you can help listeners imagine how something *sounds.* How can you use language to convey the way something *feels* (textures, shapes, temperatures)? How can language re-create a sense of how something *tastes* or *smells*? To achieve this in your speech, use colorful descriptors. They make your ideas more concrete and can arouse emotions. They invite listeners to imagine details. Here's an example about downhill skiing:

Sight: As you climb the hill, the bright winter sunshine glistening on the snow is blinding.

Touch and feel: Just before you take off, you gently slip your goggles over your eyes. They are bitterly cold and sting your nose for a moment.

Taste: You start the descent and, as you gradually pick up speed, the taste of air and ice and snow in your mouth invigorates you.

Sound: An odd silence fills the air. You hear nothing but the swish or your skis against the snow beneath your feet. At last, you arrive at the bottom of the slope. Reality hits as you hear the hustle and bustle of other skiers and instructors directing them to their next session.

Smell and feel: You enter the warming house. As your fingers thaw in the warm air, the aroma from the wood stove in the corner comforts you as you drift off into sleep.

By using colorful descriptors that appeal to the senses, you arouse and maintain listener interest and make your ideas more memorable.

Use Figures and Structures of Speech

figures of speech phrases that make striking comparisons between things that are not obviously alike

Figures of speech make striking comparisons between things that are not obviously alike and so help listeners visualize or internalize what you are saying.

Structures of speech combine ideas in a particular way. Any of these devices can serve to make your speech more memorable as long as they aren't overused. Let's look at some examples.

A **simile** is a direct comparison of dissimilar things using the word *like* or *as*. Clichés such as "He walks like a duck" and "She's as busy as a bee" are similes. If you've seen the movie *Forrest Gump,* you might recall Forrest's use of similes: "Life is like a box of chocolates. You never know what you're going to get" and "Stupid is as stupid does." A very vivid simile was used by an elementary school teacher who said that being back at school after a long absence "was like trying to hold 35 corks under water at the same time."[8] This is a fresh, imaginative simile to describe an elementary school teacher's job. Similes can be effective because they make ideas more vivid in listeners' minds. But they should be used sparingly or they lose their appeal. Clichés should be avoided because their predictability reduces their effectiveness.

A **metaphor** is an implied comparison between two unlike things, expressed without using *like* or *as*. Instead of saying that one thing is *like* another, a metaphor says that one thing *is* another. Thus, problem cars are "lemons" and the leaky roof is a "sieve." Metaphors can be effective because they make an abstract concept more concrete, strengthen an important point, or heighten emotions. Notice how one speaker used a metaphor effectively to conclude a speech: "It is imperative that we weave our fabric of the future with durable thread."[9]

An **analogy** is an extended metaphor. Sometimes, you can develop a story from a metaphor that makes a concept more vivid. If you were to describe a family member as the "black sheep in the barnyard," that's a metaphor. If you went on to talk about the other members of the family as different animals on the farm and the roles ascribed to them, you would be extending the metaphor into an analogy. Analogies can be effective for holding your speech together in a creative and vivid way. Analogies are particularly useful to highlight the similarities between a complex or unfamiliar concept with one that is familiar.

Alliteration is the repetition of consonant sounds at the beginning of words that are near one another. Tongue twisters such as "She sells seashells by the seashore" use alliteration. In her speech about the history of jellybeans, Sharla used alliteration when she said, "And today there are more than fifty fabulous fruity flavors from which to choose." Used sparingly, alliteration can catch listeners' attention and make the speech memorable. But overuse can hurt the message because listeners might focus on the technique rather than the content of your message.

Assonance is the repetition of vowel sounds in a phrase or phrases. "How now brown cow" is a common example. Sometimes, the words rhyme, but they don't have to. Neil used assonance in his call to action this way: "Global warming is, in fact, a serious problem. I ask you to act now. Let's make a real difference for the future of our world." As with alliteration, assonance can make your speech more memorable as long as it's not overused.

Onomatopoeia is the use of words that sound like the things they stand for, such as "buzz," "hiss," "crack," and "plop." In the speech about skiing, the "swish" of the skis is an example of onomatopoeia.

Personification attributes human qualities to a concept or an inanimate object. When Madison talked about her truck, "Big Red," as her trusted friend and companion, she used personification. Likewise, when Rick talked about flowers dancing on the front lawn, he used personification.

Repetition is restating words, phrases, or sentences for emphasis. Martin Luther King Jr.'s "I Have a Dream" speech is a classic example:

> I say to you today, my friends, so even though we face the difficulties of today and tomorrow, I still have a dream. It is a dream deeply rooted in the American dream.

structures of speech phrases that combine ideas in a particular way

simile a direct comparison of dissimilar things using *like* or *as*

SPEECH SNIPPET

Using Metaphors

Dan decided to use a metaphor to help explain the complex concept of bioluminescence to his listeners. He said that "bioluminescence is a miniature flashlight that fireflies turn on and off at will."

---

metaphor an implied comparison between two unlike things without using *like* or *as*

analogy an extended metaphor

alliteration repetition of consonant sounds at the beginning of words that are near one another

assonance repetition of vowel sounds in a phrase or phrases

onomatopoeia words that sound like the things they stand for

personification attributing human qualities to a concept or an inanimate object

repetition restating words, phrases, or sentences for emphasis

I have a dream that one day this nation will rise up and live out the true meaning of its creed: "We hold these truths to be self-evident: that all men are created equal."

I have a dream that one day on the red hills of Georgia the sons of former slaves and the sons of former slave owners will be able to sit down together at the table of brotherhood.

I have a dream that one day even the state of Mississippi, a state sweltering with the heat of injustice, sweltering with the heat of oppression, will be transformed into the oasis of freedom and justice.

I have a dream that my four little children will one day live in a nation where they will not be judged by the color of their skin but by the content of their character. I have a dream today.

Reprinted by arrangement with the Estate of Martin Luther King, Jr. c/o Writers House as agent for the proprietor New York, NY. Copyright 1963 Dr. Martin Luther King, Jr., copyright renewed 1991 Coretta Scott King.

antithesis combining contrasting ideas in the same sentence

Antithesis is combining contrasting ideas in the same sentence, as when John F. Kennedy said, "Ask not what your country can do for you. Ask what you can do for your country." Likewise, astronaut Neil Armstrong used antithesis when he first stepped on the moon: "One small step for man, one giant leap for mankind." Speeches that offer antithesis in the concluding remarks are often very memorable.

SPOTLIGHT ON SPEAKERS

Benazir Bhutto *I Dream of a Pakistan*

Mark Wilson/Getty Images

In 1988, Benazir Bhutto made history when she became the first female prime minister of Pakistan, a country whose Muslim religious tradition is unaccustomed to female leadership. Yet Bhutto argued against the "preconceptions about the role of women in our society." Putting this belief into action, Bhutto served two terms as prime minister, but her journey was not without turmoil and controversy.

Unconstitutionally ousted only twenty months into her first term as prime minister, Bhutto did not give up. Her message of equality and rights for all people in a culturally splintered nation won her reelection in 1993. She governed for three more years before again being dismissed from office. The platform from which she moved her country forward (or backward, as some of her critics would charge) is echoed in this excerpt from her speech "Male Domination of Women," presented at the United Nations Fourth World Conference on Women in Beijing in 1995.

Equal rights are not defined only by political values.

Social justice is a triad of freedom, an equation of liberty: Justice is political liberty.

Justice is economic independence. Justice is social equality.

Delegates, sisters, the child who is starving has no human rights. The girl who is illiterate has no future.

The woman who cannot plan her life, plan her family, plan a career, is fundamentally not free. . . .

I am determined to change the plight of women in my country. More than sixty million of our women are largely sidelined.

It is a personal tragedy for them. It is a national catastrophe for my nation. I am determined to harness their potential to the gigantic task of nation building. . . .

I dream of a Pakistan in which women contribute to their full potential. I am conscious of the struggle that lies ahead. But, with your help, we shall persevere. Allah willing, we shall succeed.

To Think About

◆ Where in the speech excerpt did Bhutto use vivid language to make her ideas more compelling?

◆ What figures or structures of speech did Bhutto use to emphasize her ideas about social justice?

◆ Do you think her word choices made her ideas more compelling? Why or why not?

Speaking Appropriately

During the past several years, we have seen much controversy over "political correctness," especially on college campuses. Although many issues germane to the debate on political correctness go beyond the scope of this chapter, at the heart of this controversy is the question of what language behaviors are appropriate—and what language behaviors are inappropriate.

Speaking appropriately means using language that adapts to the needs, interests, knowledge, and attitudes of your listeners and avoiding language that alienates audience members. Through appropriate language, we communicate our respect for and acceptance of those who differ from us. In this section, we discuss specific strategies that will help you craft appropriate verbal messages.

As you begin rehearsing your speech, you may inadvertently use language that jolts audience members in such a way that they stop listening or shift their focus to you as a person rather than the content you are presenting. So, as you consider various ways of communicating a point, beware of common pitfalls that may be distracting or detrimental to achieving your goal.

Let's consider a few important guidelines that you will want to follow as you choose ways of expressing your ideas.

speaking appropriately
using language that adapts to the needs, interests, knowledge, and attitudes of the listener and avoiding language that alienates audience members

Adapt the Formality of Language to the Occasion

Language should be appropriately formal for the occasion. Your goal is to adapt your language to the occasion and the specific audience to which you are speaking. Thus, we are likely to use more informal language when speaking to a small audience of colleagues at a department meeting and more formal language when speaking with large audiences or with people whom we know less well or who have great power and authority.

Not only is the formality of your language suggested by the occasion and audience but so is the way you present yourself through your attire. We expect Lance Armstrong to adapt his speaking to the formality of the occasion.

Some people mistakenly believe that it is appropriate to use language in a way the speaker believes the members of the audience speak. Rather than being appropriate, however, this is likely to be counterproductive. For instance, when a middle-class adult gives a speech to young teenagers and tries to use teen slang or street talk, he or she may come off as a patronizing phony. Appropriately formal language, then, reflects the audience and the occasion but does not call for the speaker to adopt language patterns that are uncharacteristic of the speaker's usual style.

Show Sensitivity

Language is appropriate when it is sensitive to usages that others perceive as offensive. Some of the mistakes in language that we make result from using expressions that others perceive as sexist, racist, or otherwise biased—that is, any language that is perceived as belittling any person or group of people by virtue of their sex, race, age, disability, or other identifying characteristic. Four of the most prevalent linguistic uses that communicate insensitivity are profanity and vulgarity, biased language, offensive humor, and hate speech.

AVOID PROFANITY AND VULGARITY

Appropriate language avoids profanity and vulgar expressions. Fifty years ago, a child was punished for saying "hell" or "damn," and adults used profanity and vulgarity only in rare situations to express strong emotions. Today, "casual swearing"—profanity injected into regular conversation—is epidemic in some language communities, including college campuses.[10] In some settings, even the crudest and most offensive terms are so commonly used that speakers and (as a result) listeners alike have become desensitized, and the words have lost their ability to shock and offend.

Despite the growing, mindless use of crude speech, many people are still shocked and offended by swearing. And people who casually pepper their speech with profanity and vulgar expressions are often perceived as abrasive and lacking in character, maturity, intelligence, manners, and emotional control.[11]

Unfortunately, profanity and vulgarity are habits that are easily acquired and hard to extinguish. If you have acquired a "potty mouth," you're going to have to work very hard to clean up your act because verbal habits are hard to break. For tips on how to "tame your tongue," use your CengageNOW for *Challenge* to access **Web Resource 10.5: Cuss Control Academy.**

DEVELOP VERBAL IMMEDIACY

verbal immediacy when the language you use reduces the psychological distance between you and your audience

"we" language the use of plural personal pronouns like "we," "our," and "us" rather than "you" or "they"

Verbal immediacy occurs when the language you use reduces the psychological distance between you and your audience.[12] In other words, choose words that enhance the connection between you and the members of your audience. Verbal immediacy can be achieved by using "we" language, by using bias-free language, by avoiding inappropriate humor, and by shunning hate speech.

"We" language, the use of plural personal pronouns like "we," "our," and "us" rather than "you" or "they," conveys a sense of connection with your listeners and involves them in the topic and occasion. Pete used "we" language to introduce his speech in this way: "Today, we'll see why Tok Pisin of Papua New Guinea should be considered a legitimate language. We'll do this by looking at what kind of language Tok Pisin is, some of the features of the Tok Pisin language, and why this language is necessary in New Guinea." When used appropriately, "we" language helps you appear more likable, friendly, and understanding to your listeners. When you are perceived as having these traits, the more open your audience will be to listening to you, believing what you say, and remembering your ideas.[13]

Bias-free language, word choices that demonstrate an ethical concern for fairness and respect with regard to race, ethnicity, gender, ability, sexual orientation, and diverse worldviews,[14] also helps to create verbal immediacy. Unfortunately, many of us routinely use generic language and nonparallel language.

Generic language uses words that may apply only to one sex, race, or other group as though they represent everyone. Generic language is a problem because, in essence, it excludes a portion of your audience. Let's consider some examples.

Traditionally, English speakers have used the masculine pronoun *he* to stand for all humans regardless of gender. This is an example of using generic language. In contrast, bias-free language avoids using male pronouns when no specific gender reference is intended. You can avoid using generic language in one of two ways. First, you can use plurals: "When people shop, they should have a clear idea of what they want to buy." Alternatively, you can use both male and female pronouns: "When a person shops, he or she should have a clear idea of what he or she wants to buy." Research shows that using "he or she," and to a lesser extent "they," gives rise to listeners' including women in their mental images, thus increasing gender balance in their perceptions.[15] These changes are small, but the resulting language is more accurate and bias-free. To read an interesting article about masculine and feminine pronouns and think about how this topic might apply to your speeches, complete the InfoTrac College Edition Exercise at the end of this chapter.

A second problem of generic language results from the traditional use of *man.*[16] Consider the term *man-made.* What this really means is that a product was produced by human beings, but its underlying connotation is that a male human being made the item. For most generic expressions, suitable bias-free alternatives exist—for instance, *police officer* instead of *policeman, synthetic* instead of *man-made,* and *humankind* instead of *mankind.* Similarly, it is more inclusive to use *flight attendant* rather than *stewardess* and *server* rather than *waitress.* Not only is bias-free language more appropriate, but it is also more accurate.

Nonparallel language is language in which terms are changed because of the sex, race, or other group characteristics of the individual. Because it treats groups of people differently, nonparallel language is also belittling. Two common forms of nonparallelism are marking and unnecessary association.

Marking is the addition of sex, race, age, or other group designations to a description. For instance, a doctor is a person with a medical degree who is licensed to practice medicine. Notice the difference between the following two sentences:

Jones is a good doctor.

Jones is a good black doctor.

In the second sentence, use of the marker "black" is offensive. It has nothing to do with doctoring. Marking is inappropriate because you trivialize the person's role by introducing an irrelevant characteristic.[17] The speaker may be intending to praise Jones, but listeners may interpret the sentence as saying that Jones is a good doctor for a black person (or a woman or an old person) but not that Jones is as good as a good white doctor (or a male doctor or a young doctor).

A second form of nonparallelism is emphasizing one person's relationship to another when that relationship is irrelevant. For example, introducing a speaker as "Gladys Thompson, whose husband is CEO of Acme Inc., is the chairperson for this year's United Way campaign" is inappropriate. Using her husband's status implies that Gladys Thompson is chairperson because of her husband's accomplishments, not her own.

---

bias-free language language that demonstrates through word choices an ethical concern for fairness and respect with regard to race, ethnicity, gender, ability, sexual orientation, and diverse worldviews

generic language language that uses words that may apply only to one sex, race, or other group as though they represent everyone

nonparallel language language in which terms are changed because of the sex, race, or other group characteristics of the individual

marking the addition of sex, race, age, or other group designations to a description

Heather had agreed to listen to a portion of Terry's speech on nutrition. Terry said to her, "I think you'll love this opening—it's a little risky, but I think it will really get people's attention: 'It's obvious that several of you are getting pretty fat—and I know that you'd like to be looking more like normal people. Well, today I'm going to talk about nutrition and how even those of you who aren't as overweight as some others in class can still profit from the following advice that I've got to offer.'"

"Whoa, Terry—are you listening to what you're saying?"

"Come on, I'm just trying to get people to take a good look at themselves. My startling statement is designed to give people a jolt. And anyway, they know me and know that I don't mean anything by it."

"Terry, saying 'It's obvious that several of you are getting pretty fat—and I know that you'd like to be

looking more like normal people' isn't funny. It's flat-out offensive, and you know it!"

"I still don't think most people would take it wrong. But okay, I'll be more politically correct. How about this: 'It's obvious that a lot of you are overweight—in fact, I'm sure that you'd like to get rid of some of that fat. Well, today I'm going to talk about nutrition and how even those of you who aren't so overweight can still profit from following the advice that I've got to offer.' There, that's better, isn't it?"

1. Is it better? Has Terry made sufficient changes in the opening?
2. If not, how can Terry revise further to get people to think about themselves but not be offended by his wording?

AVOID OFFENSIVE HUMOR

Show sensitivity by avoiding offensive humor. Dirty jokes and racist, sexist, or other "-ist" remarks may not be intended to be offensive, but if some listeners are offended, you will have lost verbal immediacy. Comedian Chris Rock used offensive humor many times during his remarks as host of the 2003 MTV music awards. For example, he introduced rapper Eminem this way: "Our next presenter saves a lot of money on Mother's Day. Give it up for Eminem!" This remark, reflecting Eminem's ongoing disputes with his mother, may have been funny to some, but it certainly offended others. Likewise, he introduced entertainment mogul P. Diddy, who had faced several lawsuits recently, as "being sued by more people than the Catholic church."[18] Again, some in his audience were probably offended. To be most effective with your formal public speeches, avoid humorous comments or jokes that may be offensive to some listeners. Being inclusive means demonstrating respect for all listeners.

SHUN HATE SPEECH

You've heard the old child's saying, "Sticks and stones will break my bones, but words will never hurt me." As children, we all knew that this statement was a lie. Still, it gave us psychological comfort in the face of cruel name-calling. Unfortunately, name-calling can take on even uglier forms in adult speech. Think of the damage caused by the use of words such as "nigger," "cracker," "kike," or "fag."

hate speech the use of words and phrases to demean another person or group and to express the speaker's hatred and prejudice toward that person or group

Hate speech is the use of words and phrases to demean another person or group and to express the speaker's hatred and prejudice toward that person or group. Under the U.S. Constitution, people are generally afforded free speech protection. From a communication perspective, however, hate speech is designed to be divisive rather than inclusive.

By monitoring yourself, you can become more sensitive in your language choices. How can you speak more appropriately? (1) Use language geared to the formality of the relationship and setting and (2) show sensitivity by avoiding profanity and vulgarity, using bias-free language, avoiding inappropriate humor, and shunning hate speech.

Summary

Your overall language goal is to develop a "personal" oral style that captures your uniqueness. Language usage should be guided by the knowledge that words are only representations of ideas, objects, and feelings. Meaning is often a product of both word denotation, or dictionary meaning, and word connotation, or the thoughts and feelings that words evoke.

Specific goals of language use in a speech are to state ideas accurately, clearly, vividly, and appropriately. Ideas are clarified through specific, concrete, precise language. Specific language clarifies meaning. Concrete language appeals to the senses. Precise words are those that narrow a larger category. The larger your vocabulary, the more choices you have to select a word you want. Ways to increase your vocabulary are to study vocabulary-building books, to look up meanings of words you don't understand, and to use a thesaurus to identify synonyms. Clarity can also be achieved by providing details and examples. A speaker must also take into account how audience members might mistake meaning if they represent a culture different from that of the speaker.

Vividness means full of life, vigorous, bright, and intense. Increase the vividness of your language by using sensory language as well as rhetorical figures and structures of speech. Appropriateness means using language that adapts to the audience's needs, interests, knowledge, and attitudes and that avoids alienating listeners. Language in a speech will be appropriate if it is suited to the audience and occasion and if the language is sensitive and avoids profanity and vulgarity while using inclusive terms, avoiding offensive humor, and shunning hate speech.

CHALLENGE ONLINE

Now that you've read Chapter 10, use your CengageNOW for *The Challenge of Effective Speaking* for quick access to the electronic resources that accompany this text. Your CengageNOW gives you access to the "Shakespeare" video clip discussed on page 192, the Web Resources featured in this chapter, Speech Builder Express, InfoTrac College Edition, and online study aids such as a digital glossary and review quizzes.

Your *Challenge* CengageNOW is an online study system that helps you identify concepts you don't fully understand, allowing you to put your study time to the best use. Using chapter-by-chapter diagnostic pretests, the system creates a personalized study plan for each chapter. Each plan directs you to specific resources designed to improve your understanding, including pages from the text in e-book format. Chapter posttests give you an opportunity to measure how much you've learned and let you know if you are ready for graded quizzes and exams.

KEY TERMS

Go to your CengageNOW for *Challenge* to access your online glossary for Chapter 10. Print a copy of the glossary for this chapter and test yourself with the electronic flash cards or complete the crossword puzzle to help you master these key terms:

accurate language (189) **analogy** (197) **assonance** (197)
alliteration (197) **antithesis** (198) **bias-free language** (201)

concrete words (191)

connotation (190)

context (190)

denotation (190)

dialect (191)

figures of speech (196)

generic language (201)

hate speech (202)

intelligible (190)

jargon (194)

marking (201)

metaphor (197)

nonparallel language (201)

onomatopoeia (197)

oral style (188)

personification (197)

precise words (192)

repetition (197)

sensory language (196)

simile (197)

slang (194)

speaking appropriately (199)

specific language (191)

Standard English (191)

structures of speech (197)

verbal immediacy (200)

vivid language (196)

vocalized pause (195)

"we" language (200)

WEB RESOURCES

Go to your CengageNOW for *Challenge* to access the Web Resources for this chapter.

10.1 WordsmartChallenge (192)

10.2 Merriam-Webster Online (193)

10.3 Slang Dictionary (194)

10.4 Speaking to International Audiences (195)

10.5 Cuss Control Academy (200)

Practicing Delivery

© T.wayne Newton/PhotoEdit

Delivery I say has the sole and supreme power of oratory.

Cicero

What's Ahead

HERE'S WHAT'S AHEAD IN THIS CHAPTER:

1. What are the characteristics of effective delivery?

2. What can you do to use your voice effectively as you deliver your speech?

3. What can you do to use your body effectively as you deliver your speech?

4. Why and how should you rehearse your speech?

**Practicing speech
wording and delivery**

B. Practice until the
delivery is animated
and conversational.
C. Continue practicing
until you can deliver
your speech
extemporaneously
within the time limit.

When Nadia finished speaking, everyone in the audience burst into spontaneous applause and whistles.

"I just don't get it, Maurice. My speech was every bit as good as Nadia's, but when I finished, all I got was the ordinary polite applause that everyone gets regardless of what they've done. Of course, I'm not as hot as Nadia."

"Come on, Sylvia, get off it. Yeah, Nadia's pretty, but that's not why the audience loved her. Your speech was good. You had an interesting topic, good information, and it was well organized. But when it comes to delivery, Nadia has it all over most of us, including you."

In leveling with Sylvia, Maurice recognized what has been well known through the ages: Dynamic delivery can make a mediocre speech appear good and a good speech great. Why? Because how well the ideas are spoken can have a major impact on the audience's interest, understanding, and memory. In fact, research suggests that listeners are influenced more by delivery than by the content of speeches.[1] A speaker's delivery alone cannot compensate for a poorly researched, organized, or developed speech, but a well-delivered speech can rise above the ordinary and capture an audience. Some people, like Martin Luther King Jr. and former President Ronald Reagan, seemed naturally gifted in delivering speeches. Other speakers must spend time practicing their speeches to be dynamic. And most of us will need to practice our speeches if we are to capture and hold our audience's attention.

In this chapter, we begin by talking about the characteristics of effective delivery. We then describe the elements of effective delivery: use of voice, use of body, and a conversational style. Next, we explain the three types of speech delivery and the settings in which each is most appropriate. Finally, we suggest a process for rehearsing your speech that will prepare you to deliver it in a dynamic, conversational style. We also describe ways to adapt to your audience while giving your speech. At the end of this chapter, we have included a sample of a first speech given by a student in a beginning public speaking course.

Characteristics of an Effective Delivery Style

Think about the best speaker you have ever heard. What made this person stand out in your mind? In all likelihood, how the speaker delivered the speech had a lot to do with your evaluation. So, all the work you have done thus far to prepare your speech will be compromised if you cannot deliver it effectively.

delivery how a message is communicated orally and visually through the use of voice and body

nonverbal communication all speech elements other than the words themselves

Delivery is how a message is communicated orally and visually through your use of voice and body. When you deliver a speech, you rely primarily on nonverbal communication; whereas the content of a speech is conveyed through the *verbal channel*, delivery of the speech is conveyed through the *nonverbal channel*. **Nonverbal communication** includes all speech elements other than the words themselves.[2] These elements include your voice, articulation, eye contact, facial expressions, gestures, body language, and even appearance. An effective delivery style makes use of all these elements to create a speech that is conversational and animated.

Use a Conversational Tone

You have probably witnessed speakers whose delivery was "over the top" so that they appeared overly dramatic, too formal, or affected. Likewise, you may have experienced speakers who simply read their speeches to you or sounded "canned." These delivery styles can put off an audience because the speaker appears more interested in performing or reading than in actually talking with the audience. Effective delivery is **conversational,** meaning that the speaker sounds spontaneous, relaxed, and informal and is engaged in talking *with*, not *at*, the audience. The hallmark of a conversational style is that the speaker's message appears spontaneous. **Spontaneity** is a naturalness of speech where what is said sounds as if the speaker is really thinking about the ideas *and* the audience as he or she speaks. A speech with a spontaneous feel does not seem rehearsed or memorized or read.

Speakers who try to memorize their speeches often have to struggle so hard to remember the words that their delivery becomes laborious. Although talented actors can make lines they have spoken literally hundreds of times sound spontaneous and informal, most novice public speakers cannot.

The secret to developing a conversational style is to learn the *ideas* of your speech rather than trying to memorize its *words*. Suppose someone asks you about the route you take on your drive to work. Because you are familiar with the route, you can present it spontaneously. You have never written out the route, and you've never memorized it—you just know it. You develop a conversational style in public speaking in the same way. Through practice, you get to know the ideas in your speech as well as you know the route you take to work. As you study your outline, you absorb the material you are going to present, and when you have effectively rehearsed your wording, vocal delivery, and bodily movements, you can really enjoy talking with the audience about your ideas. You can then focus on talking about them with the audience, adjusting your message based on the nonverbal feedback you receive.

conversational style delivery that is spontaneous, relaxed, and informal and allows the speaker to talk *with,* not *at,* an audience

spontaneity a naturalness of speech where what is said sounds as if the speaker is really thinking about the ideas *and* the audience as he or she speaks

Be Animated

Have you ever sat in a class and listened to a professor give a well-structured lecture in a quiet monotone voice, while mostly looking at the lecture notes, and with few gestures besides turning the pages of those notes? If so, you were probably bored and had trouble staying focused on what was said, even if this was a class you were really interested in. A well-prepared speech given by an expert can bore an audience unless its delivery is **animated,** lively, energetic, enthusiastic, and dynamic.

How can you be conversational and animated at the same time? The secret is to focus on conveying the passion you feel about your topic to your audience through your voice and body. In everyday life, all of us differ in how animated we are when we speak. Some of us are extroverted and naturally expressive, whereas others are introverted and more circumspect in our verbal and nonverbal expressiveness. And of course, there are cultural differences in how much animation is appropriate when we speak. Nevertheless, when we are excited to share something with someone, almost all of us become more animated in our delivery. It is this level of liveliness that you want to duplicate when you deliver your speech. To see a video clip of a student speaker with an animated delivery, use your CengageNOW for *Challenge* to access the speech "Why Pi?" in Chapter 11 resources.

animated delivery delivery that is lively, energetic, enthusiastic, and dynamic

Ironically, for most of us, appearing conversational and animated requires considerable practice. In the next two sections, we will consider how you can use your voice and body to deliver your speech effectively.

Effective Use of Voice

voice the sound you produce in your larynx, or voice box, which is used to transmit the words of your speech to an audience

Your **voice** is the sound you produce in your larynx, or voice box, which you use to transmit the words of your speech to the audience. How you sound to your audience emphasizes, supplements, and sometimes even contradicts the meaning of your words. As a result, how you use your voice affects how successful you are in getting your ideas across. As you rehearse and deliver your speech, focus on not only *what* you say but also on *how* you sound as you say it. Strive to use your voice so that what you say is intelligible and vocally expressive. You will be better prepared to do this if you understand the characteristics of your voice.

Understand the Characteristics of Voice

The four major characteristics of voice are pitch, volume, rate, and quality.

pitch the scaled highness or lowness of the sound a voice makes

Pitch is the highness or lowness of the sound of your voice on a musical scale. Pitch is created by loosening or tightening the vocal folds in the larynx, or voice box. Natural pitch varies from person to person, but men generally have lower pitched voices than women and children.

volume the degree of loudness of the tone you make

Volume is how loudly or softly you speak. You control your volume by how forcefully you expel the air through your vocal cords. When you push a lot of air through the cords, you speak loudly; when you push less air through, your volume drops.

rate the speed at which you talk

Rate is how fast you talk. In normal conversations, most people speak between 130 and 180 words per minute. We generally speak faster when we are excited and slow down when we are trying to explain difficult material.

quality the tone, timbre, or sound of your voice

Quality is the tone or timbre of your voice and what distinguishes it from the voices of others—it is "how you sound" to others. The ideal voice quality is clear and sounds like a ringing bell. Most TV announcers and film narrators have voices with exceptional quality. Difficulties with quality include nasality (talking through your nose), breathiness (too much air escaping through the vocal cords), and harshness (caused by overconstriction of the throat).

With this basic understanding of vocal characteristics, let's now explore how you can use your voice to ensure that your speech is intelligible and vocally expressive.

Speak Intelligibly

intelligible capable of being understood

To be **intelligible** means to be understandable. All of us have experienced situations in which we couldn't understand what was said because the speaker was talking too softly or too quickly or had a voice that was compromised in some way. If you're not intelligible, your listeners are bound to struggle with your verbal message. By practicing using appropriate vocal pitch, volume, rate of speech, and vocal quality, you can improve the likelihood that when you deliver your speech, it will be intelligible to your audience.

Most of us speak within a pitch range that is appropriate for us and intelligible to listeners. However, some people naturally have voices that are higher or lower in register or become accustomed to talking in tones that are above or below their natural pitch. Speaking at an appropriate pitch is particularly important if you're speaking to an audience in which some members have experienced hearing loss. People with hearing loss often find it difficult to hear a pitch that is too high or too low. As overamplified music has become widespread, hearing losses, especially in the upper register, are becoming a problem even among younger people. Intelligibility is also affected by how much a speaker fluctuates his or her pitch. In normal conversation, pitch fluctuates frequently, and perhaps even a bit more during a speech. Pitch that doesn't fluctuate often hinders intelligibility. For example, in English, a sentence that is meant to be a question is vocalized with rising pitch. If pitch doesn't rise at the end of a question, listeners may interpret the sentence as a statement instead.

Appropriate volume is the key to intelligibility. You must speak loudly enough, with or without a microphone, to be heard easily by the audience members seated in the back of the room but not so loudly as to bring discomfort to listeners seated near the front. In addition, varying your volume allows you to emphasize important information. For example, you may speak louder as you introduce each of your main points.

The rate at which you speak can determine how intelligible your message is. Speaking too slowly gives your listeners time to let their minds wander after they've processed your message. Speaking too quickly, especially when sharing complex ideas and arguments, doesn't give your listeners enough time to process the difficult information completely. Although your typical rate of speaking may be within the normal range, being nervous when giving a speech can cause you to speak more quickly or slowly. As you practice and then deliver your speech, monitor your speaking rate and slow down or speed up depending on the difficulty of the ideas and the nervousness you feel. To complete a simple test to see if your typical rate of speech is within the range that is intelligible to most people, use your CengageNOW for *Challenge* to access **Web Resource 11.1: Your Speech Rate**.

In addition to vocal characteristics, your articulation and accent can affect how intelligible your message is to your audience. **Articulation** refers to using the tongue, palate, teeth, jaw movement, and lips to shape vocalized sounds that combine to produce a word. **Accent** is the inflection, tone, and speech habits typical of the natives of a particular country, a region, or even a state or city that may differ from others who speak the same language. When you misarticulate or speak with a heavy accent during a conversation, your listeners can ask you to repeat yourself until they understand you. But in a speech setting, audience members are unlikely to interrupt to ask you to repeat what you have just said.

Many of us suffer from minor articulation and **pronunciation** problems such as adding a sound where none appears ("athalete" for *athlete*), leaving out a sound where one occurs ("libary" for *library*), transposing sounds ("revalent" for *relevant*), and distorting sounds ("truf" for *truth*). Although some people have consistent articulation problems that require speech therapy (such as always substituting *th* for *s*), most of us are guilty of careless articulation habits that are easily corrected. Exhibit 11.1 on page 210 lists many common words that people are likely to mispronounce or misarticulate.

Accent is often a major concern for second language speakers or speakers from varying subcultures or geographic areas. Everyone speaks with some kind of accent, since "accent" means any tone or inflection that differs from the way others speak. Natives of a particular city or region in the United States will speak with inflections and tones that they believe are "normal" spoken English—for instance, people from the Northeast who drop the *r* sound (saying

"LADIES AND GENTLEMEN... IS *THAT* MY VOICE?.. I NEVER HEARD IT AMPLIFIED BEFORE. IT SOUNDS SO WEIRD. HELLO. HELLO. I CAN'T BELIEVE IT'S ME. WHAT A STRANGE SENSATION. ONE, TWO, THREE... HELLO. WOW..."

© 2004 by Sidney Harris

articulation using the tongue, palate, teeth, jaw movement, and lips to shape vocalized sounds that combine to produce a word

accent the inflection, tone, and speech habits typical of the natives of a country, a region, or even a state or city

pronunciation the form and accent of various syllables of a word

EXHIBIT 11.1   Words commonly mispronounced

Word	Incorrect	Correct
arctic	ar'-tic	arc'-tic
athlete	ath'-a-lete	ath'-lete
family	fam'-ly	fam'-a-ly
February	Feb'-yu-ary	Feb'-ru-ary
get	git	get
hundred	hun'-derd	hun'-dred
larynx	lar'-nix	ler'-inks
library	ly'-ber-y	ly'-brer-y
nuclear	nu'-kyu-ler	nu'-klee-er
particular	par-tik'-ler	par-tik'-yu-ler
picture	pitch'-er	pic'-ture
recognize	rek'-a-nize	rek'-ig-nize
relevant	rev'-e-lant	rel'-e-vant
theater	thee-ay'-ter	thee'-a-ter
truth	truf	truth
with	wit or wid	with

"cah" for *car*) or people from the South who elongate their vowels and "drawl." But when they visit a different city or region, they are perceived as having an accent. If your accent is "thick" or different from that of most of your audience, practice pronouncing key words so that you are easily understood, speak slowly to allow your audience members more time to process your message, and consider reinforcing important terms with visual aids.

Use Vocal Expressiveness

vocal expressiveness variety you create in your voice through changing pitch, volume, and rate, as well as stressing certain words and using pauses

Vocal expressiveness is produced by the variety you create in your voice through changing pitch, volume, and rate, stressing certain words, and using pauses. These contrasts clarify the emotional meaning of your message and help animate your delivery. Generally, speeding up your rate, raising your pitch, or increasing your volume reinforces emotions such as joy, enthusiasm, excitement, anticipation, and a sense of urgency or fear. Slowing down your rate, lowering your pitch, or decreasing your volume can communicate resolution, peacefulness, remorse, disgust, or sadness.

monotone a voice in which the pitch, volume, and rate remain constant, with no word, idea, or sentence differing significantly from any other

A total lack of vocal expressiveness produces a **monotone**—a voice in which the pitch, volume, and rate remain constant, with no word, idea, or sentence differing significantly in sound from any other. Although few people speak in a true monotone, many severely limit themselves by using only two or three pitch levels and relatively unchanging volume and rate. An actual or near monotone not only lulls an audience to sleep but, more important, diminishes the chances of audience understanding. For instance, if the sentence "Congress should pass laws limiting the sale of pornography" is presented in a monotone, listeners will be uncertain whether the speaker is concerned with *who* should be responsible for the laws, *what* Congress *should do* with the laws, or *what* the laws should be.

Creating vocally expressive messages is a complex process. For example, Nick introduced his speech on legalizing marijuana as a painkiller this way:

Millions of Americans suffer needlessly each year. These people endure unbearable pain needlessly because, although our government is capable of helping them, it chooses to ignore their pain. Our government has no compassion, no empathy, no regard for human feeling. I'm here today to convince you to support my efforts toward legalizing marijuana as a painkiller for terminally ill patients.

To reinforce the emotional elements of anger, disgust, and seriousness, Nick gradually slowed his rate, decreased his volume, and lowered his pitch as he emphasized, "Our government has no compassion, no empathy, no regard for human feeling."

He also used **stress,** an emphasis placed on certain words by speaking them more loudly than the rest of the sentence, to shape his meaning. Read the following sentence from Nick's speech:

Millions of Americans suffer needlessly each year.

What did Nick intend the focus of that sentence to be? Without hearing it spoken, it is difficult to say because its focus would change depending on which word Nick chose to stress. Read the sentence aloud several times. Each time, stress a different word and listen to how your stress changes the meaning. If you stress *millions,* the emphasis is on the number of people affected. When you stress *Americans,* the fact that the problem is on a national scale is emphasized. When you stress *suffer,* notice how much more you feel the pain. When you stress *needlessly,* you can sense Nick's frustration with how unnecessary the suffering is. And when you stress *each year,* the ongoing nature of the unnecessary suffering becomes the focus. Thus, the words you stress in a sentence affect your meaning.

Pauses, moments of silence strategically placed to enhance meaning, can also mark important ideas. If you use one or more sentences in your speech to express an important idea, pause before each sentence to signal that something important is coming up or pause afterward to allow the ideas to sink in. Pausing one or more times within a sentence can add further impact. Nick included several short pauses within and a long pause after his line, "Our government has no compassion *(pause)*, no empathy *(pause)*, no regard for human feeling" *(longer pause)*.

Effective Use of Body

Because your audience can see as well as hear you, conversational and animated delivery are also achieved by how you use your body. The nonverbal characteristics that affect your delivery are your facial expressions, gestures, movement, posture, and appearance.

Facial Expressions

Your **facial expressions,** eye and mouth movements, convey your personableness and can help you animate your speech. When you are talking with your friends, your facial expressions are naturally animated. Your audiences expect your expressions to be similarly animated and to vary and be appropriate to what you are saying when you give a speech. Speakers who do not vary their facial expressions during their speech but who wear deadpan expressions, perpetual grins, or permanent scowls will be perceived as boring, insincere, or stern. Audiences respond positively to natural facial expressions that appear to spontaneously reflect what you're saying and how you feel about it.

Gestures

Your **gestures,** the movements of your hands, arms, and fingers, can help your speech remain intelligible. You can use gestures to describe or emphasize what you are saying, refer to presentational aids, or clarify structure. For example, as

stress emphasis placed on certain words by speaking them more loudly than the rest of the sentence

pauses moments of silence strategically placed to enhance meaning

SPEECH SNIPPET

Using Appropriate Facial Expressions

Nancy furrowed her brows and pursed her lips when she told the story of two young children who were abandoned in a parking lot—her facial expression conveyed seriousness and disgust. Thad, on the other hand, raised his eyebrows and smiled slightly as he talked about the many new forms of entertainment a domed stadium would bring to the city—his expression conveyed joy and excitement.

facial expression eye and mouth movements

gestures the movements of your hands, arms, and fingers that help you remain intelligible

movement changing the position of the entire body

motivated movement movement with a purpose

eye contact looking directly at the people to whom you are speaking

Aaron began to speak about the advantages of wireless DSL, he said, "on one hand" and emphasized his words by lifting his right hand face up. When he got to the disadvantages, he lifted his left hand face up as he said, "on the other hand."

Some of us gesture a lot in our casual conversations; others do not. If gesturing does not come easily to you, don't force yourself to gesture during a speech. Some people who normally use gestures are nervous when giving a speech, so they clasp their hands behind their backs, bury them in their pockets, or grip the speaker's stand. Unable to pry their hands free gracefully, they wiggle their elbows weirdly or appear stiff. As with facial expressions, effective gestures must appear spontaneous and natural even though they are carefully planned and practiced. When you practice and then deliver your speech, leave your hands free so that they will be available to gesture as you normally do.

Movement

Movement refers to changing the position of the entire body. During your speech, it is important to engage only in **motivated movement,** movement with a specific purpose such as emphasizing an important idea, referencing a presentational aid, or clarifying macrostructure. To emphasize a particular point, you might move closer to the audience. To create a feeling of intimacy before you tell a personal story, you might walk out from behind a lectern and sit down on a chair placed at the edge of the stage. Each time you begin a new main point, you might take a few steps in alternating directions. To use motivated movement effectively, you need to practice when and how you will move.

Avoid such unmotivated movement as bobbing, weaving, shifting from foot to foot, or pacing from one side of the room to the other because unplanned movements distract the audience from your message. Since many unplanned movements result from nervousness, you can minimize them by paying mindful attention to your body as you speak. At the beginning of your speech, stand up straight on both feet. Whenever you find yourself fidgeting, readjust and position your body with your weight equally distributed on both feet.

Eye Contact

Eye contact is looking directly at the people to whom you are speaking. In speech making, it involves looking at people in all parts of an audience throughout a speech. As long as you are looking at someone (those in front of you, in the left rear of the room, in the right center of the room, etc.) and not at your notes or the ceiling, floor, or window, everyone in the audience will perceive you as having good eye contact with them. Generally, you should look at your audience at least 90 percent of the time, glancing at your notes only when you need a quick reference point. Maintaining eye contact is important for several reasons.

1. Maintaining eye contact helps audiences concentrate on the speech. If speakers do not look at us while they talk, we are unlikely to maintain eye contact with them. This break in mutual eye contact often decreases concentration on the speaker's message.

2. Maintaining eye contact increases the audience's confidence in you, the speaker. Just as you are likely to be skeptical of people who do not look you in the eye as they converse, so too audiences will be skeptical of speakers who do not look at them. Eye contact is perceived as a sign of sincerity. Speakers who fail to maintain eye contact with audiences are perceived almost always as ill at ease and often as insincere or dishonest.[3]

3. Maintaining eye contact helps you gain insight into the audience's reaction to the speech. Because communication is two way, audience members are speaking to you at the same time you are speaking to them. In conversation, the audience's response is likely to be both verbal and nonverbal; in public speaking, the audience's response is more likely shown by nonverbal cues alone. Audiences that pay attention are likely to look at you with varying amounts of intensity. Listeners who are bored yawn, look out the window, slouch in their chairs, and may even sleep. If audience members are confused, they will look puzzled; if they agree with what you say or understand it, they will nod their heads. By monitoring your audience's behavior, you can adjust by becoming more animated, offer additional examples, or move more quickly through a point. If you are well prepared, you will be better equipped to make the adjustments and adapt to the needs of your audience.

One way of ensuring eye contact during your speech is to gaze at various groups of people in all parts of the audience throughout the speech. To establish effective eye contact, mentally divide your audience into small groups scattered around the room. Then, at random, talk for four to six seconds with each group. Perhaps start with a Z pattern. Talk with the group in the back left for a few seconds, then glance at people in the far right for a few seconds, and then move to a group in the middle, a group in the front left, and then a group in the front right, and so forth. Then perhaps reverse the order, starting in the back right. Eventually, you will find yourself going in a random pattern in which you look at all groups over a period of a few minutes. Such a pattern helps you avoid spending a disproportionate amount of your time talking with those in front of you or in the center of the room.

When speaking to large audiences of 100 or more people, you must create a sense of looking listeners in the eye even though you actually cannot. This process is called **audience contact.** You can create audience contact using the Z pattern and four- to six-second rule as you focus on different groups of people throughout the speech.

When a person speaks, we expect appropriate facial expression, gestures, and movement.

audience contact creating a sense of looking listeners in the eye when speaking to large audiences

Posture

Your **posture** refers to the position or bearing of the body. In speeches, an upright stance and squared shoulders communicate a sense of poise to an audience. Speakers who slouch may give an unfavorable impression of themselves, including the impression of limited self-confidence and an uncaring attitude. As you practice, be aware of your posture and adjust it so that you remain upright with your weight equally distributed on both feet. To read a thought-provoking discussion of how various body motions, including posture, affect audience attention during a speech, use your CengageNOW for *Challenge* to access **Web Resource 11.2: Body Motions and Audience Attention.**

During speech practice sessions, try various methods to monitor or alter your bodily action. Videotape provides an excellent means of monitoring your bodily action. You may want to practice before a mirror to see how you look to others when you speak. (Although some speakers swear by this method, others find it a traumatic experience.) Perhaps the best method is to get a willing listener to critique your bodily action and help you improve. Once you have identified the behavior you want to change, tell your helper what to look for. For instance, you might say, "Raise your hand every time I begin to rock back

posture the position or bearing of the body

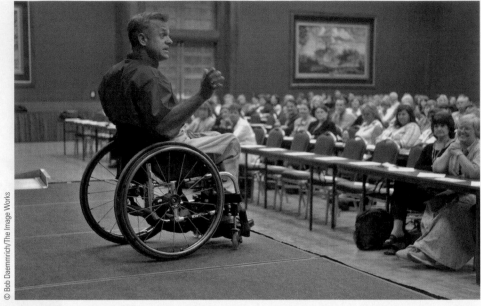
© Bob Daemmrich/The Image Works

The better you are able to maintain eye contact with all parts of the audience during your speech, the more confident they will be that you are a sincere speaker.

and forth." By getting specific feedback when the behavior occurs, you can make immediate adjustments.

To see a video clip of a student speaker using effective bodily action, use your CengageNOW for *Challenge* to access the speech "No More Sugar" in the Chapter 11 resources.

CENGAGENOW™

Appearance

appearance the way you look to others

Some speakers think that what they wear doesn't or shouldn't affect the success of their speech. But your **appearance,** the way you look to others, is important. Studies show that a neatly groomed and professional appearance sends important messages about a speaker's commitment to the topic and occasion, as well as the speaker's credibility.[4] Your appearance should complement and reinforce your message, not detract from it. Three guidelines can help you decide how to dress for your speech.

1. Consider your audience and the occasion of your speech. Dress a bit more formally than you expect the members of your audience will dress. If you dress too formally, your audience is likely to perceive you as untrustworthy and insincere,[5] and if you dress too casually, the audience may view you as uncommitted to your topic or disrespectful of them or the occasion.[6]

2. Consider your topic and purpose. In general, the more serious your topic, the more formally you should dress. For example, if your topic is AIDS and you are trying to convince your audience to be tested for HIV, you will want to look like someone who is an authority by dressing the part. But if your topic is skateboarding and you are trying to convince your audience they would enjoy visiting the new skateboard park on campus, you might dress more casually.

3. Avoid extremes. Your attire shouldn't detract from your speech. Avoid gaudy jewelry, over- or undersized clothing, or sexually suggestive attire. Remember, you want your audience to focus on your message, so your appearance should be neutral, not distracting.

Methods of Delivery

Speeches can be delivered in one of three methods that vary in the amount of content preparation and the amount of practice the speaker does ahead of time. These delivery methods are impromptu, scripted, and extemporaneous.

Impromptu Speeches

At times, you may be called on to speak on the spot. At a business meeting or in a class, you may be asked to speak with little advance warning. An **impromptu speech** is one that is delivered with only seconds or minutes of advance notice for preparation and is usually presented without referring to notes of any kind. You may have already been called on in this class to give an impromptu speech, so you know the kind of pressures and problems this type of speaking creates.

Because impromptu speakers gather their thoughts as they speak, it is difficult to carefully organize their ideas and develop what they are saying. As a result, they may leave out important information or confuse audience members. Delivery can suffer as speakers use "ahs," "ums," "like," and "you know" to buy time as they scramble to collect their thoughts.

You can improve your impromptu performances by practicing "mock" impromptu speeches. For example, if you are taking a class in which the professor calls on students to answer questions, you can prepare by anticipating the questions that might be asked and by practicing giving your answers out loud. Over time, you will become more adept at quickly organizing your ideas and "thinking on your feet."

> **impromptu speech** a speech that is delivered with only seconds or minutes of advance notice for preparation and is usually presented without referring to notes of any kind

Scripted Speeches

At the other extreme, there are situations in which a speaker carefully prepares a complete written manuscript of the entire speech text and delivers it either word for word from memory or by reading the manuscript from a printed document or a teleprompter. A **scripted speech** is one that is prepared by creating a complete written manuscript and delivered by reading a written copy.

Obviously, effective scripted speeches take a great deal of time to prepare and practice. Not only must you prepare an outline, but you must also write out the entire speech, carefully choosing language and sentence structures that sound natural when spoken. Once the manuscript is prepared, you memorize the script and then rehearse orally, or you rehearse with the written manuscript. When scripted speeches are memorized, you face the increased anxiety caused by fear of forgetting your lines. When they are read from a printed manuscript or from a teleprompter, you must become adept at looking at the script with your peripheral vision so that you can maintain eye contact with your audience. While politicians, talk show hosts, and television news anchors are usually good at achieving conversational style while reading from printed manuscripts and teleprompters, most speakers sound like they are reading or reciting and find it difficult to achieve a conversational style with a scripted speech.

Scripted speeches take the most time to prepare and to rehearse if they are to be done well. So, when people are called on to give important speeches that have grave consequences, they will take the time and make the effort to prepare a scripted speech. Political "stump" speeches, keynote addresses at conventions, commencement addresses, and CEO remarks at annual stockholder meetings are examples of occasions when a scripted speech might be appropriate.

> **scripted speech** a speech that is prepared by creating a complete written manuscript and delivered by reading a written copy or from memory

Extemporaneous Speeches

extemporaneous speech a speech that is researched and planned ahead of time, but the exact wording is not scripted and will vary from presentation to presentation

In this book, our emphasis is on the third type of delivery because, in most situations, whether at work or in the community, speeches are delivered extemporaneously. An **extemporaneous speech** is researched and planned ahead of time, but the exact wording is not scripted and will vary from presentation to presentation. When speaking extemporaneously, you may refer to speaking notes you have prepared to remind you of the ideas you want to present and the order in which you want to present them.

Extemporaneous speeches are the easiest to give effectively. Unlike impromptu speeches, when speaking extemporaneously, you are able to prepare your thoughts ahead of time and to have notes to prompt you. Yet unlike scripted speeches, extemporaneous speeches do not require as lengthy a preparation and practice process to be effective. In the next section of this chapter, we describe how to rehearse successfully for an extemporaneous speech.

Rehearsal

rehearsing practicing the presentation of your speech aloud

Rehearsing is practicing the presentation of your speech aloud. In this section, we describe how to schedule your preparation and practice, how to prepare and use notes, and guidelines for effective rehearsal.

Scheduling and Conducting Rehearsal Sessions

Inexperienced speakers often believe they are ready to present the speech once they have finished their outline. But a speech that is not practiced is likely to be far less effective than it would have been had you given yourself sufficient practice time. In general, if you are not an experienced speaker, try to complete the outline at least three days before the speech is to be presented so that you have sufficient practice time to revise, evaluate, and mull over all aspects of the speech. Exhibit 11.2 provides a useful timetable for preparing a classroom speech.

Is it really necessary to practice a speech out loud? A study by Menzel and Carrell supports this notion and concludes, "The significance of rehearsing out loud probably reflects the fact that verbalization clarifies thought. As a result, oral rehearsal helps lead to success in the actual delivery of a speech."[7]

Preparing Speaking Notes

speaking notes a word or phrase outline of your speech, plus hard-to-remember information such as quotations and statistics, as well as delivery cues designed to trigger memory

Prior to your first rehearsal session, prepare a draft of your speaking notes. **Speaking notes** are a word or phrase outline of your speech, including hard-to-remember information such as quotations and statistics, as well as delivery cues designed to

---

EXHIBIT 11.2 Timetable for preparing a speech

7 days before	Select topic; begin research
6 days before	Continue research
5 days before	Outline body of speech
4 days before	Work on introduction and conclusion
3 days before	Finish outline; find additional material if needed; have all visual aids completed
2 days before	First rehearsal session
1 day before	Second rehearsal session
Due date	Give speech

help trigger memory. The best notes contain the fewest words possible written in lettering large enough to be seen instantly at a distance. Although some speakers do so, you should not use PowerPoint slides as speaking notes. This is bad practice because it results in you and your listeners reading from the screen rather than you communicating a message; use PowerPoint slides only as visual enhancement.

To develop your notes, begin by reducing your speech outline to an abbreviated outline of key phrases and words. Then, if you have details in the speech for which you must have a perfectly accurate representation—such as a specific example, a quotation, or a set of statistics—add these in the appropriate places. Next, indicate exactly where you plan to show visual aids. Finally, incorporate cues to remind you of where you want to use delivery techniques that make use of your voice and body. For example, indicate where you want to pause, gesture, or make a motivated movement. Capitalize or underline words you want to stress. Use slash marks (//) to remind yourself to pause. Use an upward-pointing arrow to remind yourself to increase rate or volume.

Making speaking notes not only provides you with prompts when you are speaking, but it also helps in two other ways. First, the act of compiling the speaking notes helps to cement the flow of the speech's ideas in your mind. Second, as you prepare your notes, think about key ideas and phrasings. Notes don't include all the developmental material.

For a three- to five-minute speech, you will need only one or two 3-by-5-inch note cards to record your speaking notes. For longer speeches, you might need one card for the introduction, one for each main point, and one for the conclusion. If your speech contains a particularly important and long quotation or a complicated set of statistics, you can record this information in detail on separate cards. Exhibit 11.3 shows how Emming could represent his complete outline, shown on pages 159–160 of Chapter 8, on two 3-by-5-inch note cards.

During practice sessions, use the notes as you would in the speech. If you will use a lectern, set the notes on the speaker's stand or, alternatively, hold them in one hand and refer to them only when needed. How important is it to construct good note cards? Speakers often find that the act of making a note card is so effective in helping cement ideas in the mind that during practice, or later during the speech itself, they rarely use the notes at all.

Effective speakers relate better to their audience using a few note cards rather than a complete outline or manuscript.

Rehearsing the Speech

Just as with any other activity, effective speech making requires practice, and the more you practice, the better your speech will be. During practice sessions, you have three goals. First, you will practice wording your ideas so they are vivid. Second, you will practice "doing" your speech—working with your voice and body so that your ideas are delivered with enthusiasm, appropriate emphasis, and spontaneity. Third, you will practice using presentational aids. As part of each practice, you will want to analyze how well it went and set goals for the next practice session. Let's look at how you can proceed through several practice rounds.

FIRST REHEARSAL

Your initial rehearsal should include the following steps:

1. Audiotape your practice session. If you do not own a recorder, try to borrow one. You may also want to have a friend or relative sit in on your practice.

EXHIBIT 11.3 Two note cards

Note Card 1

Intro
(PAUSE and LOOK LISTENERS IN THE EYE)
How many hounded by vendors?
credit card = answer to dreams
Three criteria: 1 IR, // 2 Fee, // 3 incentives //

Body
(walk right)
1st Crit: Examine interest rates
IRs are % that a company charges to carry balance
- Average of 8%
- As much as 32%!! (Kiplinger's, Jan 2007)
- Start as low as 0% up to 12 months
  — Student cards higher (Business Week, May 21, 2001)
  — Some below 14%
IRs variable or fixed
- Variable—change month to month
- Fixed—stay same
  — Even fixed rates can be raised after late payment
(walk left to VISUAL AID)
(Considered IRs: look at next criterion)

Note Card 2

2nd C: Examine the annual fee
AF charges vary
(SHOW VISUAL AID)
- Most, no annual fee
- Some companies do have fee (AMEX)
(COVER VISUAL AID)
(walk left)
(After considered interest and fees, weigh benefits)
3rd C: Weigh incentives
- Rebates (US News, July 31, 2005)
- Freq flyer miles
- Discounts
  — Cash back on purchases
Incentives not outweigh other factors

Conclusion
(walk back to center)
So, 3 criteria: IRs, annual fees, incentives
Then your credit card may truly be the answer to dreams.

2. Read through your complete sentence outline once or twice to refresh your memory. Then put the outline out of sight and practice the speech using only the note cards you have prepared.

3. Make the practice as similar to the speech situation as possible, including using the presentational aids you've prepared. Stand up and face your imaginary audience. Pretend that the chairs, lamps, books, and other objects in your practice room are people.

4. Write down the time that you begin.

5. Begin speaking. Regardless of what happens, keep going until you have presented your entire speech. If you goof, make a repair as you would if you were actually delivering the speech to an audience.

6. Write down the time you finish. Compute the length of the speech for this first rehearsal.

ANALYSIS

Listen to the tape and look at your complete outline. How did it go? Did you leave out any key ideas? Did you talk too long on any one point and not long enough on another? Did you clarify each of your points? Did you adapt to your anticipated audience? (If you had a friend or relative listen to your practices, have him or her help with your analysis.) Were your note cards effective? How well did you do with your presentational aids? Make any necessary changes before your second rehearsal.

SECOND REHEARSAL

Repeat the six steps listed for the first rehearsal. By practicing a second time right after your analysis, you are more likely to make the kind of adjustments that begin to improve the speech.

ADDITIONAL REHEARSALS

After you have completed one full practice session, consisting of two rehearsals and an analysis, put the speech away until that night or the next day. Although you should rehearse the speech at least one more time, you will not benefit if you cram all the practices into one long rehearsal time. You may find that a final practice right before you go to bed will be very helpful; while you are sleeping, your subconscious will continue to work on the speech. As a result, you are likely to find significant improvement in your mastery of the speech when you practice again the next day.

How many times you practice depends on many variables, including your experience, your familiarity with the subject, and the length of your speech. For beginning speakers, we suggest at least three practice sessions.

SPEAKING EXTEMPORANEOUSLY

When practicing, try to learn the speech ideas, but do not memorize specific phrasings. Recall that memorizing the speech involves saying the speech the same way each time until you can give it word for word without notes. Learning the speech involves understanding the ideas of the speech but having the freedom to present the ideas differently during each practice.

To illustrate how extemporaneous presentations change from one time to the next, let's see how a short portion of the speech outline for the credit card criteria speech might be modified from one practice to the next. That portion of the outline reads as follows:

A. Interest rates are the percentages that a company charges you to carry a balance on your card past the due date.

1. Most credit cards carry an average of 8 percent.

Now let's consider three practices that focus on this small portion of the outline.

First practice: "Interest rates are the percentages that a company charges you to carry a balance on your card past the due date. Most credit cards carry an average of 8 percent. Did you hear that? 8 percent."

Second practice: "Interest rates are the percentages that a company charges you when you don't pay the balance in full and thus still owe the company money. Most credit cards carry an average of 8 percent—think of that,

8 percent. So, if you leave a balance every month, before you know it you're going to be paying a lot more money than you thought you would."

Third practice: "Interest rates are the percentages that a company charges you when you don't pay the balance in full—you can rack up a lot of debt by not paying on time. Most credit cards carry an average of 8 percent. Did you hear that? A whopping 8 percent, at a time when you can get about any kind of a loan for less than 6."

Notice that points A and 1 of the outline are in all three versions. As this illustrates, the essence of the outline will be part of all versions. But because you make slight variations using different words each time, when you finally give the speech, the extemporaneous delivery will ensure spontaneity.

SPEECH PLANNING · 6 | Delivery · ACTION STEP 6

ACTIVITY 6A Rehearsing Your Speech

The goal of this activity is to rehearse your speech, analyze it, and rehearse it again. One complete rehearsal includes (1) a practice, (2) an analysis, and (3) a second practice.

1. Find a place where you can be alone to practice your speech. Follow the six points of the first rehearsal.

2. Listen to the tape. Review your outline as you listen and then complete a speech evaluation checklist to see how well you presented your speech during this rehearsal. (You can find the Speech Evaluation Checklist: General Criteria on page 13 in Chapter 1, a more detailed checklist in this chapter, and checklists for informative and persuasive speeches in later chapters.)

   List three specific changes you will make in your next practice session.

   One: _____

   Two: _____

   Three: _____

3. Go through the six steps outlined for the first rehearsal again. Then assess: Did you achieve the goals you set for the second rehearsal?

   Reevaluate the speech using the checklist and continue to practice until you are satisfied with all of your presentation.

 You can complete this activity online, print copies of this rehearsal analysis sheet, see a student sample of a practice round, and if requested, e-mail your work to your instructor. Use your CengageNOW for *Challenge* to access Activity 6A.

Adapting to Your Audience as You Give Your Speech

Even when you've practiced your wording and delivery to the point that you know your speech inside and out, you must be prepared to adapt to your audience and possibly change course a bit as you give your speech. Remember that your primary goal as a public speaker is to generate shared understanding with your listeners, so pay attention to the audience's feedback as you speak and adjust accordingly. Here are six tips for adapting to your audience.

1. Be aware of and respond to audience feedback. As you make eye contact with members of your audience, notice how they react to what you say. For instance, if you see quizzical looks on the faces of several listeners, you may need to explain a particular point in a different way, perhaps by providing an additional example to clarify the point. On the other hand, if you see listeners nodding impatiently, recognize that you don't need to belabor your point and move on. If you notice that many audience members look bored, adjust your voice and try to rekindle their interest by showing your enthusiasm for what you are saying.

2. Be prepared to use alternative developmental material. Your ability to adjust to your audience's needs will depend on how much additional alternative information you have to share. If you have prepared only one example, you wouldn't be ready if your audience is confused and needs another. If you have prepared only one definition for a term, you may be unable to rephrase an additional definition if needed. As you prepare, try to anticipate where your audience may be confused or already knowledgeable and practice adding or dropping examples and other details.

3. Correct yourself when you misspeak. Every speaker makes mistakes. They stumble over words, mispronounce terms, forget information, and mishandle presentational aids. So expect that you will make a few mistakes—it's normal. What's important is what you do when you make that mistake. If you stumble over a phrase or mispronounce a word, correct yourself and move on. Don't make a big deal of it by laughing, rolling your eyes, or in other ways drawing unnecessary attention to it. If you suddenly remember that you forgot to provide some information, consider how important it is for your audience to have that information. If what you forgot to say will make it difficult for your audience to understand a point that comes later, figure out how and when to provide the information later in your speech. You may need to say something like, "When I was speaking earlier about X, I meant to tell you Y" or "Before going on to my third main point, I really would like to back up to my first point and tell you——." At times, however, information we forgot to share is not critical to the audience's understanding. For instance, if you forget about a second example you had planned to share and you don't think your audience will miss it, there's no need to provide it.

When you make a mistake, remember that your goal is to get your ideas across to the audience. If your mistake will prevent your audience from understanding what you are saying, correct it. Otherwise, go on. Your audience doesn't know what you had planned to say, so as long as what you do say makes sense, your audience won't notice the mistake.

4. Adapt to unexpected events. Maintain your composure if something unexpected happens, such as a cell phone ringing or someone entering the room while you're speaking. Simply pause until the disruption ceases and then move on. If the disruption causes you to lose your train of thought or has distracted the audience, take a deep breath, look at your speaking notes, and continue your speech at a point slightly before the interruption occurred. This will allow both you and your audience to refocus on your speech. You might acknowledge that you are backtracking by saying something like, "Let's back up a bit and remember where we were——."

5. Adapt to unexpected audience reactions. Sometimes, you'll encounter listeners who disagree strongly with your message. They might show their disagreement by being inattentive, heckling you belligerently, or rolling their eyes when you try to make eye contact with them. If these behaviors are limited to one or only a few members of your audience, ignore them and focus on the rest of your listeners. If, however, you find that your audience analysis was inaccurate and that the majority of your audience is hostile to what you are saying, try to anticipate and address their concerns. You might begin by acknowledging their feedback and then try to convince your audience to suspend their judgment while they listen. For example, you could say something like, "I can see that most of you don't agree with my first point. But let me ask you to put aside your initial reaction and think along with me on this next point. Even if we end up disagreeing, at least you will understand my position."

6. Handle questions respectfully. It is rare for audience members to interrupt speakers with questions during a speech. But if you are interrupted, be prepared to deal respectfully with the question. If the question is directly related to understanding the point you are making, answer it immediately. If it is not, acknowledge the question, indicate that you will answer it later, and then do so. In most professional settings, you will be expected to answer questions when you've finished your speech. Some people will ask you to clarify information. Some will ask you for an opinion or to draw conclusions beyond what you have said.

Whenever you answer a question, it is important to be honest about what you know and don't know. If an audience member asks a question you don't know the answer to, admit it by saying something like, "That's an excellent question. I'm not sure of the answer, but I would be happy to follow up on it later if you're interested." Then move on to the next question. If someone asks you to state an opinion about a matter you haven't thought much about, it's okay to say, "You know, I don't think I have given that enough thought to have a valid opinion."

Be sure to monitor how much time you have to answer questions. When the time is nearly up, mention that you'll entertain one more question to warn listeners that the question-and-answer period is almost over. You might also suggest that you'll be happy to talk more with individuals one on one later—this provides your more reserved listeners an opportunity to follow up with you.

Although you cannot predict everything that could happen during your speech, you can prepare yourself to be ready for some adjustments. The most important thing to remember is that no speech is perfect. But you will succeed if your audience understands and retains your message. That's what counts most.

| SPEECH ASSIGNMENT |  |

Presenting Your First Graded Speech

1. Based on the specific assignment of your instructor, prepare a three- to five-minute speech by completing the Speech Plan Action Step activities. You can also use Speech Builder Express as a tool to help you prepare your speech and your outline.
2. The primary criteria for evaluating this first speech are clarity of goal, clarity and appropriateness of main points, and delivery (items that are in boldface on the checklist). An example of one student's outline and speech follows.

First Graded Speech Evaluation Form

Please note that although all major criteria for evaluating any speech are included, emphasis for this first speech is placed on items in boldface (speech goal, all items of speech organization, and several items of speech presentation).

Check items that were accomplished effectively.

Content

_____ 1. **Did the speaker seem to have expertise in the subject area?**

_____ 2. **Was the goal of the speech clear?**

_____ 3. Did the speaker have high-quality information?

_____ 4. Did the speaker use a variety of kinds of developmental material?

_____ 5. Were presentational aids appropriate and well used?

_____ 6. Did the speaker establish common ground and adapt the content to the audience's interests, knowledge, and attitudes?

Macrostructure

_____ 7. **Did the introduction gain attention, state the topic of the speech, preview the main points, and lead into the speech?**

_____ 8. **Were the main points clear, parallel, and meaningful complete sentences?**

_____ 9. **Did transitions lead smoothly from one point to another?**

_____ 10. **Did the conclusion tie the speech together?**

Microstructure

_____ 11. Was the language accurate?

_____ 12. Was the language clear?

_____ 13. Was the language vivid?

Delivery

_____ 14. **Did the speaker sound enthusiastic?**

_____ 15. **Did the speaker show sufficient vocal expressiveness?**

_____ 16. **Was the presentation spontaneous?**

_____ 17. **Was the presentation fluent?**

_____ 18. **Did the speaker look at the audience?**

_____ 19. Were the speaker's pronunciation and articulation acceptable?

_____ 20. Did the speaker have good posture that communicated poise and confidence?

_____ 21. Was the speaker's movement appropriate?

Based on these criteria, evaluate the speech as (check one):

_____ excellent _____ good _____ satisfactory _____ fair _____ poor

You can use your CengageNOW for *Challenge* to access this checklist online under the resources for Chapter 11.

© Cengage Learning

Sample First Graded Speech
Chinese Fortune Telling
by Chung-yan Man*

*Used with permission of Chung-yan Man, Collin County Community College.

Read the speech adaptation plan, outline, and a transcript of a speech given by Chung-yan Man in an introductory speaking course as her first major speech. You can access a video clip of Chung-yan presenting her speech by using your CengageNOW for *Challenge*. (See the inside back cover of this book for how to access speech videos through CengageNOW.) You can also use CengageNOW to identify some of the strengths of Chung-yan's speech by preparing an evaluation checklist and an analysis. You can then compare your answers to those of the authors.

Adaptation Plan
1. **Key aspects of audience.** The majority of listeners are not familiar with Chinese culture and have had little exposure to Chinese mysticism.
2. **Establishing and maintaining common ground.** My main way of establishing common ground will be by using personal pronouns.
3. **Building and maintaining interest.** Since interest is not automatic, I will provide a variety of examples to perk audience interest.
4. **Audience knowledge and sophistication.** Since most of the class is not familiar with Chinese fortune telling, I will introduce them to the three most common forms of fortune telling. I believe that by repeating key points and by using a variety of examples, my audience will be more likely to retain the information.
5. **Building credibility.** Since I am Chinese, the audience will assume that I am familiar with the culture, and I will reinforce this as I speak.
6. **Audience attitudes.** The audience is likely to be curious but skeptical.
7. **Adapting to audiences from different cultures and language communities.** Since most audience members come from a different culture and language community than I do and are unfamiliar with these practices, I will be careful to describe these techniques in everyday language.
8. **Using presentational aids to enhance audience understanding and memory.** I will show an overhead transparency of the palm, a transparency of a face, and samples of the sticks used in joss-stick fortune telling.

Speech Outline

General goal: I want to inform my audience.

Specific goal: I want my audience to appreciate three different kinds of Chinese fortune telling.

Introduction
   I. Do you want to know what your future will be?

   II. In general, people want to know the future, because knowledge of the future means control of the future.

  III. As you know, I am from Hong Kong and I have experienced the mysterious but unique practice of fortune telling in the traditional Chinese culture.

  IV. So, today I am going to talk about three different forms of Chinese fortune telling: palm reading, face reading, and fortune-telling sticks.

Body
   I. One kind of Chinese fortune telling you may have heard of is palm reading.

     A. Palm reading, also termed as palmistry, is the process of foretelling one's future by the imprints and marks on the palm.

       1. Palmistry is based upon the interpretation of the general characteristics of one's hands.

2. Palmistry focuses on the study of lines, their patterns, and other formations and marks that appear on the palms and fingers. *(Overhead 1: Picture of palm with heart, head, life lines labeled.)*

   B. Palmistry is divided into two subfields: the palm itself and the fingers.

   1. The three principle lines on your palm are heart, head, and life lines: if lines are deep, clear, and have no interruptions, it is a sign of a smooth and successful life.

   2. Fingers are also important in palm reading: length of the index and ring figure each indicates different beliefs.

Transition: So now that you have understood the basic ideas of palm reading, let us go on to a second kind of Chinese fortune telling, face reading.

II. The Chinese believe that the face can also be used to predict the future and fortune of an individual.

   A. Face reading is the Chinese art of predicting a person's future and fortunes by analyzing the different elements of his or her face. *(Overhead 2: Simple line drawing of a Chinese face.)*

   1. The major facial features which are used in developing the fortune are nose, mouth, forehead, eyebrows, and eyes.

   2. The face shapes show the basic constitution and attributes.

   B. Balance and proportion are important in face reading, as in paintings.

Transition: In addition to palmistry and face reading, a third type of Chinese fortune telling uses joss sticks—you may be least familiar with this practice.

III. The oldest known method of fortune telling in the world is the use of fortune-telling sticks.

   A. It is to give an indication of the possibilities of the future instead of exactly what will happen.

   B. This method, which is part of religious practice, takes place in a temple.

   1. A believer selects numbered sticks from a bamboo case containing 78 sticks.

   2. Prayers burn joss sticks, then kneel before the main alter.

Conclusion

I. In conclusion, when people know more and more about Chinese fortune telling, they begin to understand that these methods are quite scientific and, to a certain extent, accurate.

II. So, I hope what you have learned today about palmistry, face reading, and joss sticks will give you an appreciation for Chinese culture and fortune-telling practices.

III. Do you want to know your future? If your answer is yes, these Chinese fortune-telling methods can help you.

Works Cited

Bright, Maura. "Chinese Face Reading for Health Diagnosis and Self Knowledge." 2001. The Wholistic Research Company. 18 Oct. 2005. http://www .wholisticresearch.com/info/artshow.php3?artid=96.

Chan, King-Man Stephen. *Fortune Telling*. May 2005. Chinese University of Hong Kong. 15 Oct. 2005. http://www.se.cuhk.edu.hk/~palm/chinese/fortune/.

"Fortune Telling." *Chinese Customs*. 2003. British Born Chinese. 17 Oct. 2005. http://www.britishbornchinese.org.uk/pages/culture/customs/fortunetelling .html.

"Most Popular." *Wong Tai Sin Temple*. 18 Oct. 2005. Hong Kong Tourism Board. 18 Oct. 2005. http://www.discoverhongkong.com/eng/touring/popular/ ta_popu_wong.jhtml.

"What Is Palmistry?" 2004. *Palmistry*. 16 Oct. 2005. http://www.findyourfate.com/ palmistry/palmistry.htm.

These opening rhetorical questions are designed to make the audience curious about the topic.

In this sentence, Chung-yan establishes her credibility.

Her thesis statement previews her three main points, the three types of Chinese fortune telling she will discuss.

Her first main point focuses on the first type of fortune telling: palm reading. Notice how she documents the definition of palmistry.

She has two subpoints that she quickly previews before explaining each.

Here she attempts to get the audience involved in identifying the nature of their own palm lines: the heart line, the head line, and the life line.

She encourages the audience to see whether these lines are deep, clear, and without breaks or interruptions. But she doesn't really develop what "interruptions" might mean. The audience is left to guess.

She goes on to note the importance of the length, shape, and spacing of the fingers in palm reading. But again, she doesn't really develop her point here.

Chung-yan's transition signals to the audience that she will begin discussing a new type of fortune telling.

Chung-yan gives a good example of how face shape is used to predict personal characteristics, but she doesn't explain how individual features or balance and proportion affect one's fortune. Again, she acknowledges the source of her information.

While better than no transition, this transition is trite and neither summarizes nor previews the main points.

Chung-yan needs to clarify the difference between a "possibility" and an "exact" future. An example would help.

Although she explains the process, this point would be made more meaningful with more detail. For example, what type of temple? Is the believer seeking an answer to a particular question, or is this a general fortune?

In her conclusion, Chung-yan claims that these practices are based on "scientific facts" and are "accurate." Yet nothing in the body of the speech supports this conclusion.

Let me ask you a question: Do you want to know what your future will be? Don't all of us want to know? A lot of people want to know what the future will bring, because knowing it means that you can control the future. I am from Hong Kong, and in China we *can* tell the future. Well, actually, we can experience the mysterious and unique practice of fortune telling that is part of traditional Chinese culture. Today I am going to talk about three different kinds of Chinese fortune telling: the palm reading, the face reading, and the fortune-telling sticks.

One kind of Chinese fortune telling is palm reading. According to Stephen Chan in his Web article "Fortune Telling," palm reading is the process of foretelling one's future by examining and interpreting the imprints, marks, and other general characteristics of one's hands. Palm reading, which is also known as palmistry, is divided into two subfields: the palm itself and each of the fingers. Take a look at your palm for a minute. The "What Is Palmistry?" page on FindYourFate.com tells us that the three principle lines on your palm are your heart, head, and life lines—the heart line is the long line up at the top of your palm; the head line is the line just below it that also runs across your palm; and the life line is the line running from the bottom of your palm and kind of arcing toward your thumb. If these lines are deep, clear, and have no breaks or interruptions, it is a sign of a smooth and successful life. The length, shape, and spacing of the fingers are also important aspects of a palm reading. For example, the lengths of the index and ring fingers indicate different aspects of your personality, such as whether or not you are a leader, artistic, or reckless in nature.

So now that you understand the basic ideas of palm reading, let's move on to a second kind of Chinese fortune telling, face reading. The Chinese believe that the face also can be used to predict the future and fortune of a person. In face reading, the fortune teller analyzes the different elements of a person's face. According to Maura Bright's webpage, the major facial features used to determine a person's fortune are the nose, mouth, forehead, eyebrows, and eyes. The shape and condition of the face indicate a person's basic constitution, personality, and attributes. For example, a long, narrow face indicates that you are a leader and an organizer, whereas a short and square face means that you are practical and reliable. The balance and proportion of all your features are also important in face reading, just as they are in paintings.

Last but not least, the Chinese also use fortune-telling joss sticks. This is the oldest known method of fortune telling in the world. Joss sticks are a type of incense, and they are used to indicate the *possibilities* of the future instead of exactly what will happen. This method of fortune telling, which is part of Chinese folk religious practice, takes place in a temple. As described on the "Most Popular" page of the Hong Kong Tourist Board's website, a believer seeking his or her fortune lights a joss stick, kneels before a main altar and makes a wish, then selects a fortune stick from a bamboo case containing 78 numbered sticks. The fortune-seeker exchanges the stick for a piece of paper with the same number on it, and his or her fortune is written on the paper.

In conclusion, when people know more and more about Chinese fortune telling, they begin to understand that these methods are actually based in scientific fact and, to a certain extent, are accurate. I hope what you have learned today about palmistry, face reading, and joss sticks will give you an appreciation for Chinese culture and traditional fortune-telling practices.

　　If you answered "yes" to my question about wanting to know your future, then these Chinese practices may be something for you to pursue.

REFLECT ON ETHICS

For the first graded assignment, Professor Graves required that students prepare an extemporaneous speech, outlined but delivered from note cards, not a complete manuscript. Any student who read the entire speech from a manuscript (or from several note cards that amounted to a manuscript) would be given a failing grade regardless of how well organized the speech was.

Tina was extremely nervous about delivering extemporaneously. But because she was majoring in theater, she knew she could "perform" if she had a script. So she outlined the speech and then wrote it out word for word and memorized it.

While presenting the speech in class, she glanced at her "props"—note cards that included key phrases from her speech outline—and for the most part, she appeared to be talking spontaneously with the audience, adapting well to their needs, and delivering the speech with great enthusiasm that engaged audience interest.

After all the students had spoken, during the evaluation portion of class, her professor praised her content, organization, adaptation, and delivery as he announced that she had given the best speech of the day.

1. Was Tina's behavior ethical? Why or why not?
2. Could Tina have used the skills that made her a good actor to reduce her nervousness and truly give an extemporaneous speech? Explain your answer.

Summary

Delivery refers to the use of voice and body to communicate the message of the speech; it is what the audience sees and hears. Effective delivery is conversational and animated.

　　The physical elements of delivery include the use of voice and use of body. By varying the four vocal characteristics of pitch, volume, rate, and quality, you can ensure that your speech is intelligible to your audience and is vocally expressive. During a speech, you can use your body through your facial expressions, gestures, movement, eye contact, posture, and attire to reinforce the emotional tone of your ideas or clarify your structure.

　　Speeches vary in the amount of content preparation and the amount of practice that the speaker does ahead of time. Although speeches may be delivered impromptu (with little advanced preparation) or scripted (memorized or delivered from a written manuscript or a teleprompter), in this course we focus on speeches that are presented extemporaneously—researched and planned ahead of time but with the exact wording varying from presentation to presentation.

Between the time the outline is completed and the speech is given, it is important to engage in rehearsal sessions consisting of a rehearsal, an analysis, and another rehearsal or rehearsals. During these rehearsal sessions, you will work on presenting ideas spontaneously and using notes effectively.

When you are finally ready to give your speech, remember that your goal is to have your audience understand your message, so be prepared to adapt to your audience during your speech.

CHALLENGE ONLINE

Now that you've read Chapter 11, use your CengageNOW for *The Challenge of Effective Speaking* for quick access to the electronic resources that accompany this text. Your CengageNOW gives you access to the video of Chung-yan Man's speech, "Chinese Fortune Telling," featured on pages 224–226, the speech evaluation checklist shown on page 223, the Web Resources featured in this chapter, Speech Builder Express, InfoTrac College Edition, and online study aids such as a digital glossary and review quizzes.

Your *Challenge* CengageNOW is an online study system that helps you identify concepts you don't fully understand, allowing you to put your study time to the best use. Using chapter-by-chapter diagnostic pretests, the system creates a personalized study plan for each chapter. Each plan directs you to specific resources designed to improve your understanding, including pages from the text in e-book format. Chapter posttests give you an opportunity to measure how much you've learned and let you know if you are ready for graded quizzes and exams.

KEY TERMS

Go to your CengageNOW for *Challenge* to access your online glossary for Chapter 11. Print a copy of the glossary for this chapter and test yourself with the electronic flash cards or complete the crossword puzzle to help you master these key terms:

accent (209)
animated delivery (207)
appearance (214)
articulation (209)
audience contact (213)
conversational style (207)
delivery (206)
extemporaneous speech (216)
eye contact (212)
facial expression (211)
gestures (211)

impromptu speech (215)
intelligible (208)
monotone (210)
motivated movement (212)
movement (212)
nonverbal communication (206)
pauses (211)
pitch (208)
posture (213)
pronunciation (209)

quality (208)
rate (208)
rehearsing (216)
scripted speech (215)
speaking notes (216)
spontaneity (207)
stress (211)
vocal expressiveness (210)
voice (208)
volume (208)

WEB RESOURCES

Go to your CengageNOW for *Challenge* to access the
Web Resources for this chapter.

11.1 Your Speech Rate (209)

11.2 Body Motions and Audience
Attention (213)

SPEECH PLANNING ACTION STEP

Access the Action Step activities for this chapter online at your CengageNOW for *Challenge*. Select the chapter resources for Chapter 11 and then click on the activity number you want. You may print your completed activities, and you should save your work so you can use it as needed in later Action Step activities.

6A Rehearsing Your Speech (222)

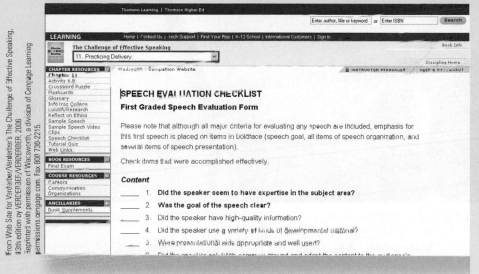

12

Informative Speaking

Any piece of knowledge that I acquire today has a value at this moment exactly proportioned to my skill to deal with it.

Ralph Waldo Emerson, "Natural History of Intellect," 1871

© Jose Luis Pelaez, Inc./Corbis

What's Ahead

HERE'S WHAT'S AHEAD IN THIS CHAPTER:

1. What is the goal of an informative speaker?

2. How can you make sure the information you include in your speech is new to your audience?

3. What strategies can you use to help your listeners understand and remember your speech?

4. Why is it important to round the cycle of learning in your informative speech?

5. What are some methods you can use to develop your informative speech?

For several months, a major architectural firm had been working on designs for the arts center to be built in the middle of downtown. Members of the city council and guests from various constituencies in the city, as well as a number of concerned citizens, were taking seats, as the long-anticipated presentation was about to begin. As Linda Garner, mayor and presiding officer of the city council, finished her introduction, Donald Harper, the principal architect of the project, walked to the microphone to begin his speech explaining the proposed design.

This is but one of many scenes played out every day when experts deliver speeches to help others understand complex information. In the previous chapters, we described the basic Speech Plan Action Steps that you will use to prepare any kind of speech. In this chapter, we go beyond the basics to focus on the characteristics of good informative speaking and the methods you can use to develop an effective informative speech.

An **informative speech** is one whose goal is to explain or describe facts, truths, and principles in a way that stimulates interest, facilitates understanding, and increases the likelihood of remembering. In short, informative speeches are designed to educate an audience. Thus, most lectures that your instructors present in class are classified as informative speeches (although, as you are aware, they may range from excellent to poor in quality). In the first section, we discuss the goal and nature of informative speaking as it relates to other types of speeches. Next, we focus on five distinguishing characteristics of informing. In the third section, we discuss five methods of informing. And finally, we discuss two common types of informative speeches and provide examples of each.

informative speech a speech whose goal is to explain or describe facts, truths, and principles in a way that stimulates interest, facilitates understanding, and increases the likelihood of remembering

The Nature of Informative Speaking

Informative speaking has as its goal to help listeners understand a topic by increasing their knowledge of the topic. Informative speaking answers questions about your topic such as "who," "when," "what," "where," "why," "how to," and "how does." So informative speaking is essentially teaching. For example, you might describe the surface of the moon, define neoconservatism, compare and contrast community colleges with liberal arts colleges and universities, narrate the myth of Pandora's box, or demonstrate how to prepare a canvas for painting. Each of these messages would be designed to educate or inform.

Informative speaking is inherently different from other speech forms such as speeches that are designed to persuade, to entertain, or for special occasions. When your goal is to inform your audience, you face some unique challenges to gain and sustain the attention of your listeners, as well as to get them to retain the information. These can be successfully met if you attend to the five characteristics of effective informative speaking and develop your speech with these in mind.

Characteristics of Effective Informative Speaking

An effective informative speech is intellectually stimulating, relevant, creative, memorable, and addresses diverse learning styles.

Intellectually Stimulating

intellectually stimulating
information that is new to audience members and is explained in a way that piques their curiosity

Information will be perceived by your audience as **intellectually stimulating** when it is new to them and when it is explained in a way that piques audience curiosity and excites their interest. When we say "new" information, we mean either that most of your audience is unfamiliar with what you present or that the way you present the information provides your audience with new insights into a topic with which they are already familiar.

If your audience is unfamiliar with your topic, you should consider how you might tap the audience's natural curiosity. Imagine you are an anthropology major who is interested in early human forms, not an interest that is widely shared by most members of your audience. You know that in 1991 a 5,300-year-old man, Ötzi, as he has become known, was found perfectly preserved in an ice field in the mountains between Austria and Italy. Even though it was big news at the time, it is unlikely that most of your audience knows much about this. However, you can draw on their natural curiosity as you present the speech "Unraveling the Mystery of the Iceman," in which you describe scientists' efforts to understand who Ötzi was and what happened to him.[1]

If your audience is familiar with your topic, you will need to identify information that is new to them. Begin by asking yourself: What about my topic do listeners probably not know? Then consider depth and breadth as you answer the question. *Depth* has to do with going beyond people's general knowledge of the topic. Jen considered depth in an informative speech about psychics. Most listeners know that psychics claim to predict the future, but they know little about the methods psychics use. So Jen focused on these methods and their roots in astrology, astronomy, and numerology. *Breadth* has to do with looking at how your topic relates to associated topics. Trace considered breadth when he informed listeners about Type 1 diabetes. He discussed not only the physical

When you speak about a familiar topic, such as how to cook a meal, your audience will be more engaged and receptive if you find a way to make the topic intellectually stimulating. For example, you might describe a helpful new technique or tool that would make a cook's life easier.

© Jeff Greenberg/PhotoEdit

and emotional effects on a person with diabetes but also the emotional and relational effects on the person's family and friends, as well as the financial effects on society. As you can see, when your topic is one that the audience is familiar with, you will need to explore a new angle on it if you are going to stimulate them intellectually.

So whether your topic is familiar or unfamiliar to the audience, your special challenge is to choose a goal and develop your speech in a way that makes it "new" to them. In doing so, your audience will feel informed rather than bored.

Relevant

As you learned in Chapter 5, it is important that the new information or insights you share are tied directly to listeners' needs and desires. Don't assume your listeners will recognize the relevance of the information. Incorporate **listener relevance links**—statements that clarify how a particular point may be important to a listener—throughout the speech. One way to come up with listener relevance links is to ask yourself how knowing the information might affect your listeners directly. How would it make them happier, healthier, wealthier, and so forth? Another way is to compare an unfamiliar topic with something the audience is familiar with and that they feel is relevant to their lives.

Creative

Creativity is the ability to produce original ideas and insights. You may never have considered yourself creative, but that may be because you have never worked to develop innovative ideas. Contrary to what you may think, creative inspiration is really just the product of perspiration. Creativity springs from raw informational material, time, and productive thinking.

To build creative informative speeches, begin with lots of research. The more you learn about the topic, the more likely you will have creative ideas to think about. If all you know about your topic is just the information that fills the time you are allotted, how can you think creatively about it? If you have read only one story, located one set of statistics, or consulted one expert, how can you do much more than present this material? Speakers who present information creatively do so because they have given themselves lots of supporting material to work with.

For the creative process to work, you have to give yourself time. If you finish your outline an hour before you are to speak, you are unlikely to come up with creative ideas for maintaining audience interest. Rarely do creative ideas come when we are in a time crunch. Instead, they are likely to come when we least expect it—when we're driving our car, preparing for bed, or daydreaming. So a simple way to increase the likelihood that you will develop creative ideas is to give yourself time by completing your outline several days before you are to speak. Then you will have time to consider how to present your ideas creatively.

Productive thinking occurs when we think about something from a variety of perspectives. Then, with numerous ideas to choose from, the productive thinker selects the ones that are best suited to a particular audience. In an article "Thinking Like a Genius," available through InfoTrac College Edition, author Michael Michalko describes eight specific strategies that can be used to become a productive thinker. To read this article, use your CengageNOW for *Challenge* to access **Web Resource 12.1: Thinking Like a Genius**.

Now let's look at how productive thought can help identify different approaches to a topic. Suppose you want to give a speech on climatic variation

listener relevance link statement that clarifies how a particular point may be important to listeners

creativity the ability to produce original ideas and insights

SPEECH SNIPPET

Making Your Informative Speech Relevant

In her speech about date rape, Jenny offered a listener relevance link to pique audience interest regarding the statistic that one in four women will be raped at some point in her lifetime. She said, "We can reason, then, that two or three of the eleven women in our classroom will be raped during her lifetime. Not only that, if you have a mother, an aunt, a sister or two, or a daughter, one of them could conceivably be raped in her lifetime."

productive thinking to think about something from a variety of perspectives

CENGAGENOW™

in the United States, and in your research, you run across the data shown in Exhibit 12.1.

With productive thinking, you can identify several lines of development for your speech. For instance, notice that the yearly high temperatures vary less than the yearly low temperatures. Most people wouldn't understand why this happens and would be curious about it. Looking at the data from another perspective, you might notice that it hardly ever rains on the west coast in the summer. In fact, Seattle, a city that most of us consider rainy, is shown as receiving less than an inch of rain in July, which is three inches less than any eastern city and five inches less than Miami. Again, an explanation of this anomaly would interest most audience members. Looking at these data yet another way reveals that although most of us might think of July as a month that is relatively dry, cities in the Midwest and on the east coast get more than one-twelfth of the average annual rainfall we would expect in July. Again, an interesting speech could be given to explain this.

Productive thought can also help us find alternative ways to make the same point. Again, using the information in Exhibit 12.1, we can quickly create two ways to support the point "Yearly high temperatures in U.S. cities vary far less than yearly low temperatures."

Alternative A: Of the thirteen cities in this table, ten cities, or 77 percent, had yearly highs between 95 and 100 degrees. Four cities, or 31 percent, had yearly lows above freezing; five cities, or 38 percent, had yearly lows between 15 and 32 degrees; and four cities, or 31 percent, had low temperatures close to zero.

Alternative B: Cincinnati, Miami, Minneapolis, New York, and St. Louis—cities at different latitudes—all had yearly high temperatures of 95 to 98 degrees. In contrast, the lowest temperature for Miami was 50 degrees, whereas the lowest temperatures for Cincinnati, Minneapolis, New York, and St. Louis were 7, 27, 2, and 9 degrees, respectively.

Memorable

If your speech is really informative, your audience will hear a lot of new information. But the audience is likely to remember only a small part of what they

EXHIBIT 12.1 Temperature and precipitation highs and lows in selected U.S. cities

City	Yearly Temperature (in degrees Fahrenheit) High	Low	Precipitation (in inches) July	Annual
Chicago	95	21	3.7	35
Cincinnati	98	7	3.3	39
Denver	104	3	1.9	15
Los Angeles	104	40	trace	15
Miami	96	50	5.7	56
Minneapolis	95	27	3.5	28
New Orleans	95	26	6.1	62
New York	98	2	4.4	42
Phoenix	117	35	0.8	7
Portland, ME	94	18	3.1	44
St. Louis	97	9	3.9	37
San Francisco	94	35	trace	19
Seattle	94	23	0.9	38

hear. So it is your responsibility to decide what the audience should remember and then to use various techniques to highlight that information. Effective informative speeches emphasize the specific goal, main ideas, and key facts so that audience members remember them. You can use several techniques to emphasize the material you want your audience to remember. For example, you might use presentational aids, vivid language, repetition, figures and structures of speech, or humor. Any of these techniques can pique listener interest as you move through your informative speech.

Addresses Diverse Learning Styles

You will recall from Chapter 5 that your audience members differ in how they prefer to learn, so effective informative speeches are developed in ways that address diverse learning styles. Consider how you might address the feeling dimension through vivid imagery that evokes emotions or through supporting material of actual experiences you've had. Likewise, you can address the watching dimension by using visual aids and by using appropriate facial expression and gestures. You can address the thinking dimension through clear macrostructure as well as definitions, explanations, and statistics. Finally, you can address the doing dimension by providing your listeners with an opportunity to do something during the speech or afterward. Rounding the cycle ensures that you address the diverse learning styles of your audience and make the speech understandable, meaningful, and memorable for all. To help you round the cycle, note in your speech outline where and how you address each dimension.

Methods of Informing

Once you have decided that the general goal of your speech will be to inform, you must decide what methods you will use to educate your audience about your topic. We can inform by describing, by defining, by comparing and contrasting, by narrating or reporting, and by showing or demonstrating. In some cases, you might choose one method of informing as the basis for organizing your entire speech. For example, when an architect presents the plans for a new building, we expect the speech to describe what the building will look like. But in most cases, you will use different methods of informing as you develop each main point.

In this section of the chapter, we explain each method of informing that you might use in developing your speeches. Later in the chapter, we will describe two of the most common types of informative speeches: process (or demonstration) speeches and expository speeches.

Description

Description method is the informative method used to create an accurate, vivid, verbal picture of an object, geographic feature, setting, event, person, or image. This method usually answers an overarching "who," "what," or "where" question. If the thing to be described is simple and familiar (like a light bulb or a river), the description may not need to be detailed. But if the thing to be described is complex and unfamiliar (like a sextant or holograph), the description will be more exhaustive. Descriptions are of course easier if you have a presentational aid, but verbal descriptions that are clear and vivid can create mental pictures that are also informative. To describe something effectively, you will want to consider explaining its size, shape, weight, color, composition, age, condition, and spatial organization. Although your description may focus on only a few of these, each is helpful to consider as you create your description.

description method the informative method used to create an accurate, vivid, verbal picture of an object, geographic feature, setting, or image

You can describe size subjectively as large or small and objectively by noting the specific numerical measurements. For example, you can describe a book subjectively as long and objectively by pointing out that it is nine by six inches with 369 pages. Likewise, you can describe Cincinnati as a medium-size city, or you can provide its actual population statistics or the square miles within the city limits.

You can describe shape by reference to common geometric forms, such as round, triangular, oblong, spherical, conical, cylindrical, or rectangular, or by reference to common objects such as a book, a milk carton, or a pitcher. Your audience will understand that most things that are described by shape do not conform perfectly, but using shapes will help them get a clearer picture of what you are describing. For example, DNA is described as a double helix, and the lower peninsula of Michigan can be described as a left-handed mitten. Shape is made more vivid by using adjectives such as smooth or jagged.

You can describe weight subjectively as heavy or light and objectively by pounds and ounces or kilograms, grams, and milligrams. As with size, descriptions of weight are clarified by comparison. So you can describe a Humvee as weighing about 7,600 pounds, or about as much as three Honda Civics together.

You can describe color as black, white, red, yellow, orange, blue, green, and brown. Since these eight basic colors will not always describe accurately, a safe way to describe color is to couple a basic color with a common familiar object. For instance, instead of describing something as puce or ocher, you might do better by describing the object as "eggplant purple" or "clay pot red."

You can describe composition as brick, concrete, wood, aluminum, steel, or plastic. Thus, if you say that a building is brick or aluminum-sided, the audience will have a reasonably clear picture. At times, you can create the most vivid image of something by describing what it seems like rather than what it is. For example, an object may best be described as "metallic" even if it is made of plastic, not metal.

You can describe something by age as old or new and by condition as worn or pristine, either of which helps the audience to visualize what is being described more clearly. Together, descriptions of age and condition can give the audience cues about the worth or value of what is being described. For example, describing a coin as old but in mint condition indicates that it may be worth far more than its face value. Similarly, describing a city as ancient and well kept gives rise to different mental pictures than does describing a city as old and decrepit.

Finally, you can describe by spatial organization, going from top to bottom, left to right, or outer to inner. A description of the Sistine Chapel might go from the floor to the ceiling; a description of a painting might proceed from foreground to background, left to right, or top to bottom; and a description of the heart might begin by explaining how the outside appears before discussing the chambers of the interior. However the description proceeds, it is important that your description is orderly and does not jump around, thus helping the audience to systematically "see" the thing you are describing.

Definition

definition method a method of informing that explains something by identifying its meaning

Definition method is a method of informing that explains something by identifying its meaning. There are four ways you can explain what something means.

First, you can define a word or idea by classifying it and differentiating it from similar ideas. For example, in a speech on vegetarianism, you might use information from the Vegan Society's website (http://www.vegansociety.com) to develop the following definition of a vegan: "A vegan is a vegetarian who is seeking a lifestyle free from animal products for the benefit of people, animals, and the environment. Vegans eat a plant-based diet free from all animal products, including milk, eggs, and honey. Vegans also don't wear leather, wool, or silk and avoid other animal-based products."

Second, you can define a word by explaining its derivation or history. For instance, a vegan is a form of vegetarian who omits all animal products from his or her diet. So where did that come from? At the Vegan Society website, we learn that "the word vegan is made up from the beginning and end of the word VEGetariAN and was coined in the UK in 1944 when the Vegan Society was founded. The derivation of the word symbolizes that veganism is at the heart of vegetarianism and the logical conclusion of the vegetarian journey in pursuit of good health without the suffering or death of any animal."[2] Offering this etymology will help your audience remember the meaning of vegan.

Third, you can define a word by explaining its use or function. When you say "a plane is a hand-powered tool that is used to smooth the edges of a wooden board," you are defining this tool by indicating its use. Not all terms can be defined by their use or function, but for those that can, it is an excellent means of definition.

The fourth and perhaps the quickest way you can define something is by using a familiar synonym or antonym. A **synonym** is a word that has the same or a similar meaning; an **antonym** is a word that is directly opposite in meaning. Synonyms for *glad* are *eager, elated, joyful, pleased,* and *delighted.* Antonyms for *fast* are *slow* and *poky.* Of course, using synonyms and antonyms will only be effective if the audience is familiar with the ones we use. So, if you wanted to give a quick definition of a *tenet,* you could use the word *principle.*

synonym a word that has the same or a similar meaning

antonym a word that is directly opposite in meaning

Comparison and Contrast

Comparison and contrast method is a method of informing that explains something by focusing on how it is similar to and different from other things. For example, in a speech on vegans, you might want to tell your audience how vegans are similar to and different from other types of vegetarians. You can point out that like all vegetarians, vegans don't eat meat, but that unlike semi-vegetarians, they also do not eat fish or poultry. Like lacto-vegetarians, they don't eat eggs, but unlike this group and the lacto-ovo vegetarians, vegans also don't use dairy products. So of all vegetarians, vegans have the most restrictive diets. As you will remember, comparisons and contrasts can be figurative or literal. So you can use metaphors and analogies in explaining your ideas as well as making actual comparisons.

comparison and contrast method a method of informing that explains something by focusing on how it is similar to and different from other things

Narration

Narration method is a method of informing that explains something by recounting events. Narration of autobiographical or biographical events, myths, stories, and other accounts can be effective ways to explain an idea. Narrations usually have four parts. First, the narration orients the listener to the event to be recounted by describing when and where the event took place and by introducing the important people or characters. Second, once listeners are oriented, the narration explains the sequence of events that led to a complication or problem, including details that enhance the development. Third, the narration discusses how the complication or problem affected key people in the narrative. Finally, the narration recounts how the complication or problem was solved. The characteristics of a good narration include a strong story line; use of descriptive language and detail that enhance the plot, people, setting, and events; effective use of dialogue; pacing that builds suspense; and a strong voice.[3]

Narrations can be presented in a first, second, or third person voice. When you use first person, you report what you have personally experienced or

narration method a method of informing that explains something by recounting events observed, using the pronouns "I," "me," and "my" as you recount the events. Your narration will be effective if your audience can identify and empathize with you and the situation and events you describe. "Let me tell you about the first time I tried to become a vegetarian . . ." might be the opening for a narrative story told in first person. When you use second person, you place your audience "at the scene" and use the pronouns "you" and "your." Second person narration can be effective because it asks the audience to recall an event that has happened to them or to become an "actor" in the story being told. "Imagine that you have just gotten off the plane in Pakistan. You look at the signs, but can't read a thing. Which way is the terminal? . . ." When you use third person, you describe to your audience what has happened, is happening, or will happen to other people. Third person narration uses pronouns like "he," "her," and "they." The effectiveness of third person narration will depend on how much your audience can identify with key people in the story.

Demonstration

demonstration method a method of informing that explains something by showing how it is done, by displaying the stages of a process, or by depicting how something works

Demonstration method is a method of informing that explains something by showing how it is done, by displaying the stages of a process, or by depicting how something works. Demonstrations range from very simple with a few easy-to-follow steps (such as how to iron a shirt) to very complex (such as demonstrating how a nuclear reactor works). Regardless of whether the topic is simple or complex, effective demonstrations require expertise, developing a hierarchy of steps, and using visual language and aids.

In a demonstration, your experience with what you are demonstrating is critical. Expertise gives you the necessary background to supplement bare-bones instructions with personally lived experience. During a demonstration, you speak from that experience as you guide your audience through. Why are TV cooking shows so popular? Because the chef doesn't just read the recipe and do what it says. Rather, while performing each step, the chef shares tips about what to do that won't be mentioned in any cookbook. It is personal experience that allows the chef to say that one egg will work as well as two or that you can't substitute margarine for butter or how to tell if the cake is really done.

In a demonstration, you organize the steps into a time-ordered hierarchy so that your audience will be able to remember the sequence of actions accurately. Suppose you want to demonstrate the steps in using a touchscreen voting machine. If, rather than presenting fourteen separate points, you group them under four headings—(1) get ready to vote; (2) vote; (3) review your choices; (4) cast your ballot—chances are much higher that the audience will be able to remember most if not all the items in each of the four groups.

Although you could explain how to do something using only words, most demonstrations involve actually showing the audience how to do something. If what you are demonstrating is relatively simple, you can demonstrate the entire process from start to finish. However, if the process to be demonstrated is lengthy or complex, you may choose to modify the demonstration and prepare material so that although all stages in the process are shown, not every step is completed as the audience watches.

Whether you demonstrate a complete process or modify your demonstration to include prepared presentational aids for some steps, you will need to practice the demonstration many times so that you can do it smoothly and easily. Remember, under the pressure of speaking to an audience, even the simplest task can become difficult (did you ever try to thread a needle with twenty-five people watching you?). As you practice, you will want to consider the size of your audience and the configuration of the room. Be sure that all of your audience can see what you are doing. You may find that your demonstration

Demonstrations of products are frequently presented at trade shows.

© Reuters/Corbis

takes longer than the time limit you have been given. In that case, you may want to prepare a step or two. We will discuss more about how to organize lengthy demonstrations in the next section.

To see a video clip of an effective demonstration from a student informative speech, use your CengageNOW for *Challenge* to access the video clip "Flag Etiquette" under the Chapter 12 resources.

Now that you understand the methods you can use when your general goal is to inform, we want to explain two speech frameworks that commonly use informative speaking: process explanation and exposition.

Common Informative Macrostructural Frameworks

Process explanations and expositions are the most common types of informative speeches. In this section, we describe each framework and then provide a sample speech given by a student as part of a basic speech course.

Process Speeches

One of the most common informative speeches is a **process speech,** which explains and shows how something is done, is made, or works. For instance, a loan officer might explain the steps in applying for a mortgage, an engineer might explain the newest design for a turbojet engine, or an author might discuss the process of writing a book. Effective process explanations require that you first carefully delineate the steps and the order in which they occur. Then you need to develop concrete explanations of each step.

A process explanation may verbally describe steps with the help of presentational aids, and it may also involve a full or partial demonstration. If the process is a simple one, such as how to get more power on a forehand table-tennis shot, you may want to try a complete demonstration, going through the entire process in front of the audience. But for relatively complicated processes, you will want to present a modified demonstration in which you

process speech a speech that explains and shows how something is done, is made, or works

exhibit completed stages of the process and only physically demonstrate small parts of each step or one or two complete steps.

For example, Allie works in a florist shop and has been asked by her former art teacher to speak on the basics of floral arrangement to a high school art class. The teacher has given five minutes for her presentation. In preparing for the speech, Allie recognized that in five minutes she could not complete arranging one floral display of any size let alone help students understand how to create various effects. So she opted to physically demonstrate only parts of the process and bring, as additional presentational aids, arrangements in various stages of completion. For example, the first step in floral arranging is to choose the right vase and frog (flower holder). So she brought in vases and frogs of various sizes and shapes to show as she explained how to choose a vase and frog based on the types of flowers used and the desired visual effect. The second step is to prepare the basic triangle of blooms, so she began to demonstrate how to place the flowers she had brought to form one triangle. Rather than hurrying and trying to get everything perfect in the few seconds she had, however, she also brought out several other partially finished arrangements that were behind a draped table. These showed other carefully completed triangles that used other types of flowers. The third step is placing additional flowers and greenery to complete an arrangement and achieve various artistic effects. Again, Allie actually demonstrated how to place several blooms, and then, as she described them, she brought out several completed arrangements that illustrated various artistic effects. Even though Allie did not physically perform all of each step, her visual presentation was an excellent demonstration of floral arranging.

Although some process speeches require you to demonstrate, others are not suited to demonstrations; instead, you can use visual aids to help the audience "see" the steps in the process. In a speech on making iron, it would not be practical to demonstrate the process; however, a speaker would be able to greatly enhance the verbal description by showing pictures or drawings of each stage.

In process speeches, the steps are the main points, and the speech is organized in time order so that earlier steps are discussed before later ones. Just as in a demonstration, speaker expertise is essential to the effectiveness of a process speech, and using vivid language when accompanied by well-prepared presentational aids ensures that the speech will be effective.

REFLECT ON ETHICS

After class, as Gina and Paul were discussing what they intended to talk about in their process speeches, Paul said, "I think I'm going to talk about how to make a synthetic diamond."

"That sounds interesting, Paul, but I didn't know that you had any expertise with that."

"I don't. But I'll bet Professor Henderson will really be impressed with my speech because my topic will be so novel."

"That may be," Gina replied, "but didn't he stress that for this speech we should choose a topic that was important to us and that we knew a lot about?"

"Sure," Paul said sarcastically. "He's going to be impressed if I talk about how to hold a golf club? No way. Trust me. Everyone's going to think I make diamonds in my basement and I'm going to get a good grade. Just watch."

1. Is Paul's plan unethical? Why?
2. What should Gina say to challenge Paul's last statement?

Process Speech

Prepare a three- to six-minute speech in which you explain how something is made, how something is done, or how something works. An adaptation plan and a complete outline are required. To help you prepare your speech and your outline, use your CengageNOW for *Challenge* to access Speech Builder Express and complete the Speech Planning Action Step Activities.

Notice that the sample Process Speech Evaluation Form shown below includes both primary criteria related to process and demonstration speeches and general criteria items that are common to all speeches.

The following topics are examples of ones that would be appropriate for a process explanation speech:

How to Do It	How to Make It	How It Works
hang wallboard	fishing flies	helicopter
grade meat	origami birds	ice cream maker
apply for a loan	plastic	asexual reproduction
organize a golf outing	spinach soufflé	cell phone

Process Speech Evaluation Form

You can use this form to critique a process speech that you hear in class. As you listen to the speaker, outline the speech. Then answer the questions below.

Primary Criteria (Content)

_____ 1. Was the specific goal appropriate for a process explanation speech?

_____ 2. Did the speaker show personal expertise with the process?

_____ 3. Did the speaker emphasize the process steps?

_____ 4. Did the speaker have good presentational aids that helped explain the process?

_____ 5. If the speaker demonstrated the process, or parts of the process, was the demonstration fluid and skillful?

_____ 6. Could the audience easily see the presentational aids or demonstration?

_____ 7. Were the demonstration or presentational aids important to understanding the main ideas?

_____ 8. Did the speaker adequately answer the overarching question of how to do it, how to make it, or how it works?

General Criteria (Structure and Delivery)

_____ 1. Was the specific goal clear?

_____ 2. Was the introduction effective in creating interest and introducing the process to be explained?

_____ 3. Was the macrostructure easy to follow?

_____ 4. Was the language clear, vivid, and appropriate?

_____ 5. Was the conclusion effective in summarizing the steps and clinching?

SAMPLE SPEECH

Sample Process Speech

Making Ethanol

by Louisa Greene*

*Used with permission of Louisa Greene.

Read the speech adaptation plan, outline, and a transcript of an informative speech given by Louisa Greene in an introductory speaking course. You can access a video clip of Louisa presenting her speech by using your CengageNOW for *Challenge.* You can also use CengageNOW to identify some of the strengths of Louisa's speech by preparing an evaluation checklist and an analysis. You can then compare your answers to those of the authors.

Adaptation Plan

1. **Key aspects of audience.** Most people in my audience have probably heard of ethanol as an alternative to fossil fuels, but don't know exactly what it is or how it's produced.

2. **Establishing and maintaining common ground.** I will begin my speech by asking the audience a question. Throughout the speech, I will refer to the audience's previous knowledge and experience.

3. **Building and maintaining interest.** Since my audience is initially unlikely to be interested in how to produce ethanol, I will have to work hard to interest them and to keep their interest through the speech. I will try to gain interest in the introduction by relating the production of ethanol, the fuel, to the production of "white lightning," the illegal alcohol, which might be of more interest to the average college student. Throughout the speech, I will use common analogies and metaphors to explain the complex chemical processes. Finally, I will use a well-designed PowerPoint presentation to capture attention.

4. **Audience knowledge and sophistication.** Since most of the class is not familiar with **ethanol**, I will introduce them to the **four-part process of making ethanol**. I believe that by **relating the process to that of making alcohol that people can drink**, my audience will be more likely to **be interested in and retain** the information.

5. **Building credibility.** Early in the speech, I will tell the audience about how I got interested in ethanol when I built a still as a science fair project in high school. I will also tell them that I am now a chemical engineering major and am hoping to make a career in the alternative fuel industry.

6. **Audience attitudes.** My audience is likely to be indifferent to my topic, so I need to capture their attention by using interesting examples. I then need to keep them interested by relating the topic to things they're familiar with.

7. **Adapting to audience from different cultures and language communities.** My audience doesn't include people from different cultures and language communities.

8. **Using presentational aids to enhance understanding and memory.** Throughout the speech, I will use color-coded PowerPoint slides with headers to reinforce the step being discussed.

Speech Outline

General goal: To inform

Specific goal: I want my audience to understand the process for making ethanol from corn.

Introduction

I. Did you know that cars were originally designed to run on ethanol?

    A. Henry Ford was an ethanol enthusiast.

    B. In World War II, about 75 percent of the German and American military vehicles were powered by ethanol.

    C. In 1978, Robert Warren built a still to produce what he called "liquid sunshine," which you may know as ethanol.

II. Both moonshine and ethanol are easily produced using the same method since both are pure or almost pure alcohol.

III. Today, I'm going to explain to you the commercial process that takes corn and turns it into alcohol.

Thesis statement: The four steps in the commercial process of making ethanol are, first, preparing the corn by making a mash; second, fermenting the mash by adding yeast to make beer; third, distilling the ethanol from the beer; and fourth, processing the remaining whole stillage to produce co-products such as animal feed. *(Slide 1. Shows the four-step flow process.)*

Body

I. The first step in the commercial process of making ethanol, preparing the mash, has two parts: milling the corn and breaking the starch down into simple sugars. *(Slide 2. Title: Preparation. Shows corn flowing from a silo into a hammer mill and then into a holding tank where yeast is added.)*

    A. The corn is emptied into a bin and passes into a hammer mill where it is ground into coarse flour.

    B. After milling, the corn flour, a starch, must be broken down so that it becomes simple sugars by mixing in water and enzymes to form thick liquid called slurry.

        1. First the water and corn flour are dosed with the enzyme alpha-amylase and heated.

        2. Then the starchy slurry is heated to help the enzyme do its work.

        3. Later gluco-amylase is added to finish the process of turning the starch to simple sugar.

II. The second step of the commercial process for making ethanol is fermenting the slurry or mash by adding yeast. *(Slide 3. Title: Fermentation. Shows yeast added to the mash in a fermenter and carbon dioxide being released to form beer.)*

    A. The mash remains in the fermenters for about fifty hours.

    B. As the mash ferments, the sugar is turned into alcohol and carbon dioxide.

III. The third step of the commercial process for making ethanol is distilling the fermented mash, now called "beer," by passing it through a series of columns where the alcohol is removed from the mash. *(Slide 4. Title: Distillation of Ethanol. Animated slide showing beer flowing into distillation tank, heat being applied to the beer, ethanol vapors being released and captured in a condenser.)*

    A. Distillation is the process of boiling a liquid and then condensing the resulting vapor in order to separate out one component of the liquid.

    B. In most ethanol production, distillation occurs through the use of cooling columns.

    C. Once the ethanol has reached the desired purity or proof, it is denatured to be made undrinkable.

IV. The fourth step in commercial production is converting the remaining whole stillage into co-products. *(Slide 5. Title: Co-product. Shows a tank with remaining whole solids flowing into a condenser with output flowing into a bin of animal feed.)*

Conclusion

I. As you can see, producing ethanol is a simple four-step process: preparing the corn into a slurry or mash, fermenting the slurry into beer, distilling the beer to release the ethanol, and processing the remaining water and corn solids into co-products. *(Slide 6: Same as Slide 1.)*

II. With today's skyrocketing gas prices, you can see why this simple process of making liquid sunshine has resulted in an increase of ethanol plants so that cars can use E-85 fuel.

Works Cited

"Industry statistics: the ethanol industry." The Renewable Fuels Association. http://www.ethanolrfa.org/industry/statistics/. Accessed 10:47 a.m. CDT 7/09/07.

"Module 2: Ethanol Science and Technology." Ethanol Business and Industry Center. Northwest Iowa Community College Help Desk. http://www.nwicc.com/pages/continuing/business/ethanol/Module2.htm. Last updated 5/07/2004. Accessed 11:05 a.m. CDT 7/3/2007.

Tham, M. T. "Distillation: an introduction." http://lorien.ncl.ac.uk/ming/distil/distil0.htm. Copyright 1997–2006. Accessed 3:30 p.m. CDT 7/05/2007.

"Tour the plant." DENCO, LLC Website. http://www.dencollc.com/DENCO%20WebSite_files/Tour.htm. Accessed 11:03 a.m. CDT 7/2/2007.

Warren, Robert. "Make your own fuel." http://running_on_alcohol.tripod.com/index.html. Last updated 8/18/2006. Accessed 2:30 p.m. CDT 7/3/2007.

Speech and Analysis

Read the following aloud at least once. Then analyze it on the basis of the primary criteria in the checklist on page 241: Process Speech Evaluation Form.

Speech

Did you know that the first Model T's were designed to run on ethanol and that Henry Ford said that ethanol was the fuel of the future? Or that in World War II about 75 percent of the German and American military vehicles were powered by ethanol since oil for gasoline was difficult to obtain? In 1978, during the first Arab oil embargo, when gas soared from 62 cents a gallon to $1.64, Californian Robert Warren and others built stills to produce what he called, no, not "white lightning" but "liquid sunshine," which we call ethanol.

I became interested in ethanol in high school when I built a miniature ethanol still as a science fair project. I'm now a chemical engineering major and hope to make a career in the alternative fuel industry. So, today, I'm going to explain to you the simple process that takes corn and turns it into liquid sunshine. Specifically, I want you to understand the process that is used to make ethanol from corn.

The four steps in the commercial process of making ethanol are, first, preparing the corn by making a mash; second, fermenting the mash by adding yeast to make beer; third, distilling the ethanol from the beer; and fourth, processing the remaining whole stillage to produce co-products like animal feed. *(Slide 1)*

The first step in the commercial process of making ethanol, preparing the mash, has two parts: milling the corn and breaking the starch down into simple sugars. *(Slide 2)*

Analysis

Louisa begins this speech with a series of rhetorical questions designed to pique the audience's interest in her topic. Since at the time she prepared the speech, gasoline prices were once again soaring, these questions coupled with the example of Robert Warren's industrious solution to a similar problem provide a provocative introduction to the general topic of ethanol.

At this point, Louisa personalizes the topic with a self-disclosure that also establishes her credibility.

Although the introduction does a good job of gaining attention and interest, it isn't really tied directly to why the audience should care about how ethanol is produced. So this transition to the thesis statement seems abrupt.

This is a clear statement of her thesis. The PowerPoint slide is a simple but effective tool to visually reinforce the verbal description.

Throughout the speech, Louisa does a good job of using signposts to help her audience follow each step of the process. Notice how Louisa has nested two steps, milling and

The corn, which has been tested for quality and stored in a silo, is emptied into a bin and passes into a hammer mill where it is ground into coarse flour. This is done to expose more of the corn's starchy material so that these starches can be more easily broken down into sugar.

In your saliva, you have enzymes that begin to break the bread and other starches you eat into sugar. In your stomach, you have other enzymes that finish this job of turning starch to simple sugar so your body can use the energy in the food you eat. In the commercial production of ethanol, a similar transformation takes place.

To break the milled corn flour starch into sugar, the milled flour is mixed with water and alpha-amylase, the same enzyme that you have in your saliva, and is heated. The alpha-amylase acts as Pac-men and takes bites out of the long sugar chains which are bound together in the starch. What results are broken bits of starch that need further processing to become glucose. So later, gluco-amylase, which is like the enzyme in your stomach, is added and these new Pac-men bite the starchy bits into simple glucose sugar molecules. Now this mixture of sugar, water, and residual corn solids, called slurry or mash, is ready to be fermented.

The second step in the commercial production of ethanol is to ferment the mash by adding yeast in an environment that has no oxygen and allowing the mixture to "rest" while the yeast "works." *(Slide 3)* This is accomplished by piping the slurry into an oxygen-free tank called a fermenter, adding the yeast, and allowing the mixture to sit for about fifty hours. Without oxygen, the yeast feeds on the sugar and gives off ethanol and carbon dioxide as waste products. Eventually, deprived of oxygen, the yeast dies.

This is similar to what happens when we add yeast to bread dough. But in bread, the carbon dioxide is trapped in the dough and causes it to rise, while the alcohol is burned off when the bread is baked.

In ethanol production, the carbon dioxide is not trapped in the watery slurry. Since it is a gas, it bubbles out of the mixture and is captured and released into the outside air. The ethanol, however, remains in the mixture that is now called "beer" with the water and the nonfermentable corn solids. At the end of the fermentation process, it is the ethanol in the mixture that retains much of the energy of the original sugar. At this point, we are now ready to separate or distill the ethanol from the other parts of the beer.

The third step in the commercial production of ethanol is distillation, which is the process of purifying a liquid by heating it and then condensing its vapor. So for example, if you boiled your tap water and condensed the steam that was produced, you would have purified water with no minerals or other impurities. But distilling ethanol is a bit more complicated since both the ethanol and the water in the beer are liquids and can be vaporized into steam by adding heat.

Luckily, different liquids boil at different temperatures, and since ethanol boils at 173°F while water boils at 212°F, we can use this boiling point difference to separate the two. So to simplify what is really a more complex process, *(Slide 4)* in the commercial distillation of ethanol, a column or series of columns are used to boil off the ethanol and the water and then to separate these vapors so that the ethanol vapors are captured and condensed back into pure liquid ethanol. The liquid ethanol is then tested to make sure that it meets the specifications for purity and proof. At this point, ethanol is drinkable alcohol and would be subject to a $20 per gallon federal excise tax. To avoid this, it is "denatured"—made undrinkable by adding gasoline to it. After this, the ethanol is ready to be transported from the plant.

The fourth step in the commercial production process is converting the whole stillage into co-products. *(Slide 5)* One of the greatest things about producing ethanol is that the water and nonfermentable corn solids which are left after the ethanol is distilled aren't just thrown out as waste. Instead, the remaining water and nonfermentable corn solids can also be processed to make co-products that are primarily used as animal feed.

So as you have seen, the process of making ethanol is really quite simple. *(Slide 6)* One, prepare the corn by milling and breaking its starch into sugar. Two, ferment the

breaking starch into sugars, under the more general heading of "Preparation." This grouping keeps the main points to a manageable number and will help her audience to remember the steps and then to remember the substeps. Her second slide is simple but effective because it reinforces the two substeps.

One thing Louisa could do better throughout the speech is to offer listener relevance links. Since the audience might not be interested in the topic, she should remind them of its relevance to them whenever possible.

Louisa helps the audience understand the unfamiliar starch to sugar conversion in ethanol production by comparing it to the familiar process of digestion.

The Pac man analogy also helps the audience to visualize what is occurring during the starch to sugar conversion.

The last sentence, mentioning slurry, is an excellent transition between the two main points.

Even though she used an effective transition statement, Louisa continues to help the audience stay with her by using the signpost, "second step." Her third slide, a visual of the "fermentation equation," nicely simplifies the complex chemistry that underlies fermentation.

By comparing fermentation in corn mash to bread making, Louisa is not only able to again make the strange familiar, but she is also able to contrast what happens to the alcohol and the carbon dioxide in ethanol production and bread.

She uses another effective transition statement to signal to her audience that she will be moving to the third step.

Again she uses a signpost to reinforce to the audience that what follows is a description of the third step. Her fourth slide is much more elaborate than the others. The animation in the slide helps the audience to visualize how distillation works. It would have been more effective, however, had she been able to control the motion so that each stage was animated as she talked about it instead of having quickly moving animation and then a static image.

The last sentence serves as an internal conclusion to the third step.

A signpost is used to mark the beginning of her abbreviated discussion of the fourth main point. The slide is so simple that it really isn't needed to aid audience understanding, but it is a visual reinforcement of this step, and the audience has been conditioned to expect one slide per point, so it would seem odd if there were not a slide for this step.

Louisa begins the conclusion with a summary of her main points. The sixth slide, a repetition of the first slide, visually "closes the loop" and reinforces the four points.

The conclusion begins with a circular reference back to Robert Warren who was introduced at the beginning of the speech. In the conclusion, she uses the statistics on ethanol production to drive home the point that ethanol is once again an important fuel

mash using yeast. Three, distill off the ethanol from the beer, and four, process the co-products.

In 1980, when Robert Warren was operating his still, only 175 million gallons of ethanol were being commercially produced in the United States. Twenty-five years later, according to the Renewable Fuels Association, 4.85 billion gallons were produced. That's a whopping 2,674 percent increase! And it is a trend that is continuing. Automobile manufacturers and service stations are gearing up to satisfy the increased demand for E-85, a fuel that is 85 percent ethanol. And, you may already own a car that is a flexible fuel vehicle. So keep an eye out at your local service station for that green handled pump. And when you see it, think of the four easy steps, preparation, fermentation, distillation, and processing co-products that were used to produce it. I'd be happy to answer any questions you may have.

Expository Speeches

expository speech an informative presentation that provides carefully researched in-depth knowledge about a complex topic

An **expository speech** is an informative presentation that provides carefully researched in-depth knowledge about a complex topic. For example, "Understanding the Health Care Debate," "The Origins and Classification of Nursery Rhymes," "The Sociobiological Theory of Child Abuse," and " Viewing Gangsta Rap as Poetry" are all topics on which you could give an interesting expository speech. Lengthy expository speeches are known as lectures. In this section, we describe four kinds of expository speeches.

All expository speeches require that the speaker use an extensive research base for preparing the presentation, choose an organizational pattern that helps the audience understand the material being discussed, and use a variety of informative methods to sustain the audience's attention and comprehension of the material presented.

Even college professors who are experts in their fields draw from a variety of source material when they prepare their lectures. So you will want to acquire your information from reputable sources. Then, as you are speaking, you will want to cite the sources for the information you present. You do so in the form

oral footnote oral reference to the original source of particular information at the point of presenting it during a speech

of **oral footnotes**—oral references to the original source of particular information at the point of presenting it during a speech. In this way, you can establish the trustworthiness of the information you present as well as strengthen your own credibility.

Expository speakers also must choose an organizational pattern that is best suited to the material they will present. Different types of expository speeches are suited to different organizational patterns. It is up to the speaker to arrange the main points of the speech thoughtfully so that they flow in a manner that aids audience understanding and memory.

Finally, a hallmark of effective expository speaking is that it uses various methods of informing for developing material. Within one speech, you may hear the speaker use descriptions, definitions, comparisons and contrasts, narration, and short demonstrations to develop the main points.

Expository speeches include those that explain a political, economic, social, religious, or ethical issue; those that explain events or forces of history; those that explain a theory, principle, or law; and those that explain a creative work.

EXPOSITION OF POLITICAL, ECONOMIC, SOCIAL, RELIGIOUS, OR ETHICAL ISSUES

Before we can solve a problem, we must understand it. So there is a need for someone to explain issues to us. In an expository speech, you have the opportunity to help the audience understand the background or context of an issue, including the forces that gave rise to the issue and continue to affect it.

An expository speech, like a classroom lecture, is an informative presentation that provides in-depth knowledge of a subject.

You may also present the various positions that are held about the issue and the reasoning behind these positions. Finally, you may discuss various ways that have been presented for resolving the issue.

The general goal of your speech is to inform, not to persuade. Therefore, you will want to present all sides of controversial issues without advocating which side is better. You will also want to make sure that the sources you are drawing from are respected experts and are objective in what they report. Finally, you will want to present complex issues in a straightforward manner that helps your audience to understand while not oversimplifying knotty issues.

For example, Mahalia has decided to give a speech on the issue of drilling for oil and natural gas in the Arctic National Wildlife Refuge. In doing her research, Mahalia needs to be careful that she consults articles and experts on all sides of this controversial issue and fairly incorporates their views in her outline. Because this is a very complex issue, if she has time, she will want to discuss all important aspects of the controversy, including the ecological, economic, political (national, state, and local), and technological aspects. If time is a factor, she may limit her discussion to just one or two of these aspects, but she should at least inform her audience of the other considerations that affect the issue.

You can identify an issue that you could use for an expository speech by reviewing the list of topics that you brainstormed earlier in this course. The following list of topic ideas might stimulate your thinking as you work with your own list.

gay marriage	stem cell research
affirmative action	universal health care
hate speech	school vouchers
media bias	teen curfews
school uniforms	home schooling
immigration	acid rain
tort reform	downloading music

EXPOSITION OF HISTORICAL EVENTS AND FORCES

It has been said that those who don't understand history may be forced to repeat it, so an important type of expository speech is one that explains historical events or forces. History can be fascinating for its own sake, but when history is explained, we can see its relevance for what is happening today. Unfortunately, there are people who think history is boring; we believe this is because many people have learned history from sources that are boring. As an expository speaker, you have a special obligation during your research to seek out stories and narratives that can enliven your speech. And you will want to consult sources that analyze the events you describe so that you can discuss what impact they had at the time they occurred and what meaning they have today. Although many of us are familiar with the historical fact that the United States developed the atomic bomb during World War II, an expository speech on the Manhattan Project (as it was known) that dramatized the race to produce the bomb and told the stories of the main players would add to our understanding of the inner workings of "secret" government-funded research projects. It might also place modern arms races and the fear of nuclear proliferation in their proper historical context. The following list of topic ideas might stimulate your thinking about historical topics you might be interested in speaking about.

slavery	Gandhi's movement
the Papacy	the colonization of Africa
Irish immigration	building the Great Pyramids
the suffrage movement	the Industrial Revolution
the Olympics	the Ming Dynasty of China
conquering Mt. Everest	the Vietnam War
the Balfour Declaration (which laid the groundwork for creating the state of Israel)	the Crusades

EXPOSITION OF A THEORY, PRINCIPLE, OR LAW

The way we live is affected by natural and human laws and principles and explained by various theories. Yet there are many theories, principles, and laws that we do not completely understand or don't understand how they affect us. An expository speech can inform us by explaining these important phenomena. As an expository speaker, you will be challenged to find material that explains the theory, law, or principle in language that is understandable to the audience. You will want to search for or create examples and illustrations that demystify esoteric or complicated terminology. Using effective examples and comparing unfamiliar ideas with those that the audience already knows can help you explain the law. For example, in a speech on the psychological principles of operant conditioning, a speaker could help the audience understand the difference between continuous reinforcement and intermittent reinforcement with the following explanation:

> When a behavior is reinforced continuously, each time people perform the behavior they get the reward, but when the behavior is reinforced intermittently, the reward is not always given when the behavior is displayed. Behavior that is learned by continuous reinforcement disappears quickly when the reward is no longer provided, but behavior that is learned by intermittent reinforcement continues for long periods of time, even when not reinforced. You can see examples of how behavior was conditioned in everyday encounters. For example, take the behavior of putting a

coin in the slot of a machine. If the machine is a vending machine, you expect to be rewarded every time you "play." And if the machine doesn't eject the item, you might wonder if the machine is out of order and "play" just one more coin, or you might bang on the machine. In any case, you are unlikely to put in more than one more coin. But suppose the machine is a slot machine or a machine that dispenses instant winner lottery tickets. Now how many coins will you "play" before you stop and conclude that the machine is "out of order"? Why the difference? Because you have been conditioned to a vending machine on a continuous schedule, but a slot machine or automatic lottery ticket dispenser "teaches" you on an intermittent schedule.

The following list of topic ideas might stimulate your thinking about topics for an expository speech on a theory, principle, or law.

natural selection	diminishing returns
gravity	Boyle's law
number theory	psychoanalytic theory
global warming	intelligent design
feminist theory	Maslow's hierarchy of needs
the normal distribution	color theory: complements and contrasts

EXPOSITION OF A CREATIVE WORK

Probably every university offers courses in art, theater, music, literature, and film appreciation. The purpose of these courses is to explain the nature of the creative work and to give the student tools by which to recognize the style, historical period, and quality of a particular piece or group of pieces. Yet most of us know very little about how to understand a creative work, so presentations designed to explain creative works such as poems, novels, songs, or even famous speeches can be very instructive for audience members.

When developing a speech that explains a creative work or body of work, you will want to find information on the work and the artist who created it. In addition, you will want to find sources that help you understand the period in which this work was created and learn about the criteria that critics use to evaluate works of this type. So, for example, if you wanted to give an expository speech on Fredrick Douglass's Fourth of July oration of 1852 in Rochester, New York, you might need to orient your audience by first reminding them of who Douglass was. Then you would want to explain the traditional expectation that was set for Fourth of July speakers at this point in history. After this, you might want to summarize the speech and perhaps share a few memorable quotes. Finally, you would want to discuss how speech critics view the speech and why the speech is considered "great."

The following list of topic ideas might stimulate your thinking about topics for an expository speech on a creative work.

jazz	the films of Alfred Hitchcock
Impressionist painting	the love sonnets of Shakespeare
salsa dancing	Kabuki theater
inaugural addresses	iconography
a postmodern critique of *A Farewell to Arms*	*Catcher in the Rye*: a coming-of-age novel
Van Gogh's *Starry Night*	Spike Lee's *Mo' Better Blues*

Expository Speech

Prepare a five- to eight-minute informative speech in which you present carefully researched in-depth information about a complex topic. To help you prepare your speech and your outline, use your CengageNOW for *Challenge* to access Speech Builder Express and complete the Speech Planning Action Step Activities.

Notice that the sample Expository Speech Evaluation Checklist that follows includes both primary criteria related to expository speeches and general criteria items that are common to all speeches.

To see sample topics that would be appropriate for this speech assignment, review the topic lists provided earlier with the descriptions of types of expository speeches.

SPEECH EVALUATION CHECKLIST

Expository Speech Evaluation Checklist

You can use this form to critique an expository speech that you hear in class. As you listen, outline the speech and identify which expository speech type it is. Then answer the questions below.

Type of expository speech

____ Exposition of political, economic, social, religious, or ethical issues

____ Exposition of historical events or forces

____ Exposition of a theory, principle, or law

____ Exposition of a creative work

Primary Criteria (Content)

____ 1. Was the specific goal of the speech to provide well-researched information on a complex topic?

____ 2. Did the speaker effectively use a variety of methods to convey the information?

____ 3. Did the speaker emphasize the main ideas and important supporting material?

____ 4. Did the speaker use high-quality sources for the information presented?

____ 5. Did the speaker use a variety of supporting material?

____ 6. Did the speaker present in-depth high-quality information?

General Criteria (Structure and Delivery)

____ 1. Was the specific goal clear?

____ 2. Was the introduction effective in creating interest, as well as introducing the topic and main points to be explained?

____ 3. Was the macrostructure easy to follow?

____ 4. Was the language simple, clear, vivid, and appropriate?

____ 5. Was the conclusion effective in summarizing the main points and clinching?

____ 6. Was the speaker's voice intelligible, expressive, and conversational?

_____ 7. Was the speaker's use of facial expressions, gestures, and movement appropriate?

Based on these criteria, evaluate the speech as (check one):

_____ excellent _____ good _____ satisfactory _____ fair _____ poor

You can use your CengageNOW for *Challenge* to access this checklist online under the Chapter 12 resources.

SAMPLE SPEECH

Sample Expository Speech

This section presents a sample expository speech given by a student in an introductory speaking course, including adaptation plan, outline, and transcript.

The Three C's of Down Syndrome

by Elizabeth Lopez*

*Used with permission of Elizabeth Lopez, Collin County Community College.

Read the speech adaptation plan, outline, and a transcript of a speech given by Elizabeth Lopez in an introductory speaking course as her first major speech. You can access a video clip of Elizabeth presenting her speech by using your CengageNOW for *Challenge*. You can also use CengageNOW to identify some of the strengths of Elizabeth's speech by preparing an evaluation checklist and an analysis. You can then compare your answers to those of the authors.

Adaptation Plan

1. **Key aspects of audience.** Because audience members have probably seen someone with Down syndrome but don't really know much about it, I will need to provide basic information.
2. **Establishing and maintaining common ground.** My main way of establishing common ground will be by using inclusive personal pronouns (we, us, our).
3. **Building and maintaining interest.** I will build interest by pointing out my personal relationship and interest in Down syndrome and through the use of examples.
4. **Audience knowledge and sophistication.** Because most of the class is not familiar with Down syndrome, I will provide as much explanatory information as I can.
5. **Building credibility.** Early in the speech, I will demonstrate credibility by mentioning my volunteer experience, educational background, and most importantly, my daughter, who has Down syndrome.
6. **Audience attitudes.** I expect my audience to be curious about Down syndrome but probably uncomfortable with the idea of interacting with people who have the syndrome. So I will give them information to help them become more knowledgeable and, I hope, less fearful.
7. **Adapt to audiences from different cultures and language communities.** Although the audience is diverse and because Down syndrome occurs in all ethnic groups and in both sexes, I won't do anything specific to adapt.
8. **Use presentional aids to enhance audience understanding and memory.** I will use several PowerPoint slides to highlight Down syndrome characteristics.

Speech Outline

General purpose: To inform

Speech goal: In this speech, I am going to familiarize the audience with the three C's of Down syndrome: its causes, its characteristics, and the contributions people with Down syndrome make.

Introduction

I. In our lifetime, we will encounter many people who, for a variety of reasons, are "different."

II. Today I want to speak to you about one of those differences—Down syndrome.

III. Why do I want to talk about this topic? Because I have a daughter who has Down syndrome.

IV. In this speech, I will discuss with you the three C's of Down syndrome. *(Slide 1: Causes, Characteristics, and Contributions)*

Body

I. To begin, let it be understood what causes Down syndrome.

    A. Although Down syndrome is a genetic condition, it is not hereditary.

        1. People with Down syndrome have forty-seven chromosomes instead of the normal forty-six (www.nads.org).

        2. This extra chromosome is caused by a random error in cell division within chromosome 21 prior to conception. *(Slide 2: Chromosome 21)*

        3. Although individuals do not inherit the mutant chromosome 21, neither parent is to blame, and once a couple has a child with Down syndrome, the likelihood of recurrence with the same two parents is increased. *(Slide 3: Genetic but Not Inherited)*

    B. There are approximately 350,000 people living in the U.S. with Down syndrome.

        1. Down syndrome occurs in one of every 800 live births, and an unknown number of fetuses with Down syndrome are aborted each year.

        2. Women over the age of thirty-five are most likely to produce Chromosome-21 altered eggs, but most children with Down syndrome are born to younger mothers because younger women have a greater percentage of babies.

Transition: Now that you know what causes Down syndrome, I want to describe the key physical and mental differences that people with this syndrome have.

II. People with Down syndrome differ from others both physically and mentally.

    A. People with Down syndrome look different, and this syndrome also can create a number of physical health problems. *(Slide 4: Characteristics: Physical and Health Differences)*

        1. The major physical differences are facial, such as a flat face, slanted eyes, and a large tongue in conjunction with a small mouth, but people with Down syndrome also experience low muscle tone.

        2. The major health concerns include heart defects, hearing loss, vision loss, and a weaker immune system.

    B. Second, people with Down syndrome are also mentally different, experiencing developmental delays, cognitive impairments, and emotional precociousness. *(Slide 5: Characteristics)*

        1. The delayed developmental characteristics of Down syndrome are speech, cognitive, and motor skills.

        2. The cognitive developmental characteristics are varied among children with Down syndrome.

        3. People with Down syndrome are emotionally precocious.

Transition: Now that you understand what Down syndrome is and how people with the syndrome differ from others, I would like to explain the special and unique ways that people with Down syndrome contribute to others.

III. People with Down syndrome positively affect their families and communities. *(Slide 6: Contributions)*

    A. What are the positive contributions people with Down syndrome make in families?

1. Families with a child who has Down syndrome often include a tighter marriage and more compassionate siblings.

2. Families with a child who has Down syndrome also tend to experience a higher degree of acceptance in their communities.

B. People with Down syndrome contribute to their communities.

1. Children with Down syndrome who are mainstreamed in classrooms teach their peers to value differences.

2. Many adults with Down syndrome in the workplace are role models of dedication and perseverance.

Conclusion

I. To review, now you know that Down syndrome is caused by a preconception change in chromosome 21 that causes people with Down syndrome to be physically and mentally different, and you also know that many people with Down syndrome make positive contributions to society.

II. So, the next time you encounter someone with Down syndrome, I hope you'll remember what you have learned so you can enjoy getting to know this person rather than being afraid.

Works Cited

Faragher, R. Down syndrome: it's a matter of quality of life. *Journal of Intellectual Disability Research,* October 2005, 49:761–765. *Academic Search Premier.* EBSCOE Host Research Databases. Collin County Community College District. Accessed October 7, 2005, at www.web27.epnet.com.

Helders, Paul. Children with Down syndrome. 2005: 141. *Academic Search Premier.* EBSCOE Host Research Databases. Collin County Community College District. Accessed October 7, 2005, at www.web27.epnet.com.

"Information and Resources," National Down Syndrome Society. Accessed October 7, 2005, at www.ndss.org.

National Association for Down Syndrome. Accessed October 7, 2005, at www .nads.org.

Rietveld, Christine. Classroom learning experiences by new children with Down syndrome. *Journal of Intellectual and Developmental Disability,* September 2005, 30:127–138. *Academic Search Premier.* EBSCOE Host Research Databases. Collin County Community College District. Accessed October 7, 2005, at www.web27.epnet.com.

Speech and Analysis

Read the following aloud at least once. Then analyze it on the basis of the primary criteria in the checklist on page 250.

Speech

In our lifetimes, we will encounter many people who, for a variety of reasons, are considered "different" by those who consider themselves "normal." Today I want to speak to you about one of those things that makes people seem different: Down syndrome. Why do I want to talk about this topic? In part, because I have volunteered with mentally disabled children for many years, I am pursuing a professional career in special education, and I'd like to share with you what I've been learning. But, more importantly, I have a toddler daughter who has Down syndrome, and I've found from personal experience that when people know more about what makes my daughter different, they're more accepting of her and of people who are different in other ways.

In this speech, I'd like to share with you some basic information about this syndrome—I call them the three C's. First, I will discuss what causes Down syndrome. Then I will explain the typical characteristics that differentiate people with Down syndrome from others. Finally, I will describe the positive contributions that people with Down syndrome make in their families and communities.

Analysis

Elizabeth opens with a statement about normal and different; then she quickly introduces her topic.

She immediately establishes her credibility by showing that she has worked with children with Down syndrome, and she also has a daughter who has the syndrome.

She concludes her introduction by using a mnemonic device, the three C's, to preview her main points.

Here Elizabeth clearly explains
that although Down syndrome is
a genetic condition, it is not an
inherited one. Her PowerPoint
slide is simple and visually reinforces her point.

Having established its genetic
cause, Elizabeth elaborates and
explains more about the prevalence of Down syndrome and
which parents are likely to have
children with Down syndrome.

Here Elizabeth uses a good transition in which she reinforces two of
her C's: causes and characteristics.

Here Elizabeth cites two of the
sources of her information.

Elizabeth could have developed
this characteristic a bit more, perhaps by giving an example.

Again, Elizabeth uses a transition
that reinforces two of the C's that
define her main points: characteristics and contributions.

Although Elizabeth begins by
telling the audience that she has a
child with Down syndrome, she
misses the opportunity to personalize this point. She might have
further developed it by giving personal examples of how her daughter has contributed to her family.

To begin, let me explain what causes Down syndrome. Contrary to what some people believe, Down syndrome is not hereditary—it is a genetic condition. According to the website for the National Association for Down Syndrome, people with Down syndrome have forty-seven chromosomes instead of the normal forty-six. This extra chromosome is produced by a random error in cell division within chromosome 21 prior to conception. Because you don't inherit the mutant chromosome 21, neither parent is to "blame," so to speak, for producing a child with Down syndrome. However, once a couple has a child with Down syndrome, the likelihood that the same two parents could have another child with the same syndrome increases.

According to the National Down Syndrome Society website, there are approximately 350,000 people with Down syndrome in the United States. Down syndrome occurs in one of about every 800 live births, and an unknown number of fetuses with Down syndrome are aborted each year. Many of us have heard that older women are more likely to have babies with Down syndrome. It's true that women over the age of thirty-five are most likely to produce Chromosome-21 altered eggs, but, really, most Down syndrome children are born to younger mothers because younger women have a greater percentage of babies.

Now that I've talked about what causes Down syndrome, let me describe the main physical and mental characteristics that differentiate people with Down syndrome from others. Of course, one of the first things people notice about people with Down syndrome is that they look different, but Down syndrome can also create a number of health problems. The major physical differences we notice first are facial characteristics, like a flat face, slanted eyes, and a large tongue in a small mouth, although not all people with the syndrome have all of these facial features. But people with Down syndrome also often experience low muscle tone and more problematic health concerns like heart defects, hearing loss, vision loss, and a weak immune system.

People with Down syndrome are also mentally different from the rest of us. According to R. Faragher in his article on Down syndrome in the *Journal of Intellectual Disability Research,* they experience developmental delays, mostly affecting their speech, cognitive, and motor skills. The degree of delays in cognitive development varies quite a bit among children with Down syndrome. As Christine Rietveld explains in her article on Down syndrome in the *Journal of Intellectual and Developmental Disability,* some children with Down syndrome are able to be mainstreamed and attend public school with other children, some need to attend special education classes in mainstream schools, and others need more specialized programs outside of regular schools.

People with Down syndrome are also emotionally precocious, which means that they often seem emotionally mature for their age and have few inhibitions about expressing their emotions. If you have spent time with a child who has Down syndrome, you know what it means to be loved unconditionally.

Now that you know a little more about what characterizes people with Down syndrome, I'd like to explain the special and unique ways that these people contribute to others. As many of us who live with people with Down syndrome know, there's no doubt that they have a positive effect on their families and communities. As R. Faragher explains, parents of a child with Down syndrome often have a very close, tightly knit marriage—they learn to come together in support of their child who has the syndrome and of their children who don't have Down syndrome, and they learn to rely on each other more to raise a child with special needs. In addition, the siblings of children with Down syndrome are often more compassionate because they understand what it's like to be viewed as "different." Families with a child who has Down syndrome also often experience a higher degree of acceptance in their communities. It's easy for people to become fond of a child with Down syndrome because they tend to be happy, loving kids who express affection easily. And when people feel fond of a child with Down syndrome, they also feel protective and accepting of the child's family.

In turn, people with Down syndrome often make important contributions to their communities, just as many of us do. For example, such children who are mainstreamed in classrooms teach their peers to value differences and to develop compassion and empathy for people who are not necessarily like everyone else. As adults, many people with Down syndrome are role models of dedication and perseverance in the workplace—I'll bet at least a few of you have encountered a cheerful and professional person with Down syndrome who has helped you in a store or who works with you in an office setting.

In review, now you know that Down syndrome is caused by a change in chromosome 21 before conception and that this results in people with Down syndrome having several different physical and mental characteristics. But you also know that people with the syndrome often make positive contributions to their families and communities. So, the next time you encounter someone with Down syndrome, I hope you'll remember what you have learned and that you enjoy getting to know this person as a unique and interesting individual.

Again, specific examples would have aided the development of her point.

In this conclusion, she reviews the three C's of causes, characteristics, and contributions, helping us remember what her speech was about. She could have made her speech more memorable, however, with a more clever clincher.

All in all, this is a well-presented, informative speech with sufficient documentation.

Summary

An informative speech is one whose goal is to explain or describe facts, truths, and principles in a way that stimulates interest, facilitates understanding, and increases the likelihood that audiences will remember. In short, informative speeches are designed to educate an audience.

Effective informative speeches are intellectually stimulating, relevant, creative, memorable, and address diverse learning styles. Informative speeches will be perceived as intellectually stimulating when the information presented is new and when it is explained in a way that excites interest. Informative speeches are creative when they produce original ideas or insights. Informative speeches stimulate audience memory and round the four-stage cycle of learning.

We can inform by describing something, defining it, comparing and contrasting it with other things, narrating stories about it, or demonstrating it.

Two common forms of informative speeches are process speeches, in which the steps of making or doing something are shown, and expository speeches, which are well-researched explanations of complex ideas. Types of expository speeches include those that explain political, economic, social, religious, or ethical issues; those that explain events or forces of history; those that explain a theory, principle, or law; and those that explain a creative work.

CHALLENGE ONLINE

CENGAGENOW™

Now that you've read Chapter 12, use your CengageNOW for *The Challenge of Effective Speaking* for quick access to the electronic resources that accompany this text. Your CengageNOW gives you access to the video of Louisa's and Elizabeth's speeches, "Making Ethanol" and "The Three C's of Down Syndrome," featured on pages 242–246 and 251–255, the speech evaluation checklists shown on pages 241 and 250, the Web Resources featured in this chapter, Speech Builder Express, InfoTrac College Edition, and online study aids such as a digital glossary and review quizzes.

Your *Challenge* CengageNOW is an online study system that helps you identify concepts you don't fully understand, allowing you to put your study time to the best use. Using chapter-by-chapter diagnostic pretests, the system creates a personalized study plan for each chapter. Each plan directs you to specific resources designed to improve your understanding, including pages from the text in e-book format. Chapter posttests give you an opportunity to measure how much you've learned and let you know if you are ready for graded quizzes and exams.

KEY TERMS

Go to your CengageNOW for *Challenge* to access your online glossary for Chapter 12. Print a copy of the glossary for this chapter and test yourself with the electronic flash cards or complete the cross-word puzzle to help you master these key terms:

antonym (237)
comparison and contrast (237)
creativity (233)
definition (236)
demonstration (238)

description (235)
expository speech (246)
informative speech (231)
intellectually stimulating (232)
listener relevance link (233)

oral footnote (246)
narration (237)
process speech (239)
productive thinking (233)
synonym (237)

WEB RESOURCE

Go to your CengageNOW for *Challenge* to access the Web Resource for this chapter.

12.1 Thinking Like a Genius (233)

From CD-ROM for Verderber/Verderber's The Challenge of Effective Speaking, 13th edition by VERDERBER/VERDERBER. 2006 Reprinted with permission of Wadsworth, a division of Cengage Learning: permissions.cengage.com. Fax 800 730-2215.

Persuasive Speaking: Reasoning with Your Audience

13

Speech is power: speech is to persuade, to convert, to compel.

Ralph Waldo Emerson, "Social Aims," 1875

What's Ahead

HERE'S WHAT'S AHEAD IN THIS CHAPTER:

1. How does knowing how people think about persuasive messages help you prepare your speech?

2. Why is it important to discover your audience's attitude about your topic?

3. How can you best phrase your persuasive speech goals?

4. What criteria do you use to evaluate your evidence?

5. What are the most effective ways to organize persuasive speeches?

6. How do you develop good reasoning for your arguments?

Eric is the oldest of several children. Growing up, he saw his younger siblings argue and fight more after they'd watched violent television programs. He wanted to give a speech on this topic but realized the audience would probably disagree with him about censoring television. He thought there must be a way to convince even this audience that he had a good solution to the problem, but how? Amanda wanted to speak on domestic violence, but like Eric, she worried that some classmates might oppose her views. She wondered if it would be better to speak about another topic. Pete wanted to raise awareness about teen suicide and convince his audience to act to prevent it, but like Eric and Amanda, he wondered if he could organize his thoughts well enough to convince his listeners.

persuasive speech a speech whose goal is to influence the attitudes, beliefs, values, or behavior of audience members

Although it is easy to get excited about a really powerful speech, real-life attempts to persuade others require the speaker to be knowledgeable about forming arguments and adapting them to the needs of the audience. A **persuasive speech** is one whose goal is to influence the attitudes, beliefs, values, and/or behavior of audience members. It is the most demanding speech challenge because it not only requires the skills you've studied so far but also means that you must understand how to convince audience members to alter their attitudes, beliefs, values, or behaviors. In this and the following chapter, we will explore what it takes to be effective in persuasive speaking.

This chapter focuses on reasoning with the audience. We begin by discussing how people process persuasive messages and what motivates them to believe persuasive messages. Then we focus on how the audience's initial attitude toward your topic affects the specific goal you select. Next we explain how to select the arguments or reasons you will use to convince your audience as well as the evidence you will want to present in support of those reasons. Then we describe how you can test the logic of your argument. After that, we present methods for organizing your material. Finally, we look at one framework used in persuasive speaking—the speech to convince—and we present the criteria that can be used to evaluate speeches of this type. The next chapter will explore the role of emotion in persuasive speaking.

How People Process Persuasive Messages: The Elaboration Likelihood Model (ELM)

Do you remember times when you listened carefully and thought about something of which someone was trying to convince you? Do you remember consciously thinking over what had been said and making a deliberate decision? Do you remember other times when you only half listened and made up your mind quickly based on your "gut" feeling about the truthfulness of what had been said? What determines how well we listen to and how carefully we evaluate the hundreds of persuasive messages we hear each day? Richard Petty and John Cacioppo developed a model that explains how likely people are to spend time evaluating information (such as the arguments that they hear in a speech) in an *elaborate* way, using their critical thinking skills, rather than processing information in a simpler, less critical manner. Called the Elaboration Likelihood Model

(ELM), this theory can be used by speakers to develop persuasive speeches that will be influential with audience members regardless of how they process.

The model suggests that people process information in one of two ways. One way is intense and more time consuming. People using this "central route" listen carefully, think about what is said, and may even mentally elaborate on the message. The second way, called the "peripheral route," is a shortcut that relies on simple cues such as a quick evaluation of the speaker's credibility or a gut check about what the listener feels about the message.

According to the ELM, what determines if we use the central or peripheral route is how important we perceive the issue to be for us. When we feel involved with an issue, we are willing to expend the energy necessary for processing on the central route. When the issue is less important, we take the peripheral route. So how closely your audience members will follow your arguments depends on how involved they feel with your topic. For example, if you have a serious chronic illness that is expensive to treat, you are more likely to pay attention to and evaluate for yourself any proposals to change your healthcare benefits. If you are healthy, you are likely to quickly agree with whatever someone you perceive to be credible suggests or go along with a proposal that seems compassionate.

The ELM also suggests that when we form attitudes as a result of central processing (critical thinking), we are less likely to change our minds than when our attitudes have been formed based on peripheral cues. You can probably remember times when in the moment you were swayed by a powerful speaker but on later reflection you regretted your action and changed your mind. Likewise, based on information you have heard and spent time thinking about, you probably have some strongly held beliefs that are not easily changed.

When you are preparing a persuasive speech, you will draw on this theory by developing your topic in such a way that you increase the likelihood that your audience members feel personally involved with the topic. You will want to develop sound reasons so that audience members who use the central critical thinking approach to your speech will find your arguments convincing. For members who are less involved, you will want to appeal to their emotions and include information that enables them to see you as credible.

The Greek philosopher Aristotle defined rhetoric as "the ability to discover in a certain case what are the available means of persuasion." He suggested that the speaker can present three types of appeals in a speech that will motivate the audience to accept the position the speaker is advocating. **Logos,** logical appeals, is the systematic way you structure your argument and the way you use reasoning to build it and support your claims with evidence. **Ethos,** which we call speaker credibility, is the sense of competence and character you are able to convey. **Pathos**, emotional appeals, refers to your ability to evoke certain feelings in your listeners. As you can see, when you are preparing a persuasive speech, part of your preparation will entail discovering what logos, ethos, and pathos you can bring to bear as you speak. The logos you create is critical to persuading audience members who use the central critical thinking approach, while the ethos and pathos appeals you create may convince listeners who are processing on the peripheral cues. Later in this chapter, we will describe each of these means of persuasion and offer insight on how to use them in your speeches. Let us now turn to the first step in planning a persuasive speech, writing a specific goal.

logos logical appeals

ethos speaker credibility

pathos emotional appeals

Constructing a Persuasive Speech Goal

The first step in preparing your persuasive speech is constructing a persuasive speech goal. In this section, we consider using audience attitude toward your topic to help you phrase your speech goal.

Adapting Your Persuasive Goal to Initial Audience Attitude

attitude a general or enduring positive or negative feeling about some person, object, or issue

As you begin considering your speech goal, you'll want to understand the current direction and strength of audience members' attitudes about your topic. An **attitude** is "a general or enduring positive or negative feeling about some person, object, or issue."[1] People express their attitudes about something when they give their opinions. So someone who states "I think physical fitness is important" is expressing an opinion that reflects a favorable attitude about physical fitness.

In Chapter 4, you learned that you can assess your audience's attitudes by surveying the audience or by referring to published surveys and extrapolating these polls to the members of your audience. So you will want to begin your persuasive speech preparation by understanding the attitudes that your audience is likely to have about your topic. Your knowledge of the audience attitude will help you phrase your goal and choose your arguments.

Audience members' attitudes (expressed by their opinions) about your speech topic can range from highly favorable to strongly opposed and can be visualized as lying on a continuum like the one pictured in Exhibit 13.1.

target audience the cluster point that represents the group of people you most want to persuade

Even though an audience will include individuals whose opinions fall at nearly every point along the distribution, generally audience members' opinions tend to cluster in one area of the continuum. For instance, the opinions of the audience represented in Exhibit 13.1 cluster around "mildly opposed," even though a few people are more hostile and a few have favorable opinions. That cluster point represents your **target audience,** the group of people you most want to persuade. Based on your target audience, you can classify your audience's initial attitude toward your topic as "in favor" (already supportive of a particular belief), "no opinion" (uninformed, neutral, or apathetic), or "opposed" (against a particular belief or holding an opposite point of view). Given that initial attitude, you can develop a speech goal and arguments designed to influence your audience's attitudes in the way you would like. In general, when your target audience is in favor, seek action. When your target audience has no opinion, seek agreement. When your target audience is opposed to your position, seek incremental change.

OPPOSED

incremental change moving reluctant listeners only a small degree in your direction

If your target audience is very much opposed to your goal, it is unrealistic to believe that you will be able to change their attitude from "opposed" to "in favor" in only one short speech. Instead, when dealing with a hostile audience, seek **incremental change,** trying to move them only a small degree in your direction, hoping for further movement later. For example, if you determine that your audience is likely to be opposed to the goal "I want to convince my audience that gay marriage should be legalized," you might rephrase your goal as "I want to convince my audience that committed gay couples should be able

---

EXHIBIT 13.1 Sample opinion continuum

Highly opposed	Opposed	Mildly opposed	Neither in favor nor opposed	Mildly in favor	In favor	Highly in favor
2	2	11	1	2	2	0

to have the same legal protection afforded to committed heterosexual couples through state-recognized civil unions." Begin by brainstorming objections, questions, and criticisms that might arise, and then shape your speech around them.

NO OPINION

If your target audience is neutral, you can be straightforward with the reasons in support of your goal. Still, it might be wise for you to consider whether they are uninformed, impartial, or apathetic about your topic. If they are **uninformed**—that is, they do not know enough about the topic to have formed an opinion—you will need to provide the basic arguments and information that they require to become informed. Make sure that each of your reasons is really well supported with good information. You may find that your audience is **impartial;** that is, the audience has no opinion. In this case, they are likely to listen objectively and accept sound reasoning. So, as with the uninformed audience, you can keep your focus on sound reasons and evidence. Finally, you may find that your audience members have no opinion because they are **apathetic.** An apathetic audience has no opinion because it is uninterested, unconcerned, or indifferent to your topic. To convince this audience type, you will need to find ways to arouse them. Look for materials that seem to relate to audience needs and incorporate listener relevance links throughout your speech.

uninformed not knowing enough about a topic to have formed an opinion

impartial having no opinion

apathetic uninterested, unconcerned, or indifferent to your topic

IN FAVOR

If your target audience is only mildly in favor of your proposal, your task is to reinforce and strengthen their beliefs. An audience whose beliefs favor your topic will still benefit from a logical explanation of the reasons for holding these beliefs. The audience may also become further committed to a belief by hearing additional or new reasons and more recent evidence that support it.

If your audience analysis reveals that your listeners strongly agree with your topic, then you can consider a speech goal that builds on that belief and moves the audience to act on it. So, for example, if the topic is gay marriage and your audience poll shows that most audience members strongly favor the idea, then your goal might be "I want my audience to write their state legislators to express their support for gay marriage." We will discuss speeches that call listeners to action in the next chapter.

When you know that your target audience is already leaning in your favor, you can focus your speech on a specific course of action.

© Jose Carrillo/PhotoEdit, Inc.

Phrasing Persuasive Speech Goals as Propositions

proposition a declarative sentence that clearly indicates the position that the speaker will advocate in a persuasive speech

In a persuasive speech, the specific goal is stated as a proposition. A **proposition** is a declarative sentence that clearly indicates the position on the topic that the speaker will advocate. For example, "I want to convince my audience that smoking causes cancer" is a proposition. From it, we know that the speaker will present arguments, reasons, and evidence to prove the validity of the proposition.

Notice how a persuasive proposition differs from an informative speech goal on the same subject: "I want to inform my audience of the research about smoking and cancer." In the informative speech, the goal is met if the audience understands and remembers what the speaker has said. In the persuasive situation, however, the audience must not only understand what has been said but accept it as true, believe it, and sometimes even take action.

The three major types of persuasive goals are stated as propositions of fact, value, or policy.

proposition of fact a statement designed to convince your audience that something did or did not exist or occur, is or is not true, or will or will not occur

A **proposition of fact** is a statement designed to convince your audience that something did or did not exist or occur, is or is not true, or will or will not occur. It takes a position on something not known but that can be argued for as true. Propositions of fact can concern the past, present, or future. Although propositions of fact may or may not be true—both positions are arguable—they are stated as true. For example, whether or not Lee Harvey Oswald acted alone when he killed President Kennedy is debatable. So you could argue a proposition of fact concerning the past in two ways: "Lee Harvey Oswald was the lone gunman who shot President John F. Kennedy" or "Lee Harvey Oswald was part of a larger conspiracy to shoot President John F. Kennedy." Examples of propositions of fact concerning the present are "I want to persuade the audience that there is a God," "I want to convince the audience that smoking causes cancer," and "I want the audience to believe that large numbers of elementary school children are illiterate." Claims of fact concerning the future are predictions. For example, "Thanks to the Internet, paperbound books will eventually cease to exist" and "E-mail will eventually replace traditional postal service" are both propositions of fact concerning the future.

proposition of value a statement designed to convince your audience that something is good, bad, desirable, undesirable, fair, unfair, moral, immoral, sound, unsound, beneficial, harmful, important, or unimportant

A **proposition of value** is a statement designed to convince your audience that something is good, bad, desirable, undesirable, fair, unfair, moral, immoral, sound, unsound, beneficial, harmful, important, or unimportant.[2] You can persuade your audience that something has more value than something else, or you can persuade your audience that something meets valued standards. For instance, "I want to convince my audience that a low-fat diet is actually better than a fat-free diet" is a proposition that will require you to prove that the nutritional value of a low-fat diet meets the American Dietetic Association standards that we value better than a fat-free diet. Similarly, the proposition "I want my audience to believe that multilingual education is beneficial to children" requires you to prove that children who receive multilingual education receive specific educational rewards that we, as a society, value.

proposition of policy a statement designed to convince your audience that they should take a specific course of action

A **proposition of policy** is a statement designed to convince your audience that they should take a specific course of action. Propositions of policy will implore listeners using words such as "do it/don't do it," "should/shouldn't," or "must/must not." "I want my audience to believe that a public speaking course *should* be required for all students at this university," "I want to persuade the audience that the United States *must* stop participating in the war in Iraq," and "I want to convince the audience that to receive a high school diploma all home-schooled children *should* be required to take and pass the same tests as public school children" are all propositions that advocate a specific policy. Sim-

EXHIBIT 13.2 Examples of persuasive speech propositions

Propositions of Fact	Propositions of Value	Propositions of Policy
Mahatma Gandhi was the father of passive resistance.	Mahatma Gandhi was a moral leader.	Mahatma Gandhi should be given a special award for his views on passive resistance.
Pharmaceutical advertising to consumers increases prescription drug prices.	Pharmaceutical advertising of new prescription drugs on TV is better than marketing new drugs directly to doctors.	Pharmaceutical companies should be required to refrain from advertising prescription drugs on TV.
Using paper ballots is a popular method for voting in U.S. elections.	Using paper ballots is better than using electronic voting machines.	Using paper ballots should be required for U.S. elections.

ilarly, "I want to convince the audience that government must do more to foster the habit of recycling" and " I want to convince the audience not to drink and drive" are propositions of policy.

Exhibit 13.2 provides several examples of how propositions of fact, value, and policy can be developed from the same topic idea.

As you begin work on your persuasive speeches, you can use the Speech Planning Action Steps and Speech Builder Express to help you organize and develop them, although some of the steps will be modified to provide you with guidance that is particular to persuasive speeches. You can use Activity 7A and the sample student response to help you develop a specific goal for a persuasive speech that is stated as a proposition.

SPEECH PLANNING   ACTION STEP 1

1 | Goals

ACTIVITY 7A Speech Planning Action Step for Persuasive Speeches

Writing a Specific Goal as a Persuasive Proposition
1. Tentatively phrase your goal as a proposition.
2. Check whether you believe that your target audience is opposed, has no opinion, or is in favor of your proposition. Why?
3. Check whether you believe that the degree of your target audience attitude makes your goal too difficult to meet or your audience is already convinced of your goal. If you've checked either of these, then rephrase your goal to adapt to that audience attitude.
4. Check whether your proposition, as stated or revised, is one of fact, value, or policy.

You can complete this activity online with Speech Builder Express. Use your Cengage-NOW for *Challenge* to access Activity 7A.

CENGAGENOW™

ACTIVITY 7A Student Response Action Step for Persuasive Speeches

Writing a Specific Goal as a Persuasive Proposition

1. Tentatively phrase your goal as a proposition.
   I want to convince members of the audience that they should not download music from the Internet.

2. Check whether you believe that your target audience is opposed, ✓, has no opinion, or is in favor of your proposition. Why?
   Although some students may be opposed or in favor of this proposition, I judge that the majority of the students in class are undecided.

3. Check whether you believe that the degree of your target audience attitude makes your goal too difficult to meet or your audience is already convinced of your goal. If you've checked either of these, then rephrase your goal to adapt to that audience attitude.
   Since my audience is neutral, my goal seems achievable.

4. Check whether your proposition, as stated or revised, is one of fact, value, or ✓, policy.

Identifying Good Reasons and Sound Evidence

Once you have identified a specific goal, you will use the research you have acquired to help you choose the main points of the speech. In a persuasive speech, the main points are reasons that support the goal, and the supporting material is evidence that buttresses the reasons.

Finding Reasons to Use as Main Points

reasons main point statements that summarize several related pieces of evidence and show *why* you should believe or do something

Reasons are main point statements that summarize several related pieces of evidence and show *why* you should believe or do something. For example, suppose you have decided to give a speech whose value proposition is, "I want the audience to believe that homeownership is good for society." After you have researched this, you might conclude that everything you have discovered can be grouped under one of six summary statements:

    I. Homeownership builds strong communities.

    II. Homeownership reduces crime.

    III. Homeownership increases individual wealth.

    IV. Homeownership increases individual self-esteem.

    V. Homeownership improves the value of a neighborhood.

    VI. Homeownership is growing in the suburbs.

Once you have identified reasons, you can weigh and evaluate each of them to select the three or four that are of the highest quality. You can judge the quality of each reason by asking the following questions:

1. Is the reason directly related to proving the proposition? Sometimes, we find information that can be summarized into a reason, but that reason doesn't directly argue the proposition. For instance, you may have uncovered a lot of research that supports the notion that "Homeownership is growing in the suburbs." Unfortunately, it isn't clear how the growth of homeownership in the suburbs benefits society as a whole. So, in choosing the reasons you will present, eliminate those that are not obviously related to your proposition.

2. Do I have strong evidence to support a reason? Some reasons sound impressive but cannot be supported with solid evidence. For example, the second reason, "Homeownership reduces crime," sounds like a good one, but can you support it? Sometimes, you may discover that the only proof you have for a reason is an opinion expressed by one person or that you haven't uncovered any widespread or systematic confirmation of this claim. In fact, in your research, you may discover that although crime is lower in areas with high homeownership, there is little evidence to suggest a cause-and-effect relationship. Because the audience will assess whether they accept your reason based on the evidence you present, eliminate reasons for which you do not have strong support.

3. Will this reason be persuasive for this audience? Suppose you have a great deal of factual evidence to support the reason "Homeownership increases individual self-esteem." This reason might be very persuasive to an audience of social workers, psychologists, and teachers but may be less persuasive to an audience of financial planners, bankers, and economists. So, once you are convinced that your reasons are related to the proposition and have strong evidence to support them, choose as main points of your speech those that you believe will be most persuasive for your particular audience. You can use Activity 7B and the sample student response to help you select reasons to support your goals.

Audiences believe reasons when there is strong evidence to support them.

SPEECH PLANNING   1 | Goals

ACTION STEP 1

ACTIVITY 7B Speech Planning Action Step for Persuasive Speeches

Selecting Reasons
1. Write the proposition that is the specific goal for this speech.
2. Try to list at least six reasons that support your specific goal. Then put asterisks (*) beside the three or four reasons that your audience analysis suggests will be most persuasive for this particular audience.
3. Write a thesis statement incorporating these reasons.

You can complete this activity online with Speech Builder Express. Use your Cengage-NOW for *Challenge* to access Activity 7B.

ACTIVITY 7B Student Response Action Step for Persuasive Speeches

Selecting Reasons

1. Write the proposition that is the specific goal for this speech.
I want to convince members of the audience that they should not download music from the Internet.

2. Try to list at least six reasons that support your specific goal. Then put asterisks (*) beside the three or four reasons that your audience analysis suggests will be most persuasive for this particular audience.
Downloading music is unethical.
* *Downloading music is extremely harmful to recording companies.*
* *Downloading music is extremely harmful to artists.*
* *Downloading music is extremely harmful to your computer.*
* *Downloading music is illegal.*
Downloading music might result in penalties.

3. Write a thesis statement incorporating these reasons.
Three good reasons for not downloading music off the Internet are that it's extremely harmful to recording companies and artists, it's harmful to your computer, and it's illegal.

Selecting Evidence to Support Reasons

Although a reason may seem self-explanatory, before most audience members will believe it, they want to hear information that backs it up. As you did your research, you may have discovered more evidence to support a reason than you will be able to use in the time allotted to your speech. So you will have to choose what evidence you will present.

As we learned in Chapter 6, verifiable factual statements are a strong type of supporting material. Suppose that in a speech whose goal is to convince people that Alzheimer's research should be better funded, you give the reason "Alzheimer's disease is an increasing health problem in the United States." The following would be a factual statement that supported this reason: "According to a 2003 article in the *Archives of Neurology,* the number of Americans with Alzheimer's has more than doubled since 1980 and is expected to continue to grow, affecting between 11.3 and 16 million Americans by the year 2050."

Statements from people who are experts on a subject can also be used as evidence to support a reason. For example, the statement "According to the surgeon general, 'By 2050 Alzheimer's disease may afflict 14 million people a year'" is an expert opinion.

Let's look at an example of how both fact and opinion evidence can be used in combination to support a proposition.

Proposition: I want the audience to believe that television violence has a harmful effect on children.

Reason: Television violence desensitizes children to violence.

Support: In Los Angeles, California, a survey of fifty children between the ages of five and ten who had just watched an episode of *Teenage Mutant Ninja*

Turtles asked the children whether or not violence was acceptable. Thirty-nine of the fifty, about 80% percent of them, responded, "Yes, because it helps you to win fights" (fact). Regardless of the rationale children express, the fact remains that viewing violence desensitizes children, and this can lead to real violence. According to Kirsten Houston, a well-regarded scholar writing in the July 1997 *Journal of Psychology,* "Repeated exposure to media violence is a major factor in the gradual desensitization of individuals to such scenes. This desensitization, in turn, weakens some viewers' psychological restraints on violent behavior" (expert opinion).

Regardless of whether the evidence is fact based or opinion based, you will want to choose the best evidence you have found to support your point. You can use the answers to the following questions to help you select evidence that is likely to persuade your audience.

1. Does the evidence come from a well-respected source? This question involves both the people who offered the opinions or compiled the facts and the book, journal, or Internet source where they were reported. Just as some people's opinions are more reliable than others, so are some printed and Internet sources more reliable than others. As we stated in Chapter 6, be especially careful of undocumented information. Eliminate evidence that comes from a questionable, unreliable, or biased source.

2. Is the evidence recent and, if not, is it still valid? Things change, so information that was accurate for a particular time period may or may not be valid today. As you look at your evidence, consider when the evidence was gathered. Something that was true five years ago may not be true today. A trend that was forecast a year ago may have been revised since then. And a statistic that was reported last week may be based on data that were collected three years ago. So, whether it is a fact or an opinion, you want to choose evidence that is valid today.

For example, the evidence "The total cost of caring for individuals with Alzheimer's is at least $100 billion, according to the Alzheimer's Association and the National Institute on Aging" was cited in a 2003 National Institutes of Health publication. But it is based on information from a study conducted using 1991 data, updated to 1994 data before being published. As a result, we can expect that annual costs would be higher today. If you choose to use this

Use evidence from a well-respected expert. Quotes from Madeleine Albright about foreign policy will be more likely to persuade than those from less reliable sources.

© Reuters/Corbis

Sara, a social worker in a homeless shelter, received a call from the president of the Lions Club asking her if she would like to speak to the group tomorrow. He was sorry for the late call, but the speaker they had scheduled had canceled. Sara was eager to do this because she wanted to ask the club to contribute "last dollars"—about $10,000 to a new family shelter that was being built. This shelter would allow the community to house homeless families as a unit rather than making them break up and go to single-sex shelters.

Her problem was that the research she had gathered and used in speeches four years ago as part of the original fund drive seemed dated. But since she was a last-minute fill-in speaker, she didn't have time to do additional research. Sara pondered her dilemma. She figured that one thing she could do would be to use the old information but obscure the actual dates. That way, the audience wouldn't really know that the evidence was old. Besides, she reasoned, it's not as though we've solved the homeless problem.

1. Is Sara's plan ethical?
2. How else might she solve her problem?

evidence, you should disclose the age of the data in the study and indicate that today the costs would be higher.

3. Does the evidence really support the reason? Just as reasons need to be relevant to the proposition, so does evidence need to be relevant to the reason. Some of the evidence you have found may be only indirectly related to the reason and should be eliminated in favor of evidence that provides more central support.

4. Will this evidence be persuasive for this audience? Finally, just as when you select your reasons, you will want to choose evidence that your particular audience is likely to find persuasive. So, if you have a choice of two quotations from experts, you will want to use the one from the person your audience is likely to find more credible.

Reasoning with Audiences

In a persuasive speech, the goal is met by arguing for your point of view using reasons that you support with evidence. In this section of the chapter, we describe how you can build and test the logic of the most common types of arguments used in presenting persuasive speeches.

Essentials of Reasoning

reasoning the mental process of drawing inferences (conclusions) from factual information

arguments the process of proving conclusions you have drawn from reasons and evidence

When you are **reasoning** with an audience, you are using the mental process of drawing inferences from factual information, providing arguments for your audience to consider. **Arguments** involve proving conclusions you have drawn from reasons and evidence.[3] Thus, when you show your friend that the engine of his car is "missing" at slow speeds and stalling at stoplights, you can reason (draw the conclusion or inference) that the car needs a tune-up. To put this in speech order, you say, "Jim, your car needs a tune-up. Why? Because the car is missing at slow speeds and stalling at stoplights."

As you prepare your speeches, you need a method for analyzing the soundness of the reasons or arguments that you are planning to make. Stephen Toulmin,[4] a philosopher and rhetorician, developed a system you can use for analyzing your arguments. The basic elements of an argument are the claim, the support, and the reasoning process, called the warrant.

CLAIM

A **claim** is a conclusion to be proven. In our simple example, one claim is "Your car needs a tune-up," which is supported by the evidence statements "It is missing at slow speeds" and "It is stalling at stoplights." But each of these statements is also a claim that must be supported by evidence if it is to be accepted and be valid as support for the larger claim "Your car needs a tune-up."

claim the proposition or conclusion to be proven

SUPPORT

You can support a claim with reasons or evidence, including facts, opinions, experiences, and observations that support the reasons. In the car example, the support for our argument includes two reasons, "missing at slow speeds" and "stalling at stoplights," and the evidence that supports each of these reasons.

In outline form, our example looks like this:

Specific goal: I want the audience to believe that the car needs a tune-up if the following situations occur. (claim)

I. The car misses at slow speeds. (reason and claim)
 A. On Tuesday, it was missing when driven below 20 mph. (evidence)
 B. On Wednesday, it did the same thing. (evidence)

II. The car stalls at stoplights. (reason and claim)
 A. It stalled three times at lights on Monday. (evidence)
 B. It stalled each time I stopped at a light yesterday. (evidence)

WARRANT

The **warrant** is the logical statement that connects the support to the claim.[5] Sometimes, the warrant of an argument is verbalized, but other times, it is simply implied. For instance, a person who claims that "the car needs a tune-up" on the basis of "missing" and "stalling at stoplights" may verbalize the reasoning process with the warrant, "Missing at slow speeds and stalling at lights *are common indications, or signs,* that the car needs a tune-up." Or the speaker may just assume you understand that these are signs of a car that needs a tune-up.

warrant the logical statement that connects the support to the claim

Although you may not actually state your warrants during the speech itself, identifying the type of warrants you are planning to use will allow you to build arguments that are persuasive.

Using C for claim (proposition or reason), S for support (reasons and evidence), and W for warrant or explanation of the reasoning process, we can write the reasoning for the proposition in our example in outline form as follows:

C I want the owner to believe that the car needs a tune-up. (specific goal)

S I. The engine misses at slow speeds. (plus evidence in support)

S II. The car stalls at stoplights. (plus evidence in support)

W (I believe this reasoning is sound because missing and stalling are *major indicators—signs*—of the need for a tune-up.) (The warrant is written in parentheses because it may not be verbalized when the speech is given.)

Types and Tests of Arguments

Although an argument *always* includes a claim and support, different logical relationships can exist between the claim and the support on which it is based. Four types of arguments commonly used in persuasive speeches are example, analogy, causation, and sign.

ARGUING FROM EXAMPLE

You **argue from example** when the support statements you use are examples of the claim you are making. For almost any topic, it is easy to find examples. So

argue from example to support your claim by providing one or more individual examples

Susan B. Anthony *Under Arrest*

In 1872, Susan B. Anthony was arrested. Her crime? She voted in a presidential election.

Today, it's hard for us to imagine a United States where people are denied the right to vote because of their gender. But imagine you were in Anthony's shoes. If you were denied the right to vote because of *your* gender, what strategy would you use to change the system? Would you file a lawsuit? Foment a rebellion? Advocate a hunger strike? Or go on the talk show circuit? What would your goal be? Shut out of making headway in the courts, Anthony hit the talk show circuit of her time, presenting public lectures in fifty-four counties in New York following her arrest. Anthony believed that mustering support for suffrage and women's rights required not only making appeals to the male voters but also encouraging other women to risk arrest by exercising their "citizen's right to vote." In this excerpt from her speech "Is It a Crime for a Citizen to Vote?" we see Anthony arguing that change to the franchise policy of the United States would come only as the result of massive civil disobedience.

> We no longer petition Legislature or Congress to give us the right to vote. We appeal to the women everywhere to exercise their too long neglected "citizen's right to vote." We appeal to the inspectors of election everywhere to receive the votes of all United States citizens as it is their duty to do. We appeal to United States commissioners and marshals to arrest the inspectors who reject the names and votes of United States citizens.

A powerful advocate for woman's suffrage, Susan B. Anthony died fourteen years before an amendment to the U.S. Constitution guaranteed women the right to vote.

---

you are likely to use arguing from example quite frequently. The warrant for an argument from example—its underlying logic—is, "What is true in the examples provided is (or will be) true in general or in other instances."

Suppose you are supporting Juanita Martinez for president of the local neighborhood council. One of the reasons you present is the claim that "Juanita is electable." In examining her résumé to find support for this claim, you find several examples of her previous victories. She was elected treasurer of her high school junior class, chairperson of her church youth group, and president of her college sorority. Each of these is an example that gives support to the claim. What would the warrant statement for this argument look like? You could say, "What was true in several instances (Juanita has been elected in three previous races) is true or will be true in general or in other instances (she will be electable in this situation)."

Let's look at this argument in speech analysis form:

C Juanita Martinez is electable.

S Juanita has won previous elections.

    A. Juanita won the election for treasurer of her high school junior class.

    B. Juanita won the election for chairperson of her church youth group.

    C. Juanita won the election for president of her sorority.

W (Because Juanita Martinez was elected to previous offices, she is electable for this office.)

When arguing from example, you can make sure your argument is valid by answering the following questions.

1. Are enough examples cited? Are three elections (junior class treasurer, youth group chairperson, and sorority president) enough examples to make your audience believe that your claim is true? Because the instances cited should represent most or all possibilities, enough must be cited to satisfy the listeners that the instances are not isolated or handpicked.

2. Are the examples typical? Are the three examples typical of all of Juanita's campaigns for office? Typical means that the examples cited must be similar to or representative of most or all within the category. If examples are not typical, they do not support the argument. For instance, because all three of these successes came in youth organizations, they may not be typical of election dynamics in community organizations. If the three examples are not typical, then the logic of the argument can be questioned. As a speaker, you might search for additional examples that are typical.

3. Are negative examples accounted for? In searching for supporting material, we may find one or more examples that are exceptions to the argument we wish to make. If the exceptions are minor or infrequent, then they won't invalidate the argument. For instance, in college, Juanita may have run for chairperson of the Sociology Club and lost. That one failure does not necessarily invalidate the argument. If, however, negative examples prove to be more than rare or isolated instances, the validity of the argument is open to serious question. For instance, if you found that Juanita had run for office twelve times and was successful on only the three occasions cited, then the argument would be invalid.

If you believe that there are not enough examples, that the examples you have found are not typical, or that negative examples are common, then you will have only weak support for the claim and should consider making a different type of argument.

ARGUING FROM ANALOGY

You **argue from analogy** when you support a claim with a single comparable example that is so significantly similar to the subject of the claim as to be strong proof. The general statement of a warrant for an argument from analogy is, "What is true for situation A will also be true in situation B, which is similar to situation A" or "What is true for situation A will be true in all similar situations."

Suppose you wanted to argue that the Cherry Fork volunteer fire department should conduct a raffle to raise money for three portable defibrillator units. You could support the claim by analogy with a single example: Mack Fire Department conducted a raffle and raised enough money to purchase four units. The form for this argument from analogy looks like this:

C Cherry Fork Fire Department should conduct a raffle to raise money for three portable defibrillator units.

S Mack Fire Department, which is very similar to Cherry Fork, raised enough money through a raffle to purchase four units.

W (What worked at a very similar volunteer fire department, Mack, will work at Cherry Fork.)

Let us return to the claim that Juanita is electable for president of the local neighborhood council to see how arguing from analogy works in a more complex situation. If you discover that Juanita has essentially the same characteristics as Paula Jefferson, who was elected president two years ago (both are very bright, both have a great deal of drive, and both have track records of successful campaigns), then you can use the single example of Paula to form a reason "Juanita has the same characteristics as Paula Jefferson, who was elected two years ago." This is analogical reasoning.

Let's look at how the Martinez argument would look in outline form:

C Juanita Martinez is electable.

S Juanita has the same characteristics as Paula Jefferson, who was elected two years ago. (This is also a claim, for which A, B, and C below are support.)

argue from analogy to support a claim with a single comparable example that is significantly similar to the subject of the claim

A. Juanita and Paula are both very bright.

B. Juanita and Paula both have a great deal of drive.

C. Juanita and Paula both have won other campaigns.

W (What was true for Paula will be true for Juanita, who is similar on the important characteristics.)

So the claim is supported through an analogy; then additional support is offered to validate the analogy.

When arguing from analogy, you can make sure that your argument is valid by answering the following questions.

1. Are the subjects being compared similar in every important way? Are intelligence, drive, and track records the most important characteristics on which to determine electability? If criteria on which the subjects are being compared are not the most important ones, or if they really don't compare well, then you can question the reasoning on that basis.

2. Are any of the ways in which the subjects are dissimilar important to the outcome? If Paula is a native of the community, whereas Juanita has only been in the area for a year, is this dissimilarity important? When the dissimilarities outweigh the subjects' similarities, then conclusions drawn from the comparisons may be invalid.

ARGUING FROM CAUSATION

argue from causation to cite events that have occurred that result in the claim

You **argue from causation** when you support a claim by citing events that have occurred that result in the claim. Reasoning from causation says that one or more of the events cited always (or almost always) brings about, leads to, or creates or prevents a predictable effect or set of effects.

The general warrant for arguments from cause can be stated as follows: If an event comes before another event and is associated with that event, then we can say that it is the cause of the event. "If A, which is known to bring about B, has been observed, then we can expect B to occur." For instance, you could develop a causal argument based on the relationship between mortgage interest rates and home sales: "Home sales are bound to increase during the next three months (claim) because mortgage interest rates have recently dropped markedly (causal event as support)."

How would you evaluate the causal claim made on this billboard?

Let's look at this type of argument in outline form:

C Home sales will increase.

S Mortgage interest rates have dropped.

W (Lower interest rates generally lead to higher home sales.)

In researching Juanita's election campaign, you might discover that (1) she has campaigned intelligently and (2) she has won the endorsement of key community leaders. If these two events are usually associated with victory, then you can form the argument that Juanita has engaged in behavior that leads to campaign victories, thus supporting the claim that she is electable. The argument would look like this:

C Juanita Martinez will be elected.

S **A.** Juanita has campaigned intelligently.

S **B.** Juanita has key endorsements.

W (Intelligent campaigning and getting key endorsements lead to [cause] electoral victory.)

When arguing from causation, you can make sure that your argument is valid by answering the following questions.

1. Are the events alone sufficient to cause the stated effect? Are intelligent campaigning and key endorsements important enough by themselves to result in winning elections? If the events are truly causes, it means that if these events were eliminated, then the effect would be eliminated as well. If the effect can occur without these events occurring, then you can question the causal relationship.

2. Do other events accompanying the cited events actually cause the effect? Are other factors (such as luck, drive, friends) more important in determining whether a person wins an election? If the other events appear equally or more important in bringing about the effect, then you can question the causal relationship between the data cited and the conclusion. If you believe that other data caused the effect, then you can question the reasoning on that basis.

3. Is the relationship between the causal events and the effect consistent? Do intelligent campaigning and key endorsements always (or usually) yield electoral victories? If there are times when the effect has not followed the cause, then you can question whether a causal relationship exists. If you believe that the relationship between the cause and effect is not consistent, then you can question the reasoning on that basis.

ARGUING FROM SIGN

If certain events, characteristics, or situations always or usually accompany something, those events, characteristics, or situations are signs. You **argue from sign** when you support a claim by providing evidence that the events that signal the claim have occurred. For instance, your doctor may claim that you have had an allergic reaction because you have hives and a slight fever.

The general warrant for reasoning from sign can be stated as follows: When phenomena that usually or always accompany a specific situation occur, then we can expect that specific situation is occurring (or will occur). So the warrant for the allergy argument can be stated as follows: "Hives and a slight fever are indicators (signs) of an allergic reaction."

Let's look at this argument in outline form:

C You have had an allergic reaction.

S **A.** You have hives.

argue from sign to cite information that signals the claim

B. You have a slight fever.

W (Hives and a slight fever are signs of an allergic reaction.)

Signs should not be confused with causes; signs accompany a phenomenon but do not bring about, lead to, or create the claim. In fact, signs may actually be the effects of the phenomenon. A rash and fever don't cause an allergic reaction; they are indications, or effects, of a reaction.

If in analyzing Juanita's campaign, you notice that she has more campaign workers than all other candidates combined and that a greater number of people from all segments of the community are wearing "Juanita for President" buttons, you may reason "Juanita's campaign has the key signs of an election victory."

A speech outline using the sign argument would look like this:

C Juanita Martinez will be elected.

S A. Juanita has more campaign workers than all other candidates combined.

  B. A greater number of community members are wearing her campaign buttons.

W (The presence of a greater number of campaign workers and buttons than the opponents have is a sign/indicator of victory.)

When arguing from sign, you can make sure that your argument is valid by answering the following questions.

1. Do the signs cited always or usually indicate the conclusion drawn? Do large numbers of campaign workers and campaign buttons always (or usually) indicate election victory? If the data can occur independently of the conclusion, then they are not necessarily indicators. If the signs cited do not usually indicate the conclusion, then you can question the reasoning on that basis.

2. Are a sufficient number of signs present? Are campaign workers and buttons enough to indicate a victory? Several signs often indicate events or situations. If enough signs are not present, then the conclusion may not follow. If there are insufficient signs, then you can question the reasoning on that basis.

3. Are contradictory signs in evidence? Are campaign buttons thrown away in great numbers? If signs usually indicating different conclusions are present, then the stated conclusion may not be valid. If you believe that contradictory signs are evident, then you can question the reasoning on that basis.

COMBINING ARGUMENTS IN A SPEECH

An effective speech usually contains several reasons that are based on various types of arguments. For a speech with the goal "I want my audience to believe that Juanita is electable," you might choose to present three of the reasons we've been working with. Suppose you selected the following:

  I. Juanita has run successful campaigns in the past. (argued by example)

   A. Juanita was successful in her campaign for treasurer of her high school class.

   B. Juanita was successful in her campaign for chairperson of her church youth group.

   C. Juanita was successful in her campaign for president of her sorority.

 II. Juanita has engaged in procedures that result in campaign victory. (argued by cause)

   A. Juanita has campaigned intelligently.

   B. Juanita has key endorsements.

III. Juanita is a strong leader. (argued by sign)

    A. Juanita has more campaign workers than all other candidates combined.

    B. Juanita has a greater number of community members wearing her campaign buttons.

Just as each of our reasons is presented as an argument, so too is the overall speech. So we need to determine what type of argument we are making. What relationship do all three of these reasons have with the overall claim? That is, how do running successful campaigns in the past, being engaged in procedures that result in victory, and being a strong leader relate to whether Juanita is electable? Are they examples of being electable? Do they cause one to be elected? Are they signs that usually accompany election? Do they distinguish a person who is electable from one who is not? As you study this, you will recognize that the warrant is best stated: "Running successful campaigns in the past, being engaged in procedures that result in victory, and being a strong leader are all signs of electability." Now you can test the soundness of the overall argument by using the tests of sign argument listed earlier.

Avoiding Fallacies of Reasoning

As you are developing your reasons and the arguments you will make, you should check to make sure that your reasoning is appropriate for the particular situation. This will allow you to avoid fallacies, or errors in reasoning. Five common fallacies to avoid are hasty generalization, false cause, either-or, straw man, and ad hominem arguments.

HASTY GENERALIZATION

A **hasty generalization** is a fallacy that presents a generalization that is either not supported with evidence or is supported with only one weak example. Because the supporting material that is cited should be representative of all the supporting material that could be cited, enough supporting material must be presented to satisfy the audience that the instances are not isolated or hand-picked. Avoiding hasty generalizations requires you to be confident that the instances you cite as support are typical and representative of your claim. For example, someone who argued, "All Akitas are vicious dogs," whose sole piece of evidence was, "My neighbor had an Akita and it bit my best friend's sister," would be guilty of a hasty generalization. It is hasty to generalize about the temperament of a whole breed of dogs based on a single action of one dog.

> **hasty generalization** a fallacy that presents a generalization that is either not supported with evidence or is supported with only one weak example

FALSE CAUSE

A **false cause** fallacy occurs when the alleged cause fails to be related to, or to produce, the effect. The Latin term for this fallacy is *post hoc, ergo propter hoc,* meaning "after this, therefore because of this." Just because two things happen one after the other does not mean that the first necessarily caused the second. Unlike people who blame monetary setbacks and illness on black cats or broken mirrors, be careful that you don't present a coincidental event as a causes unless you can prove the causal relationship. An example of a false cause fallacy is when a speaker claims that school violence is caused only by television violence, the Internet, a certain song or musical group, or lack of parental involvement. When one event follows another, there may be no connection at all, or the first event might be just one of many causes that contribute to the second.

> **false cause** a fallacy that occurs when the alleged cause fails to be related to, or to produce, the effect

EITHER-OR

An **either-or** fallacy is the argument that there are only two alternatives when, in fact, others exist. Many such cases are an oversimplification of a complex

> **either-or** a fallacy that argues there are only two alternatives when, in fact, there are many

issue. For example, when Robert argued that "we'll either have to raise taxes or close the library," he committed an either-or fallacy. He reduced a complex issue to one oversimplified solution when there were many other possible solutions.

STRAW MAN

straw man a fallacy that occurs when a speaker weakens the opposing position by misrepresenting it and then attacks that weaker position

A **straw man** argument is when a speaker weakens the opposing position by misrepresenting it in some way and then attacks that weaker (straw man) position. For example, in her speech advocating a seven-day waiting period to purchase handguns, Colleen favored regulation, not prohibition, of gun ownership. Bob argued against that by claiming "it is our constitutional right to bear arms." However, Colleen did not advocate abolishing the right to bear arms. Hence, Bob distorted Colleen's position, making it easier for him to refute.

AD HOMINEM

ad hominem argument a fallacy that occurs when a speaker attacks or praises a person making an argument rather than addressing the argument itself

An **ad hominem argument** attacks or praises the person making the argument rather than addressing the argument itself. *Ad hominem* literally means "to the man." For example, if Jamal's support for his claim that his audience should buy an Apple computer is that Steve Jobs, the founder and current president of Apple Computer, is a genius, he is making an ad hominem argument. Jobs's intelligence isn't really a reason to buy a particular brand of computer. TV commercials that feature celebrities using the product are often guilty of ad hominem reasoning.

Organizational Patterns for Persuasive Speeches

Once you have identified and tested the logic of your reasons, you are ready to organize the main points into a pattern that will enable your audience to follow your argument. The most common patterns for organizing persuasive speeches are statement of reasons, comparative advantages, criteria satisfaction, refutative, problem-solution, problem-cause-solution, and motivated sequence. In this section, we describe and illustrate each of the first four persuasive organizational patterns and identify the type of proposition for which they are most commonly used. The last three patterns, problem-solution, problem-cause-solution, and motivated sequence, will be described in the next chapter. So you can contrast the patterns and better understand their use, we will illustrate each pattern using the same topic with different propositions that use the same (or similar) reasons.

Statement of Reasons Pattern

The **statement of reasons** is a form of persuasive organization used for proving propositions of fact in which you present your best-supported reasons in a meaningful order. For a speech with three reasons or more, place the strongest reason last because this is the reason you believe the audience will find most persuasive. You will often place the second strongest reason first because you want to start with a significant point. Place the other reasons in between.

> **statement of reasons** a straightforward organization in which you present your best-supported reasons in a meaningful order

Proposition: I want my audience to believe that passing the proposed school tax levy is necessary.

   I. The income will enable the schools to restore vital programs. (second strongest)

   II. The income will enable the schools to give teachers the raises they need to keep up with the cost of living.

   III. The income will allow the community to maintain local control and will save the district from state intervention. (strongest)

Comparative Advantages Pattern

The **comparative advantages** organizational pattern shows that one of two or more alternatives (which may include the status quo) is best. You show that the advantages of your alternative outweigh the disadvantages and that its advantages surpass the advantages of the other options.[6] A comparative advantages approach to a school tax proposition would look like this:

> **comparative advantages** an organization that shows that a proposed change has more value than the status quo

Proposition: I want my audience to believe that passing the school tax levy is better than not passing it. (compares the value of change to the status quo)

   I. Income from a tax levy will enable schools to reintroduce important programs that had to be cut. (advantage 1)

   II. Income from a tax levy will enable schools to avoid a tentative strike by teachers who are underpaid. (advantage 2)

   III. Income from a tax levy will enable us to retain local control of our schools, which will be lost to the state if additional local funding is not provided. (advantage 3)

Criteria Satisfaction Pattern

criteria satisfaction an indirect organization that seeks audience agreement on criteria that should be considered when evaluating a particular proposition and then shows how the proposition satisfies those criteria

The **criteria satisfaction** pattern is an indirect organization that seeks audience agreement on criteria that should be considered when evaluating a particular proposition and then shows how the proposition satisfies those criteria. A criteria satisfaction pattern is especially useful when your audience is opposed to your proposition because it approaches the proposition indirectly by first focusing on criteria that the audience may agree with before introducing the specific proposition. A criteria satisfaction organization for the school tax proposition would look like this:

Proposition: I want my audience to believe that passing a school levy is a good way to fund our schools.

I. We all can agree that a good school funding method must meet three criteria:

   A. A good funding method results in the reestablishment of programs that have been dropped for monetary reasons.

   B. A good funding method results in fair pay for teachers.

   C. A good funding method generates enough income to maintain local control, avoiding state intervention.

II. Passage of a local school tax levy is a good way to fund our schools.

   A. A local levy will allow us to fund important programs again.

   B. A local levy will allow us to give teachers a raise.

   C. A local levy will generate enough income to maintain local control and avoid state intervention.

Refutative Pattern

refutative an organization that persuades by both disproving the opposing position and bolstering one's own

The **refutative** pattern helps you organize your main points so that you persuade by both challenging the opposing arguments and bolstering your own. This pattern is particularly useful when the target audience opposes your position. Begin by acknowledging the merit of opposing arguments and then showing their flaws. Once listeners understand the flaws, they are more receptive to the arguments you present to support your opinion. A refutative organization for the school tax proposition might look like this:

Proposition: I want my audience to agree that a school levy is the best way to fund our schools.

I. Opponents of the tax levy argue that the tax increase will fall only on property owners.

   A. Landlords will recoup property taxes in the form of higher rents.

   B. Thus, all people will be affected.

II. Opponents of the tax levy argue that there are fewer students in the school district, so schools should be able to function on the same amount of revenue.

   A. Although there are fewer pupils, costs continue to rise.

   1. Salary cost increases

   2. Energy cost increases

   3. Maintenance cost increases

   4. Unfunded federal and state government mandates

   B. Although there are fewer pupils, there are many aging school buildings that need replacing or retrofitting for this computer age.

III. Opponents of the tax levy argue that parents should be responsible for the excessive cost of educating their children.

    A. Historically, our nation flourished under a publicly funded educational system.

    B. Parents today are already paying more than our parents did.

        1. Activity fees

        2. Lab fees

        3. Book fees

        4. Transportation fees

    C. Of school-age children today in this district, 42 percent live in families that are below the poverty line and have limited resources.

SPEECH ASSIGNMENT

Persuasive Speaking

1. Prepare a four- to seven-minute speech in which you change audience belief.
2. Write a persuasive plan for adapting to your specific audience that includes:
    a. How your goal adapts to whether your prevailing audience attitude is in favor, has no opinion, or is opposed.
    b. What reasons you will use and how the organizational pattern you selected is fitting for your topic and audience.
    c. How you will organize those reasons.
3. Write a complete speech outline.

To help you prepare your outline, use your CengageNOW for *Challenge* to access Speech Builder Express.

SPEECH EVALUATION CHECKLIST

Speech to Convince Evaluation Checklist

You can use this checklist to critique a persuasive speech that you hear in class. As you listen to the speaker, outline the speech. Pay close attention to the reasoning process the speaker uses. Note the claims and support used in the arguments, and identify the types of warrants used. Then answer the questions below.

Primary Criteria

_____ 1. Did the specific goal appear to be adapted to the initial attitude of most members of the audience?

_____ 2. Was the specific goal phrased as a proposition (were you clear what position on the issue the speaker was taking)?

_____ 3. Was the proposition one of: _____ fact _____ value _____ policy?

_____ 4. Were the reasons (claims) used in the speech:

    _____ Directly related to the proposition?

    _____ Supported by strong evidence?

    _____ Persuasive for the particular audience?

_____ 5. Was the evidence (support) used to back the reasons (claims):

     _____ From well-respected sources?

     _____ Recent or still valid?

     _____ Persuasive for this audience?

     _____ Typical of all evidence that might have been used?

     _____ Sufficient (enough evidence was cited)?

_____ 6. Could you identify the types of warrants that were used?

     _____ Did the speaker argue from example? If so, was it valid?

     _____ Did the speaker argue from analogy? If so, was it valid?

     _____ Did the speaker argue from causation? If so, was it valid?

     _____ Did the speaker argue from sign? If so, was it valid?

_____ 7. Did the speaker engage in any fallacies of reasoning?

     _____ Hasty generalizations

     _____ Arguing from false cause

     _____ Ad hominem attacks

     _____ Either-or

     _____ Straw man

_____ 8. Did the speaker use an appropriate persuasive speech organizational pattern?

     _____ Statement of reasons

     _____ Comparative advantages

     _____ Criteria satisfaction

     _____ Refutative

General Criteria

_____ 1. Was the specific goal clear?

_____ 2. Was the introduction effective in creating interest and introducing the proposition?

_____ 3. Was the speech organized using an appropriate persuasive pattern?

_____ 4. Was the language clear, vivid, and appropriate?

_____ 5. Was the conclusion effective in summarizing what had been said and motivating the audience to agree or act?

_____ 6. Was the speaker's oral delivery intelligible, vocally expressive, and conversational?

_____ 7. Was the speaker's use of body poised, expressive, and appropriate?

Overall evaluation of the speech (check one):

_____ excellent _____ good _____ average _____ fair _____ poor

Use the information from this checklist to support your evaluation.

You can use your CengageNOW for _Challenge_ to access this checklist online under the Chapter 13 resources.

Sample Speech to Convince

This section presents a sample speech to convince given by a student, including an adaptation plan, an outline, and a transcript.

Downloading Music

by Tobias Varland*

*Used with permission of Tobias Varland, University of Cincinnati.

Read the speech adaptation plan, outline, and a transcript of a speech given by Tobias Varland in an introductory speaking course. You can access a video clip of Tobias presenting his speech by using your CengageNOW for *Challenge*. You can also use CengageNOW to identify some of the strengths of Tobias's speech by preparing an evaluation checklist and an analysis. You can then compare your answers to those of the authors. To watch and evaluate another persuasive speech, use your CengageNOW to access Eric Wais's speech, "Capital Punishment," under the Chapter 13 resources.

Adaptation Plan

1. Audience attitude: When I asked people about their feelings about downloading, I found that most realized that it was easy to do and that it saved them time and money. There was a general belief that downloading didn't really hurt companies that much. But most also mentioned that they realized that it was not the right thing to do, but with so many doing it, chances of being caught were pretty low. As I put these data together, I determined that although the audience was not set against downloading, they were not totally in favor of doing it either. So I put the majority in the group of undecided or not that worried about the consequences.

2. Reasons: I believe the three reasons most likely to convince the audience are that downloading is really harmful to companies, that downloading is harmful to the computer (few people even mention this as a possible downside), and that downloading is not only illegal but can be costly.

3. Selecting an organization to meet audience needs: Given that the majority of the class seemed indifferent or unworried about the consequences, I determined that a statement of reasons approach was appropriate. I have organized my speech in such a way that it will gain momentum throughout the speech, and by the end of the speech, the audience will have no choice but to consider my suggestions.

Outline

General purpose: To persuade

Speech goal: I want to convince members of the audience that they should not download music from the Internet.

Introduction

   I. Over the past few weeks, I've discovered that large numbers of people are doing something that in my mind is unbelievably stupid.

   II. They're saving approximately 99 cents for doing something that could cost them as much as $150,000.

   III. They're downloading copyrighted music off the Internet.

Thesis statement: There are three good reasons for not downloading music off the Internet: it's extremely harmful to recording companies and artists, it's harmful to computers, and it's illegal.

Body

   I. Downloading music is extremely harmful to recording companies and artists.

A. Record sales have declined radically in the last five years.

   1. About 41 percent of people are downloading music for free rather than buying records, according to *Fortune* magazine.

   2. Since 1993, average annual profit has dropped from 20 percent to less than 5 percent.

B. People are losing jobs.

   1. This year three major recording companies, BMG, EMI, and Sony Music, fired 4,200 people as a result.

II. The second reason that you should not be downloading music from the Internet is that it is harmful to your computer.

A. In order to download music from the Internet, people must use some sort of spot check program.

   1. Just one such program, His Eye, has 65 million users.

B. According to *PC Magazine,* by installing such a program, you also install several others, such as spyware.

   1. These programs monitor who you send e-mails to, copy your e-mail messages, and store them on your server.

   2. They send out spam directories that take control of your computer, lock you out of your own computer, use your computer for illegal practices, and say you are responsible.

      a. For instance, a graduate student who is writing a thesis could have it stolen and published before he or she gets a chance to print it.

   3. Saving a few dollars instead of buying CDs or buying individual songs off the Internet can put people at such huge risk that it's unbelievable that they continue to do it.

III. The third and most important reason for not downloading music is that it's illegal.

A. Music in the United States is protected by copyright law.

   1. When you download music off the Internet, you are committing theft.

B. Recording studios have filed numerous lawsuits.

   1. According to CBC News, one company just filed a lawsuit against four college students from New England who had all downloaded 1,500 songs apiece.

   2. It sought fines of $150,000 per song that these students had downloaded, according to the CBC News.

   3. Although the company didn't get the $150,000 per song, each student was forced to pay somewhere between $12,500 and $17,500 and was kicked out of school.

C. All of this happened because they wanted to save themselves 15 bucks per CD.

Conclusion

I. So, think about it: Downloading is harmful to the recording industry, it is likely to be harmful to your computer, and most of all, it could result in tremendous financial loss to you because it is illegal.

II. I would encourage you to consider these things before you download anything else. Consider whether or not it's really worth it.

Works Cited

CBC News (Web Site). http://www.cbc.ca/stories/2003/05/02/Consumers/record/lawsuit 03052.

Seith, Robert, CWK Senior Producer. "Downloading Copyrighted Music." http://www.connectingwithkids.com/tipsheet/2003/115_mar12/music.html.

"Songs in the Key of Steve." *Fortune Magazine,* May 19, 2003.

"Spyware: It's Lurking on Your Machine." *PC Magazine,* April 22, 2003.

"Study Links Burning and Downloading to Falling Music Sales." *The Write News,* June 20, 2003. www.writenews.com.

Sweeting, Paul. "Avast ye pirates! The copyright industries, particularly the record companies, are entering dangerous new waters," *Video Business,* June 30, 2003 v23 i26 p10(1).

Speech and Analysis

Speech

As I was talking with a lot of my friends and acquaintances, I discovered a pretty amazing phenomenon. I discovered that almost every person I talked to does something that in my mind is unbelievably stupid. Anyone know what I'm talking about? It's a behavior that has become extremely popular: illegally downloading copyrighted music off the Internet. Today I'd like to convince you that you should not download music on your computer. Why? For at least three reasons.

The first reason is that it's extremely harmful to recording companies and recording artists. I'm going to discuss some numbers with you—and I want you to think about them. The first number is 61. According to *The Write News,* CD record sales in the United States have dropped 61 percent in just the last year. The second number is 41. Downloading has become extremely popular, according to *Fortune* magazine. Today, about 41 percent of people who love music are downloading it for free rather than buying records. Third is a set of numbers: 20/5. Obviously, downloading is very harmful to recording companies. In 1993, recording companies made an average annual profit of just over 20 percent. Now they're making less than 5 percent profit. That's 20 to 5! The last number is 4,200. During this last year, three major recording companies, BMG, EMI, and Sony Music, have fired 4,200 people because they could not gainfully employ these people. As much as you would like to think that music is for the sake of art and people do it because they love doing it, music is a business. To get their money out of it, recording companies can't continue to produce music, the artists have no ambition in producing music, and therefore, by downloading music, most people would say, I'm trying to support this music, I want to listen to it, I want to hear it—what they're really doing is destroying an industry and insuring that there will not be as much music produced in the future.

The second reason that you should not be downloading music from the Internet is that it is extremely harmful to your computer. In order to download this music from the Internet, almost everybody uses some sort of spot check program. The most popular program right now is called His Eye, a program that has as many as 65 million users. The problem is that when you install His Eye on your computer, you install numerous other programs like spyware. This spyware does things to your computer such as monitors who you send e-mails to, copies your e-mail messages and stores them on your server, sends those addresses out to spam directories that can actually take control of your computer, locking you out of your own computer, uses your computer for illegal practices and says you are responsible for it since it is your computer. Let's look at a potential consequence. Suppose you're a graduate student and you're writing a thesis paper. It could be stolen and published before you get a chance to print it. It seems that people are doing this to save themselves a few dollars from buying CDs or buying individual songs off the Internet and putting themselves in such huge risk that it's unbelievable that they continue to do it.

The third one, and the most important reason why this should not be done, is it's illegal. Music in the United States is protected by copyright law. When you download this music off the Internet, you are committing theft. Recording companies recently have been on a kind of a rampage in catching people who've been doing this. They want to be very aggressive about it. And they just filed a lawsuit against four college students from New England who had all downloaded 1,500 songs apiece. The recording industry sought a fine of $150,000 per song that these students had downloaded. This is according to the CBC News. The recording industry didn't get the $150,000

Analysis

Tobias begins indirectly by sharing his opinions about a behavior that has become very popular. This indirect method is designed to get people interested in determining what he is going to talk about.

In his introduction he states his goal and mentions that he will focus on three reasons.

His first reason is designed to focus on one important harm that results from downloading.

Notice the presentation of information used to support his point. Throughout this section, he cites sources and gives a variety of statistics.

Here he tries to get his audience to think about what he has said. He makes a good case showing that downloading has in fact a major effect on companies and artists.

In this second reason, Tobias looks at material with which the audience may be totally unfamiliar.

He talks about side effects that result from downloading methods. Some of these side effects don't seem to be that important, but in fact, they are. He shows that allowing access enables others to take advantage of your machine.

In short, he's focusing on unnecessary risks that may result from your use of various downloading programs.

Notice how he keeps coming back to his key point: For relatively small savings, you are taking tremendous risks—and you might not even be aware of the potential harms.

Since the audience may not totally accept the importance of these first two reasons, Tobias closes with his third and most important reason—that some or much of what you're doing is not only illegal but also could be tremendously detrimental to you.

The point is that the industry is making examples of some individuals by seeing to it that they pay fines. So the costs are not $150,000, but would you be able to afford the $12,500 to per song; there's no way that these students could ever pay that much money to the recording companies. Each student was forced to pay somewhere between $12,500 and $17,500 along with being kicked out of school, and they were very lucky apparently to avoid at least a six-month jail sentence. All to save themselves 15 bucks per CD. I know that as a college student if somebody told me that I was responsible all of a sudden for paying a $15,000 fine, I'm kind of out of luck—I can't pay a $15,000 fine.

So, thinking about it, there are these three very obvious reasons that by downloading off the Internet you are costing people dollars, you're destroying some people's careers; sound engineers, that's all they know. They can't be employed anymore, because their companies are undermined by people trying to save a few dollars. You're putting your privacy and your computer at risk and making yourself further liable for damages done with your computer by other people. And you're breaking the law. In a society where people don't obey the law in one instance, what's to keep them from not obeying in another instance? How can you break this law and condemn somebody else for breaking another law? It doesn't make sense, the whole package of downloading copyrighted music off the Internet doesn't make sense, and most people just don't think about that. So I would encourage you to consider these things before you download anything else.

Summary

Persuasive speeches are designed to influence the attitudes, beliefs, values, or the behavior of audience members. The Elaboration Likelihood Model (ELM) describes how audiences process persuasive messages. Understanding this model will enable you to focus on how to use logos, ethos, and pathos appeals as you plan your speech. The first step in preparing a persuasive speech is to construct a speech goal. These goals are chosen based on the audience's initial attitude. An audience may be opposed to the proposition, have no opinion (because they are uninformed, impartial, or apathetic), or be in favor. Persuasive speech goals are phrased as propositions in which the position advocated by the speaker is clearly indicated.

The second step is to choose good reasons and sound evidence. Reasons are main point statements that support the proposition. Evidence is information (including facts and expert opinions) selected to support reasons.

The third step is to evaluate the quality of your reasons. As you reason with your audience, you will make claims that you support with evidence. The logic that links your claim and your support is called the warrant. The warrant may be voiced or just implied. Different types of warrants can be used to link claims and support. Four of the most common are arguing from example, analogy, cause, and sign. As you prepare your speech, you will want to decide which types of warrants you will use and test them to ensure that they are valid. You will also want to make sure that you avoid five common fallacies that occur in reasoning: hasty generalizations, false cause, either-or, straw man, and ad hominem arguments.

Finally, once you have selected your reasons and evidence and tested the logic of your warrants, you can choose from among seven patterns of persuasive organization: statement of reasons, comparative advantages, criteria satisfaction, refutative (discussed in this chapter), and problem-solution, problem-cause-solution, and motivated sequence (discussed in the next chapter).

Now that you've read Chapter 13, use your CengageNOW for *The Challenge of Effective Speaking* for quick access to the electronic resources that accompany this text. Your CengageNOW gives you access to the video of Tobias's speech, "Downloading Music," featured on pages 281–284, the speech evaluation checklist shown on page 279, the Web Resources featured in this chapter, Speech Builder Express, InfoTrac College Edition, and online study aids such as a digital glossary and review quizzes.

Your *Challenge* CengageNOW is an online study system that helps you identify concepts you don't fully understand, allowing you to put your study time to the best use. Using chapter-by-chapter diagnostic pretests, the system creates a personalized study plan for each chapter. Each plan directs you to specific resources designed to improve your understanding, including pages from the text in e-book format. Chapter posttests give you an opportunity to measure how much you've learned and let you know if you are ready for graded quizzes and exams.

KEY TERMS

Go to your CengageNOW for *Challenge* to access your online glossary for Chapter 13. Print a copy of the glossary for this chapter and test yourself with the electronic flash cards or complete the crossword puzzle to help you master these key terms:

ad hominem argument (276)
apathetic (261)
argue from analogy (271)
argue from causation (272)
argue from example (270)
argue from sign (273)
arguments (260)
attitude (260)
claim (269)
comparative advantages (277)
criteria satisfaction (278)

either-or (275)
ethos (259)
false cause (275)
hasty generalization (275)
impartial (261)
incremental change (260)
logos (259)
pathos (259)
persuasive speech (258)
proposition (262)
proposition of fact (262)

proposition of policy (262)
proposition of value (262)
reasoning (269)
reasons (265)
refutative (278)
statement of reasons (277)
straw man (276)
target audience (260)
uninformed (261)
warrant (269)

SPEECH PLANNING ACTION STEPS

Access the Action Step activities for this chapter online at your CengageNOW for *Challenge*. Select the chapter resources for Chapter 13 and then click on the activity number you want. You may print your completed activities, and you should save your work so you can use it as needed in later Action Step activities.

7A Writing a Specific Goal as a Persuasive Proposition (263)

7B Selecting Reasons (266)

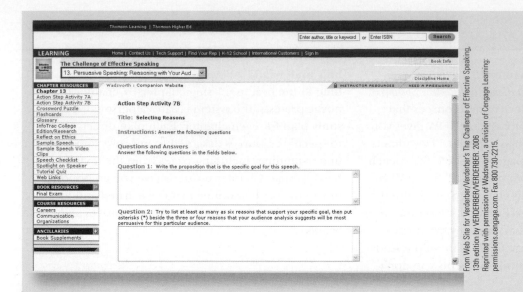

From Web Site for Verderber/Verderber's The Challenge of Effective Speaking, 13th edition by VERDERBER/VERDERBER. 2006 Reprinted with permission of Wadsworth, a division of Cengage Learning: permissions.cengage.com. Fax 800 730-2215.

Persuasive Speaking: Motivating the Audience

14

There can be no knowledge without emotion. We may be aware of a truth, yet until we have felt its force, it is not ours. To the cognition of the brain must be added the experience of the soul.

Arnold Bennett, *The Journals of Arnold Bennett,* **entry for March 18, 1897**

What's Ahead

HERE'S WHAT'S AHEAD IN THIS CHAPTER:

1. Why is it important to appeal to emotions in your persuasive speech?

2. What are strategies you might employ to appeal to emotions?

3. Why is it important to establish credibility in your persuasive speech?

4. What are strategies you might employ to establish credibility?

5. How can you organize your speech to actuate effectively?

6. What are some things to consider to ensure you develop an ethical persuasive speech?

As Steve finished his speech on "Taking Back the Neighborhood: Get Out the Vote!" the audience rose to their feet and began to chant, "No more! No more! No more! No more! . . ." It was clear to him that he had made an impact. Not only had he convinced his audience, but he could also see that they were visibly angry and ready for action. As he was leaving the platform, he heard a member of the audience shout out, "You heard him. It's time! Voting won't do any good. Let's go take what is ours. Take to the streets! Get yours!" In the riot that ensued, three neighborhood shops were ransacked, ten cars were set on fire, and twenty-three people were arrested. The next day as he toured the neighborhood and saw firsthand the wreckage his speech had led to, all he could think was, "This wasn't what I meant. This isn't what I wanted."

As this vignette suggests, you can deliver a persuasive speech that is a powerful catalyst for action. The type of persuasive speech Steve gave, a speech to actuate, moves beyond simply convincing the audience to believe something by urging the audience to take action in some specified way. As a result, when our speech calls for action on the part of audience members, we have an awesome responsibility to ensure that we use reasoning, emotional appeals, and our credibility in ethical ways.

In the previous chapter, you were introduced to the Elaboration Likelihood Model (ELM). This model suggests that when people are involved with your topic, they are more likely to evaluate the arguments you make and the support for those arguments that you provide. So you studied how to use reasoning (logos) to build a speech whose logic can convince an audience. But to get members of an audience to act requires additional speech-making skills.

In this chapter, we focus on motivating your audience to internalize the message through the use of emotional appeals (pathos) and building your credibility (ethos). Then we briefly explain how you can identify and suggest incentives that motivate your audience to act. According to the ELM, emotional appeals and appeals to credibility are also used by uninvolved listeners, so we offer ethical guidelines for using pathos and ethos in speeches to actuate. Finally, we introduce three patterns for organizing the macrostructure of speeches to actuate.

Increasing Audience Involvement Through Emotional Appeals (Pathos)

When we are involved with something, we care about it and have an emotional stake in it. **Emotions** are the buildup of action-specific energy.[1] Aristotle called appeals to emotion "pathos." We can see simple examples of this when we observe how people's facial expressions change as they receive good or bad news. Smiling is one way to release our built-up feelings of happiness. Crying is a way to release our built-up feelings of sadness. When people experience the tension associated with any emotion, they look for a way to release the energy. So as a speaker, if you can involve your audience (give them an emotional

emotions the buildup of action-specific energy

stake) in what you are saying, they are more likely to use their energy to listen carefully and internalize your speech.[2] Let's look at how research from Robin Nabi shows you can increase involvement by stimulating both negative and positive emotions in your speeches.[3]

Evoking Negative Emotions

Negative emotions are disquieting, so when people experience them, they look for ways to eliminate them. During your speech, if you can help your audience experience negative emotions, they will be more involved with what you are saying. As a result, they will be motivated to use their energy to listen carefully to you to see if you give them a way to reduce their feelings of discomfort. There are numerous negative emotions that you can tap; in the following discussion, we describe five of the most common.

negative emotions disquieting feelings that, when people experience them, they look for ways to eliminate them

FEAR

We experience **fear** when we perceive that we have no control over a situation that threatens us. We may fear physical harm or psychological harm. Fear is reduced when the threat is eliminated or when we escape. If as a speaker you can use examples, stories, and statistics that create fear in your audience, they will be more involved in hearing how your proposal can eliminate the source of their fear or allow them to escape. For example, in a speech whose goal was to convince the audience that they were at risk of developing high blood pressure, the speaker might begin by personalizing the statistics on heart disease.

fear the emotion we experience when we perceive that we have no control over a situation that threatens us

> One of every three Americans age eighteen and older has high blood pressure. It is a primary cause of stroke, heart disease, heart failure, kidney disease, and blindness. It triples a person's chance of developing heart disease, boosts the chance of stroke seven times, and the chance of congestive heart failure six times. Look at the person on your right, look at the person on your left. If they don't get it, chances are, you will. Today, I'd like to convince you that you are at risk for developing high blood pressure.

GUILT

We feel **guilt** when we personally violate a moral, ethical, or religious code that we hold dear. Guilt is especially keen in situations where the violation is

guilt the emotion we experience when we personally violate a moral, ethical, or religious code that we hold dear

When people are involved with the message, they listen attentively and process using the central route. Emotional appeals create involvement.

associated with how we believe we should conduct ourselves in relationship to others. We experience guilt as a gnawing sensation that we have done something wrong. When we feel guilty, we are energized or motivated to "make things right" or to atone for our transgression. As a speaker, you can evoke feelings of guilt in your audience so that they pay attention to your arguments. To be effective, your proposal must provide a way for the audience to repair or atone for the damage their transgression has caused or to avoid future violations. For example, in a speech designed to motivate the audience to take their turn as designated drivers, a speaker might evoke guilt like this:

> Have you ever promised your mom that you wouldn't ride in a car driven by someone who had been drinking? And then turned around and got in the car with your buddy even though you both had had a few? You know that wasn't right. Lying to your mother, putting yourself and your buddy at risk . . . (pause) but what can you do? Well, today I'm going to show you how you can avoid all that guilt, live up to your promises to mom, and keep both you and your buddy safe.

SHAME

We feel **shame** when we have violated a moral code and it is revealed to someone we think highly of. The more egregious our behavior or the more we admire the person who has found out, the more shame we experience. When we feel shame, we are motivated to "redeem" ourselves in the eyes of that person. Likewise, we can be convinced to refrain from doing something to avoid feelings of shame. If in your speech you can evoke feelings of shame and then demonstrate how your proposal can either redeem someone after a violation has occurred or prevent feelings of shame, then you can motivate the audience to carefully consider your arguments. For example, in a speech advocating thankfulness, the speaker might use a shame-based approach by quoting the old saying, "I cried because I had no shoes until I met a man who had no feet."

ANGER

When we are faced with an obstacle that stands in the way of something we want, we experience **anger.** We also experience anger when someone demeans us or someone we love. As with all emotions, the intensity of what we feel varies. We can be mildly annoyed, or we can experience a level of anger that short-circuits the reasoning process and leads to blind rage. Speakers who choose to evoke anger in their audience members must be careful that they don't incite so much anger that reasoning processes are short-circuited. You will recall that in the opening vignette, the speaker left the audience so riled up that instead of using their energy to thoughtfully probe their own beliefs, the audience responded to a rabble-rouser's call and rioted.

When we feel anger, we want to strike back at the person or overcome the situation that is thwarting our goals or demeaning us. So in your speeches, if you can rouse your audience's anger and then show how your proposal will enable them to achieve their goals or stop or prevent the demeaning that has occurred, you can motivate them to listen to you and think about what you have said. For example, suppose you want to convince the audience to support a law requiring the active notification of a community when a sex offender is released from prison and living in the neighborhood. You might arouse the audience's anger to get their attention by personalizing the story of Megan Kanka.

> She was your little girl, just seven years old, and the light of your world. She had a smile that could bring you to your knees. And she loved puppies. So when that nice man who had moved in down the street invited her in to see his new puppy, she didn't hesitate. But she didn't get to see the puppy, and you didn't ever see her alive again. He beat her, he raped her, and then he strangled her. He packaged her body in an old toy chest and dumped it in a park. Your seven-year-old princess would

never dig in a toy chest again or slip down the slide in that park. And that hurts. But what makes you really angry is she wasn't his first. But you didn't know that. Because no one bothered to tell you that the guy down the street was likely to kill little girls. The cops knew it. But they couldn't tell you. You, the one who was supposed to keep her safe, didn't know. Angry? You bet. Yeah, he's behind bars again, but you still don't know who's living down the street from you. But you can. There is a law pending before Congress that will require active notification of the community when a known sex offender takes up residence, and today I'm going to tell how you can help to get this passed.[4]

SADNESS

When we fail to achieve a goal or experience a loss or separation, we experience **sadness.** Unlike other negative emotions, whose energy is projected outward, when we feel sad, we tend to withdraw and become isolated. Because sadness, like the other negative emotions, is an unpleasant feeling, we look for ways to end it. This can happen through the actions of others when they notice our withdrawal and try to comfort us. Because we withdraw when we are sad, sadness helps us to focus inward, pondering what has happened and trying to make sense of it. As a result, when we are sad, we are already "looking for answers." So speeches that help us understand and find answers for what has happened can comfort us and help relieve this unpleasant feeling. For example, after 9/11, many Americans were sad. Yes, they were also afraid and angry, but overlaying it all was profound sadness for those who had been lost and what had been lost. The questions "Why? Why did they do this? Why do they hate us so?" capture the national melancholy. So, when politicians suggest that they understand the answers to these questions and can repair the relationships that led to 9/11, Americans listen and think about what they say.

sadness the emotion we experience when we fail to achieve a goal or experience a loss or separation

Evoking Positive Emotions

Just as evoking negative emotions can cause audience members to internalize what you are saying, so too can you increase audience involvement with your proposal by tapping **positive emotions,** which are feelings that people enjoy experiencing. With negative emotions, our goal is to show how our proposal will help the audience to reduce or avoid the feeling. With positive emotions, our goal is to help the audience sustain or develop the feeling. Five of the positive emotions that can motivate the audience to become involved in listening to your arguments are discussed next.

positive emotions feelings that people enjoy experiencing

HAPPINESS AND JOY

Happiness or **joy** is the buildup of positive energy we experience when we accomplish something, when we have a satisfying interaction or relationship, or when we see or possess objects that appeal to us. Think of how you felt when you won that ribbon in grade school or when you found out that you got an "A" on that volcano project in fourth grade. Think of how you felt when you heard that special someone say "I love you" for the very first time. Or think about the birthday when you received that toy you had been dreaming about. In each of these cases, you were happy, maybe even so happy that you were joyous. As a speaker, if you can show how your proposal will lead your audience members to be happy or joyful, then they are likely to listen and to think about your proposal. For example, suppose you want to motivate your audience to attend a couples encounter weekend where they will learn how to "rekindle" their relationship with a partner. If you can remind them about how they felt early in their relationship and then prove how the weekend can reignite those feelings, they will listen.

happiness or joy the emotion we experience when we accomplish something, when we have a satisfying interaction or relationship, or when we see or possess objects that appeal to us

PRIDE

When you experience self-satisfaction and an increase to your self-esteem as the result of something that you have accomplished or that someone you identify with has accomplished, you feel **pride.** "We're number one! We're number one!" is the chant of the crowd feeling pride in the accomplishment of "their" team. Whereas happiness is related to feelings of pleasure, pride is related to feelings of self-worth. So, if in your speech you can demonstrate how your proposal will help your audience members to feel good about themselves, they will be more involved in hearing what you have to say. For example, suppose you want to convince your audience to volunteer to work on the newest Habitat for Humanity house being constructed in your community. You might involve them by alluding to the pride they will feel when they see the house they have helped to build standing where there was once a vacant lot.

RELIEF

When a threatening situation has been alleviated, we feel the positive emotion of **relief.** In relief, the emotional energy that is experienced is directed inward, and we relax and put down our guard. Thus, relief is not usually accompanied by overt action. As a speaker, if you want to use relief as a way to motivate audience members to be involved with your arguments, then you will want to combine it with the negative emotion of fear. For example, suppose your goal is to convince the audience that they are not at risk for high blood pressure. You might use the same personalization of statistics that was described in the example of fear appeals, but instead of proving that the audience is at risk, you could promise relief. Your audience would then listen and evaluate whether they believed your arguments to experience relief from the fear of high blood pressure.

HOPE

The emotional energy that stems from believing something desirable is likely to happen is called **hope.** When you yearn for better things, you are feeling hope. Like relief, hope is a positive emotion that has its roots in a difficult situation. Whereas relief causes you to relax and let down your guard, hope energizes you to take action to overcome the situation. Hope empowers. As with relief, hope appeals are usually accompanied by fear appeals. So you can get audience members to listen to you by showing them how your proposal provides a plan for overcoming a difficult situation. In this problem-solution organization, you can embed both fear and hope appeals. For example, if your proposal is that adopting a low-fat diet will reduce the risk of high blood pressure, you can use the same personalization of statistics that were cited in the example of fear but change the ending to state: "Today, I'm going to convince you to beat the odds by adopting a low-fat diet." This offer of hope should influence your audience to listen to and adopt your plan.

COMPASSION

When we feel selfless concern for the suffering of another person and that concern energizes us to try to relieve that suffering, we feel **compassion.** Speakers can evoke audience members' feelings of compassion by vividly describing the suffering endured by someone. The audience will then be motivated to listen to see how the speaker's proposal plans to end that suffering. For example, when a speaker whose goal is to have you donate to Project Peanut Butter displays a slide of an emaciated child, claims that 13 percent of all Malawi children die of malnutrition, and states that for $10 you can save a child, he or she is appealing to your compassion.

pride the feeling of self-satisfaction and an increase to our self-esteem we experience as the result of something that we have accomplished or that someone we identify with has accomplished

relief the emotion we experience when a threatening situation has been alleviated

hope the emotion we experience when we believe something desirable is likely to happen

compassion the emotion we feel when we have selfless concern for the suffering of another person that energizes us to try to relieve that suffering

You can evoke negative emotions, positive emotions, or both as a way to encourage listeners to internalize your message. In the next section, we offer specific guidelines to do so effectively in your content, language, and delivery.

Guidelines for Appealing to Emotions

As you plan your speech, consider the following guidelines to increase your audience's emotional involvement.

1. Tell vivid stories. Dramatize your arguments by using supporting material such as stories and testimonials that personalize the issue for listeners by appealing to specific emotions. In his speech on bone marrow donation, David Slater simply could have said, "By donating bone marrow—a simple procedure—you can save lives." Instead, he dramatized both the simplicity of the bone marrow donation procedure and the lifesaving impact with a short story designed to heighten audience members' feelings of compassion.

> When Tricia Matthews decided to undergo a simple medical procedure, she had no idea what impact it could have on her life. But more than a year later, when she saw five-year-old Tommy and his younger brother Daniel walk across the stage of the *Oprah Winfrey Show*, she realized that the short amount of time it took her to donate her bone marrow was well worth it. Tricia is not related to the boys who suffered from a rare immune deficiency disorder treated by a transplant of her marrow. Tricia and the boys found each other through the National Marrow Donor Program, or NMDP, a national network which strives to bring willing donors and needy patients together. Though the efforts Tricia made were minimal, few Americans made the strides she did. Few of us would deny anyone the gift of life, but sadly, few know how easily we can help.[5]

Notice how David used a compelling example to appeal to his listeners' emotions and personalize the information for them.

Similarly, Ryan Labor began his speech on shaken baby syndrome with the following vivid story designed to raise feelings of fear, anger, and sadness:

> Last winter, two-year-old Cody Dannar refused to eat or play. He had a headache. Doctors said he just had the flu. After a couple weeks home with his mother, Cody felt better. Days later . . . Cody's headaches returned. Coming home from work the next afternoon, his parents found the babysitter frantically calling 911 and Cody lying rigid and unconscious on the floor. He didn't have the flu; in fact, he wasn't sick at all. The babysitter had caused his headaches. To quiet Cody down, she had shaken him, damaging the base of Cody's brain that now risked his life as he lay on the ground.[6]

2. Use startling statistics. Statistics don't have to be boring; instead, when used strategically, they can evoke strong emotions. To provoke emotions, statistics need to be startling. A statistic may surprise because of its sheer magnitude. For example, in a speech urging the audience to attend a local protest march organized by the Mobilization for Global Justice, Cory used the following statistic to shame and anger his audience about the global problem of wealth distribution: "Did you know that the USA has 25.4 percent of the world's wealth? And of that, the top 10 percent of Americans control 71 percent?" Sometimes, by comparing two statistics, you can increase the emotional impact. For example, during his second main point, Cory used the following comparative statistic to highlight wealth disparity. "In the U.S., not only does the top 10 percent control 71 percent of the wealth, but the bottom 40 percent of Americans control less than 1 percent!" In Ryan's speech on shaken baby syndrome, he strengthened his emotional appeal by following his vivid story with these startling statistics:

> Unfortunately, Cody isn't alone. Over one million infants and young children suffer from shaken baby syndrome annually while thousands die. . . . Only 15 percent

survive without damage. The remaining children suffer from blindness, learning disabilities, deafness, cerebral palsy, or paralysis.

3. Incorporate listener relevance links. You can also appeal to emotions by integrating listener relevance links because emotions are stronger when listeners feel personally involved. At a later point in Ryan's shaken baby syndrome speech, he appealed to emotions through listener relevance. Notice how he brings the problem close to each listener by suggesting the universality of the problem.

> Jacy Showers, director of the first National Conference on shaken baby syndrome, says "shaking occurs in families of all races, incomes, and education levels" and "81 percent of SBS offenders had no previous history of child abuse." The reason? The offenders were so young, either babysitters or new parents.

4. Choose striking presentational aids. Since "a picture is worth a thousand words," consider how you can reinforce your verbal message with dramatic presentational aids. Still pictures and short video clips can at times create an emotional jolt that is difficult to achieve with words. Johnna used several before-and-after pictures of female celebrities Nicole Richie, Calista Flockhart, and Mary Kate Olsen to reinforce her point that emaciated celebrities were contributing to the eating disorder epidemic in teenage girls. Likewise, Anton used a fifteen-second video clip from the DVD "Zoned for Slavery: The Child Behind the Label"[7] to dramatize the problem of child labor in the global textile industry. His goal was to shame his audience members into sending one postcard to the manufacturer of their favorite brand of clothing asking about the working conditions of the workers who manufacture their clothing.

persuasive punch words
words that evoke emotions

5. Use descriptive and provocative language. When developing your speech, include **persuasive punch words**—words that evoke emotion—where you can. Here's how Ryan used persuasive punch words to strengthen his emotional appeal:

> The *worst* of all *epidemics* is a silent one. With the majority of all *victims* either infants or young children, shaken baby syndrome can be classified as a *stealthy plague*. . . . When shaken, the brain is *literally ricocheted* inside the skull, *bruising the brain* and *tearing blood vessels* coming from the neck . . . *cutting off* oxygen and causing the *eyes to bulge*.

6. Use nonverbal elements of delivery to reinforce your emotional appeal. Even the most eloquently phrased emotional appeal will lose its impact unless the nonverbal parts of delivery heighten and highlight the emotional content of the message. Practice using your voice to emphasize what you are saying with the use of pauses, volume, and pitch to heighten and highlight the emotional content of your message. A dramatic pause before a startling statistic can magnify its emotional effect. Similarly, lowering or raising the volume or pitch of your voice at strategic places can create an emotional response. If you experiment as you practice out loud, you will find a combination of vocal elements that can enhance emotional appeal when delivering your speech.

7. Use gestures and facial expressions that highlight the emotions you are conveying. Your message will lose its emotional impact if you deliver it with a deadpan expression or if your demeanor contradicts the emotional content of your message. So, if you want your audience to feel angry, you should model this feeling by looking annoyed or livid or furious. You might clench your fists, furrow your brows, and frown. When you want to foster feelings of joy in your audience, you can smile, nod, and use other nonverbal gestures that are natural for you when you experience joy. Remember, as an ethical speaker, you are appealing to emotions that you yourself feel about the situation, so allow yourself to experience these emotions as you practice. Then when you give your speech, you will be more comfortable displaying your feelings for your audience.

To explore one speaker's use of emotional appeals, use your CengageNOW for *Challenge* to access **Web Resource 14.1: Terrorism and Islam: Maintaining the Faith**. To see a video clip of a student speaker appealing to her audience's emotions, use your CengageNOW to access "Environmental Racism (1)" under the Chapter 14 resources.

Cueing Your Audience Through Credibility (Ethos): Demonstrating Goodwill

Although you may try your best to emotionally involve your audience with what you are advocating, not all audience members will choose the central processing route. Some will choose to pay minimal attention to your arguments and will instead use simple cues to decide whether or not to accept your proposal. The most important cue people use when they process information by the peripheral route is the credibility of the speaker. In Chapter 5, we discussed three characteristics of a speaker (expertise, trustworthiness, and personableness) that audience members pay attention to when evaluating the speaker's credibility. We also described how, as you were speaking, you could demonstrate being expert, trustworthy, and personable. You may want to go back to Chapter 5 and review our suggestions. A fourth characteristic of credibility is especially important in persuasive settings, influencing whether audience members who are processing the speech on the peripheral route believe what the speaker is advocating. This is called goodwill.

It was the Greek philosopher Aristotle (384–322 B.C.E.) who first observed that a speaker's credibility was dependent on the audience's perception of the speaker's goodwill. Today, we define **goodwill** as a perception the audience forms of a speaker who they believe understands them, empathizes with them, and is responsive to them.[8] In other words, goodwill is the audience's take on the speaker's intentions toward them. When audience members believe in the speaker's goodwill, they are willing to believe what the speaker says. Especially in situations where the audience may not have high personal involvement with

goodwill a perception that the audience forms of a speaker who they believe understands them, empathizes with them, and is responsive to them

Throughout the September 11 crisis, then New York City Mayor Rudy Giuliani was seen as credible because of the goodwill he displayed.

the topic, their perceptions of the speaker's goodwill help determine their response to the message.

When you speak, in addition to establishing your expertise, trustworthiness, and personableness, you will want to demonstrate your goodwill toward your audience. Just as with the other dimensions of credibility, it is unethical to fake goodwill. So you should only advocate for proposals that you believe are in the best interest of the audience.

Let's take a closer look at what goodwill entails. The better you know audience members' experiences, circumstances, and desires, the better you will formulate proposals that they will see as in their best interests. A thorough audience analysis will help you. For example, in his speech at the annual conference of the Property Casualty Insurers Association of America (PCI) on November 6, 2006, Julian James, director of Worldwide Markets for Lloyds, demonstrated understanding for the membership by referencing membership facts over the past year.

> I would certainly contend that, following two consecutive record hurricane seasons, we have passed a key financial test. Debate after Katrina was largely about the detail of how we can do things better, and not about whether the industry could survive—as it was after 9/11. Not bad progress for an industry that faced almost double the value of claims from catastrophes in 2005 as it did for 9/11. . . . If we come out of this year intact, U.S. insurance industry profits in 2006 are forecast to be the best in a generation at $55 to 460 billion.[9]

empathy the ability to see the world through the eyes of someone else

Not only must you understand your audience, but speakers who show goodwill also empathize with their audience. **Empathy** is the ability to see the world through the eyes of someone else. When we empathize, we put aside our own ideas and feelings and try to experience something from another's point of view. If you do not understand your audience, you will be unable to empathize with them. But empathizing requires you to go beyond understanding to identify emotionally with your audience members' views.

Empathizing with the views of the audience doesn't mean that you accept their views as your own. It does mean that you acknowledge them as valid. Although your speech may be designed to change audience members' views, the sensitivity you show to audience members' feelings will demonstrate your goodwill. Julian James demonstrates empathy for the reputation of business and industry today:

> So far the industry's finances have rarely looked better. But not everyone is celebrating. With success in business comes greater scrutiny—just ask the oil industry.
>
> In recent weeks we have seen a growing vilification of insurers that is unprecedented and, I believe, wholly unwarranted. Take these recent headlines I came across:
>
> > From *USA Today:* "Insurance rates pummel Florida homeowners."
> >
> > From *Dow Jones Market Watch:* "Sweet are the uses of adversity: Are insurers reeling from disaster or reeling in the profits?" (No prizes for guessing which side the authors came down on in that one.)
> >
> > And from the *Niagara Falls Reporter:* "Insurance companies real villains in Hurricane Katrina's aftermath."
>
> If that is the kind of press the industry is getting in Niagara Falls, in upstate New York, you might wonder how we are being portrayed in the Gulf States.[10]

responsive showing care about the audience by acknowledging feedback from the audience, especially subtle negative cues

Finally, to demonstrate goodwill, you will want to be responsive to the audience. Speakers who are **responsive** show that they care about the audience by acknowledging feedback from the audience, especially subtle negative cues. This feedback may occur during the presentation, but it also may have occurred prior to the speech.

For example, Julian James reminded this audience about their responses to his speech at a previous PCI convention.

> When I spoke to you at this conference, I posed a challenge and asked, "Do you want to take control of the insurance cycle . . . or do you want to stay a passenger?" The reaction was very interesting. One group said, "That's so obvious, why hasn't anyone said that before?" Others said, "Ah, but you're very young, you don't understand, insurance cycles are a fact of life, and you can't do anything about them." . . . Ladies and gentlemen, four years ago, it may have felt like we were standing at the cliff edge, looking into the abyss.
>
> The good news is that, in the intervening period, we have made important progress. . . . But we put our future in grave danger if we stop here. . . . The challenges we face today may be different, but the message from 2002 remains the same: "Our thinking and behaviour must change if the insurance industry is to be a stable, secure industry for our policy holders and shareholders of the future." Let's not mess it up again.[11]

By establishing goodwill, you enhance your credibility with the audience. This is especially important for persuading those who are not personally involved with your proposal.

Guidelines for Demonstrating Credibility During Your Speech

Consider the following strategies for increasing your listeners' perception of your ethos so that your **terminal credibility,** their perception of your expertise at the end of your speech, is greater than your **initial credibility,** their perception of your expertise at the beginning of your speech.

1. Explain your competence. Unless someone has formally introduced you and your qualifications to your audience, your initial credibility will be low, and as you speak, you will need to tell your audience about your expertise. Sending these types of messages during the speech results in your achieving a level of **derived credibility** with your audience. You can interweave comments about your expertise into introductory comments and at appropriate places within the body of the speech.[12] If you've done a good deal of research on the topic, say so. If you have personal experience, say so. It's important for the audience to know why they can trust what you are saying.

2. Establish common ground. Identify with the audience by talking about shared beliefs and values related to your speech topic.[13] If the topic is controversial or your target audience is opposed to your position, establishing common ground by showing empathy for your audience's position before trying to convince them to change. In so doing, you will increase your derived credibility since the audience will feel respected and understood.

3. Use evidence from respected sources. If you are not a recognized expert on your subject, you can increase your derived credibility by using supporting material from well-recognized, unbiased, and respected sources who are experts. So, if you have a choice between using a statistic from a known partisan organization or from a dispassionate professional association, choose the professional association. Likewise, if you can quote a local expert who is well known and respected by your audience or an international scholar with limited name recognition with your audience, use the local expert's opinion.

4. Use nonverbal elements of delivery to enhance your image. Your audience establishes its assessment of your initial credibility not only from what it has heard about you before you begin speaking but also from what it has observed about you by looking at you prior to your speech. So how you look and what you do in the few minutes before you speak are important.

terminal credibility perception of credibility listeners have at the end of the speech

initial credibility perception of credibility created before you begin to speak

derived credibility messages you send about your expertise during the speech

SPEECH SNIPPET

Establishing Common Ground

In his speech arguing against the death penalty, Lester used the common ground technique in his introduction when he said: "I'm sure that you, like me, value human life."

Although professional attire enhances credibility in any speaking situation, it is particularly important for persuasive speeches. Research shows that attractive people are perceived as more competent, well organized, and confident.[14] Attire contributes to this, and persuasive speakers dressed more formally are perceived as more credible than those dressed casually or sloppily.[15] So your audience will assess your physical appearance in developing its initial judgment about your credibility. That's why it is important to "dress the part."

The audience will also notice how confident you appear as you prepare to address them. From the moment you rise to speak, you will want to convey through your nonverbal behavior that you are competent. Plant your feet firmly, glance at your notes, then make eye contact or audience contact with one person or group before taking a breath and beginning to speak. These simple behaviors create a perception of competence and confidence.

Likewise, pause and establish eye contact upon finishing the speech. Just as pausing and establishing eye contact or audience contact before the speech enhance credibility, doing so upon delivering the closing lines of the speech has the same result.

5. Use vocal expression to enhance your credibility. Research shows that credibility is strongly influenced by how you sound. Speaking fluently, using a moderately fast rate, and expressing yourself with conviction makes you appear more intelligent and competent.[16] So you will want to practice until you can smoothly and confidently deliver your speech avoiding vocal interrupters like "ums," "uhs," "you knows," and "likes," all of which make you appear unsure of what you are saying and detract from your derived credibility.

SPOTLIGHT ON SPEAKERS

Bono *Credibility and the Rock Star*

Eric Feferberg/Getty Images

Does fame derived from being a rock star give someone credibility to speak on Third World debt, AIDS, or free trade? Well, there is certainly no question that Bono, the lead singer for the band U2, arguably one of the most celebrated rock bands of our time, has used his fame to gain an audience for his views on these and other issues.

In fact, most of his time these days is spent not so much performing on stage with his *rock* group but speaking on behalf of his *humanitarian* group, DATA.org (Debt, AIDS, Trade, Africa). DATA.org raises awareness— and dollars—to fight hunger and disease and to advocate for changes to fair trade policies and for Third World debt relief. It's almost commonplace to see a news clip of Bono speaking about his relief efforts, such as those he undertook in Malawi: "I've seen the eyes of the people dying three to a bed—it's children they leave behind . . . eighteen million AIDS orphans by the end of the decade in Africa alone."*

While Bono's fame certainly gives him visibility, his credibility to speak on these issues derives not simply from his fame that gives him "personableness," but more important, it stems from his trustworthiness. In the lyrics that Bono writes, we see reflected the same deeply held beliefs he advocates through his nonprofit organization: "And today the millions cry / We eat and drink while tomorrow they die / The real battle just begun."** We see a consistency between what he sings and what he says.

Finally, Bono's advocacy is powerful because in it he demonstrates goodwill. He chooses to use his voice and the power of his fame not to further his own ambitions but rather to help those who are voiceless and powerless. So in Bono, we see how fame coupled with credibility can be a powerful tool for effecting change.

*Bono, "Make AIDS a Crucial Topic at Both Conventions" [Op-Ed], *Boston Globe,* July 25, 2004.

**U2, "Sunday. Bloody Sunday," 1982.

Motivating Your Audience to Act: The Speech to Actuate

In speeches in which your specific goal is to convince, you affect your audience members' attitudes by using emotional appeals to involve the audience so that it listens to, evaluates, and internalizes your well-reasoned arguments. Just because your audience intellectually agrees with your arguments, however, doesn't mean that they will choose to act on what you have said. Appeals to emotion can prompt audience members to be involved with your topic and to think carefully about your arguments. Demonstrating your credibility can cue audience members when they are uninvolved. But when your goal is to motivate audience members to take action, you will have to provide them with incentives to act that outweigh the costs. That is, you will have to demonstrate how, by behaving as you advocate, they can increase the likelihood that they will fulfill their unmet needs. For example, if you want your audience to vote for candidate A, you will have to show how the election of candidate A will meet needs the audience feels will leave them better off than if they didn't vote or voted for another candidate.

In this section, we turn our attention to a particular type of persuasive speech, the speech to actuate, which moves beyond affecting audience beliefs and attitudes and motivates the audience to act. In the **speech to actuate,** you not only present convincing arguments for your audience to consider but go beyond this, motivating the audience by explaining how taking the action you recommend offers incentives that will satisfy their unmet needs. We begin by discussing how incentives work in helping people meet their needs. Then we use this framework to explain how you can identify and articulate incentives for your audience. Finally, we describe three organizational patterns especially suited to speeches to actuate.

> **speech to actuate** a speech that moves beyond affecting audience beliefs and attitudes and motivates the audience to act

Understanding How Incentives Motivate Behavior

An **incentive** is a reward that is promised if a particular action is taken or goal is reached.[17] Incentives encourage us to act. Incentives can be physical rewards such as food, shelter, money, and sex. They can be psychological rewards such as positive self-concept and peace of mind. They can be social rewards such as acceptance, status, and popularity. Regardless of the type of incentive offered, if a person values it, that person will be motivated to take goal-related actions. Suppose you hear a speech whose goal is to motivate you to recycle aluminum cans. The speaker uses the incentive that you can earn a penny a can by taking aluminum cans to the local recycling center. Would hearing that you could earn a penny per can be an incentive for you to recycle? It depends. If you were destitute and hungry, you might go home, disassemble the soda pop can pyramid you and your roommate have built in the living room, take the cans to the recycling center, and head to the local market to get some food. In this case, the money offered for recycling was an effective incentive that motivated your action. Suppose, however, that you're not destitute. Even if you have lots of easy access to cans, a penny a can may not be enough to propel you into acting. However, pointing out that you can contribute to saving the environment by recycling might be an effective incentive to you.

> **incentive** a reward that is promised if a particular action is taken or goal is reached

As we evaluate the incentives that are meant to motivate us to act, we usually balance them against the costs we think we will incur. **Costs** are expenditures that we incur when we act. Like incentives, costs can be physical (time, money, energy), psychological (uncertainty, confusion), or social (ostracism, humiliation). Costs are deterrents to action.

> **costs** expenditures that we incur when we act; may be physical, psychological, or social

When Bill Gates talks about using Microsoft products, he is likely to give the audience incentives to motivate their behavior.

AFP/Getty Images

Obviously, then, people are more likely to be motivated to act by incentives if they perceive that the incentives outweigh the costs. The greater the costs associated with an action, the less likely we are to act, even if we value the incentive. According to Thibaut and Kelley, who wrote about social exchanges, each of us seeks exchange situations with a favorable cost–reward ratio (where rewards outweigh costs).[18] So we will continue our present behavior unless we are shown that by changing our behavior we can either lower our costs or raise our rewards. Let's look at an example. Suppose you are asking your audience to use some of their free time to volunteer an hour a week to help adults learn to read. The time you are asking them to give would be perceived as a cost because they would have to give up time that they usually spend relaxing. So, if you are going to motivate your audience to actually do this, you will have to describe to them the rewards that they will experience if they volunteer. For these to be incentives, the promised rewards must be perceived to outweigh the cost of giving up free time.

As a speaker, then, you must show your audience that the time, energy, or money investment for behaving as you suggest is small when compared to the rewards to be gained from acting.

Using Incentives to Meet Needs

Why was the penny a can an incentive to the hungry person and not an incentive to the sated person? Because we make our cost–reward decisions based on our needs. Incentives are likelier to motivate people when they satisfy a strong but unmet need. Various ways of categorizing needs have been developed to help us understand types of needs. One of the most widely recognized is Maslow's hierarchy of needs.

Abraham Maslow divided people's needs into five categories, illustrated in Exhibit 14.1: (1) physiological needs, including food, drink, and life-sustaining temperature; (2) safety and security needs, including long-term survival and stability; (3) belongingness and love needs, including the need to identify with friends, loved ones, and family; (4) esteem needs, ego gratification, including the quest for material goods, recognition, and power or influence; and (5) self-actualization needs, including the need to develop one's self to realize one's full potential and engage in creative acts.[19] Maslow believed that these needs

EXHIBIT 14.1 **Maslow's hierarchy of needs**

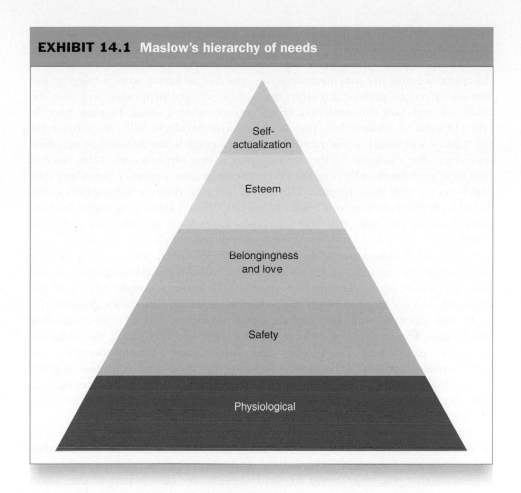

were hierarchical; that is, your "lower-order" needs had to be met before you would be motivated by "higher-order" needs. The hierarchical nature of needs is still debated because there is evidence that at times some people will sacrifice lower-order needs to satisfy higher-order ones. Nevertheless, as a speaker, if you can tie the incentives that accompany your proposal with unmet audience needs, you will increase the likelihood that the audience will take the action you are proposing.

Let's see how this could work in the volunteering for literacy speech with a college student audience. Suppose that during the speech you point out that people who volunteer thirty hours or more a year receive a recognition certificate and are invited to attend a private dinner with the stars of the hot band that will be headlining the big spring campus concert. After announcing this, you add, "I know that while most of you care about literacy, you're thinking about what else you could do with that hour. But the really cool part of spending your time as a literacy volunteer is that not only will you feel good about yourself because you have improved someone's life, but you also will be able to list this service and recognition on your résumé. And as a bonus, you'll get to brag to your friends about having dinner with several celebrities." In the first part of this short statement, you have enumerated three incentives that are tied to volunteering: a physical incentive (an award certificate), a psychological incentive of enhanced self-concept (I feel good about myself because I have helped someone else), and a social incentive (having dinner with an elite group and meeting celebrities). In the second part, you have also tied each incentive to a need that it can satisfy. With an enhanced résumé, people are likelier to get jobs that provide money for food and shelter. If by helping someone else we feel better about ourselves, then we have met a self-actualization need. And by attending the private dinner, we might satisfy both esteem needs and belongingness needs.

As you prepare your speech, you not only want to understand the needs of the audience and the incentives that are attached to acting as you suggest, but you also need to understand what the action you are proposing will cost the audience and how this cost may result in increasing a need. In your speech, you will want to address how the incentives you highlight will compensate for the cost or will result in the need that is threatened being fulfilled in an alternative way. For example, in the literacy speech, one obvious cost is the hour of free time each week, which might take away from time audience members currently spend with their friends. This could threaten their belongingness need. To address this concern, you might point out, "Now I know you might be concerned about the time this will take away from your friends, but rest your mind. Not only will your friends understand and admire you (esteem need substitute for belongingness), but at the Literacy Center, you're going to have time before the tutoring starts to meet other volunteers (belongingness) and they are some really cool people (esteem). I know a couple who just got engaged, and they met through their volunteering (big-time belongingness)."

If you discover that you cannot relate your material to basic audience needs, then you probably should reconsider what you are asking the audience to do. For example, if you discover that most of your audience members are overcommitted and have no time to take on an additional volunteer activity, then it is unrealistic to ask them to volunteer an hour a week. But you may be able to persuade them to donate a book or money to buy a book for the literacy library.

Finally, if your incentives are to motivate your audience, the audience must be convinced that there is a high likelihood that if they act as you suggest, they will receive the rewards. It is important, therefore, that you discuss only those incentives that you have strong reason to believe are closely tied to the action you are requesting and are received by almost all people who act in the recommended way. Although there is an annual award given to the literacy volunteer who has donated the most time that year, mentioning this in your speech is unlikely to motivate the audience because only one person receives it, and the cost is very high.

So, when you want to move an audience to action, you need to understand their needs and explain the rewards they can receive by taking the action you suggest. You also need to make sure that the incentives you mention fulfill unmet audience needs.

Organizational Patterns for Speeches to Actuate

Implicit in a speech to actuate is the assumption that there is a problem that audience members can help solve by taking certain actions. As a result, most speeches to actuate follow one of three organizational patterns: problem-solution, problem-cause-solution, and the motivated sequence pattern.

The Problem-Solution Pattern

problem-solution pattern a persuasive organizational pattern that reveals details about a problem and poses solutions to it

A **problem-solution pattern** explains the nature of a problem and proposes a solution. A problem-solution pattern can be used with any persuasive speech, but it is particularly useful when listeners may be unaware of the problem or how they personally can work toward a solution. A speech to actuate organized with this pattern usually has three main points. The first examines the problem, the second presents the solution(s), and the third suggests what action the listener can take.

To convince the audience that there is a problem, you will need to explore the breadth and depth of the issue, as well as provide listener relevance links. You provide breadth by showing the scope or scale of the problem, for example, the number of people it affects and proving upward trends over time, including forecasted trends if the problem is not solved. You might provide depth by showing the gravity of the problem. Both breadth and depth may be described through stories and startling statistics.

When you describe the solution, you should be detailed enough for the audience to understand how and why it will solve the problem. The call to action should provide your audience with specific steps that they can take to help implement the solution(s).

A problem-solution organization for a speech on reducing gun violence might look like this:

I. Gun-related violence is a serious problem that affects us all. *(statement of the problem)*

    A. Gun-related violence occurs in urban, suburban, and rural communities and across the country. *(breadth)*

        1. Most recent law enforcement statistics on gun-related violence in the U.S.A.

        2. Most recent law enforcement statistics on gun violence in Arizona.

        3. An example of gun violence in Tempe. *(listener relevance link)*

    B. The consequences of gun violence include injury, disability, and death. *(depth)*

        1. Statistics on gun-related injuries.

        2. Story of gun-related disability in people like the audience members.

        3. Statistics on gun-related deaths.

        4. Story of local family who died in gun-related murder-suicide.

II. Our state legislatures and the U.S. Congress should pass measures to reduce gun violence.

    A. Tighten gun ownership requirements.

        1. Require background checks at all sales points.

            a. Both public and private sales.

            b. Checks for both criminal background and evidence of mental illness.

        2. Require "proof of competence" testing for gun licensure like vehicle licensure.

            a. Evidence of gun safety procedure knowledge.

            b. Evidence of marksmanship.

        3. Require periodic relicensing of both guns and owners.

    B. Increase criminal penalties associated with violation of gun laws.

III. You should e-mail, write, or call your state and national representatives to urge them to support measures to reduce gun violence.

    A. Bills currently pending in the state legislature.

    B. Bills currently pending in Congress.

The Problem-Cause-Solution Pattern

problem-cause-solution pattern a form of persuasive organization that examines a problem, its cause(s), and solutions designed to eliminate or alleviate the underlying cause(s)

The **problem-cause-solution pattern** is similar to the problem-solution pattern but differs from it by adding a main point that discusses the causes of the problem and then proposes a solution designed to alleviate those causes. This pattern is particularly useful for addressing seemingly intractable problems that have been dealt with unsuccessfully in the past as a result of treating symptoms rather than underlying causes. In speeches to actuate, the problem-cause-solution main points are followed by a fourth main point that calls the audience to a specific action.

Margaret, who lived near a landfill and was concerned about waste overflow, wanted to convince her audience that they should recycle their garbage. As she researched the problem of overflowing landfills, she noticed that recycling was catching on nationally and that, according to 2005 statistics, 32 percent of solid waste was recycled compared to 54 percent, which went into landfills, and 13 percent, which was burned.[20] She also read articles about communities whose recycling rates were higher than average and concluded that the key to increasing recycling was to make it easy and convenient. So she developed a problem-cause-solution speech to actuate that looked like this:

I. Solid waste disposal is a problem.
   A. Landfills are overflowing.
   B. Recycling, while growing, is not widespread in our community.

II. Causes for recycling resistance.
   A. Confusion about proper recycling procedures.
   B. Lack of recycling containers.
   C. Infrequent recycling pickups.

III. Solutions to overcome recycling resistance.
   A. Promotional mailers and periodic reminders mailed to each residence to clarify and reinforce local recycling procedures and to communicate changes in local recycling programs.
   B. Grade-appropriate educational material used in local classrooms.
   C. Free recycling containers delivered to each residential address with additional containers available at convenient locations.
   D. Increased frequency of pickups planned for and implemented as recycling becomes more pervasive.

IV. Audience actions.
   A. Call your local waste management agency and inquire about recycling policies and procedures.
   B. Procure appropriate recycling containers for use in your home.
      1. Curbside containers.
      2. Containers for in-home use.
   C. Educate all family members on proper recycling techniques.
   D. Contact local school board members and urge recycling curriculum for your local school district.

The Motivated Sequence Pattern

motivated sequence a form of persuasive organization that combines a problem-solution pattern with explicit appeals designed to motivate the audience

The **motivated sequence** is an organization pattern that combines a problem-solution pattern with explicit appeals designed to motivate the audience. Allan Monroe articulated the motivated sequence as a distinct speech pattern in the 1930s. In the motivated sequence, the normal introduction, body, and conclusion are unified into a five-step sequence described as follows:

1. The attention step. The attention step replaces the traditional introduction. Like an introduction, it should begin with a statement that can generate attention. Startling statements, rhetorical questions, quotations, or short narratives will all serve this purpose. Then you should pique the audience's curiosity by talking about the value of what you are going to say. During the attention step, you might also refer to the knowledge and experiences you have that build your credibility. Finally, just as in a traditional introduction, you will want to state your purpose and preview the rest of the speech.

2. The need step. The need step should explore the nature of the problem that gives rise to the need for change. In it, you will point out the conditions that are unsatisfactory using statistics, examples, and expert opinion to bolster your argument. Then you will describe the implications or ramifications of this problem. What is happening because the condition is allowed to continue? Finally, you will allude to how the audience might be instrumental in changing the situation.

3. The satisfaction step. Having developed a rational argument that there is a need for change, in the satisfaction step you explain your solution to the problem. In this step, you will show, point by point, how what you are proposing will satisfy each of the needs that you articulated in the previous step. If there are other places where your proposal has been tried successfully, you will want to mention these. In addition, you will want to present and refute any objections to the proposal that you can anticipate.

4. The visualization step. In the visualization step, you will ask your audience to imagine what will happen if your proposal is implemented and is successful. Alternatively, you can ask the audience to visualize how things will be if your proposal is not adopted, or you can do both and have the audience experience the comparison. Obviously, the more descriptive and graphic your visualization step, the more likely it is to have an impact on the audience.

5. The action appeal step. In this final step, you might quickly review your main ideas, but then you will emphasize the specific belief or action that you are directing your audience toward. You will also state or restate your own commitment and action that you have taken. You also offer a direct call to action indicating what your listeners are to do and how. Finally, you will want to conclude with a quote, story, or other element that is emotionally compelling.

Let's look at a short outline of what a speech asking the audience to support a school tax levy would look like if it were organized using the motivated sequence.

Proposition: I want the audience to vote in favor of the school tax levy that is on the ballot in November.

   I. Attention step

     A. Comparisons of worldwide test scores in math and science show the United States continues to lose ground.

     B. I've made an extensive study of this problem, and today I'm going to tell you how you can help stop this decline.

     C. I'll start by describing the problem; then I will tell you what you should do and why it will help.

  II. **Need step:** The local schools are underfunded.

     A. The current funding is insufficient and has resulted in program cuts.

     B. Qualified teachers leave because of stagnant wages.

     C. A threatened state takeover of local schools would lead to more bureaucracy and less learning.

III. **Satisfaction step:** The proposed local tax levy is large enough to solve these problems.

   A. Programs will be restored.

   B. Qualified teachers will be compensated so they will stay.

   C. We will retain local control.

   D. You'll once again have pride in your community.

IV. **Visualization step:** Imagine the best and imagine the worst.

   A. What it will be like if we pass the levy. How will you feel?

   B. What it will be like if we don't. How will you feel?

V. **Action appeal step:** Vote "yes" for the levy in November.

   A. If you want to see schools improve and the United States catch up to the rest of the world, vote for the levy.

   B. Come join me. I'm registered, I'm ready, I'm voting for the levy.

   C. It costs to be the best in the world. Where there is pain, there is gain.

   D. They say it takes a village, so you can make a difference.

All persuasive speeches, regardless of organizational pattern, use emotional appeals, include demonstrations of speaker credibility, and can be used to change attitudes and behavior. But as you can see from the description and the sample outline, in the motivated sequence the use of emotion, credibility, and incentives is built into the structure of the speech. To see a video clip of a student speaker motivating her audience to act, use your CengageNOW for *Challenge* to access "Environmental Racism (2)" under the Chapter 14 resources.

Guidelines for Developing an Ethical Persuasive Speech

We hope that in this chapter we have motivated you to consider the various ways of motivating your audience to believe and to act. Unfortunately, some speakers get so involved in the process of motivation that they fail to remember that the use of all these forms must still meet ethical standards. In Chapter 1, we discussed the fundamental ethical behaviors of truthfulness and crediting the ideas that are used in a speech. At this point, we want to look at six additional ethical guidelines that speakers should follow when their specific goal is to convince the audience to believe a certain way or to move the audience to action.

1. Ethical persuasive speeches aim to improve the well-being of the audience by advocating the honest belief of the speaker. If you have reason to believe that the members of the audience will be hurt or disadvantaged if they believe what you say or do what you ask, then you should not give the speech. At times, we can get excited about seeing what we can do as a devil's advocate—that is, argue for a belief or action that is totally counter to anything we really believe just to stir up discussion. Although this can be fun when we're dealing with a few friends who just enjoy the spirit of debate, in the real world it is unethical for you to give a speech that calls for the audience to believe something that you do not believe. So, for your persuasive speech, phrase a proposition that you enthusiastically endorse.

2. Ethical persuasive speeches provide choice. In any speech, you are free to provide the audience with reasoning that supports your position in a way that encourages them to think about and evaluate what you have said before making up their own mind. Although it is possible to persuade an audience by manipulating their emotions, using smear tactics to attack opposite points of view (or advocates of those points of view) or coercing them with serious threats is unethical.

3. Ethical persuasive speeches use supporting information that is representative. In your persuasive speech, you will use evidence in the form of statistics, expert opinion, and examples to support your claims. You can probably find an item of "evidence" to support any claim, but ethical speakers make sure that the evidence they cite is representative of all the evidence that might be used. Although you may use an individual item to show that something is possible, or can happen, you do not want to give the impression that the item is commonplace. In short, it is unethical to misrepresent what a *body* of evidence (as opposed to a single item) would show if all of it were presented to the audience.

4. Ethical persuasive speeches use emotional appeals to engage the audience in the rational thought process. Emotional appeals are a legitimate part of a persuasive speech when they are used to increase the involvement of the audience so that audience members choose the central processing route to listen to, think about, evaluate, and personally decide whether to believe or act. When excessive emotional appeals are used as the basis of persuasion instead of logical reasons, then although the speech might be effective, it is unethical.

5. Ethical persuasive speeches honestly present the incentives and costs associated with an advocated action. Because the goal of ethical speaking is to equip the audience with the information that it needs to make a rational choice, ethical speakers are careful to present honestly all the known costs and incentives associated with a recommended action. It is unethical to downplay costs or overstate incentives.

6. Ethical persuasive speeches honestly present the speaker's credibility. Because some audience members will process what you say along a peripheral route, using your credibility as the primary factor that determines what they will believe or how they will act, as an ethical speaker you will want to present your expertise and trustworthiness honestly. It is unethical to act as if you know a great deal about a subject when you do not. In fact, most people believe it is unethical to try to convince others of something on which you are not

Ethical persuasion requires that the audience have free choice to accept or reject the ideas of the speaker without fear of retribution. Under totalitarian political systems, coercion rather than persuasion is the norm.

© AFP/Getty Images

Alexandro, a student who had worked full time for three years before returning to college for his sophomore year, decided that for his final speech he would motivate the members of his class to donate money to the Downtown Food Bank. He was excited about this topic because he had begun volunteering for the Food Bank during those last three years and had seen firsthand the face of hunger in this community.

He planned to support his speech with three reasons: (1) an increasing number of people in the community needed food; (2) government agencies were unable to provide sufficient help; and (3) a high percentage of every dollar donated to the Food Bank was spent on food. As he researched these points, he discovered that the number of families who were in need in the community had not really risen in the past two years and that government sponsorship of the Food Bank had increased. Then, when he examined the Food Bank's financial statements, he discovered that only 68 percent of every

dollar donated was actually spent on food. Faced with this evidence, he just didn't think his reasons and evidence were very strong.

Yet, because of his experience, he still thought the Food Bank was a cause that deserved financial support, so he decided to focus his entire speech on the heart-warming case of the Hernandez family. Ineligible for government assistance, over the years this family of ten had managed to survive because of the aid they received from the Food Bank. Today, several of the children had graduated from college, and one was a physician working in the barrio. By telling this heart-wrenching story of the struggle to survive, Alexandro thought he would be successful in persuading the class.

1. Would it be ethical for Alexandro to give his speech in this way? Why or why not?
2. If not, what would he need to do to make the speech ethical?

extremely well informed because you may inadvertently misrepresent the arguments and information. Finally, ethical speakers disclose interests that may have inadvertently biased their arguments and may place their interests and those of their audience at odds. You might say, for example, "I think you should know that I work for the Literacy Project as a paid intern, so even though I will do my best to give you the most accurate information possible on this subject, I may not be totally objective in my comments."

As you work on your speech, you will want to continually remind yourself of your ethical responsibilities. It's easy to get caught up in trying to build arguments and lose sight of your bigger ethical responsibility to your audience.

SPEECH ASSIGNMENT

Speech to Actuate

1. Prepare a four- to seven-minute persuasive speech in which your goal is to persuade the audience to act. To help you prepare your speech and your outline, use your CengageNOW for *Challenge* to access Speech Builder Express and complete the Speech Planning Action Step Activities.
2. As an addendum to the outline, write a persuasive speech adaptation plan in which you describe:
   a. The reasoning process for your arguments.
   b. How you will use emotional appeals to involve your audience so that they process what you are saying on the central route. List the emotions you plan to appeal to and explain why you chose these.
   c. How you will establish your credibility by demonstrating your expertise, trustworthiness, personableness, and goodwill.
   d. The incentives for action and the needs that they will satisfy.
   e. The persuasive organizational pattern that you will use and why you chose it.

Speech to Actuate Evaluation Checklist

Primary Criteria

_____ 1. Did the speaker use statistics, expert opinion, and examples that had emotional impacts on the audience?

_____ 2. Did the speaker appeal to negative emotions? If so, check all that were tapped: ___ fear ___ guilt ___ anger ___ shame ___ sadness

_____ Were the appeals very effective, somewhat effective, or ineffective?

_____ 3. Did the speaker appeal to positive emotions? If so, check all that were tapped: ___ happiness/joy ___ pride ___ relief ___ hope ___ compassion

_____ Were the appeals very effective, somewhat effective, or ineffective?

_____ 4. Did the speaker establish credibility?

_____ Did the speaker establish expertise?

_____ Did the speaker demonstrate trustworthiness?

_____ Did the speaker demonstrate personableness?

_____ Did the speaker demonstrate goodwill?

_____ 5. Did the speaker identify the incentives for taking action?

_____ Did the speaker show that incentives outweighed costs?

_____ Did the speaker show how incentives would satisfy unmet audience needs?

_____ 6. If the speaker used a problem-solution or problem-cause-solution pattern, was each element clear and thoroughly developed?

_____ 7. If the speaker used the motivated sequence, was each of the steps clearly evident?

_____ 8. Did the speaker offer a compelling call to action?

General Criteria

_____ 1. Was the specific goal clear?

_____ 2. Was the introduction effective in creating interest, involving the audience in the speech, and previewing the main points?

_____ 3. Was the speech organized using an appropriate persuasive pattern?

_____ 4. Was the language clear, vivid, and appropriate?

_____ 5. Was the conclusion effective in summarizing what had been said and mobilizing the audience to act?

_____ 6. Was the use of voice intelligible, vocally expressive, conversational, and convincing?

_____ 7. Did the use of body convey ethos (credibility) and pathos (emotional appeal)?

Based on these criteria, evaluate the speech as (check one):

_____ excellent _____ good _____ average _____ fair _____ poor

You can use your CengageNOW for Challenge to access this checklist online under the Chapter 14 resources.

Sample Speech to Actuate

Sexual Assault Policy a Must

by Maria Lucia R. Anton[21]

This sample speech was developed and presented by college student Maria Lucia R. Anton at the 1994 Interstate Oratorical Association competition. It is now published in an anthology of the winning speeches by college students that year. The speech is a good example of a speech to actuate using the motivated sequence. An adaptation plan was not required, so the one provided here has been created as an example for you to use as you create your own persuasive speech.

You can use your CengageNOW for *Challenge* to identify some of the strengths of Maria Lucia's speech by preparing an evaluation checklist and an analysis. You can then compare your answers to those of the authors. To watch and evaluate another student persuasive speech, use your CengageNOW to access Raimone's speech, "Become an Entrepreneur," under the Chapter 14 resources.

Adaptation Plan

1. **Audience analysis:** My audience is composed of traditional-age college students with varying majors and classes. Most are European Americans from working- or middle-class backgrounds.
2. **Background knowledge:** My perception is that my audience knows about sexual assaults on college campuses but not about the nuances of it.
3. **Creating and maintaining interest:** I will involve my audience by appealing to several emotions, including guilt, sadness, relief, hope, and most of all, compassion. I will use representative examples as short stories.
4. **Organization:** I have organized my speech using the motivated sequence.
5. **Building credibility:** I will build credibility by pausing and looking listeners in the eye before beginning. Throughout the speech, I will cite strong sources. I will dress professionally and sound emotionally convincing about the topic. I will provide terminal credibility by pausing and looking listeners in the eye for a moment after appealing to them with my call to action.
6. **Motivation:** The incentive I will offer is that the audience members can act to create a sexual assault policy on their campuses. Doing so will appeal to hope and safety.

Outline

General purpose: To persuade

Speech goal: I want my audience to petition the administration on their campus to formulate and implement a sexual assault prevention policy.

Attention

   I. "If you want to take her blouse off, you have to ask. If you want to touch her breast, you have to ask. If you want to move your hand down to her genitals, you have to ask. If you want to put your finger inside her, you have to ask." *(quotation from Antioch College's sexual offense policy)*

     A. The policy consists of three major points.

       1. If you have an STD, you must disclose it to a potential partner.

       2. It is not acceptable to knowingly take advantage of someone who is under the influence of alcohol or drugs.

       3. Obtaining consent is an ongoing process in any sexual interaction.

     B. The policy is designed to create a "safe" campus environment.

Need

  II. Sexual assault on college campuses is a problem across the nation.

     A. Carlton College in Northfield, Minnesota, was sued for $800,000 in damages by four university women. (*Time* magazine article)

B. Although college administration know of enrolled rapists, they need not say or do anything.

C. One in every four college women has been an assault victim. (*Ms. Magazine* survey)

D. Between 30 and 40 percent of male students reported they might force someone to have sex if they knew they would escape punishment. (*Ms. Magazine* survey)

E. The effects of sexual assault on victims are disturbing.

Transition: Many campuses are open invitations for sexual assault. The absence of a policy is a grand invitation.

Satisfaction

III. We need to push for sexual assault policies on our campuses.

A. Antioch policy example.

B. Fundamental points to any sexual assault policy.

1. Input from students, faculty, staff, and administration is crucial when developing the policy.

2. The policy must be publicized in many venues, including the student handbook, newspaper, and radio station.

3. Educational programs must be developed to educate the campus community about the sexual assault policy.

4. Campuses should outline a step-by-step procedure for reporting and addressing sexual assault perpetrators.

Transition: It is pertinent that universities provide support to victims through such policies and procedures if college campuses are to be a safe environment for all students.

Visualization

IV. All students should feel safe leaving the classroom at night.

A. The wheels of justice turn too slowly when sending victims to the local police.

B. Without a policy, there are no specific penalties to prosecute offenders.

C. With a policy, would-be offenders will think twice.

D. With a policy, there is at least a chance that justice will be served.

Action

V. We students must voice our concerns.

A. We must form petitions to demand that our universities create sexual assault policies.

B. We must not stop until we've succeeded and our campuses have sexual assault policies.

Speech and Analysis

Read the following speech aloud. Then analyze it on the basis of the primary criteria in the Speech to Actuate Evaluation Checklist on page 309.

As you examine the speech, consider the fact that it was created and delivered more than a decade ago. Does your campus have a sexual assault policy? If so, is it similar to the one Maria Lucia advocates? To what degree do you think the problem has or has not been solved today? Why? Interestingly, according to a 2005 report conducted by the U.S. Department of Justice, most colleges and universities today do not have a sexual assault response policy or could not provide it for the study. The larger four-year institutions and historically black colleges and universities in the United States tend to have policies, but they vary in clarity and thoroughness.[22]

Speech

"If you want to take her blouse off, you have to ask. If you want to touch her breast, you have to ask. If you want to move your hand down to her genitals, you have to ask. If you want to put your finger inside her, you have to ask."

Analysis
Attention catcher

This opening attracts our attention by personalizing the Antioch sexual offense prevention policy. Notice how

the emotional impact of the policy
changes as the acts described become
more intimate.

Maria Lucia draws on language specific to the Antioch policy, referring to
the "respondent" and the "primary
witness." This language could be confusing to the audience. It would have
been clearer to use the terms "aggres-
sor" and "victim."

She could have helped the audience to
better understand the purpose of the
speech if she had previewed what was
to come. As it is, the transition to the
next step in the motivated sequence is
very abrupt which makes it difficult to
see where she is headed.

Need

Maria Lucia's first subpoint in sup-
port of the need for campus sexual
offense prevention policies is an excel-
lent case example with first person
narratives that dramatize the problem
and pack a powerful emotional
punch.

Here the startling fact that adminis-
tration knew the man was a rapist
serves to heighten emotional appeal.

As the second subpoint supporting the
need for these policies on campus, the
speaker cites several startling statistics.
While the percentage of college women
who were victims of an attack is sur-
prising, and the fact that about three-
quarters of them knew their attacker is
shocking, it is the final statistic that
stuns.

These statistics from a sample of cam-
puses across the nation demonstrate
the breadth of the problem. The
increase of rapes at the University of
California, however, needs more
explanation.

The third subpoint describes the effects
of sexual assault on the victim. Maria
Lucia uses vivid language to paint a
picture of the aftermath of an attack
on the life of the victim. She could
have heightened the emotional impact
by personalizing the information using
personal pronouns as she described the
effects.

Satisfaction

The ideal satisfaction step shows in a
point-by-point fashion how the pro-
posed solution, in this case, a sexual
assault prevention policy, would sat-
isfy the needs presented earlier. Here
we would expect the speaker to tell us

What I've just quoted is part of the freshman orientation at Antioch College in Ohio. In the sexual offense policy of this college, emphasis is given to three major points: (1) If you have a sexually transmitted disease, you must disclose it to a potential partner; (2) to knowingly take advantage of someone who is under the influence of alcohol, drugs, and/or prescribed medication is not acceptable behavior in the Antioch community; (3) obtaining consent is an ongoing process in any sexual interaction. The request for consent must be specific to each act.

The policy is designed to create a "safe" campus environment, according to Antioch President Alan Guskin. For those who engage in sex, the goal is 100 percent consensual sex. It isn't enough to ask someone if they would like to have sex; you have to get verbal consent every step of the way.

This policy has been highly publicized and you may have heard it before. The policy addresses sexual offenses such as rape, which involves penetration, and sexual assault, which does not. In both instances, the respondent coerced or forced the primary witness to engage in nonconsensual sexual conduct with the respondent or another.

Sexual assault has become a reality in many campuses across the nation. Carleton College in Northfield, Minnesota, was sued for $800,000 in damages by four university women. The women charged that Carleton was negligent in protecting them against a known rapist. From the June 1991 issue of *Time* magazine:

Amy had been on campus for just five weeks when she joined some friends to watch a video in the room of a senior. One by one the other students went away, leaving her alone with a student whose name she didn't even know. "It ended up with his hands around my throat," she recalls. In a lawsuit she has filed against the college, she charges that he locked the door and raped her again and again for the next four hours. "I didn't want him to kill me, I just kept trying not to cry." Only afterwards did he tell her, almost defiantly, his name. It was on top of the "castration list" posted on women's bathroom walls around campus to warn other students about college rapists. Amy's attacker was found guilty of sexual assault but was only suspended.

Julie started dating a fellow cast member in a Carleton play. They had never slept together, she charges in a civil suit, until he came to her dorm room one night, uninvited, and raped her. She struggled to hold her life and education together, but finally could manage no longer and left school. Only later did Julie learn that her assailant was the same man who had attacked Amy.

Ladies and gentlemen, the court held that the college knew this man was a rapist. The administration may have been able to prevent this from happening if they had expelled the attacker, but they didn't. My campus has no reports of sexual assault. Is the administration waiting for someone to be assaulted before it formulates a sexual assault policy? This mistake has been made elsewhere; we don't have to prove it again.

Perhaps some statistics will help you understand the magnitude of the problem. According to *New Statesman and Society,* June 21, 1991, issue:

- A 1985 survey of sampled campuses by *Ms. Magazine* and the National Institute of Mental Health found that one in every four college women were victims of sexual assault; 74 percent knew their attackers. Even worse, between 30 and 40 percent of male students indicated they might force a woman to have sex if they knew they would escape punishment.

- In just one year, from 1988 to 1989, reports of student rape at the University of California increased from two to eighty.

These numbers are indeed disturbing. But more disturbing are the effects of sexual assault: a victim feeling the shock of why something this terrible was allowed to happen; having intense fears that behind every dark corner could be an attacker ready to grab her, push her to the ground, and sexually assault her; many waking moments of anxiety and impaired concentration as she remembers the attack; countless nights of reliving the traumatic incident in her sleep; mood swings and depression as she tries to deal internally with the physical hurt and the emotional turmoil that this attack has caused.

Many campuses are open invitations for sexual assault. The absence of a policy is a grand invitation. I have never been sexually assaulted so why do I care so much about a policy? You know why—because I could be assaulted. I won't sit and wait to be among one out of every four women on my campus to be assaulted. The first step to keep myself out of the statistics is to push for a sexual assault policy on my campus. One way to do this is through a petition to the university.

Although the Antioch policy sounds a little far-fetched and has been the target of criticism in comedy routines such as those on *Saturday Night Live,* and although students feel that formalizing such a policy is unnatural, many campuses are taking heed and revisiting their own policies. Campuses like mine don't have a sexual assault policy to revisit. Does yours?

By far the most controversial policy today is the one established at Antioch College. I'm not saying that we need one as specific as theirs, but every university has a responsibility to provide a safe environment for its students. Universities have an obligation to provide a sexual assault policy. The following points are fundamental to the safety of the students and need to be addressed by universities:

1. Every campus should have a sexual assault policy that is developed with input from students, faculty, staff, and administration. The policy then needs to be publicized in the student handbook. The school newspaper should print and the campus radio broadcast the policy periodically to heighten awareness.

2. Campuses must institute programs to educate students and other campus personnel. Examples of these policies can include discussing the sexual assault policy during mandatory student orientation and conducting special workshops for faculty and other staff.

3. Campuses should outline a step-by-step written procedure to guarantee that sexual assault victims are assisted by the university. It is pertinent that they are not without support at this very critical time.

My vision is a campus where there is no place for any sexual assault. I want to leave the classroom at night knowing that my trip from the building to the car will not be one of fear for my personal safety.

You may be saying to yourself that there are laws to handle crimes like these. In the *Chronicle of Higher Education,* May 15, 1991, issue, Jane McDonnell, a senior lecturer in women's studies at Carleton, says colleges cannot turn their back on women. "We'd be abandoning victims if we merely sent them to the police," she says. "The wheels of justice tend to grind slowly and rape has one of the lowest conviction rates of any crime."

Without a policy, most institutions lack specific penalties for sexual assault and choose to prosecute offenders under the general student-conduct code. At Carleton College, for example, Amy's attacker was allowed back on campus after his suspension, and consequently, he raped again.

Although the policy may not stop the actual assault, would-be offenders will think twice before committing sexual assault if they know they will be punished. In addition, it guarantees justice for victims of sexual assault. We need to make it loud and clear that sexual assault will not be tolerated.

Yes, universities have a big task in the struggle to prevent sexual assault.

You and I can actively assist in this task and can make a giant contribution to move it forward. On my campus, students have not only voiced their concerns, but we have also started a petition demanding that the university formulate a sexual assault policy.

The bottom line is that we need to prevent sexual assault on campus. The key to prevention is a sexual assault policy. If your university does not have a policy, then you need to petition your administration to have one. I know I won't stop my advocacy until I see a policy on my campus.

how such a policy would (1) prevent scenarios like the one at Carleton College, (2) change the statistics on date rape, (3) change male students' perceptions about the likelihood of punishment, and (4) offer support for the victim.

Maria Lucia handles this step very well, although the organization of this section could be tighter. Specifically, she should have laid out four points, not three, as "fundamental" to an effective policy. Point four would have addressed disciplinary procedures and penalties specific to sexual assault. She implies these are important but never makes the case.

Visualization

This section might have been more compelling had it been placed after the discussion of disciplinary procedures and victim support. The visualization also could have been developed a bit more. It would have been more effective had it been less "speaker specific" and instead invited the audience to visualize.

Here she points to negative visualization—that is, what we can expect if action to create sexual assault policies is not taken.

This transition to the action step doesn't really follow from the previous discussion.

Action

Here Maria Lucia offers a specific action to be taken by the audience— that is, to petition for a sexual assault prevention policy on their campuses. The way she phrases it, however, is not as compelling as it could be. She could have been more effective by replacing passive voice with active voice.

She also fails to quickly review her main points, and she doesn't provide much direction to the audience about how to go about petitioning.

The speech ends abruptly with an indirect emotional appeal to the audience's sense of guilt. She didn't really have a clincher. As such, the speech seems to "just end." Perhaps a tie-back to the opening quotation and an appeal to compassion or hope would have served her purpose more effectively.

Summary

Persuasive speeches are based on logical reasons but must also present those reasons in a way that motivates the audience to listen and to internalize what the speaker is saying. When people are personally involved with a proposition, they are more likely to be persuaded.

Because audience members become involved with an issue when they have an emotional stake in it, speakers need to use emotional appeals to create involvement. Speakers can evoke negative emotions, including fear, guilt, anger, sadness, and shame, or positive emotions such as happiness/joy, pride, compassion, relief, or hope.

Because some audience members will choose the peripheral route, persuasive speakers need to establish their credibility. In addition to demonstrating their expertise, trustworthiness, and personableness, they also need to demonstrate goodwill—the perception that they have the best interests of the audience at heart.

One type of persuasive speech, the speech to actuate, moves beyond affecting audience beliefs and asks audience members to take action. When you want to move your audience to action, you need to show them the incentives for acting and how these incentives outweigh the costs. You also need to point out how incentives meet audience members' needs. One way to understand needs is through Maslow's hierarchy, which suggests that needs can be classified as physical, safety, belongingness, esteem, and self-actualization.

Three persuasive organizational patterns, problem-solution, problem-cause-solution, and the motivated sequence, are designed for moving audiences to action. Finally, persuasive speakers must bear in mind that they have special ethical responsibilities. These include advocating the honest belief of the speaker, providing choice for the audience, using supporting information that is representative, using emotional appeals to engage audience rational thought process, presenting incentives and costs accurately, and honestly presenting speaker credibility.

CHALLENGE ONLINE

Now that you've read Chapter 14, use your CengageNOW for *The Challenge of Effective Speaking* for quick access to the electronic resources that accompany this text. Your CengageNOW gives you access to the sample persuasive speech featured on pages 310–313; the videos of the student speeches "Environmental Racism (1)," "Environmental Racism (2)," and "Become an Entrepreneur" described on pages 295, 306, and 310; the speech evaluation checklist shown on page 309; the Web Resource featured in this chapter; Speech Builder Express; InfoTrac College Edition; and online study aids such as a digital glossary and review quizzes.

Your *Challenge* CengageNOW is an online study system that helps you identify concepts you don't fully understand, allowing you to put your study time to the best use. Using chapter-by-chapter diagnostic pretests, the system creates a personalized study plan for each chapter. Each plan directs you to specific resources designed to improve your understanding, including pages from the text in e-book format. Chapter posttests give you an opportunity to measure how much you've learned and let you know if you are ready for graded quizzes and exams.

Go to your CengageNOW for *Challenge* to access your online glossary for Chapter 14. Print a copy of the glossary for this chapter and test yourself with the electronic flash cards or complete the crossword puzzle to help you master these key terms:

anger (290)
compassion (292)
costs (299)
derived credibility (297)
emotions (288)
empathy (296)
fear (289)
goodwill (295)
guilt (289)

happiness/joy (291)
hope (292)
incentive (299)
initial credibility (297)
motivated sequence (304)
negative emotions (289)
persuasive punch words (294)
positive emotions (291)
pride (292)

problem-cause-solution pattern (304)
problem-solution pattern (302)
relief (292)
responsive (296)
sadness (291)
shame (290)
speech to actuate (299)
terminal credibility (297)

WEB RESOURCE

Go to your CengageNOW for *Challenge* to access the Web Resources for this chapter.

14.1 Terrorism and Islam: Maintaining
   Our Faith (295)

© Wadsworth, a division of Cengage Learning

Ceremonial Speaking: Speeches for Special Occasions

A society emphasizing social rituals and manners requires a certain reverence for words to adequately express sentiment and feeling.

William Van O'Connor, "Robert Penn Warren, 'Provincial Poet,'" *A Southern Vanguard: The John Peale Bishop Memorial Volume,* **1945**

Masterfile Royalty Free (RF)

What's Ahead

HERE'S WHAT'S AHEAD IN THIS CHAPTER:

1. What should you include in a speech of welcome?

2. Why should a speech of introduction be brief?

3. What is your goal in a speech of nomination?

4. When might you be expected to give a speech of recognition?

5. What are some common types of speeches of tribute?

Because Ben didn't know his biological father, his grandfather had been like a father to him. He and his grandfather had spent hours playing ball, fishing, or simply watching television together. Although Ben's grandfather had lived a long and fruitful life, Ben was finding it difficult to say good-bye. Still, he wanted to give the eulogy at the funeral. How could he find the right words to do justice to his grandfather's memory?

On special occasions such as weddings and funerals, we may be called on to "say a few words." On these ceremonial occasions, your audience has distinct expectations for what they will hear. So, although the speech plan action steps you have learned will help you prepare your remarks, you also need to understand how the occasion affects how you should shape your speech.

The goal of ceremonial speeches lies somewhere between informing and persuading. In ceremonial speeches, you invite listeners to agree with you about the value of the person, object, event, or place the special occasion revolves around. Another characteristic of most ceremonial speeches is brevity: They are generally—although not always—fewer than five minutes long. This chapter describes six common types of ceremonial speeches given on special occasions: speeches of welcome, introduction, nomination, recognition, acceptance, and tribute. For each speech type, we describe the typical expectations for you to keep in mind as you prepare.

Speeches of Welcome

A **speech of welcome** is usually a very brief, formal ceremonial address that greets and expresses pleasure for the presence of a person or an organization. A speech of welcome is generally not more than two to four minutes long. You can welcome someone on your own, but more frequently, you will give a speech of welcome as the representative of a group. On some occasion, you may be asked to serve as **master or mistress of ceremonies,** an individual designated to welcome guests, set the mood of the program, introduce participants, and keep the program moving. Year-end honorary banquets, corporate dinner meetings, and local charity events typically use someone in this role.

Expectations

You must be familiar with the group that you are representing and the occasion. It is surprising how little some members of an organization, a community, or a college or university really know about their organization or community. As you prepare your welcome, you may need to do some research so you can accurately describe the group and the circumstances or occasion to the person or people you are welcoming.

A speech of welcome invites listeners to agree that the occasion is friendly and their attendance is appreciated. Do this by respectfully catching their attention and, after expressing appreciation on behalf of your group for the presence of the person or people, provide a brief description of the group and setting to which they are being welcomed. The conclusion should briefly express your hope for the outcome of the visit, event, or relationship. A typical speech of welcome might be as simple as this:

speech of welcome a brief, formal ceremonial address that greets and expresses pleasure for the presence of a person or an organization

master or mistress of ceremonies an individual designated to set the mood of the program, introduce participants, and keep the program moving

Today, I want to welcome John Sheldon, who is joining us from the North Thurston Club. John, as you are aware, we are a newer club, having been established in 2000. At that time, we had only ten members. But we had big hopes. Today, we are 127 members strong, and we raised more than $250,000 last year to support local children's organizations. We hope that our talks here today will lead to closer cooperation between the North Thurston Club and ours here in Yelm.

At times, you may be asked to give a speech that both welcomes and introduces a speaker. When this is the case, the speech can be a bit longer and should also include the type of information described in the next section.

Speeches of Introduction

speech of introduction a brief ceremonial speech that establishes a supportive climate for the main speaker, highlights the speaker's credibility by familiarizing the audience with pertinent biographical information, and generates enthusiasm for listening to the speaker and topic

A **speech of introduction** is a brief ceremonial speech that establishes a supportive climate for the main speaker, highlights the speaker's credibility by familiarizing the audience with pertinent biographical information, and generates enthusiasm for listening to the speaker and topic. Generally, a speech of introduction is not more than three to five minutes long.

Expectations

The goal of a speech of introduction is to establish the credibility of the main speaker by letting the audience know the education, background, and experience of the speaker related to the topic of the speech and to suggest why the audience should listen. At times, you will be given a résumé or brief biography of the speaker; at other times, you may need to research the speaker's background yourself. Regardless of what you have learned, before you prepare your remarks you should try to contact the speaker and ask what points in the biography the speaker would like you to emphasize.

The beginning of the speech of introduction should quickly establish the nature of the occasion, the body of the speech should focus on three or four things about the person being introduced that are critical for the audience to know, and the conclusion should mention the speaker by name and briefly identify the speaker's topic or the title of the speech. If the person is well known, you might simply say something like, "Ladies and gentlemen, the President of the United States." If the person is less well known, however, then mentioning his or her name specifically during the speech of introduction and especially at the end is imperative.

Speeches of introduction should honestly represent the person being introduced. Do not hype a speaker's credentials or overpraise the speaker. If you set the audience's expectations too high, even a good speaker may have trouble living up to them. For instance, an overzealous introducer can doom a competent speaker by saying, "This man [woman] is undoubtedly one of the greatest speakers of our time. I have no doubt that what you are about to hear will change your thinking." Although this introduction is meant to be complimentary, it does the speaker a grave disservice.

A typical speech of introduction might look like the following:

> Today, it is my pleasure to introduce our speaker, Ms. Susan Wong, the new president of the finance club. I've worked with Susan for three years and have found her to have a gift for organization, insight into the financial markets, and an interest in aligning student organizations with leaders in our community. Susan, as you may not know, has spent the last two summers working as an intern at Salomon Smith Barney, and has now laid the groundwork for more college internships for students from this university. She is a finance major, with a minor in international business. Today, she is going to talk with us about the benefits of summer internships. Let's give a warm welcome to Susan Wong!

Speech of Introduction

Prepare a three-minute speech of introduction. Assume that you are introducing the featured speaker for a specific occasion. Criteria for evaluation include creativity in establishing speaker credibility and presenting the name of the speaker and the speech title.

Speeches of Nomination

A **speech of nomination** is a ceremonial presentation that proposes a nominee for an elected office, honor, position, or award. Every four years, the Democratic and Republican Parties have speeches of nomination at their national conventions. Those speeches are rather long, but most speeches of nomination are brief, lasting only about two to four minutes.

speech of nomination a ceremonial presentation that proposes a nominee for an elected office, honor, position, or award

Expectations

The goal of a speech of nomination is to highlight the qualities that make this person the most credible candidate. To do so, first clarify the importance of the position, honor, or award by describing the responsibilities involved, related challenges or issues, and the characteristics needed to fulfill it. Second, list the candidate's personal and professional qualifications that meet those criteria. Doing so links the candidate with the position, honor, or award in ways that make him or her appear to be a natural choice. Finally, formally place the candidate's name in nomination, creating a dramatic climax to clinch your speech.

Speeches of nomination should be brief and should make clear that the nominee is well suited for the position, honor, or award. Moreover, the nominee is generally most well received when the nominator is a respected member of the organization. A speech of nomination could be as simple and brief as this:

"What's the matter, Ryan—you really look like something's bugging you!"

"Well, you know I'm introducing Spencer at the University Convocation for those running for offices. He's my friend, and I told him I'd be happy to introduce him. So I asked him to give me some information that he'd like me to include. I thought he'd summarize some of the stuff he's done, but instead, he wrote out an introduction that includes stuff about him that's mostly fiction! I'm really not sure what to do, Abby."

"So, he's the one who's running for office. You're just giving the introduction he wants you to give. Don't worry about it—nobody's going to pay attention to what you're saying anyway."

"Still, I'm giving the speech. I'm afraid that I'm going to be the one who gets blamed when and if people find out that what I've said isn't true."

"I'm telling you—your job is to do what Spencer wants. You asked him to give you information, and he did."

"I guess you're right—but I'm not going to like doing it."

1. Is Ryan violating ethical principles by agreeing to give the introduction Spencer wants as written?
2. If so, what should Ryan do about it?

I am very proud to place in nomination for president of our association the name of one of our most active members, Ms. Adrienne Lamb.

We all realize the demands of this particular post. It requires leadership. It requires vision. It requires enthusiasm and motivation. And most of all, it requires a sincere love for our group and its mission.

Adrienne Lamb meets and exceeds each one of these demands. It was Adrienne Lamb who chaired our visioning task force. She led us to articulate the mission statement we abide by today. It was Adrienne Lamb who chaired the fund-raising committee last year when we enjoyed a record drive. And it was Adrienne Lamb who acted as mentor to so many of us, myself included, when we were trying to find our place in this association and this community. This association and its members have reaped the benefits of Adrienne Lamb's love and leadership so many times and in so many ways. We now have the opportunity to benefit in even greater ways.

It is truly an honor and a privilege to place in nomination for president of our association Ms. Adrienne Lamb!

Speeches of Recognition

speech of recognition a ceremonial presentation that acknowledges someone and usually presents an award, a prize, or a gift to the individual or a representative of a group

A **speech of recognition** is a ceremonial presentation that acknowledges someone and usually presents an award, a prize, or a gift to the individual or a representative of a group. Usually, the speech is a fairly short, formal recognition of an accomplishment, although the recognition can be accompanied by a longer tribute to the individual or group. You have probably watched speeches of recognition given on awards shows such as the Academy Awards, the Grammies, or the MTV Movie Awards. Some speeches of recognition are typically quite brief (fewer than three minutes long), but occasionally, they are longer.

Expectations

A speech of recognition discusses the nature of the accomplishment or award, including its history, donor, or source, and the conditions under which it is made. Although the tangible award may be a certificate, plaque, trophy, or check symbolizing an achievement, the recognition may have a long history and tradition that you are responsible for recounting.

Because the audience wants to know why the recipient is being recognized, you must know the recognition criteria and how the recipient met them. If the recognition is based on a competition, this might include the number of contestants and the way the contest was judged. If the person earned the award through years of achievement, you will want to describe the specific milestones that the person passed.

Ordinarily, the speech begins by describing what the recognition is for, then states the criteria for winning or achieving the recognition, and finally describes how the person being recognized won or achieved the award. In some cases, the recognition is meant to be a surprise, so you will deliberately omit the name of the recipient in what you say, building to a climax when the name is announced.

There are two special considerations for the speech of recognition. First, as in a speech of introduction, you should refrain from overpraising; do not explain everything in superlatives that make the presentation seem to lack sincerity and honesty. Second, in the United States, it is traditional to shake hands with recipients as awards are received. So, if you have a certificate or other tangible award that you are going to hand to the recipient, be careful to hold it in your left hand and present it to the recipient's left hand. That way, you will be able to shake the right hand in congratulations. A typical speech of recognition may look like this:

When presenting an award, discuss the nature of the award and the recipient's accomplishments.

I'm honored to present this year's Idea of the Year Award to Rebecca Goldbloom from the installation department. As you may remember, this is an award that we have been giving since 1985 to the employee who has submitted an idea that resulted in the largest first-year cost savings for the company. Rebecca's idea to equip all installation trucks with prepackaged kits for each type of job has resulted in a $10,458 savings in the first twelve months. And in recognition of this contribution to our bottom line, I am pleased to share our savings with Rebecca in the form of a check for $2,091.60, one-fifth of what she has saved us. Good work, Rebecca.

SPEECH ASSIGNMENT

Speech of Recognition

Prepare a three- to five-minute speech in which you present a gift, a plaque, or an award to a member of your class. Criteria for evaluation include showing what the award is for, the criteria for winning, and how the person met the criteria.

Speeches of Acceptance

A **speech of acceptance** is a ceremonial speech given to acknowledge receipt of an honor or award. The goal is to sincerely convey to listeners your appreciation for the honor and the recognition and to quickly acknowledge others who have been instrumental in your success. To be effective, the speech should be brief, humble, and gracious. Generally, a speech of acceptance should be no longer than one to two minutes. Remember that the goal in a speech of acceptance is to convey appreciation in a way that makes the audience feel good about you receiving the award.

speech of acceptance a ceremonial speech given to acknowledge receipt of an honor or award

Expectations

In this speech, speakers should briefly thank the person or group bestowing the honor, acknowledge the competition, express feelings about receiving the award, and thank those who contributed to achieving the honor or award.

Most acceptance speeches are brief. Rarely, as in the case of a politician accepting a nomination, a professional accepting the presidency of a national organization, or a person receiving a prestigious award that is the focus of the gathering, an audience will expect a longer speech. As the Academy Awards program graphically illustrates, when people are honored, they can give overly long and occasionally inappropriate speeches. So, when you have the opportunity to give an acceptance speech, you will want to practice it so that you are confident that you can accomplish your purpose quickly. It is also important that you focus your remarks on the recognition you have been given or on the position you are accepting. It is inappropriate to use an acceptance speech to advocate for an unrelated cause. The following is an example of an appropriate speech of acceptance:

> On behalf of our board of directors, thank you for this award, the Largest Institutional Benefactor in Second Harvest's 1998 Food Drive. It is an honor to be a part of such a worthwhile cause, and it is really our board who should be thanking you, Second Harvest, for all the wonderful work you have done over the years. You continue to collect and distribute food to thousands of needy families and individuals, especially to our senior citizens and single mothers. Without your work, many would otherwise go hungry. You are a model of community sharing and caring.
>
> I would also like to thank our company staff—Juanita Alverez, Su Lin, Al Pouzorek, Linda Williams, and Jesus Washington—for their efforts in organizing the collection of food and money to go to Second Harvest. They were tireless in their work, persistent in their company memos and meetings requesting donations, and consistent in their positive and upbeat attitudes throughout the drive! We could not have won this award without them! Let's give them a round of applause, too.
>
> Finally, thank you, Second Harvest, for this honor—and we hope to be back next year to receive it again!

SPEECH ASSIGNMENT

Speech of Acceptance

This assignment can be paired with the speech of recognition assignment. Prepare a one- to two-minute speech of acceptance in response to another speaker's speech of recognition. The criteria for evaluation are how well you express your feelings about the recognition and your acknowledgment of the contribution of others.

Speeches of Tribute

speech of tribute a ceremonial speech that praises or celebrates a person, a group, or an event

A **speech of tribute** is a ceremonial speech that praises or celebrates a person, a group, or an event. You might be asked to pay tribute to a person or persons on the occasion of their birthday, wedding, anniversary, oath of office, retirement, or funeral. There are a variety of special types based on the specific special occasion they are meant for. The goal is to invite listeners to truly appreciate the person, group, or event by arousing their sentiments. This is achieved by focusing on the most notable characteristics or achievements of the person, group, or event with vivid stories, examples, and language that arouses sentiments. Speeches of tribute can vary in length from very brief to lengthy depending on the nature of the occasion. Let's take a closer look at two types of tribute that you are likely to be asked to give.

Toasts

toast a ceremonial speech offered at the start of a reception or meal that pays tribute to the occasion or to a person

A **toast** is a ceremonial speech offered at the start of a reception or meal that pays tribute to the occasion or to a person. On most occasions, a toast is

Daniel Inouye *Duty, Honor, Country*

Marco Garcia/Getty Images

Each year, West Point Military Academy gives an award to an American who has served the United States with distinction. Recipients of the Thayer Award, named after a celebrated West Point alum and academy superintendent, have included Colin Powell, Walter Cronkite, Barbara Jordan, and Ronald Reagan. In 2002, Hawaii Senator Daniel Inouye joined the list of those who have received this honor.

Of course, being honored with an award typically necessitates honoring, in turn, a request to give an acceptance speech. A master public speaker, Senator Inouye's speech to a sea of West Point cadets and spectators received a standing ovation and media accolades.

Inouye's warm reception was perhaps a response to his skillfully crafted use of audience-involving language. Because West Point's motto, "Duty, Honor, Country," is ingrained among the cadets, Inouye deliberately weaves their recognizable, cherished creed into his speech. In the excerpts that follow, notice the many ways he emphasizes the motto.

In the introduction: "The sacred words of West Point—'Duty, Honor, Country'—have been a part of the history of this land since the time of its birth."

As a transition: "'Duty, Honor, Country' are words that are also important in my life."

In the body: ". . . if only to prove our loyalty and demonstrate our commitment to the essence of your three sacred words: 'Duty, Honor, Country.'"

As reinforcement: "We Americans should not be reluctant or afraid to use the words 'Duty, Honor, Country,' because they are necessary if we are to continue enjoying the good life we have become accustomed to."

In closing: "I envy you because I believe you will live in a better America, a better America where the sacred words of 'Duty, Honor, Country' will have meaning and relevance."

In accepting the Thayer Award, Senator Inouye honored the traditions of the institution while challenging the audience to fully embrace "duty, honor, and country."

---

expected to be very brief (lasting less than a minute), consisting of only a few sentences and focusing on a single characteristic of the person or occasion. Usually, a short example is used to support or illustrate the characteristic. Wedding toasts, given at a rehearsal dinner or reception by a family member or member of the wedding party, are generally longer speeches (three to four minutes) that may use humor but should not embarrass the persons at whom they are directed.

A toast should be sincere and express a sentiment that is likely to be widely shared by those in attendance. The person giving the toast often stands or in some other way separates from the rest of the people. Generally, the person giving the toast and all other attendees have a drink in hand, which they raise and sip from at the conclusion of the toast. So, before offering a toast, it is customary to make sure that drinks are refreshed so that all can participate. If particular people are being toasted, the toast is drunk in their honor, so they do not drink.

A typical toast by a daughter given to honor her mother's college graduation might be:

> Tonight, I'd like to offer a toast to a woman I admire and respect. My mom has always supported my brother and me. So, when she told me that she wanted to go back and finish college, I was worried about how we'd all manage. But I shouldn't have worried. Mom not only finished her degree in less than two years, but she also continued to work full time, and what's more, she's even had time to coach my brother's Little League team. Here's to you, Mom—you're amazing!

Special occasions such as weddings, birthdays, and retirements call for toasts that are presented with sincerity and sensitivity to the situation.

Chev Wilkinson/Getty Images

Toast

Prepare a one-minute toast to a specific person or persons on a specific occasion. Criteria for evaluation include how well you illustrate a quality or behavior of the person you are celebrating.

Eulogies

eulogy a ceremonial speech of tribute during a funeral or memorial service that praises someone's life and accomplishments

A **eulogy** is a ceremonial speech of tribute during a funeral or memorial service that praises someone's life and accomplishments. Your goal is to comfort the mourners by focusing on positive memories of the deceased person. Based on what you know about the person, select three or four positive personal characteristics of the person to use as the main points and then use personal stories you have collected about the person to provide support. Your audience will enjoy hearing new stories that exemplify the characteristics as well as revisiting widely shared stories. Incidents that reveal how a personal characteristic helped the person overcome adversity will be especially powerful. To see an example of a eulogy, use your CengageNOW for *Challenge* to access the video of Oprah Winfrey's eulogy for civil rights activist Rosa Parks under the Chapter 15 resources.

commencement address a speech of tribute praising graduating students and inspiring them to reach for their goals

commemorative address a speech of tribute that celebrates national holidays or anniversaries of important events

keynote address a ceremonial speech that both sets the tone and generates enthusiasm for the topic of a conference or convention

dedication a speech of tribute that honors a worthy person or group by naming a structure, monument, or park after them

farewell a speech of tribute honoring someone who is leaving an organization

speech to entertain a humorous speech that makes a serious point

Eulogy

Prepare a four- to six-minute eulogy. Criteria for evaluation include how well you identify and develop the person's laudable characteristics and accomplishments.

Other Ceremonial Speeches

Other occasions that call for ceremonial speeches include graduations, holidays, anniversaries of major events, and special events. A **commencement address,** for example, is a speech of tribute praising graduating students and inspiring them to reach for their goals. A **commemorative address** is a ceremonial speech of tribute that celebrates national holidays or anniversaries of important events. A **keynote address** is a ceremonial speech that both sets the tone and generates enthusiasm for the topic of a conference or convention. A **dedication** is a speech of tribute that honors a worthy person or group by naming a structure such as a building, monument, or park after the honoree. A **farewell** is a ceremonial speech of tribute honoring someone who is leaving an organization. A **speech to entertain** is a humorous speech that makes a serious point. To learn more about each of these types of ceremonial speeches, use your CengageNOW for *Challenge* to access "Other Ceremonial Speeches" under the Chapter 15 resources.

Summary

In addition to informative and persuasive speeches, you are likely to have occasion to give speeches to welcome, introduce, nominate, recognize, accept, and tribute. A welcoming speech expresses pleasure at the presence of a person or an organization. A speech of introduction serves to introduce a speaker. In a speech of recognition, you present an award, a prize, or a gift to an individual or to a group. A speech of acceptance is a response to a speech of recognition. A speech of tribute celebrates an occasion, person, or event. Toasts are offered before a meal or reception to celebrate an occasion, person, or people. A eulogy celebrates a person during a funeral or memorial service.

Other ceremonial speeches include commencement addresses, commemorative addresses, keynote addresses, dedications, farewells, as well as speeches to entertain.

CHALLENGE ONLINE

Now that you've read Chapter 15, use your CengageNOW for *The Challenge of Effective Speaking* for quick access to the electronic resources that accompany this text. Your CengageNOW gives you access to the video of Oprah Winfrey's eulogy for Rosa Parks described on page 324, Speech Builder Express, InfoTrac College Edition, and online study aids such as a digital glossary and review quizzes.

Your *Challenge* CengageNOW is an online study system that helps you identify concepts you don't fully understand, allowing you to put your study time to the best use. Using chapter-by-chapter diagnostic pretests, the system creates a personalized study plan for each chapter. Each plan directs you to specific resources designed to improve your understanding, including pages from the text in e-book format. Chapter posttests give you an opportunity to measure how much you've learned and let you know if you are ready for graded quizzes and exams.

KEY TERMS

Go to your CengageNOW for *Challenge* to access your online glossary for Chapter 15. Print a copy of the glossary for this chapter and test yourself with the electronic flash cards or complete the crossword puzzle to help you master these key terms:

commemorative address (324)
commencement address (324)
dedication (324)
eulogy (324)
farewell (324)
keynote address (324)

master or mistress of ceremonies (317)
speech of acceptance (321)
speech of introduction (318)
speech of nomination (319)
speech of recognition (320)

speech of tribute (322)
speech of welcome (317)
speech to entertain (324)
toast (322)

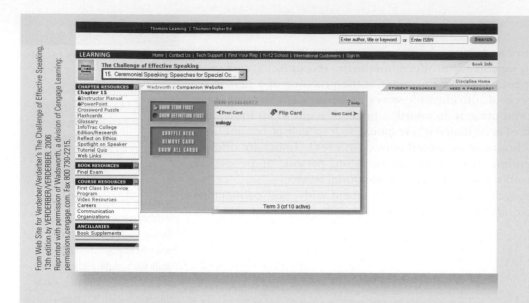

Developing and Delivering Group Presentations

© Steve Chenn/Corbis

Men are never so likely to settle a question rightly as when they discuss it freely.

Thomas Babington, Lord Macaulay, *Southey's Colloquies*

What's Ahead

HERE'S WHAT'S AHEAD IN THIS CHAPTER:

1. Why is teamwork becoming so popular as a means for solving problems?

2. What does it mean to be a responsible group member?

3. How can you solve problems effectively in groups?

4. How do you prepare a group presentation?

5. How can you evaluate group work?

WORK SESSION 1: Julio, Kristi, Luke, Bryn, and Nick have been asked to work as a small group to prepare a persuasive presentation that will count for one-third of the grade in their public speaking course. As the other members see it, Nick is a troublemaker because he has contradicted the instructor several times during previous class sessions. Their impression might be compounded by the fact that Nick drives a Harley-Davidson motorcycle to school and wears black leather most days. Nick has also been absent several times and seems less than fully committed to earning a good grade. In short, the other members are worried that Nick will cause them to earn a lower grade than they would earn without him in their group.

WORK SESSION 2: After the instructor refused to move Nick to another group, Julio, Kristi, Luke, and Bryn decide to restrict Nick's participation by not asking him for substantive help even though that means he'll get a better grade than he deserves. As the full group begins discussing their topic—the mandatory seat belt law—Nick explains that he has a lot of material on it since he is a fairly vocal opponent of the helmet law, which involves similar issues. Kristi and Luke become disgruntled because they plan to argue in support of the law, and as they suspected, Nick opposes it. Kristi asks Bryn: "How do YOU feel about this conflict?" Much to Kristi's surprise, Bryn replies, "Actually, I'd like to hear more from Nick before I decide. Nick, tell us more." Nick goes on to share highly relevant information that would eventually be used to strengthen the group's speech. The group soon realizes the hastiness of their judgments about Nick.

Perhaps you have already been part of a group whose task was to prepare a joint presentation. If so, the opening scenario probably sounds familiar. In fact, when asked to work in small groups on a class or work project, many people respond—as Julio, Kristi, Luke, and Bryn did—with resistance. Their reasons usually focus on concerns that a few members will end up doing most of the work, that the group process will slow them down, that they'll earn a lower grade than if they worked alone, or that they will be forced to work on a topic that they aren't interested in or take a position they don't agree with.

Although working in a group to develop and deliver a presentation has its disadvantages, it is the preferred approach in business and industry.[1] These work teams begin as **problem-solving groups:** groups comprised of four to seven people that are formed to carry out a specific task or solve a particular problem. Usually at the end of their deliberations, they present their analysis, findings, and recommended solutions to others in the organization. Whether you want to or not, you can expect to work in a group or on a team in your professional life, sometimes in face-to-face settings and often in virtual settings through e-mail, chat rooms, discussion boards, and video conferences.[2] Leaders in business and industry have come to realize that the advantages of work

problem-solving group four to seven people who work together to complete a specific task or solve a particular problem

teams far outweigh the disadvantages. The advantages include deeper analysis of problems, greater breadth of ideas and of potential solutions, improved group morale, and increased productivity.

You can also expect to be asked to present group findings in formal presentations whether in the form of a progress report, sales presentation, proposal, or staff report.[3] So it makes sense to learn how to work effectively in problem-solving groups and how to present your group findings orally. In this chapter, we begin by talking about the responsibilities of group members in effective problem-solving groups and describing an effective method for solving problems in small groups. Then we discuss how to prepare group presentations and describe three public presentation formats. Finally, we explain how you can evaluate your group's effectiveness.

Responsibilities of Group Members

When problem-solving groups work well, the product is better than what any one member could have accomplished alone. This is known as **synergy.** Your goal when working in a small group is to achieve synergy. We believe small groups usually fail when members do not understand or follow through with the ethical responsibilities shown in Exhibit 16.1. When met by all members, these five responsibilities result in shared leadership where every member and their contributions are valued and synergy can occur.

synergy when the result of group work is better than what one member could achieve alone

1. Be committed to the group goal. Being committed to the group goal means finding a way to align your expertise with the agreed-upon goal of the

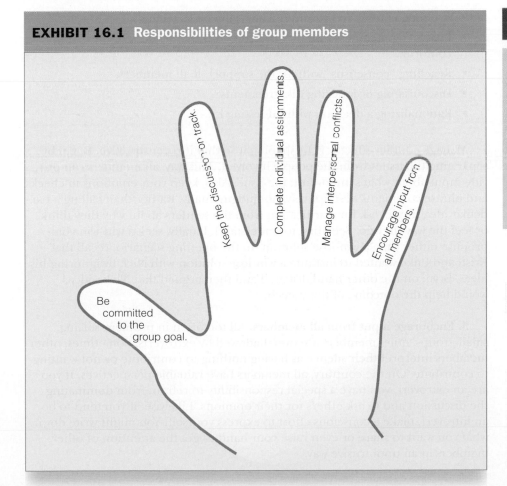

EXHIBIT 16.1 **Responsibilities of group members**

Keep the discussion on track.

Complete individual assignments.

Manage interpersonal conflicts.

Encourage input from all members.

Be committed to the group goal.

SPEECH SNIPPET

Committing to the Group Goal

Luke wanted to do the group speech on legalizing marijuana for medical purposes. Once his group decided to focus on the mandatory seat belt law, however, he let go of the marijuana idea and supported the agreed-upon goal instead.

group. So, for a class project, once your group decides on a topic, you need to be a good team member. This might mean working together on a topic that wasn't your first choice. Once the decision has been agreed upon, it is no longer appropriate to dredge up old issues that have already been settled. (For information about setting group goals, use your CengageNOW for Challenge to access **Web Resource 16.1: Setting Group Goals**.)

2. Keep discussions on track. It is every member's responsibility to keep the discussion on track by offering only comments that are relevant and by gently reminding others to stay focused if the discussion starts to get off track. It is unproductive to talk about personal issues during the team's work time. Moreover, it is unethical to try to get the discussion off track because you disagree with what is being said.

3. Complete individual assignments on time. One potential advantage of group work is that tasks can be divided among members. However, each member is responsible for completing his or her tasks thoroughly and on time.

4. Manage conflict among members. All small groups experience some **conflict**—disagreement or clash among ideas, principles, or people. If managed appropriately, conflict can actually be beneficial to the group goal by stimulating thinking, fostering open communication, encouraging diverse opinions, and enlarging members' understanding of the issues.[4] In fact, groups that *don't* experience some conflict risk the problem of **groupthink**—when group members accept information and ideas without subjecting them to critical analysis.[5] Behaviors that signal groupthink include:

- Avoiding conflict to prevent hurting someone's feelings.
- Pressuring members who do not agree with the majority of the group to conform.
- Reaching "consensus" without the support of all members.
- Discouraging or ignoring disagreements.
- Rationalizing a decision without testing it.

Manage conflict effectively by shaping it so that it is constructive. Begin by separating the issues from the people involved. This way, all members can provide input about what's important: the issue. Also, keep your emotions in check and phrase comments descriptively, not judgmentally. Rather than calling a particular idea stupid, ask for clarification from the senders about why they think or feel the way they do. Seek first to understand. Finally, seek a win-win compromise rather than a win-lose solution. In the opening scenario, recall that Kristi and Luke wanted to institute a win-lose solution with Nick by ignoring his ideas. Bryn, on the other hand, listened and then argued that Nick's ideas would help the outcome of the speech.

5. Encourage input from all members. All too often in problem-solving small groups, quiet members are overshadowed by extroverts. Sometimes, other members interpret their silence as having nothing to contribute or not wanting to contribute. On the contrary, all members have valuable perspectives. If you are an extrovert, you have a special responsibility to refrain from dominating the discussion and to ask others for their opinions. Likewise, if you tend to be an introvert, make a conscious effort to express yourself. You might write down what you want to share or even raise your hand to get the attention of other members in an unobtrusive way.

SPEECH SNIPPET

Keeping the Discussion on Track

When Luke and Kristi began talking about attending the upcoming football game, Bryn gently reminded them that the group had only thirty minutes to figure out how to proceed and finish the speech, due next week.

conflict disagreement or clash among ideas, principles, or people

groupthink when group members accept information and ideas without subjecting them to critical analysis

SPEECH SNIPPET

Encouraging Input from All Group Members

Bryn tends to be quiet during group discussions, yet when Kristi asked for her opinion, Bryn helped the group realize that Nick had a valuable contribution to make.

"You know, Sue, we're going to be in deep trouble if the group doesn't support McGowan's resolution about dues reform."

"Well, we'll just have to see to it that all the arguments in favor of that resolution are heard—but in the end, it's the group's decision."

"That's very democratic of you, Sue, but you know that if it doesn't pass, you're likely to be out on your tail."

"That may be, Heather, but I don't see what I can do about it."

"You don't want to see. First, right now, the group respects you. If you would just apply a little pressure on a couple of the members—you'd get what you want."

"What do you mean?"

"Look, this is a good cause. You've got something on just about every member of the group. Take a couple aside and let them know that this is payoff time. I think you'll find that some key folks will see it your way."

Heather may well have a point about how Sue can control the outcome.

1. Should Sue follow Heather's advice?
2. Why or why not?

Systematic Group Problem-Solving Method

To be effective, a problem-solving group needs a concrete approach for arriving at a productive solution in a short amount of time. One effective means for doing so is the **systematic problem-solving method.**[6] Although this method was created nearly a century ago, its staying power is evidenced in classrooms across the country still today.[7] The method consists of six steps.

systematic problem-solving method an efficient six-step method for finding an effective solution to a problem

1. Identify and define the problem. The first step is to identify the problem and define it in a way all group members understand and agree with. Groups might begin by coming up with a number of problems or needs and then narrow them to a particular one. Posing questions can also help identify and define a problem: What is the problem? What is its history? Who is affected by it and how does it affect them? How many people are affected, in what ways, and to what degree? These questions help a group realize what kinds of information must be gathered to help define the problem. To ensure that your group is focusing on the problem itself and not just the symptoms of the problem, don't rush through this step. For more information about defining the problem, use your CengageNOW for *Challenge* to access **Web Resources 16.2: What's Your Problem?**

2. Analyze the problem. To analyze the problem, you must find out as much as possible about it. Most groups begin by sharing the information that individual members have acquired through their experience. You will need to examine published materials available through the library and on the Internet. You might also consult experts or conduct a survey to gather information from a particular target group. You might consider using questions to guide you in analyzing the problem: Can the problem be subdivided into a series of smaller problems? Why has the problem occurred? What are the symptoms? What methods already exist for dealing with it? What are the limitations of those methods? One important element of this step when working in problem-solving small groups is to share new information with your other group members as you discover it.

3. Determine criteria for judging solutions. Criteria are standards used for judging the merits of proposed solutions—a blueprint for evaluating them. Without clear criteria, groups may select solutions that don't adequately address

criteria standards used for judging the merits of proposed solutions

the real problem or, perhaps, solutions that create a host of new problems. Questions that might guide your thinking about criteria include: Exactly what must the solutions achieve? Are there any factors that might limit the choice of solutions (e.g., cost, feasibility, location, complexity, expedience, risk–benefit ration, etc.)? Once you've established criteria, prioritize the list. Which criteria are most important? Which are least important?

4. Generate a host of solutions. At this point, you'll want to brainstorm for possible solutions. **Brainstorming,** you'll recall, is an uncritical, nonevaluative process of generating alternatives by being creative, suspending judgment, and combining or adapting the ideas of others. It involves verbalizing your ideas as they come to mind without stopping to evaluate their merits. At least one member should record all solutions as they are suggested. To ensure that creativity is not stifled, no solution should be ignored, and members should build on the ideas presented by others. You might come up with twenty or more solutions. As a minimum, try to come up with eight to ten solutions before moving to the next step. For more on brainstorming, use your CengageNOW for *Challenge* to access **Web Resource 16.3: Rules for Brainstorming**.

5. Select the best solution(s) based on the criteria. Here you need to evaluate the merits of each potential solution based on the criteria established by the group. Consider each solution as it meets the criteria and eliminate solutions that do not meet them adequately. In addition to applying the criteria, the group might also ask questions such as: How will the solution solve the problem? How difficult will it be to implement? What problems might be caused as a result of implementing the solution? Once each potential solution has been thoroughly evaluated based on the criteria, the group must select the best one(s).

6. Implement the agreed-upon solution. Finally, the group implements the agreed-upon solution or, if the group is presenting the solution to others for implementation, makes recommendations for how the solution should be implemented. The group has already considered implementation in terms of selecting a solution but now must fill in the details. What tasks are required by the solution(s)? Who will carry out these tasks? What is a reasonable time frame for implementation generally and for each of the tasks specifically?

Preparing Group Presentations

Once the group has worked through the systematic problem-solving method, it's time to prepare a group presentation. Doing so involves a five-step process that starts with dividing the topic into areas of responsibility and ends with practicing the presentation.

1. Divide the topic into areas of responsibility. As a group, determine the thesis and macrostructure for the presentation. Each member can then be responsible for researching and organizing the content necessary to develop a particular main point. If there are more group members than main points, assign more than one person to a main point or assign one person to develop and integrate presentational aids.

2. Draft an outline of your topic area. Each group member should construct an outline for his or her main point. Even though the outline is for only part of the presentation, it must still be thorough, so follow the steps for creating an outline you learned in Chapter 7.

3. Combine member outlines to form a group outline. Once the individual outlines are completed, the group is ready to combine them into a single outline. Members should share their individual outlines and then, as a group,

brainstorming an uncritical, nonevaluative process of generating alternatives by being creative, suspending judgment, and combining or adapting the ideas of others

develop the transitions between main points and make any other changes needed for continuity and consistency. If no member was responsible for developing the introduction and conclusion, the group should create them now. Likewise, presentational aids should be integrated at this point.

4. Finalize the details of delivery. Because this is a group presentation, more than the usual number of decisions must be made about delivery. For example, which presentation format will you use? (The next section in this chapter shows various presentation formats.) Who will speak when? Who will introduce the speakers and when? Where will group members sit when they are not speaking? How will presentational aids be displayed, and who will be responsible for displaying them?

5. Practice your presentation. It is crucial to practice both individually and as a group, using the delivery guidelines described in Chapter 11. Because group presentations pose additional complexities, there are more tasks to be done to complete the speech. As a result, there is even more need for practice if you are to succeed at conveying one seamless message to your listeners.

Public Group Presentation Formats

Although your group problem solving will be done in private—without the presence of an onlooking or participating audience—occasionally you will have the opportunity to share your issues in a public forum. At times, this means conducting your group discussion with nonparticipating observers present; at other times, it means presenting your group's conclusions to an audience. As such, public group presentations have much in common with traditional public speaking. Three common formats for public group presentations are the symposium, the panel discussion, and the town hall meeting.

Symposium

A **symposium** is a discussion in which a limited number of participants (usually three to five) present individual speeches of approximately the same length dealing with the same subject. After delivering their planned speeches, the participants in the symposium respond to questions from the audience. Unfortunately, a symposium often omits the interaction necessary for a good discussion. However, if the participants make their prepared speeches short enough to allow sufficient time for questions and answers, a symposium can be interesting and stimulating.

In a symposium, all speakers typically are seated in front of the audience. One person acts as moderator, offering the introductory and concluding remarks and providing transitions between speakers. In a way, the moderator provides the macrostructure for the group presentation. When introduced by the moderator, each speaker moves from his or her seat to the lectern to deliver a speech on the aspect of the topic he or she is covering. Although each speech can stand on its own, all fit together to present the larger picture of the issue. After all speakers have finished, the moderator returns to the lectern to offer concluding remarks and to facilitate the question-and-answer session. Questions can be directed to individuals in the group or to the group as a whole.

The way the group divides the content among speakers depends on how the material was organized. For example, each speaker might focus on one step of the problem-solving process or on one major issue related to the overall topic. If the presentation is persuasive, successive speakers might focus on the problem, the causes, and the solutions. Or one might focus on the need,

symposium a discussion in which a limited number of participants present individual speeches of approximately the same length dealing with the same subject and then discuss their reactions to what others have said and answer questions from the audience

another on the plan for meeting the need, another on visualization of the future, and another on a call to action. To see sample outlines for a persuasive group symposium speech, use your CengageNOW for *Challenge* to access the online resources for Chapter 16. There you can see the outlines prepared by a group of students for their symposium "The Dirty Truth About Antibacterial Products," in which the motivated sequence organizational pattern is used to organize the order of the speeches given by each group member.

Panel Discussion

panel discussion a problem-solving discussion in front of an audience

A **panel discussion** is a problem-solving discussion in front of an audience. After the formal discussion, the audience is often encouraged to question the participants. Perhaps you've seen or heard a panel of experts discuss a topic—for example, on radio or television talk shows like *SportsCenter* or *The View*. The group is typically seated in a semicircle to allow the audience to see all participants. One person serves as moderator, introduces the topic, and provides the macrostructure by asking a series of planned questions that panelists answer. Their answers and the interaction between them provide the supporting evidence. A well-planned panel discussion seems spontaneous and interactive but requires careful planning and rehearsal to ensure that all relevant information is presented and that all speakers are afforded equal speaking time. To see a transcript of the panel discussion of "The Dirty Truth About Antibacterial Products," use your CengageNOW for *Challenge* to access the online resources for Chapter 16.

Town Hall Meeting

town hall meeting an event in which a large number of people who are interested in a topic convene to discuss, and at times to decide, an issue

A **town hall meeting** is an event in which a large number of people who are interested in a topic convene to discuss, and at times to decide, one or more issues. In the New England states, many small towns use town hall meetings of residents to decide community issues. In a town hall meeting, one person who is respected by other participants is selected to lead the discussion. The leader announces the ground rules for the discussion, introduces the issues to be discussed, calls on participants for comments, ensures that divergent opinions are expressed, periodically summarizes the discussion, and oversees the decision

Town hall-style meetings are often used by communities to discuss controversial issues that affect the well-being of residents.

© Jeff Greenberg/PhotoEdit

making. Because town hall meetings involve large numbers of people, the leader strictly controls taking turns. In your public speaking course, your instructor may have the entire class participate in a town hall meeting on a particular topic. You may be asked to consult with other students and as a group to represent a particular type of stakeholder. Your group task will be to research your stakeholder's position and then to represent these ideas in the larger forum.

Evaluating Group Effectiveness

Just as preparing and presenting are a bit different for group speeches than for individual speeches, so is the process of evaluating effectiveness. Evaluations should focus on group dynamics during the preparation process as well as on the effectiveness of the actual presentation.

Evaluating Group Dynamics During the Preparation Process

To be effective, groups must work together as they define and analyze a problem, generate solutions, and select a course of action. They also need to work together as they prepare their written report, which in some public speaking classrooms is a formal group outline, and practice the oral presentation.

So it is important to evaluate how effectively each member works in the group. This notion of how individuals work together as a team toward a common goal is known as **group dynamics.** You can evaluate group dynamics by judging the merit of each member's efforts in terms of the five group member responsibilities discussed earlier in this chapter. In addition, each group member could prepare a "reflective thinking process paper," which details in paragraph form what each member did well and could improve upon in terms of the five member responsibilities. In the final paragraph of the paper, each member should provide a self-evaluation of what they did and what they could do to improve the group process in future sessions. To complete a reflective thinking process paper online, use your CengageNOW for *Challenge* to access **Web Resource 16.4: Reflective Thinking Process Paper.**

Like the evaluations business managers make of employees, these evaluations serve to document the efforts of group members. They can be submitted to the instructor, just as they would be submitted to a supervisor. In business, these documents provide a basis for determining promotion, merit pay, and salary adjustments. In the classroom, they can provide a basis for determining one portion of each member's grade.

group dynamics how individuals work together as a team toward a common goal

Evaluating Effectiveness of the Group Presentation

Effective group presentations depend on quality individual presentations as well as quality overall group performance. So evaluations of group presentations should consist of both an individual and a group component. Exhibit 16.2 shows a form you can use to evaluate the effectiveness of a group presentation.

Evaluating Your Effectiveness

Effective group presentations depend on the combined efforts of individuals. So it's also a good idea to conduct a self-evaluation to determine whether you could be doing something better during the group problem-solving process, while preparing the group presentation, and when giving your portion of the group speech. Exhibit 16.3 is an example of a form used to evaluate your own efforts.

EXHIBIT 16.2 Sample evaluation form for group presentations

Group Member Name:_____

Critic (your name):_____

Directions: Evaluate the effectiveness of each group member according to each of the following criteria for effective presentations individually and as a group.

Rating Scale:

1	2	3	4	5	6	7
(poor)						(excellent)

INDIVIDUAL PERFORMANCE CRITIQUE

_____ **Delivery** (Use of voice and use of body)
(rating) Critique (Provide a rationale for the rating you gave):

_____ **Structure** (Macrostructure and microstructure/language)
(rating) Critique (Provide a rationale for the rating you gave):

_____ **Content** (Breadth and depth and listener relevance)
(rating) Critique (Provide a rationale for the rating you gave):

GROUP PERFORMANCE CRITIQUE

_____ **Delivery** (Teamwork? Cooperation? Fluency? Use of aids?)
(rating) Critique (Provide a rationale for the rating you gave):

_____ **Structure** (Balanced? Transitions? Flow? Attn/Clincher?)
(rating) Critique (Provide a rationale for the rating you gave):

_____ **Content** (Thematic? Focused? Thorough? Construction of presentational aids?)
(rating) Critique (Provide a rationale for the rating you gave):

Overall Comments:

_____

SPEECH ASSIGNMENT

Public Group Presentation

At your instructor's request during class, divide into groups of four to six. Each group will prepare a symposium or a panel based on their findings from engaging in the problem-solving process. Present the symposium or the panel in the form of a twenty-five- to thirty-minute presentation followed by five to ten minutes of audience questions and answers. Each group member must help identify an appropriate issue, participate in the problem-solving process, and take part in the presentation.

EXHIBIT 16.3 Sample self-critique form for group presentations

Directions: Complete the items below with regard to your presentation in the group symposium.

1. In terms of delivery, I did the following things well in my oral presentation:

   a.

   b.

2. In terms of content, I did the following things well in my oral presentation:

   a.

   b.

3. In terms of structure, I did the following things well in my oral presentation:

   a.

   b.

4. If I could do my portion of the oral presentation over again, I would do the following things differently:

   a.

   b.

   c.

5. In terms of my role as a group member, I am most proud of how I:

6. In terms of my role as a group member, I am least proud of how I:

7. Overall, I would give myself a grade of _____ for the group speech because:

Summary

Today, working and speaking in groups are popular not only in the classroom but also in business and industry. Effective problem-solving groups produce better products than individuals can do on their own. Groups are ineffective when some members fail to fulfill their responsibilities as group members. These responsibilities include being committed to the group goal, keeping the discussion on track, completing individual assignments, managing conflict among group members, and encouraging input from all members.

One effective process for solving problems in groups is systematic problem solving. Members work together to identify and define a problem, analyze the problem, determine criteria for judging solutions, generate many solutions, select the best solution based on the criteria, and implement the agreed-upon solution.

Once a group has worked through the problem-solving process, members must work together to prepare the public presentation. Groups can present their findings in a symposium, panel discussion, or town hall meeting.

Finally, evaluating group effectiveness includes an evaluation of each individual's public speaking portion of the presentation. It should also include an evaluation of group dynamics and group performance as well as self-evaluation.

Now that you've read Chapter 16, use your CengageNOW for *The Challenge of Effective Speaking* for quick access to the electronic resources that accompany this text. Your CengageNOW gives you access to the symposium and panel discussion outlines discussed on pages 333–334, Speech Builder Express, InfoTrac College Edition, and online study aids such as a digital glossary and review quizzes.

Your *Challenge* CengageNOW is an online study system that helps you identify concepts you don't fully understand, allowing you to put your study time to the best use. Using chapter-by-chapter diagnostic pretests, the system creates a personalized study plan for each chapter. Each plan directs you to specific resources designed to improve your understanding, including pages from the text in e-book format. Chapter posttests give you an opportunity to measure how much you've learned and let you know if you are ready for graded quizzes and exams.

KEY TERMS

Go to your CengageNOW for *Challenge* to access your online glossary for Chapter 16. Print a copy of the glossary for this chapter and test yourself with the electronic flash cards or complete the crossword puzzle to help you master these key terms:

brainstorming (332)
conflict (330)
criteria (331)
group dynamics (335)

groupthink (330)
panel discussion (334)
problem-solving groups (328)
symposium (333)

synergy (329)
systematic problem-solving method (331)
town hall meeting (334)

WEB RESOURCES

Go to your CengageNOW for *Challenge* to access the Web Resources for this chapter.

16.1 Setting Group Goals (330)
16.2 What's Your Problem? (331)

16.3 Rules for Brainstorming (332)

16.4 Reflective Thinking Process Paper (335)

Notes

Chapter 1 Introduction to Public Speaking

1. Stephen W. Littlejohn, *Theories of Human Communication* (Belmont, CA: Thomson Wadsworth, 2002).

2. K. Kellerman, "Communication: Inherently Strategic and Primarily Automatic," *Communication Monographs* 59 (1992): 288–300.

3. Mark. L. Knapp and Gerald R. Miller, eds., *Handbook of Interpersonal Communication* (Thousand Oaks, CA: Sage, 1994).

4. Ibid.

5. Marshall Scott Poole, "The Small Group Should Be the Fundamental Unit of Communication Research," in *Communication: Views from the Helm for the Twenty-First Century*, J. Trent, ed. (Needham Heights, MA: Allyn & Bacon, 1998): 94.

6. Dennis J. Devine, Laura D. Clayton, Jennifer L. Phillips, Benjamin B. Dunford, and Sarah B. Melner, "Teams in Organizations: Prevalence, Characteristics, and Effectiveness," *Small Group Research* 30 (1999): 678–711.

7. John C. Reinard, "The Empirical Study of the Persuasive Effects of Evidence," *Human Communication Research* 15 (1988): 3–59.

8. Vernon Jensen, "Teaching Ethics in Speech Communication," *Communication Education* 34 (1985): 324–330.

9. Bert Decker, *You've Got to Be Believed to Be Heard* (New York: St. Martin's Press, 1992).

10. Randall S. Hansen and Katharine Hansen, "What Do Employers *Really* Want? Top Skills and Values Employers Seek from Job-Seekers" @ http://www.quintcareers.com/job_skills_values.html (accessed February 27, 2007).

11. "More Than Three-Quarters of Americans Have a Pessimistic View of the Current State of Ethics and Morality, and Even Fewer See It Getting Better According to a New Gallup Poll," *Christian Century* (June 28, 2003): 17.

12. Supid K. Das, "Plagiarism in Higher Education: Is There a Remedy? Lots of Instruction and Some Careful Vigilance Could Work Wonders," *Scientist* (October 20, 2003): 8.

13. "Web Plagiarism Keeps Rising," *Curriculum Review* (November 2003): 5.

14. Caroline McCullen, "Tactics and Resources to Help Students Avoid Plagiarism," *Multimedia Schools* (November–December 2003): 40–43.

15. Delivered in speech class, North Dakota State University. Used with permission of Kris Treinen.

Chapter 2 Developing Confidence through the Speech Planning Process

1. J. C. Hahner, M. A. Sokoloff, and S. L. Salisch, *Speaking Clearly: Improving Voice and Diction*, 6th ed. (New York: McGraw-Hill, 2001).

2. Virginia P. Richmond and James C. McCroskey, *Communication Apprehension, Avoidance, and Effectiveness,* 5th ed. (Scottsdale, AZ: Gorsuch Scarisbrick, 1997).

3. R. R. Behnke and L. W. Carlile, "Heart Rate as an Index of Speech Anxiety," *Speech Monographs* 38 (1971): 66.

4. Michael J. Beatty and R. R. Behnke, "Effects of Public Speaking Trait Anxiety and Intensity of Speaking Task on Heart Rate During Performance," *Human Communication Research* 18 (1991): 147–176.

5. Richmond and McCroskey, *Communication*.

6. Michael J. Beatty, James C. McCroskey, and Alan D. Heisner, "Communication Apprehension as Temperamental Expression: A Communibiological Paradigm," *Communication Monographs* 65 (September 1998): 200.

7. James C. McCroskey and Michael J. Beatty, "Communication Apprehension," in *Communication and Personality: Trait Perspectives*, James C. McCroskey, John A. Daley, Michael M. Martin, and Michael J. Beatty, eds. (Cresskill, NJ: Hampton Press, 1998): 229.

8. Richmond & McCroskey, *Communication*.

9. A. Bandura, *Social Learning Theory* (Englewood Cliffs, NJ: Prentice Hall, 1973).

10. John A. Daly, J. P. Caughlin, and L. Stafford, "Correlates and Consequences of Social-Communicative Anxiety," in *Avoiding Communication: Shyness, Reticence, and Communication Apprehension*, 2nd ed., John A. Daly, James C. McCroskey, Joe Ayres, Tim Hopf, and Debbie M. Ayres, eds. (Cresskill, NJ: Hampton Press, 1997): 27.

11. Diane White, "Smile When You Say That," *Working Woman* (September 1998): 94–95.

12. Gerald M. Phillips, "Rhetoritherapy Versus the Medical Model: Dealing with Reticence," *Communication Education* 26 (1977): 37.

13. Michael Motley, "COM Therapy," in *Avoiding Communication: Shyness, Reticence, and Communication Apprehension,* 2nd ed., John A. Daly, James C. McCroskey, Joe Ayres, Tim Hopf, and Debbie M. Ayres, eds. (Cresskill, NJ: Hampton Press, 1997): 382.

14. Phillips, "Rhetoritherapy": 37.

15. Motley, "COM Therapy": 382.

16. Ibid.: 380.

17. Joe Ayres and Theodore S. Hopf, "The Long-Term Effect of Visualization in the Classroom: A Brief Research Report," *Communication Education* 39 (January 1990): 77.

18. Phil Scott, "Mind of a Champion," *Natural Health* 27 (January–February 1997): 99.

19. Joe Ayres, Tim Hopf, and Debbie M. Ayres, "An Examination of Whether Imaging Ability Enhances the Effectiveness of an Intervention Designed to Reduce Speech Anxiety," *Communication Education* 43 (July 1994): 256.

20. Richmond and McCroskey, *Communication:* 98.

21. Ibid.

22. K. Griffin, "Beating Performance Anxiety," *Working Woman* (July 1995): 62–65, 76.

23. Lynne Kelly, Gerald M. Phillips, and James A. Keaten, *Teaching People to Speak Well: Training and Remediation of Communication Reticence* (Cresskill, NJ: Hampton Press, 1995): 11.

24. Ibid.: 11–13.

25. Karen Kangas Dwyer, "The Multidimensional Model: Teaching Students to Self-Manage High Communication Apprehension by Self-Selecting Treatments," *Communication Education* 49 (January 2000): 79.

26. "Study Shows How Sleep Improves Memory," *Science Daily,* June 29, 2005, *http://www.sciencedaily.com/releases/ 2005/06/050629070337.htm* (accessed May 9, 2007).

Chapter 3 Listening Effectively

1. International Listening Association, 1996, @*http://www .listen.org/* (accessed March 2, 2007).

2. Laura A. Janusik and Andrew D. Wolvin, *24 Hours in a Day: A Listening Update to the Time Studies.* Paper presented at the meeting of the International Listening Association, Salem, OR, 2006.

3. International Listening Association, *Listening Factoid,* 2003, @*http://www.listen.org/pages/factoids/html.*

4. Sue DeWine and Tom Daniels, "Beyond the Snapshot: Setting a Research Agenda in Organizational Communication," in *Communication Yearbook* 16, S. A. Deetz, ed. (Thousand Oaks, CA: Sage, 1993): 252–230.

5. Jennifer J. Salopek, "Is Anyone Listening?" *Training and Development* 53(9) (1999): 58–60.

6. Andrew Wolvin and Carolyn Gwynn Coakley, *Listening,* 5th ed. (New York: McGraw-Hill, 1996).

7. M. Stephens, "The New TV: Stop Making Sense," in *Impact of Mass Media: Current Issues,* 4th ed., Ray E. Hiebert, ed. (White Plains, NY: Longman, 1999): 16–22.

8. "Sharpening Your Listening Skills," *Teller Vision* 0895-1039 (October 2002): 7.

9. Roni S. Lebauer, *Learning to Listen, Listen to Learn: Academic Listening and Note-Taking,* 2nd ed. (White Plains, NY: Longman, 2000): 49.

10. Wolvin and Coakley, *Listening.*

Chapter 4 Identifying an Audience-Centered Speech Goal

1. D. Callison, "Concept Mapping," *School Library Media Activities Monthly* 17(10) (2001): 30–32.

2. D. J. Canary and K. S. Hause, "Is There Any Reason to Research Sex Differences in Communication?" *Communication Quarterly* 41 (1993): 129–144; M. L. Hummert, J. L. Shaner, T. A. Garstka, and C. Henry, "Communication with Older Adults: The Influence of Age Stereotypes, Context, and Communicator Age," *Human Communication Research* 25(1) (1998): 124–153; M. Iino, "The Trap of Generalization: A Case of Encountering a New Culture," *Working Papers in Educational Linguistics* 9 (1993): 21–45; C. Thimm, "Age Stereotypes and Patronizing Messages: Features of Age-adapted Speeches in Technical Instructions to the Elderly," *Journal of Applied Communication Research* 26(1) (1998): 66–83.

Chapter 5 Adapting to Audiences

1. W. Barbe and R. H. Swassing, *The Swassing-Barbe Modality Index* (Columbus, OH: Waner-Bloser, 1979); A. A. Canfield, *Learning Styles Inventory Manual* (Ann Arbor, MI: Humanics Inc., 1980); R. Dunn, K. Dunn, and G. E. Price, *Learning Styles Inventory* (Lawrence, KS: Price Systems, 1975); H. Gardner, *Frames of Mind: The Theory of Multiple Intelligences* (New York: Basic Books, 1983); D. Kolb, *Experiential Learning: Experience as the Source of Learning and Development* (Englewood Cliffs, NJ: Prentice Hall, 1984).

2. Kolb, *Experiential Learning.*

3. Ibid.

4. *The World Almanac and Book of Facts* (New York: World Almanac Books, 2004): 798, 850.

Chapter 6 Researching Information for Your Speech

1. M. Miller, *The Lycos Personal Internet Guide* (Indianapolis, IN: Que Corporation, 1999): 187.

2. Craig Tengler and Frederic M. Jablin, "Effects of Question Type, Orientation, and Sequencing in the Employment Screening Interview," *Communication Monographs* 50 (1983): 261.

3. Shirley Biagi, *Interviews That Work: A Practical Guide for Journalists,* 2nd ed. (Belmont, CA: Wadsworth, 1992): 94.

4. David Munger, Daniel Anderson, Bret Benjamin, Christopher Busiel, and Bill Pardes-Holt, *Researching Online,* 3rd ed. (New York: Longman, 2000): 5.

5. Ibid.

6. Jim Kapoun, "Teaching Undergraduates Web Evaluation: A Guide for Library Instruction," 1/25/2000, //www.ala.org/acrl/undwebev.htm (accessed October 17, 2001).

7. Munger et al., *Researching Online:* 17.

8. Donald Baeder, "Chemical Wastes," *Vital Speeches of the Day* (June 1, 1980): 497.

9. The Princeton Language Institute, ed., *21st Century Dictionary of Quotations* (New York: Bantam Doubleday, 1993).

10. P. Frances, "Lies, Damned Lies . . . ," *American Demographics* 16 (1994): 2.

11. John Ahladas, "Global Warming," *Vital Speeches* (April 1, 1989): 382.

12. D. Shalala, "Domestic Terrorism: An Unacknowledged Epidemic," *Vital Speeches* (May 15, 1994): 451.

13. J. A. Howard, "Principles in Default: Rediscovered and Reapplied," *Vital Speeches* (August 1, 2000): 618

14. Steven Trachtenberg, "Five Ways in Which Thinking Is Dangerous," *Vital Speeches* (August 15, 1986). 653.

15. G. Michael Durst, "The Manager as a Developer," *Vital Speeches* (March 1, 1989): 309–310.

16. Hans Becherer, "Enduring Values for a Secular Age: Faith, Hope and Love," *Vital Speeches* (September 15, 2000): 732.

17. Cynthia Opheim, "Making Democracy Work: Your Responsibility to Society," *Vital Speeches* (November 1, 2000): 60.

Chapter 8 Completing the Outline: Creating the Introduction and the Conclusion

1. Trenholm, S. *Persuasion and Social Influence.* (New Jersey: Prentice-Hall, 1989); Crano, W. D. "Primacy Versus Recency in Retention of Information and Opinion Change." *The Journal of Social Psychology* 101 (1977): 87–96.

2. Humes, J. C. *Standing Ovation: How to Be an Effective Speaker and Communicator* (New York: Harper & Row, 1988).

3. Cole, B. "The Urgency of Memory: The Arts Give Us History." *Vital Speeches of the Day* (July 2002): 563–565.

4. Mason, S. "Equality Will Someday Come." *Vital Speeches* (April 2007): 159–163.

5. The Princeton Language Institute, ed. *21st Century Dictionary of Quotations* (New York: Laurel, 1993).

6. Moyers, B. "You Have a Fight Ahead of You." *Vital Speeches* (March 2007): 120–127.

7. Walker, D. M. "America at a Crossroads." *Vital Speeches* (December 2006): 752–762.

Chapter 9 Constructing and Using Presentational Aids

1. D. Cyphert, "Presentation Technology in the Age of Electronic Eloquence: From Visual Aid to Visual Eloquence," *Communication Education* 56, no. 2 (April 2007), 168–192.

2. B. Tversky, "Memory for Pictures, Maps, Environments, and Graphs," in *Intersections in Basic and Applied Memory Research,* David G Payne and Frederick G. Conrad, eds. (Hillsdale, NJ: Erlbaum. 1997), 257–277.

3. D. Kolb, *Experiential Learning: Experience as the Source of Learning and Development* (Englewood Cliffs, NJ: Prentice Hall, 1984); C. Gallo, "Presentations with Something for Everyone," *Business Week Online.*

4. J. Hanke, "The Psychology of Presentation Visuals," *Presentations* 12, no. 5 (1998), 42–47.

5. J. Ayers, "Using Visual Aids to Reduce Speech Anxiety," *Communication Research Reports* (1991), 73–79; K. Dwyer, *Conquer Your Speechfright* (Orlando, FL: Harcourt Brace, 1991).

6. D. D. Booher, *Speak with Confidence [electronic resources]: Powerful Presentations That Inform, Inspire, and Persuade* (New York: McGraw-Hill, 2003)

7. Kolb, *Experiential Learning;* Long, *Visual Aids and Learning.*

8. A. Wahl, "PowerPoint of No Return." *Canadian Business* 76, no. 22, November 23, 2003); J. R. Brandt, "Missing the (Power)point: When Bullet Points Fly, Attention Spans Die," *Industry Week* (January 2007) //www.industryweek.com.

9. E. R. Tufte, *The Cognitive Style of PowerPoint* (Cheshire, CT: Graphics Press, 2003); Brandt, "Missing the (Power)point."

10. L. F. Szul and D. E. Woodland, "Does the Right Software a Great Designer Make?" *T.H.E. Journal* 25, no. 7 (1998), 48–49.

11. Hanke, "The Psychology of Presentation Visuals."

12. M. Y. Rabb, *The Presentation Design Book,* 2nd ed. (Chapel Hill, NC: Ventana, 1993).

13. M. Brody, *Seeing Is Believing and Content Counts* (Presenters University, 2003) //www.presentersuniversity.com/visuals_designforclose_visuals_seeing.php.

Chapter 10 Practicing Speech Wording

1. S. W. Duck, *Meaningful Relationships* (Thousand Oaks, CA: Sage, 1994). See also J. Shotter, *Conversational*

Realities: The Construction of Life Through Language (Newbury Park, CA: Sage, 1993).

2. C. K. Ogden and I. A. Richards, *The Meaning of Meaning* (London: Kegan, Paul, Trench, Trubner, 1923).

3. Adam Robinson, *Word Smart: Building an Educated Vocabulary,* 3rd ed. (Princeton, NJ: Princeton Review, 2001).

4. W. Rader, "The Online Slang Dictionary" (2007) http://www.ocf.berkeley.edu/~wrader/slang/b.html (accessed May 20, 2007).

5. W. B. Gudykunst and Y. Matsumoto, "Cross-Cultural Variability of Communication in Personal Relationships," in *Communication in Personal Relationships Across Cultures,* W. B. Gudykunst, S. Ting-Toomey, and T. Nishida, eds. (Thousand Oaks, CA: Sage, 1996), 21.

6. G. Hofstede, *Cultures and Organizations: Software of the Mind* (New York: McGraw-Hill, 1991), 67.

7. D. Levine, *The Flight from Ambiguity* (Chicago: University of Chicago Press, 1985), 28.

8. C. W. Hensley, "Speak with Style and Watch the Impact," *Vital Speeches of the Day* (September 1, 1995): 703.

9. Robert H. Schertz, "Deregulation: After the Airlines, Is Trucking Next?" *Vital Speeches* (November 1, 1977): 40.

10. D. D. DuFrene and C. M. Lehman, "Persuasive Appeal for Clean Language," *Business Quarterly* 65 (March 2002): 48.

11. J. V. O'Connor, "FAQs #1 Cuss Control Academy" (2000) http://www.cusscontrol.com/faqs.html.

12. P. L. Witt, L. R. Wheeless, and M. Allen, "A Meta-analytical Review of the Relationship Between Teacher Immediacy and Student Learning," paper presented at the annual meeting of the International Communication Association, San Diego (May 2007) http://www.allacademic.com/meta/p112238_index.html (accessed May 21, 2007).

13. C. C. Edwards, "Verbal Immediacy and Androgyny: An Examination of Student Perceptions of College Instructors" *Academic Exchange Quarterly,* 6 (2002), 180–185; J. Gorham, "The Relationship Between Teacher Verbal Immediacy Behaviors and Student Learning," *Communication Education* 37 (1988), 40–53; R. G. Powell and B. Harville, "The Effects of Teacher Immediacy and Clarity on Instructional Outcomes: An Intercultural Assessment," *Communication Education* 39 (1990), 369–379.

14. D. Braithwaite and C. Braithwaite, "Viewing Persons with Disabilities as a Culture," in *Intercultural Communication: A Reader* (8th ed.), L. Samovar and R. Porter, eds. (Belmont, CA: Wadsworth, 1997), 154–164; K. Treinen, and J. Warren, "Antiracist Pedagogy in the Basic Course: Teaching Cultural Communication as If Whiteness Matters," *Basic Communication Course Annual* 13 (2001), 46–75.

15. L. P. Stewart, P. J. Cooper, A. D. Stewart, and S. A. Friedley, *Communication and Gender,* 4th ed. (Boston: Allyn & Bacon, 2003), 63.

16. J. Gastil, "Generic Pronouns and Sexist Language: The Oxymoronic Character of Masculine Generics," *Sex Roles* 23 (1990), 629–643; M. C. Hamilton, "Masculine Bias in the Attribution of Personhood: People = Male, Male = People," *Psychology of Women Quarterly* 15 (1991), 393–402; J. W. Switzer, "The Impact of Generic Word Choices: An Empirical Investigation of Age- and Sex-related Differences," *Sex Roles* 22 (1990), 69–82.

17. Treinen and Warren, "Antiracist Pedagogy in the Basic Course."

18. MTV Video Music Awards (August 28, 2003) http://www.mtv.com/onair/vma/2003/ (accessed September 18, 2003).

Chapter 11 Practicing Delivery

1. B. Decker, *You've Got to Be Believed to Be Heard* (New York: St. Martin's Press, 1992).

2. P. Watzlawick, J. B. Bavelas, and D. D. Jackson, *Pragmatics of Human Communication* (New York: Norton, 1967).

3. Judee K. Burgoon, Deborah A. Coker, and Ray A. Coker, "Communicative Effects of Gaze Behavior: A Test of Two Contrasting Explanations," *Human Communication Research* 12 (1986): 495–524.

4. B. Bates, *Communication and the Sexes* (Prospect Heights, IL: Waveland Press, 1992); P. D. Cherulnik, *Physical Attractiveness and Judged Suitability for Leadership,* Report No. CG 021 893 (1989), Chicago: Annual Meeting of the Midwestern Psychological Association (ERIC Document Services No. ED 310 317); S. G. Lawrence and M. Watson (1991), "Getting Others to Help: The Effectiveness of Professional Uniforms in Charitable Fund Raising," *Journal of Applied Communication Research* 19, 170–185; J. T. Malloy, *Dress for Success* (New York: Warner, 1975); and L. E. Temple and K. R. Loewen, "Perceptions of Power: First Impressions of a Woman Wearing a Jacket," *Perceptual and Motor Skills* 76 (1993): 339–348.

5. P. A. Phillips and L. R. Smith, *The Effects of Teacher Dress on Student Perceptions,* Report No. SP 033 944 (1992), (ERIC Document Services No. ED 347 151).

6. T. L. Morris, J. Gorham, S. H. Cohen, and D. Huffman, "Fashion in the Classroom: Effects of Attire on Student Perceptions of Instructors in College Classes," *Communication Education,* 45 (1996): 135–148.

7. K. E. Menzel and L. J. Carrell, "The Relationship Between Preparation and Performance in Public Speaking," *Communication Education* 43 (1994): 23.

Chapter 12 Informative Speaking

1. Ice Man @ *http://www.digonsite.com/drdig/mummy/22.html* (accessed July 21, 2007).

2. Vegan Society's website @ *http://www.vegansociety.com* (accessed July 21, 2007).

3. Based on "Narrative" by Diane Baerwald, Northshore School District. @ *http://ccweb.norshore.wednet.edu/writingcorner/narrative.html*

Chapter 13 Persuasive Speaking: Reasoning with Your Audience

1. Richard E. Petty and John Cacioppo, *Attitudes and Persuasion: Classic and Contemporary Approaches* (Boulder, CO: Westview, 1996): 7.

2. Bill Hill and Richard W. Leeman, *The Art and Practice of Argumentation and Debate* (Mountain View, CA: Mayfield, 1997): 135.

3. R. M. Perloff, *The Dynamics of Persuasion* (Hillsdale, NJ: Erlbaum, 1993).

4. Stephen Toulmin, *The Uses of Argument* (Cambridge, England: Cambridge University Press, 1958).

5. Toulmin, *The Uses of Argument*.

6. G. W. Ziegelmueller, J. Kay, and C. A. Dause, *Argumentation: Inquiry and Advocacy*, 2nd ed. (Englewood Cliffs, NJ: Prentice Hall, 1990): 186.

Chapter 14 Persuasive Speaking: Motivating the Audience

1. Herbert L. Petri and John M. Govern, *Motivation: Theory, Research, and Application*, 5th ed. (Belmont, CA: Wadsworth, 2004): 376.

2. A. H. Eagly and S. Chaiken, *The Psychology of Attitudes* (Fort Worth, TX: Harcourt Brace, 1993); S. R. Maloney, *Talk Your Way to the Top* (Englewood Cliffs, NJ: Prentice Hall, 1992).

3. Robin L. Nabi, "Discrete Emotions and Persuasion," in *The Persuasion Handbook: Developments in Theory and Practice*, James P. Dillard and Michael Pfau, eds. (Thousand Oaks, CA: Sage, 2002): 291–299.

4. "Megan's Law" @ http://www.parentsformeganslaw.com/html/questions.lasso (accessed July 25, 2007).

5. David Slator, "Sharing Life," in *Winning Orations* (Mankato, MN: Interstate Oratorical Association, 1998): 63–66.

6. Ryan Labor, "Shaken Baby Syndrome: The Silent Epidemic," in *Winning Orations* (Mankato, MN: Interstate Oratorical Association, 1998): 70–72.

7. "Zoned for Slavery: The Child Behind the Label," (DVD), National Labor Committee, 1995.

8. James C. McCroskey and Jason J. Teven, "Goodwill: A Reexamination of the Construct and Its Measurement," *Communication Monographs* 66 (March 1999): 92.

9. Julian James, "No Time for Complacency," *Vital Speeches of the Day* 73 (January 2007): 26–29.

10. James, "No Time for Complacency," *Vital Speeches*.

11. James, "No Time for Complacency," *Vital Speeches*.

12. R. Stewart, "Perceptions of a Speaker's Initial Credibility as a Function of Religious Involvement and Religious Disclosiveness," *Communication Research Reports* 11 (1994): 169–176.

13. R. M. Perloff, *Dynamics of Persuasion* (Hillsdale, NJ: Erlbaum, 1993): 145–149.

14. For example, see S. Buck and D. C. Tiene, "The Impact of Physical Attractiveness, Gender, and Teaching Philosophy on Teacher Evaluations," *Journal of Educational Research* 82 (1989): 172–177; P. D. Cherulnik, *Physical Attractiveness and Judged Stability for Leadership* (Report No. CG 021 893). Chicago: Annual Meeting of the Midwestern Psychological Association, 1989 (ERIC Document Services No. ED 310 317); L. M. Drogosz and P. E. Levy, "Another Look at the Effects of Appearance, Gender and Job Type on Performance-based Decisions," *Psychology of Women Quarterly* 20 (1996): 437–445.

15. T. L. Morris, J. Gorham, S. H. Cohen, and D. Huffman, "Fashion in the Classroom: Effects of Attire on Student Perceptions of Instructors in College Classes," *Communication Education* 45 (1996): 135–148; K. Treinen, *The Effects of Gender and Physical Attractiveness on Peer Critiques of a Persuasive Speech,* unpublished master's thesis (Fargo: North Dakota State University, 1998).

16. Perloff, *Dynamics of Persuasion*.

17. Herbert L. Petri, *Motivation: Theory, Research, and Applications,* 4th ed. (Belmont, CA: Wadsworth, 1996): 3.

18. John W. Thibaut and Harold H. Kelley, *The Social Psychology of Groups* (New York: Wiley, 1959): 10.

19. Abraham H. Maslow, *Motivation and Personality* (New York: Harper & Row, 1954): 80–92.

20. "Facts Pages: History and Statistics of U.S. Waste Production and Recycling," *Tufts Recycles* @ http://www.tufts.edu/tuftsrecycles/USstats.htm/ (accessed June 15, 2007).

21. Maria Lucia R. Anton, "Sexual Assault Policy a Must," in *Winning Orations* (Mankato, MN: Interstate Oratorical Association, 1994).

22. A. R. Gonzalez, R. B. Schofield, and G. R. Schmitt, *Sexual Assault on College Campuses: What Colleges and Universities Are Doing About It* (Washington, DC: U.S. Department of Justice, 2005) @ http://www.ojp.usdoj.gov/nij (accessed June 20, 2007).

Chapter 16 Developing and Delivering Group Presentations

1. D. O'Hair, J. O'Rourke, and M. O'Hair, *Business Communication: A Framework for Success* (Cincinnati, OH: South-Western, 2001); Bill Snyder, "Differing Views Cultivate Better Decisions," *Stanford Business* (2004) @ http://www.gsb.stanford.edu/NEWS/bmag/sbsm0405/feature_workteams_gruenfeld.shtml (accessed June 14, 2007); "Teams That Succeed," *Harvard Business Review* (Boston: Harvard Business School Press, 2004).

2. W. Tullar and P. Kaiser, "The Effect of Process Training on Process and Outcomes in Virtual Groups," *Journal of Business Communication* 37 (2000): 408–427.

3. R. Lesikar, J. Pettit Jr., and M. Flately, *Basic Business Communication,* 8th ed. (New York: McGraw-Hill, 1999).

4. M. A. Rahim, *Managing Conflict in Organizations,* 3rd ed. (Westport, CT: Greenwood Press, 2001).

5. I. L. Janis, *Groupthink: Psychological Studies of Policy Decision and Fiascos,* 2nd ed. (Boston: Houghton Mifflin, 1982).

6. J. Dewey, *How We Think* (Boston: Heath, 1933).

7. B. J. Duch, S. E. Groh, and D. E. Allen, eds., *The Power of Problem-Based Learning* (Sterling, VA: Stylus, 2001); K. M. Edens, "Preparing Problem Solvers for the 21st Century Through Problem-Based Learning," *College Teaching* 48, no. 2 (2000): 55–60; B. B. Levin, ed., *Energizing Teacher Education and Professional Development with Problem-Based Learning* (Alexandria, MN: Association for Supervision and Curriculum Development, 2001).

Glossary

accent the inflection, tone, and speech habits typical of the natives of a country, a region, or even a state or city

accurate language words that convey your meaning precisely

action an attention-getting act designed to highlight your topic or purpose

active listening identifying the organization of ideas, asking questions, silently paraphrasing, attending to nonverbal cues, and taking notes

actual object an inanimate or animate sample of the idea you are communicating

ad hominem argument a fallacy that occurs when a speaker attacks or praises a person making an argument rather than addressing the argument itself

adaptation reaction the gradual decline of your anxiety level that begins about one minute into the presentation and results in your anxiety level's declining to its prespeaking level in about five minutes

alliteration repetition of consonant sounds at the beginning of words that are near one another

analogy an extended metaphor

anecdotes brief, often amusing stories

anger the emotion we experience when we are faced with an obstacle that stands in the way of something we want

animated delivery delivery that is lively, energetic, enthusiastic, and dynamic

anticipation reaction the level of anxiety you experience prior to giving the speech, including the nervousness you feel while preparing and waiting to speak

antithesis combining contrasting ideas in the same sentence

antonym a word that is directly opposite in meaning

apathetic uninterested, unconcerned, or indifferent to your topic

appeal to action a statement in a conclusion that describes the behavior you want your listeners to follow after they have heard your arguments

appearance the way you look to others

argue from analogy to support a claim with a single comparable example that is significantly similar to the subject of the claim

argue from causation to cite events that have occurred that result in the claim

argue from example to support your claim by providing one or more individual examples

argue from sign to cite information that signals the claim

arguments the process of proving conclusions you have drawn from reasons and evidence

articulation using the tongue, palate, teeth, jaw movement, and lips to shape vocalized sounds that combine to produce a word

assonance repetition of vowel sounds in a phrase or phrases

attending paying attention to what the speaker is saying regardless of extraneous interferences

attitude a general or enduring positive or negative feeling about some person, object, or issue

audience the specific group of people to whom the speech is directed

audience adaptation the process of tailoring your speech's information to the needs, interests, and expectations of your listeners

audience analysis a study made to learn about the diverse characteristics of audience members and then, based on these characteristics, to predict how audience members are apt to listen to, understand, and be motivated to act on your speech

audience-centered considering who your listeners are and how your message can best be tailored to their interests, desires, and needs

audience contact creating a sense of looking listeners in the eye when speaking to large audiences

audience feedback nonverbal and verbal cues that indicate audience members' reaction to what the speaker is saying

bar graph a diagram that uses vertical or horizontal bars to show relationships between two or more variables at the same time or at various times on one or more dimensions

bias-free language language that demonstrates through word choices an ethical concern for fairness and respect with regard to race, ethnicity, gender, ability, sexual orientation, and diverse worldviews

brainstorming an uncritical, nonevaluative process of generating alternatives by being creative, suspending judgment, and combining or adapting the ideas of others

chart a graphic representation that distills a lot of information and presents it to an audience in an easily interpreted visual format

claim the proposition or conclusion to be proven

clincher a one- or two-sentence statement in a conclusion that provides a sense of closure by driving home the importance of your speech in a memorable way

closed questions narrow-focus questions that require only very brief answers

cognitive restructuring a process designed to help you systematically rebuild your thoughts about public speaking

commemorative address a speech of tribute that celebrates national holidays or anniversaries of important events

commencement address a speech of tribute praising graduating students and inspiring them to reach for their goals

common ground the background, knowledge, attitudes, experiences, and philosophies that audience members and the speaker share

communication orientation viewing a speech as just an opportunity to talk with a number of people about a topic that is important to the speaker and to the audience

communication orientation motivation (COM) techniques designed to reduce anxiety by helping the speaker adopt a "communication" rather than a "performance" orientation toward the speech

comparative advantages an organization that shows that a proposed change has more value than the status quo

comparison illuminating a point by showing similarities

comparison and contrast method a method of informing that explains something by focusing on how it is similar to and different from other things

compassion the emotion we feel when we have selfless concern for the suffering of another person that energizes us to try to relieve that suffering

concept mapping a visual means of exploring connections between a subject and related ideas

concrete words words that appeal to the senses or conjure up a picture

conflict disagreement or clash among ideas, principles, or people

confrontation reaction the surge in your anxiety level that you feel as you begin your speech

connotation the feelings or evaluations we associate with a word

constructive critique an analysis of a speech or presentation that evaluates how well a speaker meets a specific speaking goal while following the norms for good speaking and that recommends how the presentation could be improved

context the position of a word in a sentence and its relationship to other words around it

contrast illuminating a point by highlighting differences

conversational style delivery that is spontaneous, relaxed, and informal and allows the speaker to talk *with,* not *at,* an audience

costs expenditures that we incur when we act; may be physical, psychological, or social

creating suspense wording an attention getter so that what is described generates initial uncertainty or mystery and excites the audience

creativity the ability to produce original ideas and insights

credentials your experiences or education that qualifies you to speak with authority on a specific subject

credibility the perception that you are knowledgeable, trustworthy, and personable

crediting ideas giving the sources of information you use

criteria standards used for judging the merits of proposed solutions

criteria satisfaction an indirect organization that seeks audience agreement on criteria that should be considered when evaluating a particular proposition and then shows how the proposition satisfies those criteria

critical analysis the process of evaluating what you have heard to determine a speech's completeness, usefulness, and trustworthiness

cultural setting the values, beliefs, meanings, and social mores of specific groups of people to which your audience members belong

dedication a speech of tribute that honors a worthy person or group by naming a structure, monument, or park after them

definition method a method of informing that explains something by identifying its meaning

definition a statement that clarifies the meaning of a word or phrase

delivery how a message is communicated orally and visually through the use of voice and body

demographic diversity the range of demographic characteristics represented in an audience

demonstration method a method of informing that explains something by showing how it is done, by displaying the stages of a process, or by depicting how something works

denotation the explicit meaning a language community formally gives a word

derived credibility messages you send about your expertise during the speech

description method the informative method used to create an accurate, vivid, verbal picture of an object, geographic feature, setting, or image

diagram a type of drawing to show the whole and its parts

dialect a regional variety of a language

direct question a question that demands an overt response from the audience, usually by a show of hands

either-or a fallacy that argues there are only two alternatives when, in fact, there are many

emotions the buildup of action-specific energy

empathy the ability to see the world through the eyes of someone else

ethics a set of moral principles that a society, group, or individual holds that differentiate right from wrong and good behavior from bad behavior

ethos speaker credibility

eulogy a ceremonial speech of tribute during a funeral or memorial service that praises someone's life and accomplishments

examples specific instances that illustrate or explain a general factual statement

expert opinions interpretations and judgments made by authorities in a particular subject area

expository speech an informative presentation that provides carefully researched in-depth knowledge about a complex topic

extemporaneous speech a speech that is researched and planned ahead of time, but the exact wording is not scripted and will vary from presentation to presentation

eye contact looking directly at the people to whom you are speaking

facial expression eye and mouth movements

factual statements information that can be verified

false cause a fallacy that occurs when the alleged cause fails to be related to, or to produce, the effect

farewell a speech of tribute honoring someone who is leaving an organization

fear the emotion we experience when we perceive that we have no control over a situation that threatens us

figures of speech phrases that make striking comparisons between things that are not obviously alike

flipchart a pad of paper mounted on an easel

flowchart a chart that diagrams a sequence of steps through a complicated process

follow-up questions questions designed to pursue the answers given to primary questions

general goal the overall intent of the speech

generic language language that uses words that may apply only to one sex, race, or other group as though they represent everyone

gestures the movements of your hands, arms, and fingers that help you remain intelligible

goodwill a perception that the audience forms of a speaker who they believe understands them, empathizes with them, and is responsive to them

graph a diagram that presents numerical comparisons

group dynamics how individuals work together as a team toward a common goal

groupthink when group members accept information and ideas without subjecting them to critical analysis

guilt the emotion we experience when we personally violate a moral, ethical, or religious code that we hold dear

happiness or joy the emotion we experience when we accomplish something, when we have a satisfying interaction or relationship, or when

we see or possess objects that appeal to us

hasty generalization a fallacy that presents a generalization that is either not supported with evidence or is supported with only one weak example

hate speech the use of words and phrases to demean another person or group and to express the speaker's hatred and prejudice toward that person or group

hearing the biological process that occurs when the brain detects sound waves

historical setting events that have already occurred that are related to your speech topic, to you as a speaker, to previous speeches given by you with which audience members are familiar, or to other encounters that audience members have had with you

hope the emotion we experience when we believe something desirable is likely to happen

hypothetical examples specific instances based on reflections about future events

impartial having no opinion

impromptu speech a speech that is delivered with only seconds or minutes of advance notice for preparation and is usually presented without referring to notes of any kind

incentive a reward that is promised if a particular action is taken or goal is reached

incremental change moving reluctant listeners only a small degree in your direction

informative speech a speech whose goal is to explain or describe facts, truths, and principles in a way that stimulates interest, facilitates understanding, and increases the likelihood of remembering

initial audience disposition the knowledge of and opinions about your topic that your listeners have before they hear you speak

initial credibility perception of credibility created before you begin to speak

intellectually stimulating information that is new to audience members and is explained in a way that piques their curiosity

intelligible capable of being understood

Internet an international electronic collection of thousands of smaller networks

interviewing the skillful asking and answering of questions

jargon unique technical terminology of a trade or profession that is not generally understood by outsiders

joke an anecdote or a piece of wordplay designed to be funny and make people laugh

keynote address a ceremonial speech that both sets the tone and generates enthusiasm for the topic of a conference or convention

knowledge and expertise how well you convince your audience that you are qualified to speak on the topic

LCD multimedia projector a projection unit that connects to a VCR player, a DVD player, or a computer and projects images from them onto a screen

leading questions questions phrased in a way that suggests the interviewer has a preferred answer

learning style a person's preferred way of receiving information

line graph a diagram that indicates changes in one or more variables over time

listener relevance links statements of how and why your speech relates to or might affect your listeners

listening the process of receiving, attending to, constructing meaning from, and responding to spoken or nonverbal messages

logical reasons order organizing the main points of a persuasive speech by the reasons that support the speech goal

logos logical appeals

macrostructure the overall framework you use to organize your speech content

main points complete-sentence statements of the two to five central ideas that will be used in the thesis statement

marginalizing ignoring the values, needs, and interests of certain audience members, leaving them feeling excluded from the speaking situation

marking the addition of sex, race, age, or other group designations to a description

master or mistress of ceremonies an individual designated to set the mood of the program, introduce participants, and keep the program moving

metaphor an implied comparison between two unlike things without using *like* or *as*

microstructure the specific language and style choices you use as you frame your ideas and verbalize them to your audience

model a three-dimensional scaled-down or scaled-up version of an actual object

monotone a voice in which the pitch, volume, and rate remain constant, with no word, idea, or sentence differing significantly from any other

motivated movement movement with a purpose

motivated sequence a form of persuasive organization that combines a problem-solution pattern with explicit appeals designed to motivate the audience

movement changing the position of the entire body

multiple-response items survey items that give the respondent several alternative answers from which to choose

narration method a method of informing that explains something by recounting events

narrative order organizing the main points as a story or series of stories

narrative/personal experience speech a presentation in which you recount an experience you have had

and the significance you attach to that experience

narratives accounts, personal experiences, tales, or lengthier stories

negative emotions disquieting feelings that, when people experience them, they look for ways to eliminate them

neutral questions questions phrased in ways that do not direct a person's answers

newsgroup (bulletin board) an electronic gathering place for people with similar interests

nonparallel language language in which terms are changed because of the sex, race, or other group characteristics of the individual

nonverbal communication all speech elements other than the words themselves

onomatopoeia words that sound like the things they stand for

open questions broad-based questions that ask the interviewee to provide perspective, ideas, information, or opinions

open-ended items survey items that encourage respondents to elaborate on their opinions without forcing them to answer in a predetermined way

oral footnote oral reference to the original source of particular information at the point of presenting it during a speech

oral style the manner in which one conveys messages through the spoken word

organizational chart a chart that shows the structure of an organization in terms of rank and chain of command

panel discussion a problem-solving discussion in front of an audience

parallel when wording of points follows the same structural pattern, often using the same introductory words

paraphrase a statement in your own words of the meaning you have assigned to a message

pathos emotional appeals

pauses moments of silence strategically placed to enhance meaning

performance orientation viewing public speaking as a situation demanding special delivery techniques to impress an audience aesthetically or viewing audience members as hypercritical judges who will not forgive even our minor mistakes

periodicals magazines and journals that appear at fixed periods

personableness the extent to which you project an agreeable or pleasing personality

personal pronouns "we," "us," and "our"—pronouns that directly link the speaker to members of the audience

personal reference a brief story about something that happened to you or a hypothetical situation that listeners can imagine themselves in

personalize to present information in a frame of reference that is familiar to the audience

personification attributing human qualities to a concept or an inanimate object

persuasive punch words words that evoke emotions

persuasive speech a speech whose goal is to influence the attitudes, beliefs, values, or behavior of audience members

physical setting the location, size of room, seating arrangement, distance between audience and speaker, time of day, room temperature, and lighting

pie graph a diagram that shows the relationships among parts of a single unit

pitch the scaled highness or lowness of the sound a voice makes

plagiarism the unethical act of representing another person's work as your own

positive emotions feelings that people enjoy experiencing

posture the position or bearing of the body

precise words words that narrow a larger category

presentation software a computer program that enables you to electronically prepare and store your visual aids using a computer

presentational aid any visual, audio, or audiovisual material used in a speech

pride the feeling of self-satisfaction and an increase to our self-esteem we experience as the result of something that we have accomplished or that someone we identify with has accomplished

primacy-recency effect the tendency to remember the first and last items conveyed orally in a series than the items in between

primary questions questions the interviewer plans ahead of time

primary research the process of conducting your own study to acquire the information you need

primary source a document that details a firsthand account

problem-cause-solution pattern a form of persuasive organization that examines a problem, its cause(s), and solutions designed to eliminate or alleviate the underlying cause(s)

problem-solution pattern a persuasive organizational pattern that reveals details about a problem and poses solutions to it

problem-solving group four to seven people who work together to complete a specific task or solve a particular problem

process speech a speech that explains and shows how something is done, is made, or works

productive thinking to think about something from a variety of perspectives

pronunciation the form and accent of various syllables of a word

proposition a declarative sentence that clearly indicates the position that the speaker will advocate in a persuasive speech

proposition of fact a statement designed to convince your audience that something did or did not exist or occur, is or is not true, or will or will not occur

proposition of policy a statement designed to convince your audience that they should take a specific course of action

proposition of value a statement designed to convince your audience that something is good, bad, desirable, undesirable, fair, unfair, moral, immoral, sound, unsound, beneficial, harmful, important, or unimportant

proximity the relevance of information to personal life space

psychological setting the feelings, attitudes, and beliefs of individual audience members that affect how your speech message is perceived

public speaking apprehension a type of communication anxiety; the level of fear a person experiences when anticipating or actually speaking to an audience

public speaking skills training systematic teaching of the skills associated with the processes involved in preparing and delivering an effective public speech with the intention of improving speaking competence as a means of reducing public speaking apprehension

public speech, or oration a sustained formal presentation made by a speaker to an audience

quality the tone, timbre, or sound of your voice

quotation a comment made by and attributed to someone other than the speaker

rate the speed at which you talk

reasoning the mental process of drawing inferences (conclusions) from factual information

reasons main point statements that summarize several related pieces of evidence and show *why* you should believe or do something

refutative an organization that persuades by both disproving the opposing position and bolstering one's own

rehearsing practicing the presentation of your speech aloud

relevance adapting the information in a speech so that audience members view it as important to them

relief the emotion we experience when a threatening situation has been alleviated

remembering being able to retain and recall information that you have heard

repetition restating words, phrases, or sentences for emphasis

responsive showing care about the audience by acknowledging feedback from the audience, especially subtle negative cues

rhetorical questions questions phrased to stimulate a mental response rather than an actual spoken response on the part of the audience

sadness the emotion we experience when we fail to achieve a goal or experience a loss or separation

scaled items survey items that measure the direction and/or intensity of an audience member's feeling or attitude toward something

scripted speech a speech that is prepared by creating a complete written manuscript and delivered by reading a written copy or from memory

secondary research the process of locating information that has been discovered by other people

secondary source a document written about a topic, citing both primary sources and other secondary sources

section transitions complete sentences that show the relationship between, or bridge, major parts of a speech

self-talk thoughts about success or failure that go through one's mind prior to or during a particular situation

sensory language language that appeals to the senses of seeing, hearing, tasting, smelling, and feeling

setting the location and occasion for a speech

shame the emotion we experience when we have violated a moral code and it is revealed to someone we think highly of

signposts words or phrases that connect pieces of supporting material to the main point or subpoint they address

simile a direct comparison of dissimilar things using like or as

skimming a method of rapidly going through a work to determine what is covered and how

slang informal, nonstandard vocabulary and nonstandard definitions assigned to words by a social group or subculture

speaker the source or originator of the speech

speaking appropriately using language that adapts to the needs, interests, knowledge, and attitudes of the listener and avoiding language that alienates audience members

speaking context the physical, cultural, historical, and psychological factors in the setting in which your speech is presented

speaking conversationally Sounding as though you are having a spontaneous conversation with your audience rather than simply reading to them or performing in front of them

speaking expressively Using various vocal techniques so you sound a bit more dramatic than you would in casual conversation

speaking notes a word or phrase outline of your speech, plus hard-to-remember information such as quotations and statistics, designed to trigger memory

speaking situation the circumstances under which you deliver your speech

specific goal a single statement that identifies the exact response the speaker wants from the audience

specific language words that clarify meaning by narrowing what is understood from a general category

to a particular item or group within that category

speech effectiveness the extent to which audience members listen to, understand, remember, and are motivated to act on what a speaker has said

speech goal a statement of what you want your listeners to know, believe, or do

speech making the process of presenting a speech to the intended audience

speech of acceptance a ceremonial speech given to acknowledge receipt of an honor or award

speech of introduction a brief ceremonial speech that establishes a supportive climate for the main speaker, highlights the speaker's credibility by familiarizing the audience with pertinent biographical information, and generates enthusiasm for listening to the speaker and topic

speech of nomination a ceremonial presentation that proposes a nominee for an elected office, honor, position, or award

speech of recognition a ceremonial presentation that acknowledges someone and usually presents an award, a prize, or a gift to the individual or a representative of a group

speech of tribute a ceremonial speech that praises or celebrates a person, a group, or an event

speech of welcome a brief, formal ceremonial address that greets and expresses pleasure for the presence of a person or an organization

speech plan a strategy for achieving your goal

speech planning process the system that you use to prepare a speech

speech to actuate a speech that moves beyond affecting audience beliefs and attitudes and motivates the audience to act

speech to entertain a humorous speech that makes a serious point

spontaneity a naturalness of speech where what is said sounds as if the speaker is really thinking about the ideas *and* the audience as he or she speaks

Standard English form of English described in the dictionary or an English handbook

startling statement a sentence or two that grabs your listeners' attention by shocking them in some way

statement of reasons a straightforward organization in which you present your best-supported reasons in a meaningful order

statistics numerical facts

stereotyping assuming all members of a group behave or believe alike simply because they belong to the group

story an account of something that has happened (actual) or could happen (hypothetical)

straw man a fallacy that occurs when a speaker weakens the opposing position by misrepresenting it and then attacks that weaker position

stress emphasis placed on certain words by speaking them more loudly than the rest of the sentence

structures of speech phrases that combine ideas in a particular way

subject a broad area of expertise, such as movies, cognitive psychology, computer technology, or the Middle East

supporting material developmental material that will be used in the speech, including personal experiences, examples, illustrations, anecdotes, statistics, and quotations

survey a canvassing of people to get information about their ideas and opinions, which are then analyzed for trends

symposium a discussion in which a limited number of participants present individual speeches of approximately the same length dealing with the same subject and then discuss their reactions to what others have

said and answer questions from the audience

synergy when the result of group work is better than what one member could achieve alone

synonym a word that has the same or a similar meaning

systematic desensitization a method that reduces apprehension by gradually having people visualize increasingly more frightening events

systematic problem-solving method an efficient six-step method for finding an effective solution to a problem

target audience the cluster point that represents the group of people you most want to persuade

terminal credibility perception of credibility listeners have at the end of the speech

thesis statement a one- or two-sentence summary of the speech that incorporates the general and specific goals and previews the main points

time order organizing the main points of the speech in a chronological sequence or by steps in a process

timeliness showing how information is useful now or in the near future

toast a ceremonial speech offered at the start of a reception or meal that pays tribute to the occasion or to a person

topic some specific aspect of a subject

topic order organizing the main points of the speech by categories or divisions of a subject

town hall meeting an event in which a large number of people who are interested in a topic convene to discuss, and at times to decide, an issue

transitions words, phrases, or sentences that show a relationship between, or bridge, two ideas

trustworthiness the extent to which the audience can believe that what

you say is accurate, true, and in their best interests

two-sided items survey items that force the respondent to choose between two answers, such as yes/no, for/against, or pro/con

understanding the ability to assign accurate meaning to what was said

uninformed not knowing enough about a topic to have formed an opinion

verbal immediacy when the language you use reduces the psychological distance between you and your audience

visual aid a form of speech development that allows the audience to see as well as hear information

visualization a method that reduces apprehension by helping speakers develop a mental picture of themselves giving a masterful speech

vivid language language that is full of life—vigorous, bright, and intense

vocal expressiveness variety you create in your voice through changing pitch, volume, and rate, as well as stressing certain words and using pauses

vocalized pause unnecessary words interjected into sentences to fill moments of silence

voice the sound you produce in your larynx, or voice box, which is used to transmit the words of your speech to an audience

volume the degree of loudness of the tone you make

warrant the logical statement that connects the support to the claim

"we language" the use of plural personal pronouns like "we," "our," and "us" rather than "you" or "they"

word chart a chart used to preview, review, or highlight important ideas covered in a speech

Index